# Corruption and Human Rights

# Corruption and Human Rights

Sachin Verma

RANDOM PUBLICATIONS
NEW DELHI (INDIA)

**Corruption and Human Rights**

ISBN 978-93-5111-390-4


Published in 2014 in India by

**RANDOM PUBLICATIONS**

4376-A/4B, Gali Murari Lal, Ansari Road
New Delhi-110 002
Phone : +91-11-43580356, +91-11-23289044
e-mail: randomexports@gmail.com, sales@randompublications.com, info@randompublications.com

*Type Setting by* : Keystoneprintads, Delhi-110051
*Digitally Printed at* : Replika Press Pvt. Ltd.

# Preface

In recent years, the subject of corruption has received considerable attention. Work on governance has brought it into the light and it is no longer taboo. Corruption is being addressed by financial institutions, government agencies, bilateral donors, international organisations, non-governmental organisations (NGOs) and development professionals. Its causes have been measured empirically, as have its impacts on human development. Institutions and administrative procedures have been overhauled. Countries have negotiated and signed international anti-corruption conventions. The United Nations Office on Drugs and Crime (UNODC) Global Programme against Corruption has acted as a catalyst, helping countries to implement the United Nations Convention against Corruption (UNCAC). Transparency International (TI) and other civil society actors have created a large forum for discussion and advocacy around its many forms; an international coalition of NGOs has emerged, challenging corruption.

Yet corruption clearly remains a challenge. Despite countless policy diagnoses, public campaigns to raise awareness, and institutional and legal reforms to improve public administration, research shows that it continues to flourish. Indeed, opinion polls suggest that the public is more pessimistic than before about the likelihood of eliminating it. Combating corruption requires strong collective efforts from different sectors in society acting in coordinated ways. The aim of this book is to encourage and assist individuals and institutions which work to promote and protect human rights to engage with corruption issues and collaborate more closely with anti-corruption organisations. It may also assist those who combat corruption to recognize the value of human rights to their work and the advantages of closer collaboration with human rights organisations. The book may help to raise awareness among key stakeholders and the public of the links between corruption and human rights, thereby diminishing public tolerance of corruption and strengthening public support for anticorruption measures. It suggests some additional tools that individuals can use to denounce corruption as well as to protect those who combat it. The term is often applied loosely, and different definitions and classifications have been used by different organisations in various contexts. The book then elaborates upon the different acts of corruption as they have been defined by the UNCAC. Then, it examines where the human rights framework could add value to the anti-corruption work. Special attention is given to the impact of corruption on the human rights of groups exposed to particular risks, including women and children.

Subsequently, the book examines more closely the ways in which corrupt practices may violate specific human rights and the protection of human rights of anti-corruption advocates. Finally, it explores the possibilities of collaboration between human rights and anti-corruption organisations, and where such collaboration will create opportunities and obstacles. It provides some recommendations for human rights organisations that wish to work on corruption. It is hoped that, if the links between corruption and human rights are made clear, organisations and agencies working in the field of human rights may see the value of collaborating more closely with national and international anticorruption agencies, and vice versa. This is therefore not a scholarly treatise but a book written mainly for human rights specialists and organisations who want to know how they might effectively address corruption and the harm it causes.

I thank all members of my team who have helped in the preparation of the book. My special thanks go to "Random Publications" who have published the book.

– ***Sachin Verma***

# Contents

# 1

# Human Rights, Power and Welfare Conditionality

Over the last 10 to 15 years, talk about economic and social rights has become part of social policy debates in developed countries. Rights-based approaches emphasise participation, yet the debate around economic and social rights is largely driven. This article examines the extent to which the values which underpin rightsbased approaches are consistent with the values of those whom such an approach is designed to help. The values underlying rights-based approaches and those with experience of poverty are identified and then compared in three ways: in general; in relation to the specific issue of welfare conditionality; and as prescriptions for action. The comparative analysis is facilitated by linking the discussion of values to discussion of the forms of power relationships involved in rights-based approaches and what is valued by those with experience of poverty. While there is considerable overlap between rights-based approaches and what is valued by those with experience of poverty, there are also subtle differences which should not be ignored.

## INTRODUCTION

Towards the end of the 20th century, talk about rights, particularly economic and social rights, entered social policy discourse. Even in Australia, where all attempts to establish guarantees of rights within the legal system have failed, the influence of UN treaties or conventions can be seen in policy statements and documents in specific policy sectors. For example, one of the most important elements of the Convention on the Rights of the Child is set out in Art 12, which calls on state parties to 'assure the child who is capable of forming his or her own views the right to express those views freely in all matters affecting the child'. While consultation with children can be tokenistic or undermined by bureaucratic structures, the principle of seeking children's views has become part of policy rhetoric, if not practice. For example, one of the four rights set out in the South Australian Charter of Rights for Children and Young People in Care is 'the right to understand and have a say in decisions that affect you'. Rights-based approaches differ from past practice in the emphasis on obligation, in particular the obligation of the state to ensure its citizens are able to exercise their economic and social rights and by acknowledging that all citizens are entitled to exercise such rights. Thus the Office of the High Commissioner for Human Rights defines a rights-based approach as one that 'links poverty reduction to questions of obligation rather than welfare or charity'.

Governments become 'duty-holders' who are obliged to guarantee the rights of all citizens, including those who are marginalised or disadvantaged. Welfare recipients become rights-holders who are assisted by the state, not as an act of paternalistic benevolence, but as an entitlement. As with any normative framework, rights talk has generated a mixed response.

For some, rights-based approaches provide a powerful social instrument for challenging the sites and uses of power. Others point to the fact that institutionalising human rights is a social process which itself involves the use of power. Compared to civil and political rights, economic and social rights require a much greater level of active intervention by government before such rights can be realised.

The International Covenant on Economic, Social and Cultural Rights recognises that the adoption of legislative measures may be highly desirable in many instances, but leaves it up to individual states to determine whether legislation is necessary. The belief that legislation, though important, is not sufficient to ensure a full realisation of rights is reflected in the covenant, which for some rights lists the steps to be taken by state parties in order to achieve full realisation of a particular right. In all cases, the steps refer to broad policy goals and programmes rather than specific legislative measures. For example, in relation to the right to work, the covenant lists 'technical and vocational guidance and training programs' and 'policies and techniques to achieve steady economic development and full and productive employment' as some of the steps to be taken.

Furthermore, guidelines governing the type of reporting required under the covenant clearly indicate that states should provide details of non-legislative measures such as policies, programmes or techniques, as well as all relevant laws. In establishing the principle of progressive achievement,1 the covenant also recognises that full realisation of economic and social rights requires a significant amount of resources and state parties are given considerable discretion in determining the level of financial resources devoted to policies and programmes designed to achieve realisation of economic and social rights.

Thus, economic and social rights are contingent on available resources and progressively realised through a range of measures, not all of which will be based on legislation and give rise to enforceable rights. Cox notes that governments are increasingly relying on activities which are not codified in law, citing the example of aged care in Denmark, where elderly people enjoy the right to be cared for in their own home, but this right is not stated in law and its realisation is dependent on the amount of money local communities, which fund home care activities, allocate to aged care. Carney argues that a similar process is underway in Australia, where recent welfare-to-work reforms have converted rule-based norms into discretionary powers under the control of government departments. Increasing levels of conditionality applied to welfare entitlements are seen to further erode the 'rights' of social security clients. Given the debate around rights-based approaches and, in particular, the claim that rights-based approaches have the potential to challenge existing power structures, it is worth considering the extent to which the values which underpin rights-based approaches are consistent with the values of those whom such an approach is intended to help. In this article, I have taken the views of people with experience of poverty about what they want from government and service providers as indicative of what they value. The remainder of this article is organised as follows. First, four general principles or values underlying all rights-based approaches are identified. This is followed by a discussion of what is valued by those with experience of poverty.

The values underlying rights-based approaches are then compared to the values of those with experience of poverty, first in general, then in relation to a specific issue — welfare conditionality — and finally as a prescription for action. Linked to the discussion of values is discussion of the forms of power involved in rights-based approaches and what is valued by those with experience of poverty.

## RIGHTS-BASED APPROACHES

As noted earlier, the realisation of economic and social rights requires a range of different forms of intervention by government, and under the ICESCR governments have considerable discretion in how they choose to institutionalise such rights. While there is no single agreed rights-based approach, all rights-based approaches derive from the international human rights framework from which a set of common principles or values can be identified.

The first of these is that the inherent dignity of the human person is the basis of all rights. The second is that participation is the way in which individuals are able to live with dignity. Consequently, the Office of the High Commissioner for Human Rights has suggested that in terms of the policymaking process, this principle obliges governments to facilitate participation by affected groups at all stages of the policy process, from initial conception through to implementation and evaluation. Thus, empowering rights-holders to be active participants in decision-making processes that affect their lives is a key component of rights-based approaches, with some political theorists arguing that participation is a basic right upon which all other rights rest. From a rights-based perspective, participation should not be confined to decision-making at the local level, but should encompass broader decision-making forums that impact on policy-making at the national and international level. In addition, duty-holders have an obligation to encourage right sholders to pursue the legal defence of their rights within national and international jurisdictions. While the ICESCR provides for gradual realisation of economic and social rights, taking into account the level of financial resources available to individual governments, the third principle underlying rights-based approaches is that realisation of economic and social rights must start from the bottom up. That is, governments are obliged to concentrate their efforts on the most vulnerable or disadvantaged groups in society.

The fourth principle concerns governmental accountability. Geiringer and Palmer argue that the stipulation in Art 2(1) of the ICESCR that state parties use 'all appropriate means' in moving towards full realisation of economic and social rights requires some degree of governmental accountability to its own citizens in addition to its periodic reports to the United Nations. These principles illuminate the type of power relationships involved in rights based approaches.

Larmour identifies seven types of power relationships, of which five are relevant to this discussion of human rights approaches — that is, first dimensional or coercive power, where one party has the power to force another to do something that they would rather not do; second dimensional or agenda setting power; infrastructural power, which involves the transfer of resources in order to empower the recipient; disciplinary power, where one party tries to make the other party want what they want so that the second party takes responsibility for achieving the desired outcome; and, finally, the form of power that is linked to knowledge and expertise. Clearly, the most important type of power relationship involved in rights-based approaches is infrastructural power. Governments exercise infrastructural power when they provide resources that enhance the capacity of rights-holders to participate in decision-making processes that affect their lives. However, genuine participation, which equates to the top three rungs of Arnstein's ladder of citizen participation,2 involves a rebalancing of second dimensional power. In addition, the principle of governmental accountability has the potential to shift the balance of second dimensional power slightly from governments towards rights-holders as governments are forced to report on progress towards full realisation of economic and social rights.

## WHAT DO PEOPLE WITH EXPERIENCE OF POVERTY WANT FROM GOVERNMENT AND SERVICE PROVIDERS?

When asked about their life experiences and what they want from government and service providers, the desire for dignity and respect is almost always mentioned — regardless of the age of respondents, their gender or where they live. For example, the UK Commission on Poverty, Participation and Power noted that 'the lack of respect for people living in poverty was one of the clearest and most heartfelt messages which came across to us'.

The same message was received by the Hume City Council when they talked to people from Indigenous communities, people from culturally diverse communities, women, those not in the workforce, people with a disability, older people and younger people:

- The desire for respect was by far the most important theme that emerged from discussions with those people who are experiencing, or who belong to particular community groups that are at a higher risk of experiencing poverty.

Clients of a range of welfare services in NSW and Victoria identified dignity and respect as two essential ingredients of a decent life, the desire for which was fuelled by the demeaning nature of interactions with government officials, an experience shared by people in the United Kingdom:

- Complaints were not about the quantity of payments ... the problem was punitive and disrespectful treatment. Governments were not just at fault because they didn't deliver but because what they delivered came at such a heavy price in terms of self-respect and dignity.
- You shouldn't have to be made to feel as though you are useless. I feel very angry sometimes that people are ignorant of the fact that we are humans as well and we do need to be respected.

Being treated with dignity and respect means being recognised as a person rather than a 'problem' and being listened to without being judged.

*Clients of welfare services clearly identify the importance of this form of emotional support:*

- People often think it is all about money. I don't necessarily need money, I need help dealing with being on welfare, I need help with all the shit about being worthless and useless and doing nothing. I need someone who knows what I'm going through, to sit down with me and sort all of this crap out.

While being accepted and being listened to are important, people with experience of poverty want more than a passive form of listening. People living in poverty want their expertise to be acknowledged and heard.

For example, in the many conversations Mark Peel had with people living in Inala in Brisbane, in Broadmeadows in Melbourne and in Mount Druitt in Sydney, this desire came through very strongly:

- Justice was about being respected, trusted and listened to because what you had to say was important ... What mattered to them was acknowledgment of capacity and intelligence.
- If they wanted one thing to change, it was that they be treated as knowledgeable, that outsiders should expect to learn and to listen.

Being listened to because what you have to say is considered valuable is a sign of respect and an acknowledgment of competency, both of which are valued by those with experience of poverty.

For example, for participants in a personal loan pilot in Melbourne run by the Brotherhood of St Laurence and Community Sector Banking:

- ... Obtaining a loan was more than just money, dignity, inclusion, trust and respect. It was an opportunity to not be just a passive recipient of welfare, but to gain some self-esteem by taking a positive active role in the process.

Thus, agency — the ability to take control of your life — is clearly linked to dignity and respect, and being treated with dignity and respect can increase feelings of selfrespect and a sense of agency.

*As one participant in the personal loan pilot explained, having a relationship with a mainstream bank:*

- ... Gave me the confidence to go ask somewhere else for credit ... this time I walked in with my head high and I said I want this and that.

People with experience of poverty often identify feelings of powerlessness and a lack of control over their lives. Choice is therefore important, because in choosing individuals are able to exercise control and agency. Thus, pensioners living in residential care in Melbourne experience greater financial stress than do pensioners living in rental accommodation, because they retain control over much less of their pension.

Access to services, such as affordable public transport, is valued because being able to use these services increases people's choices. When people with experience of poverty talk about receiving resources, they do so in instrumental terms — that is, the resources are valued because they increase agency. For example, clients of welfare services in New South Wales and Victoria are critical of the lack of access to dental services, because having bad teeth makes it harder to compete for jobs. The desire of many welfare recipients for information and assistance before their lives reach a crisis point is further evidence of the value placed on agency:3 People with experience of poverty often identify feelings of powerlessness and a lack of control over their lives.

Choice is therefore important, because in choosing individuals are able to exercise control and agency. Thus, pensioners living in residential care in Melbourne experience greater financial stress than do pensioners living in rental accommodation, because they retain control over much less of their pension. Access to services, such as affordable public transport, is valued because being able to use these services increases people's choices.

When people with experience of poverty talk about receiving resources, they do so in instrumental terms — that is, the resources are valued because they increase agency. For example, clients of welfare services in New South Wales and Victoria are critical of the lack of access to dental services, because having bad teeth makes it harder to compete for jobs. The desire of many welfare recipients for information and assistance before their lives reach a crisis point is further evidence of the value placed on agency:3

- I know what has happened and I know what I want to do, I just need someone to help me get the right information ... what I need to do to get there.

The high priority placed on receiving information and getting access to resources which will increase agency indicates that those with experience of poverty are happy with governments exercising infrastructural power — power which is exercised in order to 'empower' the powerless. However, individuals with experience of poverty place an even higher priority on being able to exercise power that is linked to knowledge and expertise.

Those with experience of poverty want their knowledge and expertise to be recognised; they want to be able to exercise the form of power linked to knowledge and expertise, because exercising this form of power is a powerful symbol of their worth as a human being, as well as a means of exercising second dimensional power. However, the desire to exercise second dimensional power is not absolute. Those with experience of poverty are not seeking to dominate or control negotiations to the exclusion of all other interests.

*What is important is a rebalancing of second dimensional power. As Mark Peel observed:*

- People did not expect to receive the world on a platter. As they said only the rich presume that as their right. They did not expect immediate changes in their situation but they did expect to be listened to, to play some part in defining what they needed and to be treated with respect.

Children and young people also want to exercise this nuanced form of second dimensional power. Few young people and fewer children want to be given sole decision-making responsibility, but most want to have their say and have their wishes taken into account when decisions are being made, rather than being asked to endorse a course of action decided by others.

*As a 12-year-old boy who had experienced the care and protection system put it:*

- I might want to see my grandma. I might want to see my cousins. I might want to see my uncles or my aunties. I should be able to say 'yes, I do' or 'no, I don't'. I should have some say.

## COMPARING THE TWO

It is clear from the considerable overlap between the values underpinning rights-based approaches and what is valued by those with direct experience of poverty. Rights-based approaches recognise the dignity of the human person as the basis of all rights and, for people with experience of poverty, being treated with dignity and respect is more important than anything else:

- You can put up with the struggle, you know, just get by, if you get respect and if you're treated right.

Similarly, the principle of governmental accountability is consistent with the desire of people with experience of poverty for:

- … 'Someone to make and keep a promise'. In their version of social justice, powerful people should be held to account in the same way they were … 'You see, the difference is we pay for our mistakes. They don't. We have to understand limitations and forgive them and be reasonable and make the best of it. They don't. That's not fair.'

Participating in decision-making processes that affect their lives is clearly important to those with experience of poverty who value choice and agency, but the emphasis on encouraging rights-holders to pursue a legal defence of their rights is not necessarily shared by those with experience of poverty.

Indeed, the language of rights seems to be largely confined to the non-poor. People with experience of poverty do not talk about claiming a legally defensible 'right' to a job, accessible public transport or health services; they talk instead about 'fair' access to resources and opportunities, which more closely equates to the principle that realisation of economic and social rights must start from the bottom up. Those with experience of poverty place greater emphasis on receiving information or accessing resources which will increase agency — for example, receiving information about services which may help them get a job — than claiming their 'right' to a job.

For example, in a 1997 telephone survey of 6897 jobseekers which gathered information about jobseekers' needs and expectations of service quality, as well as those aspects of service most valued by jobseekers, the desire for dignity and respect and the desire for information that would help them gain employment were all valued highly. Of much less importance was information about rights and information about rules and regulations.

So far, discussion of rights-based approaches and what is valued by those with experience of poverty has been confined to general principles. But these general principles are only ever given force in specific contexts. Discussion now turns to a specific issue, that of welfare conditionality, which is regarded by many as incompatible with rights-based approaches but is a defining characteristic of Australia's welfare system. In residualist systems, welfare conditionality is used as a rationing device — a way of ensuring that benefits and payments go to those in greatest need. Using welfare conditionality in this way is consistent with the principle that, when faced with resource constraints, realisation of economic and social rights has to begin with those most in need.

However, more recently a second layer of conditionality has been added to residualist welfare systems, with conditionality being used as a way of modifying behaviour— that is, some welfare payments have become dependent on an individual accepting their responsibility to undertake certain activities deemed socially desirable, such as actively looking for paid employment or ensuring their children attend school. The legitimacy of linking rights and responsibilities in this way has been widely debated with many arguing that rights-holders have a right to health, employment or an adequate standard of living simply by virtue of their humanity, and consequently do not have to do anything to 'earn' such rights. Others argue that conditionality imposes additional burdens on the most vulnerable and disadvantaged, such as the homeless or those with multiple disabilities, or on 'third parties', particularly the children of those who are penalised for not meeting benefit requirements, such as applying for jobs or attending job interviews.

While it is not the intention of this article to resolve the debate about whether welfare conditionality is a legitimate part of rights-based approaches, it is clear that in imposing conditionality with the aim of modifying behaviour, governments are exercising different forms of power from those associated with the key elements of rights-based approaches.

When governments introduce conditions, such as participation in the Work for the Dole programme, as a requirement for receipt of unemployment benefits, they are exercising a disciplinary form of power — that is, governments want welfare recipients to take responsibility for themselves for ensuring that they are 'work ready'. This disciplinary power can be exercised through first dimensional power — as, for example, when those deemed to have demonstrated a pattern of work avoidance are obliged to undertake 'full-time' Work for the Dole — or it can be exercised in a non-coercive way — as, for example, when individuals volunteer to have a portion of their welfare payments managed on their behalf by Centrelink. Justifications for conditionality fall into three main camps.

Contractualist justifications centre on the belief that there is an implied contract between citizens and the state, where the state agrees to support its citizens in times of need if the citizen accepts their responsibilities, of which the most important is the responsibility to work. On the other hand, paternalistic justifications are based on the belief that imposing conditions is in the best interests of those in receipt of welfare payments because such individuals are so defeated by poverty and disadvantage that they are incapable of fulfilling their own desire to work or to look after their family without the threat of penalties or sanctions.

Unlike contractualist arguments, paternalistic justifications do not emphasise the reciprocal obligations of the state — that is, welfare recipients are obliged to meet the conditions imposed upon them by the state because doing so will improve their lives, not because the state has already provided services and programmes that will enable welfare recipients to overcome poverty and disadvantage.

The third justification for welfare conditionality, derived from the writings of communitarian theorists, is based on the belief that people have a responsibility to be good parents, neighbours or citizens — not because the state has provided certain benefits or support, but because of the responsibility individuals owe to each other. But what do recipients of social welfare services believe? For a sample of welfare service users living in Bradford in the north of England, the legitimacy of welfare conditionality is dependent on the specific policy sector. While accepting that individual behaviour could be a contributing factor to the need for health care, the overwhelming majority of respondents believed access to health care should be unconditional:

- I feel there are just too many different criteria on which to apply a value judgment, it would be impractical to apply it. You can't just take an isolated thing whether it be smoking, weight or age or nice person/bad person ... The universal thing is the only real way out of it. You could say that people who do dangerous sports or whatever are endangering their health so there is nowhere to draw the line really.

On the other hand, conditionality in the housing sector was considered appropriate, particularly in situations where individuals repeatedly reneged on agreements, ignored warnings and continued to engage in behaviour which had a negative impact on their neighbours:

- If they have been notified of the rule and they are a nuisance, yes I think that the council or housing association has got a right to evict them ... I think they should get a warning first, not just throw them out. There should be a procedure like.

Support for conditional unemployment payments fell between the two, with more than half believing it was reasonable to expect those receiving unemployment benefits to accept specific work or training responsibilities because this would increase their chance of finding a job, or because respondents believed it was desirable that those in receipt of a benefit contribute in some way to the community.

However, a substantial minority, who tended to see unemployment in terms of structural rather than individual failings, did not believe it was appropriate to make the receipt of unemployment benefits conditional on fulfilling certain duties or obligations:

- If there are no jobs people should be paid unemployment benefits.

This nuanced approach to conditionality is consistent with Australian studies of community attitudes. For example, Eardley, Saunders and Evans found that support for conditionality was high when applied to young unemployed people, but only 36 per cent of those surveyed believed an unemployed parent should be forced to undertake mutual obligation activities and only 25 per cent of those surveyed believed it was appropriate to impose obligations on unemployed people who had a disability.

While elements of contractualist, paternalist and mutualist justifications can be found in the views of welfare service recipients, what these studies indicate is that users of social welfare services would agree with White's conclusion that:

- ... There is nothing intrinsically objectionable about welfare contractualism ... legitimacy ... is difficult to assess in isolation from the character of the rest of the welfare system, indeed of the rest of the economic system as a whole.

In other words, those who are often subject to the exercise of coercive power as part of the provision of assistance do not automatically condemn the use of such power. Indeed, criticisms of the compulsory nature of mutual obligation in workfare schemes such as the Work for the Dole programme are largely confined to commentators, advocacy and service delivery agencies.

Participants are more concerned with the lack of flexibility in programme design and implementation, which means the programme is unable to meet individual needs. For example, some older job seekers want access to accredited training so that they can move into new areas of employment while others do not, preferring wage subsidy schemes that would enable them to work in a real workplace in the private sector where they could demonstrate their skills and abilities to employers.

Once again, the emphasis of those with experience of poverty is centred on the ways in which the programme can help them achieve their goal — getting a job — rather than concern about the exercise of first dimensional power. Rights-based approaches can be seen both as an international system of treaties, visionary statements and commitments and as a conceptual framework that allows policy-makers to 'recharacterise and guide what we do and how we do it'. The remainder of this section of the article considers what would need to change in 'what we do and how we do it', if the values of those with experience of poverty are taken as a conceptual framework. The biggest challenge facing policy-makers and service providers lies in allowing those with experience of poverty to exercise the form of power that is linked to knowledge and expertise. Policy-makers and service providers are comfortable with the exercise of infrastructural power, but allowing service users to exercise the form of power that is linked to knowledge and expertise cuts across the strong streak of paternalism that still exists in the social welfare sector.

In other words, it challenges the belief of all professionals involved in delivering social welfare programmes that they know what is best for their clients, just as it challenges the belief of academics and policy experts that their ideas or the latest policy fad will solve particular policy problems. Allowing those with experience of poverty to exercise the form of power that is linked to knowledge and expertise means policy-makers and professionals involved in the delivery of social welfare services must at times surrender control over outcomes, even if placing power in the hands of individuals means that outcomes are less than what policy-makers and welfare professionals believe they could be. There are agencies already doing this, in spite of the ongoing frustration experienced by their staff when clients choose not to make changes that the staff believes would be beneficial. For example, staff involved in Anglicare Tasmania's Acquired Injury and Home Support Service are committed to the principle of treating their clients with dignity and respect, which means giving them choice — choice over who is employed as their personal support worker and choice over how allocated hours are used.

Even when staff members see clients who choose to make goal-oriented plans for how allocated hours are used improve their quality of life while others do not do so well, they remain committed to the principle of letting clients decide. As the preceding example illustrates, clients want different things. Some clients want personal support workers who are trained to care for people with spinal cord injuries; others are more concerned about the personality of the support worker whether they 'hit if off'. Therefore, making assumptions about what clients want is dangerous. As Renee, a young Aboriginal woman who was interviewed for Judith Brett and Anthony Moran's book Ordinary People's Politics, explains, even well-meaning assumptions which incorporate sessions from past policy failures do not always hold true:

- My sister doesn't want to be part of the Aboriginal community any more. She thinks it is destructive, and that the violence and abuse has caused all her problems ... [M]y sister's happy to be removed. She'd rather be in care because she's getting all the things Mum couldn't provide. It's not that she doesn't like Mum, but she'd rather be out of there.

*For Renee, the answer lay in treating each person as an individual and listening to what they wanted for their life:*

- Renee ... stressed repeatedly that people trying to help should talk with the children and have more faith in their resilience, and that the current situation should not just be seen in terms of the previous generation's experience.

Treating everyone as an individual and allowing them to choose means that services have to be flexible — flexible in terms of both what is provided and how long assistance is provided. This level of flexibility is often difficult to achieve in an environment where services are under-resourced and accountability frameworks emphasise upward accountability, rather than downward accountability.

But, as noted earlier, for those with experience of poverty, exercising the form of power that is linked to knowledge and expertise is a means of rebalancing, not dominating, the exercise of second dimensional power. Therefore, finding a balance between the demands of upward and downward accountability should not be impossible.4 Re-orienting service provision to fully reflect the values of those whom the service is designed to assist would require greater emphasis on the provision of information to clients or programme participants about available services, and how to access these services as a way of strengthening the exercise of infrastructural power. As noted earlier, individuals want this sort of information and the success of service models based on care in the community requires it.

*Unfortunately, clients and programme participants often report difficulties in accessing relevant information:*

- Unless you actually enquire about what services are available then people are not normally keen to tell you. So you actually have to do a lot of prying and literally ask specific questions about what is available and what is not. There is never one person. It is always several people and you will find a lot of people will do a lot of buck passing and say 'we don't handle that' and they will say you need to speak to this person or that and before you know it you have spoken to fourteen different people and you still don't have the answers you need.

Giving clients choice, providing flexible services which are responsive to individual needs and placing greater emphasis on the provision of information are all consistent with rights-based approaches. This indicates that, far from being yet another imposition on 'the poor' by experts who believe that they know best, rights-based approaches provide a conceptual framework that allows policy-makers and those involved in the delivery of social welfare services to recharacterise what they do and how they do it in ways that are largely consistent with the values of those whom they are trying to help.

## CONCLUSION

In setting forth arguments for the development of an Australian system for the protection of human rights, Hilary Charlesworth characterises human rights as 'a framework for debate over basic values and conceptions of a good society'. Recognising that this debate should be conducted by all groups in society, not just those with the power to influence what is done and how it is done, this article asked: To what extent are the values which underpin rights-based approaches consistent with the values of those such an approach is intended to help?

A comparison of the general principles underlying all rights-based approaches to what is valued by those with experience of poverty reveals considerable overlap. Those with experience of poverty value dignity and respect above all else and place a high priority on choice and agency and on receiving information which will enhance their capacity to exercise choice and agency, all of which is consistent with rights based approaches, where the inherent dignity of the human person is seen as the basis of all rights and participation in decision-making processes is seen as the way in which individuals are able to live with dignity.

However, as Arnstein noted in her analysis of forms of citizen participation, genuine participation involves a redistribution of power, and when the forms of power involved in rights-based approaches and what is valued by those with experience of poverty are compared, slight differences emerge. For those with experience of poverty, it is important to participate in decisionmaking processes through the exercise of power that is linked to knowledge and expertise.

In other words, those with experience of poverty want to be treated as knowledgeable and to participate in decision-making processes because their knowledge and expertise are respected, rather than — as would be the case under rights-based approaches — because they have a 'right' to participate. While the outcome — participation — is the same, the basis for that participation is different. This difference is also evident when attitudes to welfare conditionality are examined. For many advocates of rights-based approaches, welfare conditionality is not consistent with such an approach because individuals have a right to health or employment and therefore should not have to do anything to earn what is theirs by right.

On the other hand, with the exception of health, those with experience of poverty are less concerned about claiming something by right and more concerned about enhancing their capacity to achieve their goals. But what are the practical implications of this difference? The discussion of what would need to change if the values of those with experience of poverty are taken as a conceptual framework revealed that the recommended actions are entirely consistent with rights-based approaches. The considerable overlap between the values which underpin rights-based approaches and what those with experience of poverty value means that those committed to a human rights framework for the development of social policy do not have to make major changes to what they do and how they do it if they wish to fully reflect the values of those with experience of poverty.

What is needed, however, is an awareness of the sources of second dimensional power and an increased understanding of what is already being done, as well as what could be done, to incorporate the knowledge and expertise of those with experience of poverty into the process of policy-making, implementation and evaluation.

# 2

# Capabilities

## INTRODUCTION

The moral appeal of human rights has been used for varying purposes, from resisting torture and arbitrary incarceration to demanding the end of hunger and of medical neglect. There is hardly any country in the world— from China, South Africa and Egypt to Mexico, Britain and the United States — in which arguments involving human rights have not been raised in one context or another in contemporary political debates. However, despite the tremendous appeal of the idea of human rights, it is also seen by many as being intellectually frail — lacking in foundation and perhaps even in coherence and cogency.

The remarkable co-existence of stirring appeal and deep conceptual scepticism is not new. The American Declaration of Independence took it to be 'self-evident' that everyone is "endowed by their Creator with certain inalienable rights", and 13 years later, in 1789, the French declaration of 'the rights of man' asserted that "men are born and remain free and equal in rights". But it did not take Jeremy Bentham long to insist, in Anarchical Fallacies, written during 1791–1792, that "natural rights is simple nonsense: natural and imprescriptible rights, rhetorical nonsense, nonsense upon stilts".

That division remains very alive today, and there are many who see the idea of human rights as no more than "bawling upon paper". The concepts of human rights and human capabilities have something of a common motivation, but they differ in many distinct ways. It is useful to ask whether considering the two concepts together — capabilities and human rights — can help the understanding of each. I will divide the exercise into four specific questions. First, can human rights be seen as entitlements to certain basic capabilities, and will this be a good way of thinking about human rights? Second, can the capability perspective provide a comprehensive coverage of the content of human rights? Third, since human rights need specificity, does the use of the capability perspective for elucidating human rights require a full articulation of the list of capabilities? And finally, how can we go about ascertaining the content of human rights and of basic capabilities when our values are supposed to be quite divergent, especially across borders of nationality and community? Can we have anything like a universalist approach to these ideas, in a world where cultures differ and practical preoccupations are also diverse?

## HUMAN RIGHTS AS ENTITLEMENTS TO CAPABILITIES

It is possible to argue that human rights are best seen as rights to certain specific freedoms, and that the correlate obligation to consider the associated duties must also be centred around what others can do to safeguard and expand these freedoms. Since capabilities can be seen, broadly, as freedoms of particular kinds, this would seem to establish a basic connection between the two categories of ideas. We run, however, into an immediate difficulty here.

I have argued elsewhere that 'opportunity' and 'process' are two aspects of freedom that require distinction, with the importance of each deserving specific acknowledgement. While the opportunity aspect of freedoms would seem to belong to the same kind of territory as capabilities, it is not at all clear that the same can be said about the process aspect of freedom. An example can bring out the separate relevance of both substantive opportunities and freedom of processes. Consider a woman, let us call her Natasha, who decides that she would like to go out in the evening. To take care of some considerations that are not central to the issues involved here, it is assumed that there are no particular safety risks involved in her going out, and that she has critically reflected on this decision and judged that going out would be the sensible — indeed the ideal — thing to do.

Now consider the threat of a violation of this freedom if some authoritarian guardians of society decide that she must not go out and if they force her, in one way or another, to stay indoors. To see that there are two distinct issues involved in this one violation, consider an alternative case in which the authoritarian bosses decide that she must — absolutely must — go out. There is clearly a violation of freedom even here though Natasha is being forced to do exactly what she would have chosen to do anyway, and this is readily seen when we compare the two alternatives 'choosing freely to go out' and 'being forced to go out'.

The latter involves an immediate violation of the process aspect of Natasha's freedom, since an action is being forced on her. The opportunity aspect may also be affected, since a plausible accounting of opportunities can include having options and it can inter alia include valuing free choice. However, the violation of the opportunity aspect would be more substantial and manifest if she were not only forced to do something chosen by another, but in fact forced to do something she would not otherwise choose to do. The comparison between 'being forced to go out' and, say, 'being forced to polish the shoes of others at home' brings out this contrast, which is primarily one of the opportunity aspect, rather than the process aspect. In the incarceration of Natasha, we can see two different ways in which she is losing her freedom: first, she is being forced to do something, with no freedom of choice; and second, what Natasha is being obliged to do is not something she would choose to do, if she had any plausible alternative.

It is important to recognise that both processes and opportunities can figure powerfully in the content of human rights. A denial of 'due process' in being, say, sentenced without a proper trial can be an infringement of human rights and so can be the denial of opportunity of medical treatment, or the opportunity of living without the danger of being assaulted. The idea of 'capability' can be very helpful in understanding the opportunity aspect of freedom and human rights. Indeed, even though the concept of opportunity is often invoked, it does require considerable elaboration, and capability can help in this elucidation.

*For example, seeing opportunity in terms of capability allows us to distinguish appropriately between:*

- Whether a person is actually able to do things she would value doing, and
- Whether she possesses the means or instruments or permissions to pursue what she would like to do.

By shifting attention, in particular, towards the former, the capability-based approach resists an overconcentration on means that can be found in some theories of justice. The capability approach can help to identify the possibility that two persons can have very different substantial opportunities even when they have exactly the same set of means: for example, a disabled person can do far less than an able-bodied person can, with exactly the same income and other 'primary goods'. The disabled person cannot, thus, be judged to be equally advantaged — with the same opportunities — as the person without any physical handicap but with the same set of means or instruments. The capability perspective allows us to take into account the parametric variability in the relation between the means, on the one hand, and the actual opportunities, on the other.

*Differences in the capability to function can arise even with the same set of personal means for a variety of reasons, such as:*

- Physical or mental heterogeneities among persons (related, for example, to disability, or proneness to illness);
- Variations in non-personal resources (such as the nature of public health care, or societal cohesion and the helpfulness of the community);
- Environmental diversities (such as climatic conditions, or varying threats from epidemic diseases or from local crime); or
- Different relative positions vis-a'-vis others (well illustrated by Adam Smith's discussion, in the Wealth of Nations, of the fact that the clothing and other resources one needs "to appear in public without

shame" depends on what other people standardly wear, which in turn could be more expensive in rich societies than in poorer ones).

I should, however, note here that there has been some serious criticism of describing these substantive opportunities (such as the capability to live one kind of a life or another) as 'freedoms', and it has been argued that this makes the idea of freedom too inclusive. For example, in her illuminating and sympathetic critique of my Development as Freedom, Susan Okin has presented arguments to suggest that I tend "to overextend the concept of freedom".

She has argued: "It is hard to conceive of some human functionings, or the fulfilment of some needs and wants, such as good health and nourishment, as freedoms without stretching the term until it seems to refer to everything that is of central value to human beings". There is, certainly, considerable scope for argument on how extensively the term freedom should be used. But the particular example considered in Okin's counter-argument reflects a misinterpretation.

There is no suggestion whatever that a functioning (*e.g.* being in good health or being well nourished) should be seen as freedom of any kind, such as capability. Rather, capability concentrates on the opportunity to be able to have combinations of functionings (including, in this case, the opportunity to be well-nourished), and the person is free to make use of this opportunity or not.

A capability reflects the alternative combinations of functionings from which the person can choose one combination. It is, therefore, not being suggested at all that being well-nourished is to be seen as a freedom. The term freedom, in the form of capability, is used here to refer to the extent to which the person is free to choose particular levels of functionings (such as being well-nourished), and that is not the same thing as what the person actually decides to choose. During India's struggle for independence from the Raj, Mahatma Gandhi famously did not use that opportunity to be well fed when he chose to fast, as a protest against the policies of the Raj.

In terms of the actual functioning of being well-nourished, the fasting Gandhi did not differ from a starving famine victim, but the freedoms and opportunities they respectively had were quite different. Indeed, the freedom to have any particular thing can be substantially distinguished from actually having that thing. What a person is free to have — not just what he actually has — is relevant, I have argued, to a theory of justice.

A theory of rights also has reason to be involved with substantive freedoms. Many of the terrible deprivations in the world have arisen from a lack of freedom to escape destitution. Even though indolence and inactivity had been classic themes in the old literature on poverty, people have starved and suffered because of a lack of alternative possibilities. It is the connection of poverty with unfreedom that led Marx to argue passionately for the need to replace "the domination of circumstances and chance over individuals by the domination of individuals over chance and circumstances". The importance of freedom can be brought out also by considering other types of issues that are also central to human rights.

Consider the freedom of immigrants to retain their ancestral cultural customs and lifestyles. This complex subject cannot be adequately assessed without distinguishing between doing something and being free to do that thing. A strong argument can be constructed in favour of an immigrant's having the freedom to retain her ancestral lifestyle, but this must not be seen as an argument in favour of her pursuing that ancestral lifestyle whether she herself chooses that pursuit or not.

The central issue, in this argument, is the person's freedom to choose how she should live — including the opportunity to pursue ancestral customs — and it cannot be turned into an argument for that person specifically pursuing those customs in particular, irrespective of the alternatives she has. The importance of capability — reflecting opportunities — is central to this distinction.

## THE PROCESS ASPECT OF FREEDOM AND INFORMATION PLURALISM

In the discussion so far I have been concentrating on what the capability perspective can do for a theory of justice or of human rights, but I would now like to turn to what it cannot do. While the idea of capability has considerable merit in the assessment of the opportunity aspect of freedom, it cannot possibly deal adequately with the process aspect of freedom, since capabilities are characteristics of individual advantages, and they fall short of telling us enough about the fairness or equity of the processes involved, or about the freedom of citizens to invoke and utilise procedures that are equitable.

The contrast of perspectives can be brought out with many different types of illustrations; let me choose a rather harsh example. It is, by now, fairly well established that, given symmetric care, women tend to live longer than men. If one were concerned only with capabilities (and nothing else), and in particular with equality of the capability to live long, it would have been possible to construct an argument for giving men more medical attention than women to counteract the natural masculine handicap.

But giving women less medical attention than men for the same health problems would clearly violate an important requirement of process equity, and it seems reasonable to argue, in cases of this kind, that demands of equity in process freedom could sensibly override a singleminded concentration on the opportunity aspect of freedom (and on the requirements of capability equality in particular). While it is important to emphasise the relevance of the capability perspective in judging people's substantive opportunities (particularly in comparison with alternative approaches that focus on incomes, or primary goods, or resources), that point does not, in any way, go against seeing the relevance also of the process aspect of freedom in a theory of human rights — or, for that matter, in a theory of justice. In this context, I should comment briefly also on a misinterpretation of the general relevance of the capability perspective in a theory of justice.

A theory of justice — or more generally an adequate theory of normative social choice — has to be alive both to the fairness of the processes involved and to the equity and efficiency of the substantive opportunities that people can enjoy. In dealing with the latter, capability can indeed provide a very helpful perspective, in comparison with, say, the Rawlsian concentration on 'primary goods'. But capability can hardly serve as the sole informational basis for the other considerations, related to processes, that must also be accommodated in normative social choice theory.

Consider the different components of Rawls's (1971) theory of justice. Rawls's 'first principle' of justice involves the priority of liberty, and the first part of the 'second principle' involves process fairness, through demanding that 'positions and offices be open to all'. The force and cogency of these Rawlsian concerns (underlying his first principle and the first part of the second principle) can neither be ignored nor be adequately addressed through relying only on the informational base of capabilities.

We may not agree with Rawls's own way of dealing with these issues, but these issues have to be addressed, and they cannot be sensibly addressed within the substantive boundaries of capability accounting. On the other hand, the capability perspective comes into its own in dealing with the remainder of the second principle; namely, 'the Difference Principle' — a principle that is particularly concerned with the distribution of advantages that different people enjoy (a consideration that Rawls tried to capture, I believe inadequately, within the confines of the accounting of 'primary goods'). The territory that Rawls reserved for primary goods, as used in his Difference Principle, would indeed, I argue, be better served by the capability perspective. That does not, however, obliterate in any way the relevance of the rest of the territory of justice (related to the first principle and the first part of the second principle), in which process considerations, including liberty and procedural equity. A similar plurality of informational base has to be invoked in dealing with the multiplicity of considerations that underlie a theory of human rights. Capabilities and the opportunity aspect of freedom, important as they are, have to be supplemented by considerations of fair processes and the lack of violation of people's right to invoke and utilise them.

## LISTING CAPABILITIES

I turn now to the controversial question of the listing of capabilities. In its application, the capability approach allows considerable variations in application. Martha Nussbaum has discussed powerfully the advantages of identifying an overarching 'list of capabilities', with given priorities. My own reluctance to join the search for such a canonical list arises partly from my difficulty in seeing how the exact lists and weights would be chosen without appropriate specification of the context of their use (which could vary), but also from a disinclination to accept any substantive diminution of the domain of public reasoning.

The framework of capabilities helps, in my judgement, to clarify and illuminate the subject matter of public reasoning, which can involve epistemic issues (including claims of objective importance) as well as ethical and political ones. It cannot, I would argue, sensibly aim at displacing the need for continued public reasoning.

Indeed, I would submit that one of the uses of the capability perspective is to bring out the need for transparent valuational scrutiny of individual advantages and adversities, since the different functionings have to be assessed and weighted in relation to each other, and the opportunities of having different combinations of functionings also have to be evaluated. The richness of the capability perspective broadly interpreted, thus, includes its insistence on the need for open valuational scrutiny for making social judgements, and in this sense it fits in well with the importance of public reasoning. This openness of transparent valuation contrasts with burying the evaluative exercise in some mechanical — and valuationally opaque — convention (*e.g.* by taking marketevaluated income to be the invariable standard of individual advantage, thereby giving implicit normative priority to institutionally determined market prices).

The problem is not with listing important capabilities, but with insisting on one pre-determined canonical list of capabilities, chosen by theorists without any general social discussion or public reasoning. To have such a fixed list, emanating entirely from pure theory, is to deny the possibility of fruitful public participation on what should be included and why.

I have, of course, discussed various lists of capabilities that would seem to demand attention in theories of justice and more generally in social assessment, such as the freedom to be well nourished, to live disease-free lives, to be able to move around, to be educated, to participate in public life, and so on. Indeed, right from my first writings on using the capability perspective, I have tried to discuss the relevance of specific capabilities that are important in a particular exercise.

The 1979 Tanner lecture went into the relevance of "the ability to move about", along with other basic capabilities, such as "the ability to meet one's nutritional requirements, the wherewithal to be closed and sheltered, the power to participate in the social life of the community". The contrast between lists of capabilities and commodities was a central concern in Commodities and Capabilities.

The relevance of many capabilities that are often neglected were discussed in my second set of Tanner Lectures, given at Cambridge University under the title The Standard of Living. My scepticism is about fixing a cemented list of capabilities that is seen as being absolutely complete and totally fixed. I am a great believer in theory, and certainly accept that a good theory of evaluation and assessment has to bring out the relevance of what we are free to do and free to be, as opposed to the material goods we have and the commodities we can command. But I must also argue that pure theory cannot 'freeze' a list of capabilities for all societies for all time to come, irrespective of what the citizens come to understand and value. That would be not only a denial of the reach of democracy, but also a misunderstanding of what pure theory can do, completely divorced from the particular social reality that any particular society faces.

Along with the exercise of listing the relevant capabilities, there is also the problem of determining the relative weights and importance of the different capabilities included in the relevant list. Even with a given list, the question of valuation cannot be avoided. There is sometimes a temptation not only to have one fixed list, but also to have the elements of the list ordered in a lexicographic way. But this can hardly work.

For example, the ability to be well-nourished cannot in general be put invariably above or below the ability to be well-sheltered (with the implication that the tiniest improvement of the higher ranked capability will always count as more important than a large change in the lower ranked one). The judgement must take into account the extent to which the different abilities are being realised or violated. Also, the weighting must be contingent on circumstances.

We may have to give priority to the ability to be well-nourished when people are dying of hunger in their homes, whereas the freedom to be sheltered may rightly receive more weight when people are in general well-fed, but lack shelter and protection from the elements. Some of the basic capabilities (with which my 1979 Tanner Lecture was particularly concerned) will no doubt figure in every list of relevant capabilities in every society.

But the exact list to be used will have to take note of the purpose of the exercise. There is often good sense in narrowing the coverage of capabilities for a specific purpose. Jean Dre`ze and I have tried to invoke such lists of elementary capabilities in dealing with 'hunger and public action', and in a different context, in dealing with India's economic and social achievements and failures. I see Martha Nussbaum's powerful use of a given list of capabilities for some minimal rights against deprivation as being extremely useful, in the same practical way. For another practical purpose, we may need quite a different list. For example, when my friend Mahbub ul Haq asked me, in 1989, to work with him on indicators of human development, and in particular to help develop a general index for global assessment and critique, it was clear to me that we were involved in a particular exercise of specific relevance. So the 'Human Development Index' was based on a very minimal listing of capabilities, with a particular focus on getting at a minimally basic quality of life, calculable from available statistics, in a way that the Gross National Product or Gross Domestic Product failed to capture.

Lists of capabilities have to be used for various purposes, and so long as we understand what we are doing (and, in particular, that we are getting a list for a particular reason, related to assessment, evaluation, or critique), we do not put ourselves against other lists that may be relevant or useful for other purposes. All this has to be contrasted with insisting on one 'final list of capabilities that matter'. To decide that some capability will not figure in the list of relevant capabilities at all amounts to putting a zero weight on that capability for every exercise, no matter what the exercise is concerned with, and no matter what the social conditions are. This could be very dogmatic, for many distinct reasons. First, we use capabilities for different purposes. What we focus on cannot be independent of what we are doing and why (*e.g.* whether we are evaluating poverty, specifying certain basic human rights, getting a rough and ready measure of human development, and so on). Second, social conditions and the priorities that they suggest may vary.

For example, given the nature of poverty in India as well as the nature of available technology, it was not unreasonable in 1947 (when India became independent) to concentrate on elementary education, basic health, and so on, and to not worry too much about whether everyone can effectively communicate across the country and beyond. However, with the development of the internet and its wide-ranging applications, and the advance made in information technology (not least in India), access to the web and the freedom of general communication has become a very important capability that is of interest and relevance to all Indians. Third, even with given social conditions, public discussion and reasoning can lead to a better understanding of the role, reach and the significance of particular capabilities. For example, one of the many contributions of feminist economics has precisely been to bring out the importance of certain freedoms that were not recognised very clearly — or at all — earlier on; for example, freedom from the imposition of fixed and time-honoured family roles, or immunity from implicit derogation through the rhetoric of social communication.

To insist on a 'fixed forever' list of capabilities would deny the possibility of progress in social understanding, and also go against the productive role of public discussion, social agitation, and open debates. I have nothing against the listing of capabilities (and take part in that activity often enough), but I have to stand up against any proposal of a grand mausoleum to one fixed and final list of capabilities.

## PUBLIC REASONING, CULTURAL DIVERSITY AND UNIVERSALITY

I turn now to the final question. If the listing of capabilities must be subject to the test of public reasoning, how can we proceed in a world of differing values and disparate cultures? How can we judge the acceptability of claims to human rights and to relevant capabilities, and assess the challenges they may face? How would such a disputation — or a defence — proceed? I would argue that, like the assessment of other ethical claims, there must be some test of open and informed scrutiny, and it is to such a scrutiny that we have to look in order to proceed to a disavowal or an affirmation.

The status that these ethical claims have must be ultimately dependent on their survivability in unobstructed discussion. In this sense, the viability of human rights is linked with what John Rawls has called 'public reasoning' and its role in 'ethical objectivity'. Indeed, the role of public reasoning in the formulation and vindication of human rights is extremely important to understand. Any general plausibility that these ethical claims — or their denials — have is, on this theory, dependent on their ability to survive and flourish when they encounter unobstructed discussion and scrutiny (along with adequately wide informational availability).

The force of a claim for a human right would be seriously undermined if it were possible to show that they are unlikely to survive open public scrutiny. But contrary to a commonly offered reason for scepticism and rejection, thc case for human rights cannot be discarded simply by pointing to the possibility that in politically and socially repressive regimes, which do not allow open public discussion, many of these human rights are not taken seriously at all. Open critical scrutiny is essential for dismissal as well as for defence.

The fact that monitoring of violations of human rights and the procedure of 'naming and shaming' can be so effective (at least, in putting the violators on the defensive) is some indication of the wide reach of public reasoning when information becomes available and ethical arguments are allowed rather than suppressed. It is, however, important not to keep the domain of public reasoning confined to a given society only, especially in the case of human rights, in view of the inescapably universalist nature of these rights. This is in contrast with Rawls's inclination, particularly in his later works, to limit such public confrontation within the boundaries of each particular nation for determining what would be just, at least in domestic affairs. We can demand, on the contrary, that the discussion has to include, even for domestic justice (if only to avoid parochial prejudices and to examine a broader range of counter-arguments), views also from 'a certain distance'.

*The necessity of this was powerfully identified by Adam Smith:*

- We can never survey our own sentiments and motives, we can never form any judgment concerning them; unless we remove ourselves, as it were, from our own natural station, and endeavour to view them as at a certain distance from us. But we can do this in no other way than by endeavouring to view them with the eyes of other people, or as other people are likely to view them.

Questions are often raised about whether distant people can, in fact, provide useful scrutiny of local issues, given what are taken to be 'uncrossable' barriers of culture. One of Edmund Burke's criticisms of the French declaration of the 'rights of man' and its universalist spirit was concerned with disputing the acceptability of that notion in other cultures. Burke argued that "the liberties and the restrictions vary with times and circumstances, and admit of infinite modifications, that cannot be settled upon any abstract rule".

The belief that the universality that is meant to underlie the notion of human rights is profoundly mistaken has, for this reason, found expression in many other writings as well. A belief in uncrossable barriers between the values of different cultures has surfaced and resurfaced repeatedly over the centuries, and they are forcefully articulated today.

The claim of magnificent uniqueness — and often of superiority — has sometimes come from critics of 'Western values', varying from champions of regional ethics (well illustrated by the fuss in the 1990s about the peerless excellence of 'Asian values'), or religious or cultural separatists (with or without being accompanied by fundamentalism of one kind or another).

Sometimes, however, the claim of uniqueness has come from Western particularists. A good example is Samuel Huntington's (1996) insistence that the "West was West long before it was modern", and his claim that "a sense of individualism and a tradition of individual rights and liberties" are "unique among civilized societies". Similarly, no less a historian of ideas than Gertrude Himmelfarb has argued that ideas of 'justice', 'right', 'reason' and 'love of humanity' are "predominantly, perhaps even uniquely, Western values".

I have discussed these diagnoses elsewhere. Contrary to cultural stereotypes, the histories of different countries in the world have shown considerable variations over time as well as between different groups within the same country. When, in the twelfth century, the Jewish philosopher Maimonedes had to flee an intolerant Europe and its Inquisitions to try to safeguard his human right to stick to his own religious beliefs and practice, he sought shelter in Emperor Saladin's Egypt and found an honoured position in the court of this Muslim emperor. Several hundred years later, when, in Agra, the Moghal emperor of India, Akbar, was arguing — and legislating — on the government's duty to uphold the right to religious freedom of all citizens, the European Inquisitions were still going on, and Giordano Bruno was burnt at the stake in Rome, in 1600.

In his autobiography, Long Walk to Freedom, Nelson Mandela describes how he learned about democracy and individual rights, as a young boy, by seeing the proceedings of the local meetings held in the regent's house in Mqhekezweni:

- Everyone who wanted to speak did so. It was democracy in its purest form. There may have been a hierarchy of importance among the speakers, but everyone was heard, chief and subject, warrior and medicine man, shopkeeper and farmer, landowner and laborer.

Not only are the differences on the subject of freedoms and rights that actually exist between different societies often much exaggerated, but also there is, typically, little note taken of substantial variations within each local culture — over time and even at a point of time. What are taken to be 'foreign' criticisms often correspond to internal criticisms from non-mainstream groups.

If, say, Iranian dissidents are imprisoned by an authoritarian regime precisely because of their heterodoxy, any suggestion that they should be seen as 'ambassadors of Western values' rather than as 'Iranian dissidents' would only add serious insult to manifest injury. Being culturally non-partisan requires respecting the participation of people from any corner of the earth, which is not the same thing as accepting the prevailing priorities, especially among dominant groups in particular societies, when information is extremely restricted and discussions and disagreements are not permitted. Scrutiny from a 'distance' may have something to offer in the assessment of practices as different from each other as the stoning of adulterous women in the Taliban's Afghanistan and the abounding use of capital punishment in parts of the United States.

This is the kind of issue that made Smith insist that "the eyes of the rest of mankind" must be invoked to understand whether "a punishment appears equitable". Ultimately, the discipline of critical moral scrutiny requires, among other things, "endeavouring to view with the eyes of other people, or as other people are likely to view them". Intellectual interactions across the borders can be as important in rich societies as they are in poorer ones.

The point to note here is not so much whether we are allowed to chat across borders and to make crossboundary scrutiny, but that the discipline of critical assessment of moral sentiments — no matter how locally established they are — requires that we view our practices inter alia from a certain distance. Both the understanding of human rights and of the adequacy of a list of basic capabilities, I would argue, are intimately linked with the reach of public discussion — between persons and across borders. The viability and universality of human rights and of an acceptable specification of capabilities are dependent on their ability to survive open critical scrutiny in public reasoning.

## CONCLUSIONS

To conclude, the two concepts — human rights and capabilities — go well with each other, so long as we do not try to subsume either entirely within the other. There are many human rights for which the capability perspective has much to offer. However, human rights to important process freedoms cannot be adequately analysed within the capability approach. Furthermore, both human rights and capabilities have to depend on the process of public reasoning, which neither can lose without serious impoverishment of its respective intellectual content. The methodology of public scrutiny draws on Rawlsian understanding of 'objectivity' in ethics, but the impartiality that is needed cannot be confined within the borders of a nation. We have to go much beyond Rawls for that reason, just as we also have to go beyond the enlightenment provided by his use of 'primary goods', and invoke, in that context, the more articulate framework of capabilities. The need for extension does not, of course, reduce our debt to John Rawls. Neither human rights nor capabilities would have been easy to understand without his pioneering departures.

# 3

# Human Rights and Economics

## INTRODUCTION

The relationship between the disciplines of human rights theory and economics is often awkward and at times openly hostile. Departing from contrasting conceptions of 'the good', mainstream economists and rights theorists have tended to talk past, rather than to, each other. Language also gets in the way, as each discipline has its own highly specialised, technical vocabulary. Disagreement over terminology extends to the meaning of the word 'development'.

The majority of UN bodies have stated a commitment to a rights-based approach to development that defines progress in terms of the fulfilment of social, political, economic, cultural and civil rights. Societies that do not create the conditions for their citizens to realise these rights cannot be said to be 'developed'. This is not a definition that most economists are prepared to sign up to. For them, development is measured in terms of people's command over goods and services, usually expressed as preferred commodity bundles.

Whether their rights are violated or not is a political question that is at best tangential to their understanding of development progress and at worst – following Bentham's famous characterisation of the Rights of Man – 'nonsense on stilts'. For example, Gauri raises questions over the practical relevance of rights-based approaches to health and education in developing countries:

- Do these criticisms mean that a human rights approach to healthcare and education in developing countries is vague, impractical or self-defeating? If rights are understood as binding constraints on government action, it is hard to avoid those conclusions. Governments in developing countries cannot provide or assure adequate levels of healthcare and education. Given that legal systems in most developing countries are inequitable and underdeveloped and that enforcement mechanisms are weak, allowing citizens to make legal claims of inadequate service provision will further politicise courts, weaken their capacity to adjudicate existing rights, and possibly increase government spending even where it is inequitable or inefficient.

Thus, for many economists, any attempt to posit and enforce a human right to basic services is either fanciful or counterproductive, or both. Human rights theorists counter that economists are too quick to hide behind the impracticality of realising rights, particularly economic and social rights, when in many cases violations are primarily the result of explicit political decisions rather than resource scarcity or other physical or institutional limitations.

Despite these deeply rooted disagreements, human rights theory and economics do share some important things in common. As twin branches from the trunk of enlightenment thought, they share a commitment to the autonomy of the individual and a methodology that approaches social questions through the aggregation of individual circumstances. Whether the focus is on rights or preferences, the individual reigns supreme, with all the methodological advantages and disadvantages that this implies for the study of society.

Economists recognise that the rational agents who motivate their microeconomic models could not freely express their preferences without the prior realisation of at least some rights. That set includes property rights, the realisation of which, as with rights more generally, assumes the prior existence of the required legal infrastructure to establish and protect them. For their part, rights advocates know that individuals cannot realise their rights without access to a minimum level of income. This article argues that human rights theory and economics are not as incompatible as is often imagined.

Although differences in approach do divide the two disciplines, there is an increasing awareness, at least among some theorists, that disagreements have often been overstated while insufficient attention has been paid to potential complementarities. Moreover, the absence of a constructive dialogue between rightsbased and economic approaches to development has devalued both and represents an obstacle to a fuller understanding of the development process.

We argue that economists should broaden the array of rights considered essential to individual choice beyond property rights to include other essential human rights. Moving beyond property rights to incorporate other rights in the minimum institutional set-up for social choice would enable economists to address questions of exploitation and power relations that are assumed away in most welfare models. We further argue that those working on human rights need to broaden the array of tools at their disposal to analyse and understand economic and social situations that impinge upon the realisation of rights.

## DEFINITIONS

The human rights theorists that we refer to in this article include writers who either subscribe to a collection of ideas that ascribe rights to all people on the basis of their individual humanity, or are concerned with the application of human rights law, whether international, regional or national. Neither human rights theorists so defined nor welfare economists have arrived at a consensus on the proper scope, methods and analytical core of their respective disciplines.

We need therefore to begin with a few key definitions. Human rights theory consists of two related branches. The first is ethical or philosophical, the second legal. While both have historical antecedents at least reaching back to the nineteenth century, and arguably considerably further back, the modern understanding of human rights is largely a construct of the twentieth century. The adoption of the language of human rights as the lingua franca of ethical consideration in international relations, and to an increasing extent in national policy-making and sociopolitical dialogue, is a relatively recent phenomenon.

The decision of the founders of the United Nations to adopt a human rights framework to express the new organisation's economic, social and political agenda was an important milestone in the application of rights language to international affairs. The ethical or philosophical branch of human rights theory is essentially a deontological moral theory which holds that actions and choices should be judged on the basis of their adherence to particular rules or norms, rather than their outcomes.

*Thus Michael Sandel notes that:*

- In its moral sense, deontology opposes consequentialism; it describes a firstorder ethic containing certain categorical duties and prohibitions which take unqualified precedence over moral and practical concerns. In its foundational sense, deontology opposes teleology; it describes a form of justification in which first principles are derived in a way that does not presuppose any final human purposes or ends, nor any determinate conception of the human good.

This presents an immediate contrast with the usual perspective of welfare economics, under which, just as to one of its leading practitioners, 'the violation or fulfilment of basic liberties or rights tends to be ignored ... not just because of its consequentialist focus, but particularly because of its "welfarism" whereby consequent states of affairs are judged exclusively by the utilities generated in the respective states'.

The ethical branch of human rights theory thus maintains that all human beings are endowed, as a result of their humanity, with a set of rights that imply obligations and duties in other people. This characteristic of focusing on obligations and duties is a core feature of a human rights perspective, sometimes viewed by critics as an over-eagerness to assign blame even when responsibility for a given state of affairs is collective or when for institutional or structural reasons responsibility cannot be apportioned to specific people or groups.

Economists are quick to question attempts to hold individuals or even institutions accountable for the outcomes produced by the decentralised economic decisions of the market. The second, legal approach to human rights forms a branch of public international law, including the standards of international human rights instruments such as UNsponsored human rights law, or regional human rights law, as well as human rightsrelated provisions of customary international law.

These sit alongside the provisions of national legislation, much of which addresses human rights considerations laid out in international and regional human rights instruments through either direct incorporation or other expressions. Legal positivists contend that 'human rights' can only be understood as the rights prescribed by law, therefore rejecting the idea of the so-called 'natural' or 'pre-legal' rights. Ethical human rights theorists respond that the laws themselves are derived from each society's ethical norms.

At the very least, the two approaches do not appear to be entirely separate from one another conceptually, since the provisions of international human rights law are generally aligned with the ethical prescriptions of human rights theory. Within the economics discipline, neoclassical welfare economics represents the dominant approach to the assessment of alternative public policies.

*The following propositions constitute the basic premises of welfare theory:*

- *Welfarism*: Alternative policies should be assessed in relation to their impact on individual and aggregate utility, normally defined as the satisfaction of preferences. Welfarism is a narrower form of utilitarian consequentialism, in which utility is measured solely in terms of access to things of economic value.
- *Ordinal Utility*: To avoid the methodological problem of measuring utility in an objective manner, welfare economists rely on rank orderings of personal preferences, generally consisting of alternative bundles of commodities. This implies that we cannot make interpersonal comparisons of utility.
- *Pareto Criterion*: The basic choice rule in welfare economics is Pareto optimality, under which a policy change is to be preferred if it leaves at least one person better-off and no one worse-off than other possibilities.
- *Compensation*: Since most real world decisions involve losers as well as winners, welfare economists weaken the Pareto criterion to admit solutions under which winners could hypothetically compensate losers, leaving everyone at least as well-off as before the policy change.
- *Social Welfare Functions*: The compensation principle does not provide a choice procedure to differentiate among the many possible solutions that pass the weak Pareto test. Social welfare functions

> produce these rank orderings of possible outcomes, but only through the introduction of externally generated ethical criteria. For example, the social welfare function could treat all individuals the same, or it could assign larger weights to the utility of the least well-off or some other group.

Welfare economics is normative in the sense that it offers judgements as to which policies are best from society's perspective, but it can only do so when ethical principles are introduced exogenously – for example, the weights assigned to various groups in the social welfare function. Practitioners see the ethical agnosticism of welfare economics as a strength: whatever ultimate ends are chosen through the political process, society should still opt for policies that achieve these objectives as efficiently as possible.

Yet the apparatus described above does implicitly favour certain ethical positions. The Pareto criterion privileges the status quo, since it selects options that do not result in losses. Economists' commitment to the principle that voluntary exchange will automatically generate socially optimal outcomes too often leads them to the unwarranted conclusion that existing arrangements must be optimal because they were arrived at voluntarily.

Thus economists are poorly equipped theoretically to deal with issues of exploitation and domination. Bromley's example of the Factory Acts is instructive. Viewed from the Pareto perspective, limiting the working hours of children could be viewed as an inefficient institutional change, reducing national competitiveness and lowering the incomes of families with working children.

Child workers who had not been compelled to work, except by economic necessity, could be said to be acting on their preferences, or perhaps the preferences of their parents. Reformers could only argue that herding children into factories for twelve to sixteen hours a day was uncivilised by some a priori standard, but clearly not one that had moved the public to action. A neoclassical welfare economist present at the time might have argued that the Factory Acts were just another instance of special interests manipulating the political system to reduce aggregate social welfare.

Similarly, economists' reliance on revealed preferences as a measure of utility suggests a political libertarianism that sees no role for social norms and standards to condition individual behaviour. Privileging preferences begs the question of how preferences are formed in the first place. Welfare economists operate from an atomistic and static view of preference formation, one that does not accord with our everyday experience of decision-making.

Some people prefer not to wear seat-belts in automobiles, but society has good reason to regard this initial preference as illegitimate. And over time, we can expect their habits and preferences to change, perhaps in response to peer pressure, new information or changing social norms. Amartya Sen's influential critique of welfarism is based on the potential for incompatibility between liberal rights – in his example, the right to read a controversial book – and the Pareto criterion. Public controversy surrounding issues such as women's reproductive rights, state support for stem cell research and the legal status of pornography and recreational drug use shows quite clearly that the realisation of certain rights results in situations that do not necessarily please all of the people all of the time. Welfare economists may respond that resolution of these problems belongs appropriately in the political sphere, but this move only serves to narrow the applicability of welfare economics to a very limited range of uncontentious policy issues.

## HUMAN RIGHTS, ECONOMICS AND DEVELOPMENT

Historically, development has been concerned primarily with economic growth. Social equity concerns came into the development discourse in the 1970s, and human development in the 1990s. Yet development theory has largely remained the preserve of economists, and development economists have remained preoccupied with the problem of economic growth in poor countries. Human rights as a discipline has concerned itself with the outcomes of development for some time.

The 1948 Universal Declaration of Human Rights, which is not legally binding, sets out rights to food, shelter, education and the various other goods which are the agreed desirable outcomes of the development process. This is elaborated in the legally binding International Covenant on Economic, Social and Cultural Rights and further developed by the jurisprudence of the Committee on Economic, Social and Cultural Rights established under that treaty inter alia.

More recently, particularly over the last decade, the links between human rights and development have become more prominent in the development discourse, with the emergence of a putative 'rights-based approach to development' and at least the juxtaposition of human rights alongside development considerations in documents such as the Millennium Declaration. Conceptual approaches to the relationship between development and human rights vary, but two poles are discernible at the extremes of the debate. The first views human rights as an input into the development process. This position, which is implicit in the approach adopted by the Development Assistance Committee of the Organisation for Economic Co-operation and Development, suggests that the protection of human rights has a positive economic impact.

The second sees rights as an output, perhaps even an unintended output, of development. From this perspective human rights can be seen as a luxury that citizens of better-off countries may enjoy as incomes rise, given appropriate, and largely contingent, political preconditions. The 'mutual reinforcement' view combines the two approaches, arguing that poverty generates conflict and human rights violations, but improvements in the human rights situation can pay off in the form of economic benefits. Both the input and output interpretations of the relationship between human rights and development are influenced by a narrow view of 'human rights' as consisting only of civil and political rights, such as the rights to freedom of speech and due process of law.

Even where a broader set of rights, including those to health, education or food, is recognised, these are considered more aspirational and less concrete or real than civil and political rights.

*A good example of the standard form of this position was neatly expressed in the Economist of 22 May 2007, which complained:*

- Food, jobs and housing are certainly necessities. But no useful purpose is served by calling them 'rights'. When a government locks someone up without a fair trial, the victim, perpetrator and remedy are pretty clear. This seldom applies to social and economic 'rights'. It is hard enough to determine whether such a right has been infringed, let alone who should provide a remedy or how. Who should be educated in which subjects for how long at what cost in taxpayers' money is a political question best settled at the ballot box … no economic system known to man guarantees a proper job for everyone all the time: even the Soviet Union's much-boasted full employment was based on the principle 'they pretend to pay us and we pretend to work'.

The pervasiveness of this partial understanding of human rights partly reflects the influence of the US government in shaping the international rights discourse, and the comparatively greater success of civil society movements and organisations concerned with these rights in comparison with advocates of economic, social and cultural rights.

In a world accustomed to vast differences in wealth and life chances, political and civil rights have achieved an aura of universality – even as they remain unfulfilled for most of the earth's inhabitants – while social and cultural rights are seen as impractical at best and at worst a harking back to the failed project of state socialism. There is some truth in the perception that a human rights perspective, understood in terms of the entirety of human rights described in international human rights law, does indeed sit more comfortably with the views of the political and economic left than the political and economic right.

*Donnelly recognises this, arguing that:*

- Free markets are an economic analog to a political system of majority rule without minority rights. Like pure democracy, free markets sacrifice individuals and their rights to a 'higher' collective good. The welfare state, from this perspective, is a device to ensure that a minority that is disadvantaged in or deprived by markets is treated with minimum economic concern and respect.

But even as these polar positions on the role of human rights in development have gained currency, the idea of development itself has begun to change. The persistence of poverty and exploitation and the increase in social inequality evident in some rapidly growing developing countries – and in high-income countries like the United States – demonstrated that treating economic growth and development as synonymous risks confusing means with ends.

Similarly, the poor economic performance of some highly unequal societies and the rapid growth of the relatively equal East Asian countries suggested to some development specialists that the line of causality ran from social progress to growth, another version of the 'input' approach to rights that would conveniently obviate the need for a more fundamental rethinking of traditional approaches to economic development.

This view ultimately proved no more convincing than the conventional and converse assertion that the early stages of development required more rather than less inequality. More careful analysis has revealed the fragility of statistical relationships between equality and economic growth. Meanwhile, the East Asian financial crisis has taken some of the gloss off the only recently proclaimed 'East Asian Miracle', and rapid economic growth in China has generated social inequality on the scale of Brazil or Pakistan.

From the perspective of rights theory, to regard the social, economic and cultural rights of the International Covenant on Economic, Social and Cultural Rights as an input into or an output of the growth process is to confuse the instrumental with the fundamental, and thereby trivialise rights. The human rights perspective on development requires more than a reordering of inputs and outputs or the substitution of a new growth model. The replacement of a commodities-based with a rights-based definition of development denotes a shift in values from the satisfaction of needs to the realisation of rights. In contrast to the consequentialist utilitarianism of welfare economics, rights theorists reject certain outcomes even if they make most people better-off. From the rights perspective, certain classes of rights deprivation are inadmissible under any circumstances. In effect, the rights-based approach delegitimises social choices that deny rights to a minority in the hopes of generating growth for the majority.

Albert Camus wrote in his critique of Marxism that 'responsibility towards History releases one from responsibility towards human beings.' Human rights theorists argue that responsibility towards growth does not release one from responsibility towards human rights. This proposed shift from needs satisfaction to rights realisation immediately raises a number of objections from neoclassical welfare economists. The fulfilment of economic, social and cultural rights is hard to imagine without the prior achievement of development outcomes such as poverty reduction. But unlike the growth-oriented approach, recognition of these rights does not specify the means through which the rights can be realised.

It merely states that responsible actors – in the ethical understanding all people and in the legal understanding States Parties to the relevant treaties – must do the best they can with the resources available to them. Hence the principle in human rights law of 'progressive realisation', which acknowledges that in the context of resource constraints certain rights primarily from the sphere of economic, social or cultural rights cannot be realised immediately and must be realised progressively.

Similarly, the obligations arising from these rights are for their progressive rather than immediate realisation: rights theory and law understands that there is little value in demanding that people or governments achieve the impossible. Thus a State Party to the Convention on the Rights of the Child is not necessarily in breach of its treaty obligations because some children under its jurisdiction are not in school.

The issue is rather whether or not the government is doing the most that it can, given the circumstances and resources at its disposal. Since extremely poor societies cannot realise every citizen's human rights simply through redistribution, this approach implicitly suggests that growth is a prerequisite for the realisation of rights: states must promote economic growth to fulfil their duties to their people. Economists argue that rights advocates in this way smuggle the growth-oriented view back into the development discourse through the back door.

Similarly, welfare economists ask if the shift from consequentialism to rights implies a shift from market to state. Neoclassical welfare economists insist on the separation of equity and efficiency concerns: competitive markets produce unique, efficient outcomes, but equity can only be achieved through the prior redistribution of assets, presumably by an all-powerful state. To the extent that the rights-based approach entails a redistribution of resources to the least well-off members of society, are human rights theorists of necessity proponents of Big Government and strong states? Do these disagreements mean that economics and rights theory are incompatible in practice?

To address this question we must ask whether each side of the debate has a proper understanding of what the other discipline. After all, economists and protagonists of human rights are concerned with similar things, such as access to food, clothing, housing, health and education. Economists start from the recognition of the 'concerns of all individuals to have these things', while human rights protagonists start from 'a concern that all individuals should have them'. Does this generate incompatibility or complementarity?

## HUMAN RIGHTS AND THE ECONOMIC MODEL

Human rights theory is deontological, meaning that it assesses choices with respect to rules and norms rather than results. In its simplest expression, a rights statement has the form 'A has the right to B against C because of D'. The most common terminology used is that A is the rights holder, B the object of the right, C the duty-bearer and D the justification. There are various different justifications, or 'Ds', in different schools of human rights theory, but they tend to generate fairly similar lists of 'Bs' or objects.

These justifications share the premise that rights are inherent to the human person, that we are born 'free and equal in dignity and in rights'. From the perspective of human rights law, 'D' is reduced to 'because it is prescribed in human rights law', making the list of 'Bs' identical to the rights laid out in human rights instruments, and the 'As' the individuals covered by those instruments. For example, in UN-sponsored human rights law rights holders are individuals under the jurisdiction of States Parties to that law. 'Cs' are generally government authorities or institutions in the case of UN-sponsored human rights law. In standard models of a rights-based approach to development, the list of 'Cs' goes beyond the state, identifying key actors with a duty arising from particular individuals' rights. In standard human rights theories the list of 'Cs' is necessarily all other human beings with relevant agency. In contrast to the consequentialism of welfare economics, the rights of human rights theory and law are not contingent on the outcomes arrived at by their application. On the contrary, rights cannot be overridden on the basis of an argument about their consequences. That human rights advocates would like to see children in school, the sick provided with medical care and everyone enjoying adequate shelter does not mean that all who share those concerns are, conversely, automatically human rights advocates.

*As Nelson puts it:*

- The rights-based approach begins ... from aspects of human well-being: health, nutrition, education and other desirable conditions. For human rights practitioners however ... human rights standards are not indicators or goals, but ... statements about rights to which humans are entitled by virtue of their humanity.

*Gauri highlights this with particular regard to the examples of healthcare and education:*

- ... The mechanisms and processes for the delivery of health and education services are, in the rights approach, themselves morally compelling ... On the other hand, the economic approach views those processes instrumentally: they could in principle be reconciled with authoritarian styles in medicine and school governance if those lowered mortality and raised literacy.

Another difference is that human rights theory actively rejects the idea that human rights can be ranked in terms of the relative importance whether of particular rights or of the rights of one person versus those of another. It does so for two main reasons. With regard to prioritising one right over another, it is clear that to do so would require resort to some logically prior, presumably ethical, principle; if one right is prioritised over another, it must be done on some basis. Whatever that basis is, it must represent a principle that could at any time be drawn upon to 'trump' rights claims, making those claims secondary and vulnerable to being overridden at any time on the basis of that prior principle. With regard to prioritising rights between people, to do so not only violates the idea that people are equal in rights, but also allows a 'calculus' of human rights, whereby the rights of a minority can be sacrificed to achieve enjoyment of the rights of a majority. Thus ranking by its nature undermines the rights framework by making rights either contingent on logically prior principles or subject to a calculus that allows them to be overridden by 'greater good' arguments.

If one considers recent historical experience of the Great Depression of the 1930s and the Holocaust when the UN Charter was framed infused with the language of human rights, the attraction of a human rights framework with its central characteristic of 'non-ranking' is clear. Constructs such as John Rawls' second principle of justice suggest ways in which inequality of outcomes between people could be incorporated into a rights-compatible normative model, but this is not the same as endorsing inequalities with respect to rights.

Economists, by way of contrast, reject prior reference to rules and norms in favour of rank orderings of market or social outcomes. The value attached to any situation can only be measured relative to the existing situation, and then only in terms of marginal improvements in the ability of individuals to satisfy their preferences. In the extreme, an economist would have no basis on which to differentiate between an additional 500 calories of energy obtained by a starving child or an overweight adult.

Reference to an objective 'social welfare function' can steer us away from such obvious absurdities, but such solutions must be introduced as a deus ex machina that overrides individuals' preferences. It is legitimate to propose that all good things should be available to everyone at all times, but given that they are not, and are unlikely to be soon, economists justifiably ask for rules that establish priorities for action. Economists' social-welfare functions rank outcomes just as to their relative success in satisfying individual preferences. The human rights objection to the consequentialism of welfare economics is that some actions are inherently wrong even if they result in a desirable outcome. A consequentialist would struggle to explain why use of rape as a weapon of war is ethically wrong if it ultimately speeds the conclusion of the war itself and thus a reduction in the overall amount of human suffering.

The human rights advocate accepts the inconvenience of a theory which fails to resolve all or even the majority of possible dilemmas in exchange for not being forced into conclusions that are intuitively morally abhorrent. Yet this leaves human rights theorists open to the criticism levied by economists that they do not have a methodological vehicle to resolve trade-offs. Some economists and human rights theorists conclude on the basis of these differences that the two perspectives are simply incompatible. Yet this conclusion may be premature. The comparison of the strengths and weaknesses of the two approaches suggests that, when confronted with real life choices, we intuitively seek to reconcile these perspectives. Although we seek the reassurance of conformity with a priori moral principles, we also appreciate the necessity of a metric that allows us to make choices between competing options.

*Harvey describes this struggle with regard to employment, noting that:*

- Affirmation of an individual right to work is an uncomfortable principle for either economists or the public to embrace if the real goal of public policy is the maintenance of unemployment at a high enough level to keep inflation in check. At the same time, it is not easy to deny the right to work outright. The harms suffered by the unemployed are too great to countenance an express denial of the right. The result is a certain evasiveness in public policy discussions concerning the ultimate goal of employment policy ... Efforts to reduce unemployment are universally applauded, but securing the right to work is rarely mentioned as a policy goal ... this conflict between majoritarian public preferences for policies that use unemployment to combat inflation and government obligations to strive to secure the right to work constitutes a real-world example of a ... problem [that] arises from the possibility that utility-maximisation and human rights protection may conflict with one another as public policy goals.

One important characteristic of this qualitative difference is that economics portrays itself as a positive science, whereas the human rights perspective is fundamentally normative. Even welfare economics, as the more normative branch of the discipline, does not claim more than an intention to choose the most efficient option, given an ethical framework imported from the political system. Pareto optimality is a weak choice criterion that is irrelevant to most real world cases, even with the introduction of the principle of hypothetical compensation.

Economics may see itself as the science of social choice, but it voluntarily limits itself to the mechanics of choice rather than its normative content. Thus, neoclassical welfare economists are most comfortable advocating policies on efficiency grounds, for example policies intended to bring the economy closer to a competitive equilibrium and hence Pareto optimality. As in Bromley's example of the Factory Acts, they are on shakier ground when it comes to championing policies such as ending child labour or achieving universal access to healthcare and education.

The only normative justification for these policies to be found within welfare economics is of the input kind: that is, universal access to healthcare and education is efficient because healthy, better educated workers are more productive. But this is surely to trivialise rights that we consider central to our conception of a civilised society.

Any other normative justification must be imported from the political system and imposed upon the social welfare function. Welfare economics says nothing about whether people being unhappy, having limited capacities or having their rights denied are good or bad things, or whether good or bad things are best defined in terms of unhappiness, capabilities or rights. Thus, the only rights that fit easily into the framework of welfare economics are property rights, which are considered essential to the achievement of a competitive equilibrium and Pareto optimality.

The absence of well-specified property rights – for example, to clean air and water – is considered a market imperfection, to be contrasted with the mythical perfect market. Property rights are therefore an essential input into the economic decision-making process.

As we have already seen, economists who adopt an input view of rights may also see restrictions on the freedom of speech or the right to education as conducive to growth and development. But these rights are not as fundamental to the theory as property rights, which are its sine qua non of utility maximisation.

The emphasis of economic theory on property rights to the exclusion of other rights is logically consistent, but does not accord with the historical experience of the development of capitalism. This is not to say that the development of the market economy always requires civil and political – let alone social – rights, a proposition that anyone vaguely familiar with conditions in the developing and post-communist world would reject on empirical grounds.

But the theoretical proposition that slavery, arbitrary arrest, restrictions on mobility, starvation and illiteracy do not undermine the social, political and legal bases of the market economy departs from a particularly blinkered understanding of the development of capitalism. This leads to an important conclusion about the nature of the two disciplines.

Human rights is concerned with the principles by which different choices are assessed, while economics is concerned with assessing choices just as to specified principles. Just as measuring how tall someone is requires a standard and a measuring tool does the business of choice-making require both a normative framework like human rights and an analytical framework such as economics? If so, are the human rights and economics perspectives actually complementary rather than incompatible?

## THE PURSUIT OF HUMAN RIGHTS AND THE PRACTICE OF ECONOMICS

One consequence of the insertion of human rights considerations into the development space is the entry of human rights specialists into national development planning, a domain that has traditionally been dominated by economists. This was a departure from the previous division of labour whereby human rights practitioners occupied themselves with laws and the legislative processes and structures, while economists worked on national development plans and their associated expenditure frameworks.

It also reflected, in some quarters, a general unease among human rights proponents and activists about the whole construct of development and its association with governments of which they were at best mistrustful and institutions with which they were frequently disappointed. In many countries, the national development plan is the principal policy framework for development, usually understood narrowly as economic development. But plans have increasingly encompassed legislative changes, as recognition has grown of the importance of the rule of law to institution-building and economic progress.

Legislation is no longer just a tool for addressing 'new' problems identified by the rights approach, such as corporal punishment in schools, but also an important prerequisite to the realisation of economic development plans. In some areas, economists must yield to rights advocates because they lack a suitable framework of their own. For example, exploitative child labour might be growth-promoting, but most people consider it wrong, regardless of its economic consequences.

In the pursuit of economic growth, the existence of corporal punishment in schools might be simply irrelevant. A human rights perspective offers different insights or an additional, missing element. Many of these missing elements come from the realisation that welfare economics has devised ever more elaborate methods to address the single and at times not particularly relevant issue of the efficiency of resource allocation.

The occasional complaint by human rights activists, protesting against the privations or consequences of a particular economic policy, that economists are somehow immoral misses the mark. Instead, economics is inherently amoral, equally applicable to the most progressive or exploitative policies. Since morality is a necessary component of public policy, the juxtaposition of a human rights perspective with an economic perspective provides an essential additional dimension. There are a number of examples that demonstrate both this complementarity and the paucity of economic concepts, as contributions to policy lack an accompanying normative framework of the type provided by human rights theory and law.

## EXAMPLES OF A COMBINED PERSPECTIVE

The benefits of a combined approach emerge most clearly in relation to development issues within which the process of voluntary exchange is unlikely to generate results that are satisfactory from a human rights perspective. The assumption in most economic theorising that individuals are autonomous decision-makers unconstrained by inequalities in social, political and indeed economic power not only renders much of welfare economics irrelevant to real world situations but in many important cases generates perverse policy recommend-ations.

Human rights theory can help economists arrive at a more realistic understanding of power dynamics, particularly as they relate to gender, race, ethnicity and class, and, on the basis of this understanding, include tradeoffs that reach beyond the voluntary exchanges of the Pareto criterion. Gender equality issues provide a number of telling examples. Economists can easily incorporate input and output approaches to gender equality into their models: after all, productivity inevitably suffers if half of the population is under-educated, in poor health or excluded from the labour market. On the output side, a weak relationship does exist between levels of income per capita and the economic and political status of women. Yet input and output approaches trivialise rights, reducing them to either instruments or positive externalities of growth. Crucially, they fail to deal explicitly with domination and exploitation. Women's access to wage employment is an important case. Field research indicates that children of mothers in regular full-time employment are more likely to be well-fed and in school than children of mothers who work sporadically or in selfemployment.

In many societies a key obstacle to female participation in wage employment is control by men over women's labour time. Men use violence and other forms of coercion to redirect female labour to the household farm or domestic work, and in doing so they violate women's rights to autonomy and control over their labour power.

Welfare economists, whose analytical framework assumes free exchange and autonomous decision-making, construct models in which women choose to abstain from employment outside the household, either because risk-adjusted returns to intra-household activities are presumed to be higher or because women 'trade off' income against leisure time.

The imposition of a labour-leisure trade-off on situations of domination and extreme deprivation generates policy recommendations that do not work to reduce the exploitation of women, and may in some cases intensify it. A human rights perspective emphasising women's rights to control their labour and to be free from domestic violence is a necessary supplement to economic models in which the decisions of individuals are not constrained by power imbalances.

Development planning provides numerous illustrations of the need to supplement economic analysis with a careful consideration of power dynamics. Welfare economists have developed sophisticated techniques to measure the economic, social, environmental and even political costs and benefits of investment projects. These tools provide information on the likely impact of specific projects to help politicians decide among alternative investments. Rights advocates seeking to universalise the right to clean water and sanitation can employ economists' social cost-benefit analysis methods to find ways of realising this right in the quickest, most cost-effective manner. By the same token, factoring rights into this welfare calculus can add a vital dimension to investment planning.

A large and positive net present value cannot justify a project that requires forced eviction of the local population without due compensation. Projects should not be entertained that fail to meet minimum standards of public participation in planning, implementation and evaluation. This is not to say that the overlaying of a human rights framework somehow resolves public policy choices.

Instead, it provides a measure against which those policy options can be assessed, and without which qualitative enquiry is not possible. While alternative normative frameworks could be substituted, they would not enjoy the force of international law or the degree of consensus of the human rights framework. Another example is user fees for basic services. Welfare economists are attracted to user fees because people tend to overconsume freely provided goods and services, resulting in scarcity, queues and misallocation. But human rights protagonists argue that some kinds of services, like health and education, are qualitatively different from others.

Electricity and water are not the same as primary education. The point is not that a human rights framework provides an incontestable answer to the problem of achieving equity and efficiency in the provision of basic services, but that the combined application of positive economics and a normative human rights framework is superior to either approach taken in isolation. Economics helps us to understand some of the behavioural consequences of policy choices. Human rights provide the best available framework against which to judge those choices. Neither on its own is adequate for decision-making.

## CONCLUSION

The human rights and economics perspectives are similar in many ways. Both adopt the individual as the unit of analysis. Both human rights advocates and economists want to see children in school and people healthy and well-fed and free to choose how to live their lives to the greatest extent possible. At the same time, there are fundamental differences. A human rights perspective is normative, while economics is a positive science.

The economics perspective is inherently consequentialist and concerned with outcomes, while the human rights perspective is deontological and concerned with principles that remain important regardless of their consequences, and that cannot be discarded because of calculations suggesting that they may lead to sub-optimal or inefficient outcomes. It is rare for practitioners of either discipline to take much interest in the other, and as a result misconceptions abound. Some human rights practitioners presume that economists have no care for the ethical consequences of their policies; they bemoan the lack of concern for the negative consequences of growth or for those left behind in the pursuit of growth.

Some economists see the human rights perspective as little more than a wish-list, with no practical benefit and certainly no relevance to the important business of choice-making. This lack of shared understanding and common conceptual framework is particularly unfortunate in the field of development. Neither economists nor human rights practitioners can honestly claim to have arrived at a thorough understanding of the complex interactions between the moral and material aspects of development.

Economists, having struggled to explain development failures solely in economic terms, increasingly refer to the political and legal preconditions for growth. Yet, in the absence of a normative framework, the tendency to treat politics instrumentally can generate perverse outcomes. Meanwhile, rights theorists should not be tempted to use the principle of progressive realisation as a 'get-out-of-jail card' that excuses them from difficult choices between consumption today and investment for tomorrow, or between equally plausible rights claims. This article has argued that the human rights and economics perspectives, as much because of these similarities as because of these differences, are inherently complementary. We have suggested that human rights cannot function on its own as a policy tool because it is by its nature not good at dealing with choices and outcomes. We have also suggested that economics cannot serve as a framework for policy choices because it lacks a means by which to apply our values and beliefs about how human beings should be treated.

Economists' faith that socially optimal outcomes will arise spontaneously from voluntary exchange too often leads to the unwarranted conclusion that existing situations are both optimal and a product of people's voluntary choices. Thus, each discipline inherently addresses and responds to the shortcomings of the other.

*Each makes the other useful*: A human rights perspective directs the tools of economics in a direction that aligns them with the principles we share and which are articulated in international law; economic understanding and tools empower those who believe in human rights to pursue their realisation more effectively. The eighth Millennium Development Goal calls upon the world to 'develop a global partnership for development'. The marriage of the economics and human rights perspectives is surely not just a contribution to, but even a prerequisite for, exactly that.

# 4

# Human Rights and Social Development

## HR: COPENHAGEN DECLARATION ON SOCIAL DEVELOPMENT AND PROGRAMME OF ACTION

The Copenhagen Declaration on Social Development recognizes the urgent need to.address profound social problems, especially poverty, unemployment and social exclusion that affect every country and sets as the task of the governments to address both their underlying and structural causes and their distressing consequences in order to reduce uncertainty and insecurity in the life of people.

It adopts a broad view of social development, as meeting the.material and spiritual needs of individuals, their families and the communities in which they live. This can only be achieved through social and people centered sustainable development. As an aspect of sustainable development, there is a commitment to the protection of the environment. Social development is inextricably connected with economic development, for some of its primary goals the eradication of poverty, unemployment and social exclusion depend on it.

The Declaration identifies a number of factors that have prevented the goals of social development from being achieved: chronic hunger, malnutrition, illicit drug trade, organized crime, corruption, foreign occupation, armed conflicts, illicit arms trafficking, terrorism, intolerance, xenophobia and incitement to racial, ethnic, religious and other hatreds. Many of these factors are connected with the violation of human rights. It is therefore not surprising that the Declaration places considerable emphasis on human rights and democracy in order to achieve these goals.

Indeed more than any other international declaration, with the exception of the Declaration on the Right to Development the Declaration places human rights at the centre of development. It states, for example, that.democracy and transparent and accountable governance and administration in all sectors of society are indispensable foundations for the realization of social and people centered sustainable development. At another point it refers to the acknowledgement that social and economic development cannot be secured in a sustainable way without the full participation of women and that equality and equity between women and men is a priority for the international community and as such must be at the centre of economic and social development. The Declaration places particular emphasis on the eradication of poverty, and this is perhaps its closest connection with human rights.

Poverty is the greatest cause of the denial of human rights. It is obvious that poor people enjoy a disproportionately small measure of economic rights such as education, health and shelter. However, they are equally unable to exercise civil and political rights, which would require not only an understanding of the dynamics of society and access to public institutions, but also confidence in them.

They are for the most part unable to use the legal process to vindicate their human and legal rights. Nothing destroys confidence so much as poverty. Poverty also compels people into the violation of the rights of others, particularly of their own children and women. Child labour is essential to the survival of millions of families throughout the Third World and, increasingly, so is prostitution.

Bonded labour is a direct result of poverty, and its exploitation by the well off. Poverty produces massive inequalities, and the subordination of some groups to others in circumstances that deny them their basic dignity. The first of the principles and goals enunciated in the Declaration, and a central theme of the Programme of Action, is a commitment to.a political, economic, ethical and spiritual vision for social development that is based on human dignity, human rights, equality, respect, peace, democracy, mutual responsibility and cooperation, and full respect for the various religious and cultural backgrounds of people. More specifically, governments have agreed to.promote democracy, human dignity, social justice and solidarity at the national, regional and international levels; ensure tolerance, nonviolence, pluralism and nondiscrimination, with full respect for diversity within and among nations.

They have undertaken to promote universal respect for, and observance and protection of, all human rights and fundamental freedoms for all, including the right to development, and to ensure that disadvantaged and vulnerable persons and groups are included in social development. Particular mention is made of the right of self-determination of all peoples, in particular of peoples under colonial or other forms of alien domination or foreign occupation and support for indigenous people in their pursuit of economic and social development, with full respect for their identity, traditions, forms of social organization and cultural values.

Without trying to exhaust the references to human rights in the Declaration, the last paragraph of the first Commitment is worth quoting: As suggested, reaffirm and promote all human rights, which are universal, indivisible, interdependent and interrelated, including the right to development as a universal and inalienable right and an integral part of fundamental human development, and strive to ensure that they are respected, protected and observed.

Several points about these formulations are worth noting. First, the importance of the language of rights. Repeated references to them might indicate a broad international consensus on human rights and freedoms and attest to the moral and political force of the idea of human rights or at least of its rhetoric. In recent decades the idea of respect for human rights seems to have become a driving force in international and regional policies and conduct, as in the intervention of the United Nations in the restoration of rights and democracy in Bosnia and Herzegovina, Cambodia, East Timor, Haiti and Nicaragua; or in the more specific regional mediations and interventions by the Organization for Security and Cooperation in Europe.

Extensive references to democracy and human rights in the Declaration are evidence of the desire, if perhaps not necessarily the feasibility, of using human rights as a framework for sustainable development and solving other ailments of humankind. All of this enthusiasm and commitment to human rights must be taken with some caution, for the international human rights movement has been distinguished more by rhetoric than practice.

Human rights are understood differently in different places, and the apparent consensus on rights conceals profound differences on and even conflicts over, values and goals. Second, the frequent invocation of rights in the different contexts in the Declaration attests to the enlarged scope of the concept and content of human rights. Rights have travelled a long distance from their origins in the emerging liberal economic orders of Europe and the United States since the seventeenth century, when the focus was on civil and political rights as the means to restrict the power of the government and enhance that of economic entrepreneurs.

Their philosophical foundations have broadened, fed by various political and intellectual traditions. A large and diverse number of groups and interests have advanced their claims in the language of rights. The first additions to the classical liberal category of rights were economic, social and cultural rights. Since then specialized instruments have dealt with the claims and rights of vulnerable groups, such as women, children, refugees, migrants, indigenous peoples and people with disabilities.

More broadly, but also ambiguously, there is the right to development, and notions of the preservation of the environment are being woven into the regime of rights. There is now a rich menu of rights, perhaps too rich as some complain, and the rights do not appear to be seamless. The regime of rights guarantees democracy and participation, and the accommodation of diversity.

A fundamental assumption of contemporary human rights is social justice, and thus the alleviation of poverty, which is a primary concern of the Declaration. Social justice has also promoted the idea of equity as between men and women, between groups, and between generations. There is a considerable widening of the range of entitlements of citizens and others, transforming people from supplicants into citizens.

The broadening of human rights has focused attention on the state not merely as facilitator but also as provider. The logic of social, economic and cultural rights is positive obligations of the state, necessitating an active role, to ensure basic needs of people, and thus their dignity. It is not surprising that these developments in the concept and scope of human rights have produced controversy. Behind the seeming consensus on the formulations in the Declaration on rights and democracy lurk several disagreements. How far the apparent disagreements reflect genuine differences of values is hard to say, for there is considerable hypocrisy and posturing in the position of governments.

Human rights have become one of the frameworks for international relations, and the debates about them have become highly politicized. Having said that, it is possible to identify differences in approaches to human rights, and to their contents. These differences have been a major obstacle to a genuine consensus and the feasibility of consistent and effective international action to promote and protect human rights. The challenge to human rights of the Declaration is to achieve coherence of rights, founded on common values and understandings as to their purpose.

There are considerable advantages in using the human rights framework for social development. Despite the controversies that have prevented unified action on human rights, they seem to attract broad international support and few governments publicly condemn their values. The language of rights has the capacity to evoke a response and to provide moral and legal justification for certain forms of action. The ideology of and claims based on, human rights have become increasingly effective ways to pressure governments and the international community. The regime of rights provides a basis for international or regional action and justifies the imposition of sanctions and, in extreme cases, humanitarian intervention.

Human rights standards can also compensate for the weakness of international political institutions and machinery. In contradistinction to the growth of the idea and substance of rights in national systems where they followed the establishment of the apparatus of the state in the international system rights have developed with remarkable speed and are well ahead of the development of political institutions. However, that does not mean there is not sufficient authority or mechanism for their international enforcement.

The framework of rights is feasible because rights are now being defined in detailed terms and there are numerous decisions of courts and other tribunals that have elaborated the parameters of rights and their implications. They are no longer abstract formulations. Moreover, the regime of rights is now complex and multilayered, dealing with different kinds of claims and interests.

It speaks to a variety of concerns, and provides doctrines as well as mechanisms for striking a balance between different claims. Rights are a way to mobilize and empower the disadvantaged, and in many parts of the world this is their principal function. The language of rights makes people conscious of both their oppression and the possibility of change Rights have been extraordinarily effective as a basis of networking in and across states and have demonstrated the possibility of international solidarity, particularly for women and indigenous peoples.

Many nongovernmental organizations justify their existence by the need to promote rights and it is the regime of rights that has enabled them to perform their promotional and investigative role, which has generally proved more effective than internal state mechanisms for accountability. It would be fair to say that the human rights regime has sustained civil society in its confrontation with the state. Even more fundamentally, the regime of rights is crucial because it speaks in the language of entitlements. Poverty is not just a matter of a deprived economic situation; it is defined and sustained, on the part of the poor, by a sense of helplessness and dependence, and by a lack of opportunities, self-confidence and self-respect. It is increasingly being recognized that poverty can only be eradicated if the poor are given a greater share in decisions about programmes of poverty alleviation and their implementation. The language of rights makes it clear that the poor are not the subject of charity or benevolence, but are entitled to a decent standard of living and that civil and political rights are the vehicles for their participation and empowerment.

The effectiveness of the rights regime is, however, diminished by the fact that not all of them have been integrated into the international economic or financial systems, which are market oriented and primarily protect the interests of capitalists. Many types of rights are not favoured by the capitalist system. Historically only those rights have been upheld that support the interests of the dominant classes thus civil and political rights were propounded by a bourgeoisie coming into power.

Today's economic and social rights speak to the claims of the oppressed and the powerless, and the chances of their fulfilment are slim. Developments in human rights have been at the level of rhetoric and to some extent the establishment of institutions, but they have not led to the redistribution of resources or to building the economic base that favours economic justice.

Although norms of the human rights regime represent a serious challenge to the international market system, and an alternative vision, the material forces of the international market system are more powerful than the moral claims and rhetoric of human rights.One further point needs to be made to establish the context for a rights oriented strategy: it concerns.globalization.. The Declaration correctly identifies the contradictory nature of globalization, on one hand opening up possibilities of increased economic growth, and on the other foreclosing options central to the Copenhagen aspirations, such as those of income redistribution, alleviation of poverty, employment opportunities and equity. It states that.the global transformations of the world economy are profoundly changing the parameters of social development in all countries.

The challenge is how to manage these processes and threats so as to enhance their benefits and mitigate their negative effects upon people. There are grave doubts as to whether this challenge can be met successfully. The inherent tendency of economic globalization is to diminish democracy and to privilege marketoriented rights, reducing the importance and feasibility of social and solidarity rights.

It is impossible to discuss the salience of the human rights strategy for the Copenhagen social development envisioned in Copenhagen without taking on board the impact of globalization and the redistributions of power that it has produced.

## THE HUMAN RIGHTS SYSTEM

In order to explore the potential of the human rights framework to achieve social development, it is necessary to briefly describe the human rights system. The essential components of the system are ideology, substantive rights, functions, beneficiaries, actors, institutions, procedures and the levels at which it operates. The human rights system is rich in texts, rhetoric and institutions, but it is lacking in material resources to make rights effective. States place interests such as national security or economy, and the cultivation of international relations, human rights. Popular consciousness of rights is often dulled by ethnic conflicts or the burden of.traditional values and authority.

### IDEOLOGY

Surprisingly, there is no great consensus on the ideology of rights. There is substantial agreement that the purpose of human rights is to protect human dignity, but there are different views on the source of that dignity. The principal difference lies between those who seek a religious basis for that dignity, and those who seek a secular basis.

There is a widespread perception that the origins of the concept of human rights lie in Western, individualist or liberal philosophy and for that reason some in the East argue that it is alien to their own cultures. Even in the West there is criticism of the individualistic bias of human rights. There are also historical and pragmatic explanations for rights the former consisting of an analysis of the growth of classes and their relationship to the state, and the latter justifying rights in terms of fairness, stability and peace.

These differences bear on the acceptance and realization of rights, but perhaps their importance has diminished with the elaboration of rights under the auspices of the United Nations. It has been possible to reach broad agreement on the scope and substance of rights, and the key international instruments have been ratified by a large number of countries adhering to differing religions and cultural traditions.

The ideology of human rights is one of the most powerful forces today largely at the level of rhetoric, but also as justification for action, particularly the collective interventions by the international community in oppressive states. The ideology of rights and the acceptance that the international community has the overriding responsibility for their protection has been invoked to justify limits on state sovereignty, a cornerstone of the international system.

## LEVELS: INTERNATIONAL, REGONAL AND NATONAL

The national, regional and international levels constitute the global system of rights. Historically, the concept and practice of human rights developed in national systems. Before the establishment of the United Nations, a number of states provided for the protection of rights in their constitutions. The League of Nations and the International Labour Organization facilitated the internationalization of specific rights of workers and minorities, but it is only since the existence of the United Nations that there has been an exponential growth in international human rights law. The United Nations Charter committed its members to the promotion and protection of human rights. The United Nations marked its entry into this area in 1948 by adopting the Universal Declaration of Human Rights since then many conventions have been negotiated and ratified by member states.

The growth of conventions and institutions at the international level was paralleled by the establishment of the European Convention of Human Rights, providing the first instance of the protection of rights at the regional level. The Convention is enforced by the European Court of Human Rights.

Since then, regional systems of human rights have been established for Africa and the Americas, though there are differences in the scope of rights and the method of enforcement. Another regional system has developed in recent years under the auspices of the OSCE, in which Canada and the United States also participate so far the progress has been in developing norms and in the method of persuasion.

There are many advantages in having regional systems: for instance, they take the load off the international system, and bring the pressure of friendly, neighbouring states to bear on offending states. Equally important, they represent the consensus of the states as to the standards of government behaviour acceptable in the region.

Perhaps the absence of regional systems in Asia and PacificAustralasia is due to the lack of this regional consensus. Consequently, regional systems are uneven, with Europe's being the best integrated and certainly the most effective. The third level is the national. It is the most important level for giving legal effect to human rights norms, which is done by guarantees in the constitutions and laws, and by giving effect to international or regional treaties. It is also the most important level for the enforcement of rights; most violations of rights are dealt with, at least in the first instance, in national courts or other human rights institutions. It is at this level that the key struggle for human rights is conducted and the resistance to it waged. The different levels are being integrated through a regime of treaties that are effective at the national level but supervised at the regional or international level, and through the respect paid by national governments and judiciaries to elaborations of rights by regional or international tribunals. Nevertheless, there is a division of labour between these levels as regards the different functions of the human rights system, to which I now turn.

## FUNCTIONS

One of the most important functions is developing a consensus on rights and interests to be protected. This is often done by interest groups women, minorities, migrants, corporations and so on. In recent years NGOs have played an important role in lobbying for the recognition of particular interests many norms on indigenous peoples, minorities and protection against torture owe their origin to the efforts of NGOs. Sometimes regional or international conferences have also performed this role.

Once there is a substantial consensus, the task of norm setting can be undertaken. This involves the elaboration of treaties or legislation and has historically been the role of national governments and legislatures. However, in recent years the international system has played a crucial role. The United Nations has provided the forum for negotiating treaties on human rights. By its nature, norm setting is the responsibility of official bodies, but NGOs have also played a significant role in developing treaties or legislation.

The promotion of respect for rights consists of various activities including information on and education about human rights, and support for the institutions that uphold them. This function is the responsibility of official and nonofficial bodies. In many countries official human rights commissions have a special responsibility for the propagation of rights. In more authoritarian states, the primary responsibility is discharged by NGOs and social groups, including trade unions. Closely connected to the respect for rights is mobilization of groups on the basis of rights. Claims of rights have constituted forms of protest and challenges to authority. In so far as one function of rights is the empowerment of vulnerable groups, mobilization is crucial and, since the aim of mobilization is to organize social groups and challenge authorities, human rights defenders are often harassed or even oppressed.

Human rights also provide the basis for networking, nationally and internationally. Indigenous peoples and women have been particularly successful in networking, which is almost always the preoccupation of nonofficial bodies. Protecting rights is the primary responsibility of the state which together with other official bodies is generally bound to respect human rights and most legal actions are directed at the state's violations of rights.

*Protecting rights takes various forms, ensuring that:*

- There is law and order in which people can enjoy their rights;
- The police and army are trained in human rights norms, and respect and uphold people's rights;
- Institutions in the front line of securing rights, like the judiciary and human rights commissions, are independent and adequately resourced; and
- There are effective sanctions against those who violate the rights of others.

The United Nations has played a limited role in protecting rights. The principal UN agency for this purpose formerly the United Nations Centre for Human Rights, now incorporated into the Office of the United Nations High Commissioner for Human Rights has had very limited resources, and had a low profile until the appointment of the current Human Rights Commissioner, Mary Robinson. Unlike other UN agencies, it had no field offices until recently it now has over 20, supervising the protection of rights and offering technical assistance. The task that receives most attention is enforcing rights, most typically through the judicial process.

In recent years other institutions, such as ombudsmen, and human rights or equality commissions, have been established for the protection of human rights. These institutions tend to follow less adversarial procedures than courts, and offer mediation and reconciliation. Access to these bodies is also easier, cheaper and more informal than it is to courts, and they tend to be multifunctional, with information and education being a primary responsibility.

However, courts remain the final arbiters of violations, and the ultimate authorities for the interpretations of human rights provisions. Therefore the interpretation of judges and legal practitioners, who have a key role in access to the courts, and a well functioning legal system are indispensable for an effective system of enforcement of rights. The primary institutions for the enforcement of rights are national, but in countries that are part of a regional system of human rights, regional commissions or courts can play an important, supplementary role.

The role of the European Court of Human Rights is crucial in that it makes the final interpretations of the European Convention, which are binding on national governments and courts. The international system plays little role in the enforcement of rights. The first steps in international enforcement have been taken with the establishment of tribunals for war crimes in Rwanda and the former Yugoslavia, and with the imminent establishment of the permanent international tribunal as agreed in Rome three years ago.

The international system has an important, or, more accurately, a potentially important, role in the supervision of the protection and enforcement of rights. This supervision takes two forms: one is primarily political and is the responsibility of the OHCHR and the mechanisms associated with it, such as special rapporteurs for countries including Afghanistan and Cambodia, or on themes such as extrajudicial killings, disappearances and violence against women. The other form of supervision is more judicial the task being performed by specialist, independent bodies set up under human rights treaties.

Most major treaties provide for periodic reports to these bodies; this is the principal means of supervising a state's performance of its treaty obligations. But some treaties also provide for a complaints mechanism, either at the insistence of another state or of a person who alleges that his or her rights have been violated. Even when there is a complaints procedure, the decision of the body is not strictly enforceable, although it provides a valuable opportunity for the body to elaborate the provisions of the treaty and explain the scope of rights protected by it and the permissible derogations.

This has been a particularly valuable aspect of the work of the United Nations Human Rights Committee, set up under the International Covenant on Civil and Political Rights. However, the potential of the supervisory role of the international system has yet to be realised. Until now meager resources have been provided to the United Nations and the treaty bodies, many of who can only meet once or twice a year for a fortnight or so and have inadequate secretariat support and virtually no follow-up machinery.

This state of affairs is ample evidence of the low priority accorded to human rights by the international community, as is the fact that the international supervisory system is highly fragmented, incoherent and largely ineffective. Supervision is also exercised at the regional level for states that are members of regional systems, and also at the national level.

Some national human rights commissions may be required to produce an annual report but more often this task is performed by national and international NGOs. Of the latter, Amnesty International and Human Rights Watch are well known. It is also worth mentioning that the United States Department of State produces an annual report on the state of human rights in other countries which is an important aspect of its foreign policy.

## ACTORS AND INSTITUTIONS

The preceding subsections have given some account of the actors and institutions that form part of the human rights system. Here it is sufficient to recapitulate that actors exist at various levels and include official and unofficial bodies. There has been considerable emphasis on strengthening national institutions for the protection of rights since the World Conference on Human Rights, held in Vienna in 1993. The OHCHR has played an important role in the promotion of human rights commissions. As discussed in the upcoming subsection on Democratization: The record, considerable foreign assistance has been given for the strengthening of judicial and legal institutions.

A significant set of actors are.civil society. institutions, which operate nationally and internationally. The framework of human rights has provided a powerful basis for their growth and networking, and they have played an important role in popular mobilization and aggregating demand. In authoritarian states, they have kept alive the demand for democratization, and brought violations of rights to world attention. They are an important lobby for the protection of human rights, and play a significant supervisory role. They were once seen as.troublemakers. by governments and international agencies, but now enjoy considerable legitimacy in official circles, and are accepted as an indispensable partner in the pursuit of human rights.

## BENEFICIARIES OF RIGHTS

The beneficiaries of rights are human beings. However, most legal systems extend.human. rights to corporations and other entities at least to the extent that they are capable of exercising them. It used to be that rights were traditionally restricted to citizens, and many constitutions still so restrict their scope. International instruments are ambiguous; they speak as if rights belong to.everyone., with only the political rights being restricted to citizens, but they do not seem capable of enforcing the wider view of entitlement to rights.

However, an increasing number of states extend nonpolitical rights to all residents, although some still discriminate against immigrants in civil, economic and social rights. In a globalizing world, the restriction of rights to citizens, especially when citizenship is conceived of in narrow racial or ethnic terms, is a serious limitation on people's exercise of rights. So long as rights were attached to citizenship, there was a notion of a uniform set of rights. After the international covenants on civil and political, and on economic, social and cultural rights were adopted, available to.everyone., the international community turned its attention to specific groups of people. Conventions for the protection of vulnerable groups racial minorities, women, children, indigenous peoples and migrant workers were adopted.

For the most part, they reiterate the rights that these groups allegedly already enjoy under the two Covenants, but provide a basis for affirmative action, special policies and protective institutions, and networking. These developments were in some cases presaged in national systems for example, India, which adopted special constitutional protection of historically disadvantaged minorities.

The concern with vulnerable groups, particularly minorities, has promoted the concept of group rights. In the classical traditions of human rights, only individuals had rights; those who adhere to this approach are uncomfortable with rights of groups and newfangled ideas such as the right to development. But the notion of group rights has assumed a particular importance in multiethnic societies, where it has in some cases become the organizing matrix of society.

## INTERNATIONALIZATION OF HUMAN RIGHTS AND STATE SOVEREIGNTY

From the perspective of the Declaration and the prospects of international action, the degree of internationalization of human rights is a significant factor. The expression internationalization of human rights. refers to the process whereby human rights are encapsulated in international instruments, most of which have become binding on signatory states.

The process encompasses the elaboration of human rights, binding states to respect and enforce these rights, and setting up an international system of supervision and enforcement of the obligations of states in respect of human rights. Internationalization of rights also refers to the norms by which states conduct their relations with other states and which international organizations must follow in their work, and it is deemed to have established a new international morality. Because international human rights have been established in what passes for a consensual process, it is often assumed that they are universally valid, as opposed to, for example, democracy, where it is conceded that there is no uniform, universal form.

The result is that states may be more willing to intervene to promote or protect rights than to support democracy or criticize political systems that look authoritarian. The process has resulted in the translation into international instruments of human rights originally developed in national systems and adopted in several state constitutions. The inscription of these rights in international instruments has expanded the scope of the operation of human rights, bringing an important change in the character and purpose of international law and making individuals and their rights its central concern.

The manner in which a state treated its citizens used to be regarded as an internal affair; it was no business of other states or international organizations. The concept of state sovereignty provided a shield for states against external intervention and even external comment. State sovereignty and nonintervention in the domestic affairs of a state are still the cornerstone of the international order under the United Nations Charter. But the notion of what is domestic has changed under the Charter's imperative to promote and protect human rights. International instruments have placed special responsibilities on the state with regard to minorities and indigenous peoples, and other vulnerable communities or groups. This change in international law has been reinforced by international and regional instruments, which have placed obligations on states to respect human rights and to account to the international community for the performance of this responsibility.

A number of institutions and procedures have been established since the United Nations was founded to address the question of the violation of human rights by a state. The right of states, regional organizations and the international community to criticize states that violate the human rights of their nationals is increasingly recognized. The eruption of civil wars, often centering on ethnic conflicts, has increased the involvement of the international community in the affairs of states; this involvement is most dramatically manifested in humanitarian intervention, but also takes the form of mediation and conciliation, strengthening national capacity for the promotion of and respect for human rights, monitoring the observance of treaty obligations, and imposing sanctions. The lack of immunity for heads of state for torture and similar crimes, and the establishment of an international criminal court, reinforces this trend.

However, it is important to note that this qualification on state sovereignty is not universally accepted. A number of states, among them those that have been victims of imperialism, argue that state sovereignty and a strong state is essential for the protection of the rights of citizens. Foremost among the proponents of this view is China. Sometimes this pragmatic argument is combined with a doctrinal view of state sovereignty, drawing its inspiration from pre-UN days. Russia has, for example, tried to fend off criticism of its conduct in unleashing a brutal war on the Chechens on the grounds that what it does to its own citizens is its own business, squarely within its sovereignty.

The Association of South-East Asian Nations refused to condemn Indonesia for the atrocities that its troops perpetrated in East Timor. The resistance of states to the notion that human rights anywhere is a matter of international concern, justifying international action, is a serious impediment to the enforcement of human rights. It prevents speedy remedial action by or through the United Nations Security Council. Sanctions or interventions follow only upon brutal repression of groups, resulting in great loss of life.

An international consensus on the grounds and modalities for intervention is necessary to prevent extreme violations of human rights. Hesitation about a forthright commitment to the role of the international community in the enjoyment of rights, particularly humanitarian intervention, is no doubt induced by anxieties about the hegemonic power of some states, and the fear that interventions will be selective to serve the interests of powerful countries like the United States.

## THE HUMAN RIGHTS INDUSTRY

Despite the complex structure of the human rights system, those involved in the propagation and promotion of human rights form a small group. At the unofficial level, there are a handful of international NGOs that dominate the scene, enjoy a favoured status with the United Nations and receive most of the media publicity. National NGOs are frequently de pendent on them as interlocutors for fundraising and for guidance on tactics and organization. There are also a small number of Western foundations that sustain this movement and thus exercise a disproportionate influence on the orientation and even the possibility of the human rights movement and a small number of official international, regional and national organizations with human rights mandates. There is a considerable circulation of personnel between these NGOs, foundations and organizations, and a strong bonding.

The term.human rights industry. is often used, pejoratively, to refer to the self-interest of the aforementioned groups and the way they organize the production, dissemination and implementation of rights. It suggests that their primary commitment is to their own organizations and their dominance of the system, not the protection of rights. There is no need to buy into all of this cynicism, but there is little doubt that the human rights movement has become highly bureaucratized, hierarchical, even narrow.

The industry having become highly legalistic due to the proliferation of rights, and the mushrooming of the jurisprudence of courts, tribunals and committees, the leadership has passed to lawyers, who for the most part are less concerned with mobilizing mass social movements around rights than with advocacy and lobbying. The framework of human rights will serve the agenda of the Social Summit only if it is carried to the people, if they believe that their own oppression is clearly linked to the violation of rights, and if they are organized to claim their rights and to base their agenda and organization on them. It is ironic that the people in whose name the legitimacy of rights is claimed are for the most part isolated from participation in human rights movements.

## DIFFERENCES AND CONTROVERSIES OVER HUMAN RIGHTS

Early differences surrounded the relative claims of civil/political and economic/social rights, and led to their bifurcation and separation into two covenants. The water that has since flowed under the bridge has done little to dilute the opposition of the United States to economic and social rights. At the same time, many governments in Africa and Asia justify their resistance to civil and political rights on the grounds that they are less important and urgent than economic and social rights. The separation does little to strengthen arguments for the indivisibility of rights and freedoms, or for the equal attention of the world community to them. It laid the foundation for continuing controversy about priorities, sequence and legitimacy of rights. Since then other controversies have come to the fore.

### COMMUNITARAN CHAENGE TO RGHTS

The statement in the Declaration, which proclaims rights as.universal, indivisible, interdependent and interrelated, is now the official United Nations view of human rights. Powerful cultural and intellectual arguments have been marshalled against this proposition. The very approach, which gives primacy to human rights, is being contested. Various government leaders in Africa and Asia claim that the traditions of their societies place, and have always placed, special importance on duties, as opposed to the Western preoccupation with rights.

The same emphasis, it is said, is explicit in all the world's major religious and spiritual beliefs. Variations of this argument are espoused by communitarians in Western countries; they favour social organization and engagement on the basis of responsibilities, not rights to which some communitarians attribute many ills of contemporary society. The argument that rights promote individualism, selfishness and litigiousness, and undermine the cohesion of the community, brings these two groups together. Although these groups seriously misunderstand the nature and dynamics of rights, which are increasingly concerned with peace and justice, and underrate the extent to which the regime of rights incorporates notions of responsibility and the collective good, their opposition to human rights can undermine the goals reflected by human rights.

## CULTURAL RELATIVIST CHALLENGE TO HUMAN RIGHTS:.ASIAN VALUES

Closely connected to this approach is an even more formidable objection to the idea of universal human rights the objection of cultural relativism. The essence of this argument is that human rights are based on culture and, since cultural values vary, there cannot be any universal human rights. A version of this approach that has received a great deal of public attention is what has been called.Asian values..

The strongest proponents of this approach are a few leaders in Southeast Asia, who argue that the values of Asian, particularly Confucian, culture have provided political stability and economic development, and that these values are oriented to the community. They claim that Asian values emphasize harmony, unlike the confrontation that arises from the exercise of rights. These leaders were able to persuade Asian governments assembled in Bangkok in April 1993 prior to the World Conference on Human Rights in Vienna to endorse a declaration that is often taken to represent the Asian view of rights, although it did not support all doctrines connected with Asian values.

Once one gets past the ritualistic homage to human rights, there are four major purposes of the 1993 declaration made in Bangkok encompassed by the overarching objective of placing the question of rights within an international relations framework:

- To emphasize the rights of states. It reaffirms.the principles of respect for national sovereignty, territorial integrity and noninterference in the internal affairs of states. and the importance of the right to development, which the proponents of Asian values see as premised on the sovereignty of states.
- To condemn practices associated with the West and the imbalance in the world system. The references to colonialism and apartheid are clearly directed at the West. Asian states such as China, Indonesia

or Myanmar with colonies or other forms of foreign occupation, are fully absolved of any wrongdoing. The 1993 declaration deplores.Any attempt to use human rights as a conditionality for extending development assistance or as.an instrument of political pressure. The West is also targeted indirectly for creating an unjust international economic order and, presumably, poverty, which are the primary causes of the violation of rights.

- To establish that the state is the appropriate framework for the definition and enforcement of rights. The clearest statement appears in paragraph 9, which recognizes that.states have the primary responsibility for the promotion and protection of human rights through appropriate infrastructure and mechanisms., and that remedies must be sought and provided primarily through such mechanisms and procedures..
- To establish a framework for the analysis of rights themselves. On one hand, it suggests that, all the talk of universality and indivisibility notwithstanding, rights are to be understood in the context of national or regional particularities and various historical, cultural and religious backgrounds, and condemns the.imposition of incompatible standards.. On the other hand, it draws attention to the contribution Asian states can make to the World Conference.with their diverse and rich cultures and traditions. Second, it hints at the priority of economic development for the enjoyment of rights, and states that.economic and social progress facilitates the growing trend towards democracy and the promotion and protection of human rights.

There is little evidence that Asian economic success is due to family or community structures or to any other aspect of Asian values. Instead it is the resources and structures of the state that have played a decisive role in private accumulation and production. Those of us who live in the more economically successful parts of Asia are not struck by the cohesion of the community, or by the care that the community or family provides, or by benevolent governments, or by a public disdain for democracy.

Instead we notice the displacement of the community by the pretensions and practices of the state. Far from promoting reconciliation and consensus, the state punishes its critics, suppresses the freedom of expression. without which dialogue is not possible and relies on armed forces rather than persuasion. The doctrine of Asian values thrives on the perception of those who are perched on the higher reaches of the state and the market. The 1993 NGO Declaration on Human Rights may be contrasted with a statement issued at the same time by Asian NGOs in Bangkok, which was subsequently elaborated in the Asian Human Rights Charter. First, the NGOs emphasize the international provenance of rights and contend that, since rights are universal in concern and value, they override national sovereignty. They state:.We are entitled to join hands in solidarity to protect human rights worldwide.. International solidarity transcends the national order, to refute claims of State sovereignty and noninterference in the internal affairs of State..

Second, the NGOs believe in the universality and indivisibility of rights. This conclusion is drawn partly from their views on the purpose of rights the promotion of human and humane development and peace. Development should be informed by rights and democracy so as to ensure.a harmonious relationship between humanity and the natural environment. NGOs strongly support democratization at national and international levels, and favour a broad meaning of self-determination in the national context. For this and other reasons, they deplore the.increasing militarization through the region., which is incompatible with peace and human rights. Like the states, the NGOs see a relationship between rights and culture, but they see cultures enriching our experiences and understanding of rights, producing a cosmopolitan and hence truly universal view of rights, rather than retreating behind the barricades of relativism.

They see the empowerment of people as a function of rights, particularly the vulnerable groups, including indigenous peoples, whose right to self-determination has been systematically denied; women; children, whose welfare should be.a paramount concern of every state, regardless of considerations of state capacity and security; internally displaced people and refugees, whose rights are violated.as a direct result of militarization and armed conflict and peasants and workers, who all too often.endure the worst cases of human rights abuses in the region.

## THE FUNDAMENTALIST CHALLENGE

Religion occupies an ambiguous position in relation to human rights. Some people claim that it constitutes the foundation of rights and that without the religious notion of the sacredness of the individual there cannot be a concept of inalienable human rights. Others, preferring a secular and humanistic justification for rights, attribute the violation of rights to religious beliefs and indeed there is much historical evidence that religions have acquiesced to or justified slavery, massacres, intolerance and other forms of oppression.

In contemporary times, a fundamental challenge to human rights comes from fundamentalists of all kinds, who deny the equality of all human beings and support many practices that violate principles, norms and procedures of human rights. This is most obvious in the case of Muslim fundamentalists, who have based the organization and laws of their states on.Islamic. principles. A number of Muslim states, which have ratified international human rights conventions, have entered blanket reservations that subordinate these conventions to religious teachings.

However, a number of Islamic scholars and Islamic organizations have used religious texts for interpretations that make Islam compatible with human rights, and have employed that compatibility to mobilize support for human rights. But it is at the ideological level that religions have posed the major challenge to human rights. Like cultural relativism, religion juxtaposes an alternative normative framework for the organization of society and authority.

Cultural and religious relativism rules out both common action and the criticism of the mores and practices of a society by reference to standards external to the society; and hence the project of universal rights. This approach has a static and unjustified view of culture and ignores the commonality between and the interaction of cultures. It misunderstands the purpose of contemporary human rights, which it conceives of as the ideology underpinning privilege and hierarchy instead of promoting change. But it does respond to a sense on the part of many people in poorer regions of the world of an economic and intellectual hegemony of stronger states, and of their own marginalization.

It is essential to engage with rather than dismiss cultural and religious relativism if human rights are to provide a common framework of interaction and policy, even though many more people in poorer countries are attracted to the egalitarian and redistributive dimensions of human rights, on which the Copenhagen Declaration builds its programme of action.

## IDENTITY POLITICS

The United Nations version of human rights as universal and indivisible has come under attack from what has been called.identity politics.. Identity politics are an attack on what is assumed to be the mores of the dominant group in society, masquerading as the universal. The attack has come from ethnic as well as social minorities, such as women and homosexuals. Women point to many aspects of the regime of rights that merely reflect patriarchy and the interests of men, and homosexuals argue that many of the.values. of society are grounded in a particular view of sexuality that ignores their own orientation. The recognition of differences of this kind is not necessarily a challenge to the orthodox view of human rights, and indeed the rights of women and homosexuals can be, and in many jurisdictions have been, accommodated within that view. However, there is one version of the recognition of difference that does not sit so comfortably with that orthodox view, and it has to some extent inspired international conventions on the rights of indigenous peoples. It has also gained some currency in Canada and is particularly associated with the writings of Kymlicka and Taylor. Their arguments start from the premise of the autonomy and authenticity of the individual under liberal theory. Liberalism regards the individual as the centre of society. There are two aspects of individualism that seem to deny special measures for minorities. The first is the equality of all individuals, or at least of all citizens, who must be equal bearers of rights and obligations under the law or, at least in the public sphere, must meet as equals. The second aspect is that, in order for the individual to find his or her authenticity and exercise his or her autonomy, the public sphere should be.neutral. in terms of values, culture and religion. Kymlicka and Taylor challenge the conclusion that is drawn from the liberal premise of the centrality of the individual. They argue that individuals do not develop their values or identity in isolation from others, but in association with them.

*Taylor contrasts the ideal of equality with the politics of difference, based on the modern notion of identity:*

- With the politics of equal dignity, what is established is meant to be universally the same, an identical basket of rights and immunities; with the politics of difference, what we are asked to recognize is the unique identity of this or that individual or group, their distinctiveness from every one else. The idea is that it is precisely this distinctiveness that has been ignored, glossed over, assimilated to a dominant or majority identity. And this assimilation is the cardinal sin against the ideal of identity.

Kymlicka considers that culture is absolutely essential to the feeling of belonging and participation, and that is the most important of all bearings that a person needs to negotiate his or her way through life. He says.Cultural membership affects our very sense of personal identity and capacity. The authenticity of one.s culture cannot be replaced by other cultures, even if one is given the opportunity to learn its language and medium.

The broader position taken by Kymlicka has been influential and controversial. He regards culture as the most important defining feature of a community; he assumes a consensus within the community on the values of the community; he regards culture as unchanging; and he seems to believe in conflicts between cultures. In all these assumptions he is wrong.

There are serious implications of recognizing the isolation of communities and entrenching their cultures in this way. What justifies discrimination against other cultures that are implicit in this approach? How do we define culture? Can we say that the cultures of Hindus and Muslims are different and antagonistic, when so many customs, habits and much of history unite them, and give them a common identity? Nor does Kymlicka.s model acknowledge multiple identities that are so characteristic of the contemporary period. It would seem better to build on this overlapping of identities and values than to foster separation and antagonism, which are the inevitable result of Kymlicka.s approach.

## INDIVISBLE AND INTERDEPENDENT

Nor can it be said that rights are indivisible and interdependent, except as a rhetorical device. As the scope of rights and freedoms has expanded, the tensions and even contradictions between different sets of rights or at least the tensions surrounding the achievement thereof have become obvious. These tensions do not arise only between civil and political rights, on one hand, and economic, social and cultural rights, such as between the right to private property and the right to education or shelter, on the other.

They also arise within each set of rights, for example the tension between the freedom of expression and the protection against hate speech or incitement to war. Nor must we ignore the varying interests, national and corporate, that are served by different rights. There is no agreement among scholars on the effect of civil and political rights on economic development, or vice versa. This has cast doubt on the interdependence of the two sets of rights. A simplistic or high minded approach that ignores these tensions and contradictions is unlikely to produce an effective policy on human rights that has the capacity to reconcile the various goals of social development.

### SEARCH FOR CONSENSUS

Such agreement as there is has been secured through a variety of compromises. Sometimes it is done by putting together seemingly incompatible claims and propositions. A version of this strategy appears in the Declaration where the commitment to human rights is bracketed with.full respect for the various religious and ethical values and cultural backgrounds of people. Another strategy is to pair the traditional bundle of rights with the right to development. This strategy was endorsed at the 1993 World Conference on Human Rights, where the West withdrew its objections to the.right to development in return for the acceptance by Asian states of the hallowed formula of.universal, indivisible, and interdependent.. At an earlier stage, the right to self-determination played a similar role in the rapprochement of liberal rights and decolonization. It now plays a somewhat different role, as the foundation for democracy. The right to development, which can also be central to the Copenhagen aspirations, is still problematic, conceptually and practically. Attempts to reconcile different approaches and interests have been made by scholars, who emphasize the common values of different cultures and religions, and attempt a synthesis where values differ. It is clear that, despite the formulations in the Declaration and these efforts, there is no effective consensus on human rights and democracy that can be counted on to underpin the strategy of the Declaration.

## DEMOCRACY

### THE RIGHT TO DEMOCRACY: THE LEGAL FOUNDATIONS

One of the great achievements of the United Nations in the field of human rights was to bring colonial empires to an end. The primary foundation for its work was the principle of self-determination. Both the Covenants contain the right of all peoples to self-determination by.virtue of which... they freely determine their political status and freely pursue their economic, social and cultural development.

Despite this broad promise, self-determination did not lead to democracy; it protected against foreign, but not domestic, tyranny. Once colonial rule ended, state sovereignty trumped democracy. However, in recent years self-determination has been revived as a principle for the internal organization of a state based on the right of a people to choose their form of government and to elect and participate in it. Self-determination has been linked to article 25 of the ICCPR.

*This article guarantees all citizens, without discrimination, three kinds of rights that are important for the Copenhagen agenda:*

- The right and the opportunity. to.take part in the conduct of public affairs, directly or through freely chosen representatives.;
- To vote and to be elected at genuine periodic elections which shall be by universal and equal suffrage and shall be held by secret ballot, guaranteeing the free expression of the will of electors.; and
- To have access, on general terms of equality, to public service in [their] country.

The basis of this right was stated more forthrightly in the Universal Declaration of Human Rights: the will of the people shall be the basis of the authority of governments. The ICCPR also contains a number of rights that are essential to democratic politics, such as freedom of expression, the right of assembly, the right of association, freedom of belief and conscience and the protection of the rule of law.

Article 25 was not always considered the basis of democracy. The word democracy itself is not used. There is no reference to pluralism, which is deemed to be an essential attribute of democracy. It has been argued that elections under single party systems could satisfy the requirements of the article. In any case, even free elections should not be equated with democracy, which also includes notions of continuing accountability, the rule of law and respect for human rights, especially those of minorities.

However, with the collapse of the Soviet Union it has been possible to read a broader meaning into the article. But it needs to be emphasized that, while today's interpretation favours the broader view, it does not justify intervention by the international community to enforce democracy on a recalcitrant state. Regional and bilateral sanctions can be imposed if a state's conduct in denying democracy is strongly disapproved of.

In combination with regional declarations, it has also been used to require a degree of democratization as a precondition of the membership of an organization. One may compare this approach with that in Asia, where ASEAN clearly repudiated democracy as a criterion of membership when it welcomed Myanmar and Viet Nam to its ranks.

## RIGHTS OF MINORITIES TO POLITICAL PARTICIPATION

The orientation towards democracy has been reinforced by the favourable development of the rights of minorities from the low point of the ICCPR, which only grudgingly recognized the existence of linguistic, religious and cultural minorities and imposed no positive obligations on the state towards them. When the United Nations began work on an international regime of rights, it emphasized individual rights and carefully avoided giving rights, particularly political rights, to groups.

There are trends now, however, towards a greater recognition of cultural and ethnic bases of autonomy. Article 27 of the ICCPR, until recently the principal United Nations provision on minorities, was drafted to exclude collective rights and was narrowly interpreted. However, in recent years the United Nations Human Rights Committee has interpreted the article in a more positive way, using it to develop.collective rights of minorities., including a measure of autonomy, and some positive obligations on the states.

In a series of decisions, the Committee has interpreted the article as a basis for collective rights 96 ILR 637: No. 197/1985), as a basis for the preservation of the culture and way of life of a minority group and as a basis for protecting and developing traditional ways of life. Efforts have also been made by that Committee and others to interpret the right to self-determination to mean, where relevant, internal autonomy rather than secession.

This broader approach is reflected in the United Nations Declaration on the Rights of Minorities adopted by the General Assembly in 1992. Unlike the ICCPR, it places positive obligations on the state to protect the identity of minorities and encourage.conditions for the promotion of that identity. The Declaration states that.persons belonging to minorities have the right to participate effectively in public life. and the.right to participate effectively in decisions on the national and, where appropriate, regional level concerning the minority to which they belong or the regions in which they live.

It does not go so far as to require autonomy for minorities, but it lays the foundation for it by recognizing community rights and the importance of identity. Several initiatives have been taken in Europe, through the OSCE, the Council of Europe and the EU to promote the concept of autonomy and the right of minorities to political participation, although its impact is so far restricted to Europe. This is manifested both in formal declarations and, where appropriate, interventions to solve ethnic conflicts in Europe. Article 35 of the Declaration on the Human Dimension of the CSCE recognizes.appropriate local or autonomous administrations. as one of the possible means. for the promotion of the.ethnic, cultural, linguistic and religious identity of certain minorities. The principal instrument of the Council of Europe is the Framework Convention for the Protection of National Minorities, which protects various rights of minorities, obliges the state to facilitate the enjoyment of these rights, and recognizes many rights of.identity..

It obliges state parties to.create the conditions necessary for the effective participation of persons belonging to national minorities in cultural, social and economic life and in public affairs, in particular those affecting them. There is no proclamation of a right to autonomy, but the exercise of some of these rights implies a measure of autonomy. The Declaration and statements of principle by the Council of Europe, although not strictly binding, have been used by the OSCE High Commissioner for Minorities and other mediating bodies as a basis for compromise between contending forces, and have thus influenced practice, in which autonomy has been a key factor.

The European Community now EU, has also used conformity with the Declaration as a precondition for the recognition of new states in Europe. The ability of existing states to confer recognition on entities, especially breakaway states, can be a powerful weapon to influence their constitutional structure. When various republics were breaking away from the Federal Republic of Yugoslavia and the Soviet Union split up, the EC issued a Declaration on the Guidelines on the Recognition of New States in Eastern Europe and in the Soviet Union, although it was not applied in all cases. Among the conditions a candidate had to satisfy before it would be recognized was that its constitution contain.guarantees for the rights of ethnic and national groups and minorities in accordance with the commitments subscribed to in the framework of the CSCE. Entities requesting recognition were asked to submit evidence that their constitutions conformed to the guidelines and recognition was granted only if the evidence satisfied an EC constitutional tribunal set up for this. Similar principles have been used for admission to the Council of Europe and the EU. The greater involvement of the United Nations or consortia of states in the settlement of internal conflicts has also helped to develop the concept of self-determination as implying autonomy in appropriate circumstances, such as in Bosnia, Eastern Europe and Kosovo.

However, the birth of new states, following the collapse of the communist order in the Soviet Union, Eastern Europe and the Balkans, has removed some taboo against secession, and the international community seems to be inching towards some consensus that extreme oppression of a group may justify secession. This position has served to strengthen the internal aspect of self-determination, for a state can defeat the claim of separation if it can demonstrate that it respects political and cultural rights of minorities.

A further, and far-reaching, gloss has been placed on this doctrine by the Canadian Supreme Court, which decided in 1999 that Quebec had no right under either the Canadian Constitution or international law to unilateral secession, but that if Quebec were to decide on secession through a referendum, Ottawa and provinces would have to negotiate with Quebec on future constitutional arrangements.

Such a view of self-determination has some support in certain national constitutions, indicating no more than a trend at this stage. Often constitutional provisions for autonomy are adopted during periods of social and political transformation, when an autocratic regime is overthrown, or a crisis is reached in minority majority conflicts, or there is intense international pressure. Propelled by these factors, a number of constitutions now recognize some entitlement to self-government, such as the Philippines in relation to two provinces, one for indigenous peoples and the other for a religious minority; Spain, which guarantees autonomy to three regions and invites others to negotiate with the centre for autonomy; Papua New Guinea, which authorizes provinces to negotiate with the central government for substantial devolution of power; Fiji, which recognizes the right of indigenous peoples to their own administration at the local level; and recently Ethiopia, which gives its.nations, nationalities, and peoples. the right to seek wide-ranging powers as states within a federation and guarantees them even the right to secession.

In the wake of the break up of the Soviet Union, the Russian Constitution of 1993 provides for extensive autonomy to its constituent parts, whether republics or autonomous areas. The Chinese Constitution entrenches the rights of ethnic minorities to substantial self-government, although in practice the dominance of the Communist Party negates their autonomy. In other instances, the constitution may authorize, but not require, the establishment of autonomous areas, with China again an interesting example, in order to provide a constitutional basis for.One Country Two Systems..

## INDIGENOUS PEOPLES

The International Labour Organization Indigenous and Tribal Peoples Convention, adopted in 1989, represented a reversal of paternalistic and assimilations approach followed in the 1957 Indigenous and Tribal Populations Convention. Convention No. 169 recognizes the.aspirations of these peoples to exercise control over their own institutions, ways of life and economic development and to maintain and develop their identities, languages and religions, within the framework of the States in which they live..

It notes that their cultural and religious values, institutions and forms of traditional social control are to be preserved. The system of land ownership and the rules for the transmission of land rights are to be protected. The Draft United Nations Declaration on the Rights of Indigenous Peoples goes even further and proclaims their right to self-determination, under which they may.freely determine their political status and freely pursue their economic, social and cultural development.

The principle of self-determination gives them the.right to autonomy or self-government in matters relating to their internal and local affairs., which include social, cultural and economic activities, and the right to control the entry of nonmembers. It recognizes their.collective rights and the right to maintain and strengthen their distinct political, economic, social and cultural characteristics.

These ideas have already formed the basis of negotiations between indigenous peoples and the states in which they live, giving recognition not only to their land rights but also to forms of autonomy, although African and Asian governments deny the existence of indigenous peoples in their states and the instruments have had little impact there.

*Indigenous peoples, particularly in North America, also base their claims on other legal bases:*

- Their.inherent sovereignty, which predates colonization and
- Treaties with incoming powers.

The United Nations and the international community have shown a concern for the fate of vulnerable communities that was not envisaged in the United Nations Charter. Then the preoccupation was with decolonization, as reflected in the establishment of the Trusteeship Council. Once a major UN department, its role has diminished. It has been suggested that the change in the emphasis of the United Nations should be registered by transforming the Trusteeship Council into a Council on Diversity, Representation and Governance, with major responsibility for minorities and indigenous peoples.

## DEMOCRATIZATION: THE RECORD

There is no doubt that more countries enjoy democracy now than, say, a decade ago. A number of Eastern and Northern European countries turned to constitutional democracy after the collapse of communism, with considerable assistance from Western Europe and the United States. South Africa achieved a miraculous transition to democracy and a regime of rights; Mozambique put both civil war and authoritarianism behind it; and the largest African state, Nigeria, saw the end of a particularly obnoxious military regime. Northern Ireland is having an uncertain transition to peace, stability and power sharing.

Even the United Kingdom, with a long and cherished tradition of parliamentary supremacy, has devolved significant power to Scotland and Wales, and has adopted a Bill of Rights. Fiji overcame a military regime and its racist successor to achieve a constitution strong on political stability, power sharing, rights and social justice. But in general the picture is less rosy in Africa, Asia and Latin America and, even when there are elections, there is no particular commitment to pluralism, rights, transparency or accountability.

Governments are headed by powerful presidents with few limitations on their power. Constitutional limits on the number of terms that a person may be head of government are ignored or repealed. Restrictions continue on rights, often spuriously in the name of national security or public order. What is particularly depressing is that China, the only permanent member of the Security Council from Asia, Africa and Latin America, has neither democracy nor respect for rights and is a vigorous defender of its authoritarianism. Another member of the Security Council, Russia, has wreaked terrible suffering on the Chechens, committing gross violations of fundamental rights with impunity.

There has been great progress in civil and political rights at the level of constitutions and laws no modern constitution is without an elaborate bill of rights, there are increasing numbers of institutions for the promotion and protection of rights; judicial bodies have developed new doctrines and jurisprudence to strengthen rights; and there are many more meetings on rights, regionally and internationally. But experience also shows that democracy, in the narrow sense of elections and the operation of parliamentary institutions, does not ensure respect for human rights. It also often coexists with corruption, the lack of accountability and the persecution of minorities.

In the area of ethnic difference traditionally the source of great conflict, instability and oppression there has been some progress. Concepts and rules have emerged or are emerging that recognize group identity and confer collective and political rights on minorities. Several ethnic and other civil wars have been brought to an end through negotiated settlements, although many continue and cause great suffering to numerous peoples. Indeed it must be acknowledged that ethnic conflict, or what passes for ethnic conflict, is still the greatest cause of the violation of rights, political instability and oppression.

## EXTERNAL ASSISTANCE FOR DEMOCRACY AND RIGHTS

It is not my purpose to draw a balance sheet of democratization. The Copenhagen Declaration on Social Development is directed importantly to international assistance and cooperation towards its goals, and I want to focus on these efforts for democratization. The end of the Cold War, which to an extent freed major powers from the.need. to buttress their client states and to destabilize.unfriendly states, encouraged the West to invoke the international democracy norms to mount a democratization campaign.

The propping up of dictators became an embarrassment to them, and the people they had oppressed for so long felt emboldened to demand democracy and accountability. It would be wrong, however, to assume that the foreign policy interests of major powers took second place to democracy and human rights; even today foreign interests dominate their policies. Assistance has also come from private foundations and international NGOs, as well as from associations of states, such as the EU, and lately from the United Nations and other international organizations. Only a handful of states are involved in these efforts the most active being Denmark, the Netherlands, Sweden, the United Kingdom and the United States.

External involvement has taken several forms ranging from pressure and sanctions on, or incentives to, recalcitrant dictators; encouragement and support to democratic forces, particularly NGOs; to technical assistance and equipment. To a large extent, the forms of assistance have reflected the West's experience with democracy. The development or invigoration of civil society has been a major aim, to raise public awareness of rights and entitlements, to raise a sense of responsibility, and to strengthen the capacity of civil society to put pressure on governments to adhere to public morality. Typical forms of assistance to civil society are the establishment or granting of support to NGOs, particularly women's groups; the provision of assistance to professional groups, such as the legal profession and human rights organizations; the strengthening of the media as a vehicle for public debate; and the promotion of freedom of expression and scrutiny of government. A key role is envisaged for NGOs in the strategy of establishing or mobilizing civil society.

When a government decides to democratize, it is offered assistance to frame a national constitution consistent with a state's prerogative to devise its own constitution. These states have been encouraged to follow a participatory form of constitution making. Most new constitutions contain guarantees of human rights, provide for independent institutions and many other features of constitutionalism. Several constitutions provide for the diffusion of power, in the form of devolution or decentralization.

International assistance has focused particularly on the holding of elections, less so on the electoral system itself. Many official and private groups, local as well as international, are recruited or offer to act as election monitors to ensure the fairness of the process. For a while, democratization was equated to holding elections. It is now being recognized that, while free and periodic elections are a necessary ingredient of democracy, they are far from being sufficient. So assistance has been provided for the strengthening of institutions, particularly those of accountability, including the legislature. Bilateral and multilateral assistance has been forthcoming for human rights commissions and similar bodies. Major programmes have been undertaken with the help of foreign aid to modernize and strengthen the legal system.

This assistance has taken the form of rebuilding courts, especially in states where they were destroyed in civil war; computerizing court facilities; training judges and legal practitioners; promoting the professional association of lawyers; upgrading legal libraries; making legislation and law reports easily available; legal aid; and reform of law and procedure. This approach is motivated by the belief that the rule of law is central to the exercise of democracy, control of corruption and other abuses of power, and the protection of rights.

## FRAGMENTED ASSISTANCE FOR HUMAN RIGHTS AND DEMOCRACY

The current system of assisting democratization and the protection of rights is fragmented. A considerable number of programmes have been undertaken by the Organisation for Economic Cooperation and Development countries, principally on a bilateral basis; there is some coordination through the EU mechanisms. The efforts of international bodies are even more uncoordinated and lacking in direction. The principal economic institutions, the International Monetary Fund and the World Bank, have until recently claimed to be nonpolitical and thus desisted from aiding progressive political initiatives while at the same time supporting other kinds of capitalistoriented, political policies. Their recent concern with good governance is connected less with democratic reform than with providing legal and economic conditions for opening markets to foreign capital.

United Nations Secretary General Kofi Annan has taken some lead in centering UN work on human rights. The OHCHR has provided some coordination, with the present High Commissioner attempting to play a leading role in the promotion of rights. Of the UN agencies, the United Nations Development Programme has made the clearest commitment to.mainstreaming. human rights in its programmes. The more specialized agencies have reviewed their policies to reflect greater engagement with human rights, but the results so far are unimpressive.

## ASSESSMENT OF EXTERNAL ASSISTANCE TO DEMOCRATIZATION

It is too early to pronounce a verdict on external assistance to democratization since these efforts are beginning to be evaluated to determine what methods and institutions work, but some tentative conclusions can be stated. Perhaps the most important point is that external assistance can play only a facilitative role. It can use aid conditionalities to put pressure on the national government, but unless there is overwhelming local demand for democracy backed by effective institutions and popular mobilization, these external pressures are unlikely to yield lasting progress. Rights and democracy have to be struggled for.

One reason that South Africa is off to such promising start is that the struggle for democracy was the people's struggle, and the politicization of civil society enables the electorate to put pressure on the government to honour the commitment to democracy and fairness. Foreign governments and international organizations cannot really play a significant role in persuading reluctant presidents to democratize that task has to be left to the people.

Within the scope of assistance that foreign donors can provide, the record is mixed. NGOs, which are the primary engine for change in the face of official resistance, have generally failed, or often have not tried, to mobilize the people. They are essentially lobbying groups, without a mass base of their own, and are excessively dependent on external donors for funding. Thus strategies and projects that appeal to external donors are taken up by the NGOs, often without critical evaluation of their usefulness or effectiveness in the national context. They are accountable to foreign donors as part of their contractual relationship with them and therefore lay themselves open to the charge of being instruments of foreign governments. It has become fashionable to criticize NGOs for the self-interest of their staff, but there is no doubt that NGOs have made valuable contributions and attracted competent and dedicated people, and there is clearly a role for them as human rights watchdogs.

However, it does mean that the mobilization functions tend to be ignored. Nor do foreign governments keep faith with NGOs. They are more interested in working with governments, and if they have a chance to do so, tend to shift funds away from NGOs. Indeed an astute government can greatly weaken support for NGOs, and the NGOs themselves, by seeming to espouse human rights and democracy.

The limitations of elections for democratization have already been commented on. The broadening of aid to overcome the limitations of elections has had an impact, but not enough to significantly deepen democracy. The media, even where responsible and professional, have not always had the expected results. One example is the press in Kenya, which has been very critical of the president, alleging the most serious corruption and violations of rights, but it does not seem to have embarrassed him or eroded his support among those who have traditionally voted for him basically his ethnic vote. The same can be said about the press in Cambodia.

Reform of the legal system has also had mixed results. The process may have increased the professionalism of the system, but not access to courts and lawyers. Traditional systems of dispute resolution have been downgraded and, while these are not without their own problems, they did provide easy access to the system, the system was understood by the people, and for the most part accepted by them.

Professionalization increases the costs of the system of justice; affects different groups. access unequally, particularly favouring corporations that are able to hire the best lawyers; increases the time lag between the filing and hearing of cases; and makes the system alien and intimidating to most people. Legal reform has tended to focus on changes that favour the market mechanism and the integration of the national economy into the global, which frequently affects poorer sections of the population adversely.

The context of efforts to promote democratization determines their orientation. The collapse of communism was welcomed as a triumph of liberal democracy. But many more saw it as the triumph of the market. It is not easy to distinguish support for democracy from support for markets in the efforts of individual or collective Western states to promote rights and democracy abroad. Indeed, it can be said that the support for markets is stronger; the rationale for that support is more powerfully presented than for democracy. The IMF and the World Bank have hijacked democracy and rights through the advocacy of the narrower concept of governance, which is at the bottom of the charter of political and legal institutions for capitalism. In this way, political rights of participation and accountability are not only subordinated to the market, but are actually undermined. Another weakness of the external support for democratization has been inadequate attention to reinforcing strengthening of economic and social rights.

Democracy is often justified by the benefits it brings to the people, through political stability and economic development. Unless people see economic advantages for themselves, their enthusiasm for democracy is likely to wane;

economic betterment is what confers legitimacy on a democratic order. External assistance is, of course, provided for health, water, agricultural development and so on, but it is not clearly tied to individual or group entitlements, and is often not enough to improve the lives of most people. Experience has shown that with democratization there is no automatic change for the better in the economy.

Donorrecipient relationships are always difficult, but they are particularly sensitive in the context of assistance for democracy and human rights. They involve an element of pressure, if not direct coercion, at least the coercion that comes from the recipient's knowledge that other forms of assistance by the donor may be at stake if overtures on democratization are not accepted.

In some cases, of course, human rights conditionalities have been imposed by the donors. The evidence suggests that donors who provide assistance across a range of areas are more effective in influencing the recipient's human rights and democracy policies than those who tend to focus principally on rights and democracy. Assistance in this area touches on many points that are closely connected to a state's.sovereignty, the election and operation of government, the workings of the legislature, judicial reforms and modernization of the legal system. It also involves the donor's engagement with and assistance to, and sometimes management of, civil society. Moreover, it is all too easy for the recipient to dismiss rights and democracy as.foreign ideas, and to feel or feign particular irritation at the disregard of its own cultural, historical and political traditions. This active and extensive engagement of donors in the politics of the recipient state is likely to cause great tensions, and therefore the extent and modalities of external engagement need to be handled with great care and delicacy, but also firmness when appropriate.

### WHAT MAKES FOR SUCCESS OR FAILURE

In summary, external assistance can play a useful, but supplementary, role in promoting democracy and respect for rights. It can strengthen the status and resources of civil organizations and state bodies committed to democratization and rights. But the role that external assistance can play is limited and contingent on a firm commitment of the people or government, or both, to democracy and rights. In the end, the establishment and deepening of democracy depends on the people and government of a state; it has to be endogenously driven to be sure of lasting success.

## SOCIAL JUSTICE: ECONOMIC, SOCIAL AND CULTURAL RIGHTS

### THE LEGAL FOUNDATIONS

In adopting the framework of human rights, the Copenhagen Declaration, in conformity with United Nations orthodoxy, places equal importance on all human rights. But realistically, it is economic and social rights that are essential to the Copenhagen agenda.

Civil and political rights are undoubtedly important in organizing demands for greater equity and in themselves for facilitating an open and accountable society. But the evidence that these rights also lead to economic and social development is not conclusive. So economic and social rights that directly provide housing, food, education and clothing are crucial.

Unfortunately, economic and social rights are so far the Cinderella of rights; they are attacked, conceptually, for lacking the qualifications to be called rights, as the beneficiaries and providers are not easily identified, and even when identified the legal process cannot enforce rights. They are also attacked politically, as increasing state power, and interfering with the autonomy, and assets, of individuals.

Thus in so far as economic and social rights are central to the achievement of the Copenhagen agenda, considerable research and lobbying will be necessary to transform these rights into clear and enforceable targets and standards. This will require some intellectual ingenuity and political will, but that it can be done is clear from countries, such as Sri Lanka, that have been able to provide many of these rights despite a relatively poor economy.

The United Nations Charter committed its members to promote.higher standards of living, full employment, and conditions of economic and social progress and development. and.solutions of international economic, social, health and related problems, and international cultural and educational cooperation. The Universal Declaration of Human Rights contains a number of economic, social and cultural rights: the right to social security, and economic, social and cultural rights indispensable for the individual's dignity and the free development of the individual's personality; the right to work, free choice of employment, just and favourable conditions of work and protection against unemployment, including the right to join trade unions; the right to rest and leisure; the right to a standard of living adequate for family health and wellbeing, including food, clothing, housing, medical care and necessary social services; the right to education; and the right to participate in the cultural life of the community, to enjoy the arts and to share in scientific advancement and its benefits.

These rights formed the core of the ICESCR, but the formulation is too broad to provide sufficient guidance on implementation and the machinery for implementation and supervision is much weaker than for the ICCPR, typified by the omission of any complaints procedure.

These rights also find their way into conventions for the protection of women, children, indigenous peoples and migrant workers, and form one of the core components of the Declaration on the Right to Development in the following expression:

- States should undertake, at the national level, all necessary measures for the realization of the right to development and shall ensure, inter alia, equality of opportunity for all in their access to basic resources, education, health services, food, housing, employment and the fair distribution of income. Effective measures should be undertaken to ensure that women have an active role in the development process. Appropriate economic and social reforms shall be carried out with a view to eradicating all social injustices.

Several national constitutions require or urge the state to provide similar services, although for the most part they are mandatory only for disadvantaged groups. India and South Africa are two outstanding examples, where the obligations on the state are based on the moral and political recognition of past injustices to particular ethnic or social groups.

The recent Fiji Constitution imposes a legal obligation on the government to institute schemes for preferential policies for poorer communities and groups. Several other countries such as Australia, Canada, Malaysia and the United States, as well as Northern Ireland, also have preferential policies. However, these policies have not always helped the really disadvantaged. the resources having been appropriated by the better-off in the various communities, and used for political and patronage purposes. In any case, the resources allocated for these policies are too limited to make a major impact on poverty.

## THE RECORD

These provisions have not been used to provide assistance for economic, social and cultural rights in the post-Cold War era in the way political rights in the ICCPR were seized on to promote democracy. A 1998 UNDP report notes that.fifty years after the adoption of the Universal Declaration of Human Rights, one third of the developing world's people are enslaved by a poverty so complete that it denies them fundamental human rights.... Nearly 12 million children die each year before their fifth birthday. More than 800 million people go hungry.

It also notes that 30 per cent of all children under five are malnourished and that 38 per cent of all adult women are illiterate. Another report observes that nearly 100 million people are homeless, and the number of those without adequate housing exceeds one billion. It is often claimed that economic, social and cultural rights are different from other rights in that they are not justifiable and cannot be enforced in courts. State obligations under the ICESCR or national constitutions are not enforceable rights of the people.

Moreover, because the ICESCR commits member states to.take steps, individually and through international assistance and cooperation, especially economic and technical, to the maximum of its available resources, with a view to achieving progressively the full realization of the rights recognized in the present Covenant by all appropriate means, some national courts have taken the view that the Covenant is not directly applicable in their states but requires national legislation.

However, the United Nations Committee on Economic, Social and Cultural Rights has declared that at least some rights in the Covenant were intended for and are capable of immediate and direct application. Most arguments advanced about the difficulties of making social and economic rights enforceable are not persuasive nor is it productive to think of rights only in terms of judicial enforcement. It is more valuable to focus on the obligations of states; as has been pointed out a state's obligation in relation to all categories of rights may be seen as involving different types of obligations that can be fulfilled variously by positive action, by refraining from acting, or by creating an environment in which rights can be achieved.

There is no reason why the beneficiaries of these rights should not be involved in the planning and implementing of programmes for achieving the rights, or why their access to the appropriate institutions responsible for implementing rights should not be guaranteed.

The fact is that the no enforceability of economic and social rights springs from the low regard in which these rights are held by dominant national and international groups. Philip Alston has pointed to the low priority given to these rights and the limited resources devoted to their implementation.

He says that.denials of the most fundamental economic and social rights continue on a massive scale that affects hundreds of millions of people and offers various explanations for the neglect of economic, social and cultural rights:

- Preeminent among them was the impact of the Cold War and of the ideological struggles between communism and capitalism. This factor changed what was a rational and balanced debate between 1944 and 1947 into a struggle that encouraged the taking of extreme positions and prevented objective consideration of the key issues raised by the concept of economic and social rights.

Another reason is that the implementation of these rights requires skills and expertise that are alien to.what has been termed the normative judicial model of human rights implementation.. The result is that the human rights lawyers, the diplomatic representatives, the secretariat officials and the NGO representatives who have come to dominate human rights discussions will feel distinctively ill at ease and ill-equipped to deal with many of the most pressing issues arising from a concern with economic, social and cultural rights.

Finally.the proposition that minimum core economic and social rights ought to be accorded to every individual is still automatically made subject by decision makers to an economic calculus that will often culminate in various economically compelling reasons as to why such rights simply cannot be recognized. Little attempt has been made to establish criteria for measuring the success of the.progressive implementation. of these rights.

However, in recent years increasing attention has been paid to economic and social rights as a result of a series of world conferences such as those on women, children and social development. The 1973 Human Rights Conference endorsed the right to development. The current United Nations Secretary General, Kofi Annan, has tried to make human rights a core concern of the United Nations and its agencies, which has stimulated thinking about the means of mainstreaming human rights into development.

The High Commissioner for Human Rights has entered into agreements with UNDP and other agencies to promote human rights in their work. The World Food Summit of 1996, convened by the Food and Agriculture Organization of the United Nations, noted the appallingly low standards of nutrition of millions of people, particularly children and women, and the terrible consequences of malnutrition and hunger, observing that the problem was not so much the lack of food as the access to it.

The governments of the world pledged themselves to achieving food security for all and as an immediate objective to reducing the number of undernourished people to half the 1996 level by 2015. The OECD has a commitment, together with member states, to reduce the level of poverty by half by 2015.

A number of recent national constitutions have incorporated social and economic rights. National courts had already begun to develop jurisprudence facilitating litigation on these rights. Important impetus to their realization was given with the establishment of the United Nations Committee on Economic, Social and Cultural Rights in 1986, which has done valuable work to clarify and elaborate the provisions of the Covenant, and is developing a system of reporting and supervision. A number of NGOs have been formed to promote these rights.

Courts are now more willing to read ICESCR-type rights into the more justifiable provisions of the ICCPR-type rights. Thus the Indian courts have given a wide definition to the right to life. In one case the Indian Supreme Court held that the right to life.includes the right to live with human dignity and all that goes with it, namely, the bare necessities of life such as adequate nutrition, clothing and shelter over the head and facilities for reading, writing and expressing oneself in diverse forms, freely moving about and mixing and commingling with fellow human beings.. In another case the Supreme Court explicitly used Directive Principles of State Policy to interpret the scope of the right to life, giving it a broad meaning to include protection of health, provision of education, and just and humane conditions of work. A recent Indian Supreme Court decision has declared that the right to life guarantees access to medical services, especially in an emergency. The Court said that the state cannot ignore its constitutional obligation to provide adequate medical services to preserve human life on account of financial constraints, which it must take into account in allocating funds for medical services.

The Bangladesh Supreme Court has decided that the right to life is not limited to the protection of life and limb necessary for the full enjoyment of life, but also includes, among other things, the protection of the health and normal longevity of ordinary human beings. Despite these bold moves, the judiciary is neither particularly qualified nor willing to establish entitlements to economic and social benefits and, particularly in Bangladesh or India, unable to enforce judgments that do recognize social and economic rights.

The right to nondiscrimination has also provided the basis for the enforcement of social and economic rights. The Canadian Supreme Court has declared that hospitals that run government schemes for health care are in breach of section 15 of the Charter of Rights if they do not provide sign interpreters for deaf patients, for lack of de facto equality. The Court said that the.principle that discrimination can accrue from a failure to take positive steps to ensure that disadvantaged groups benefit equally from services offered to the general public is widely accepted in the human rights field. The Court reiterated its earlier view that.a government may be required to take positive steps to ensure the equality of people or groups who come within the scope of section 15. The United Nations Human Rights Committee has declared that the rights to equality under the ICCPR extend to all rights guaranteed in the ICESCR. National jurisprudence on economic and social rights will, in conjunction with the General Comments of the United Nations Committee on Economic, Social and Cultural Rights, help to establish or refine details of these rights, which in both the Covenant and national laws tend to be rather general. Hopefully this clarification and standard setting will increase pressure on governments and international organizations to implement these rights.

It is partly with this view that the Committee has undertaken interpretations of key social rights; it has so far issued guidelines on the rights to housing and food, and is well advanced on the guidelines on education. In 1991 it provided an explanation of what constituted the right to adequate housing as guaranteed in article 11(1) of the Covenant. The Committee defined the right to housing as not only having a roof over one.s head, but also the right to live in security, peace and dignity.

*It then outlined the following features of the right:*

- Legal security of tenure;
- Availability of services, materials, facilities and infrastructure (for example, access to water, sanitation, light and cooking facilities);
- Affordability (so that, for example, the percentage of housing related costs is commensurate with income levels);
- Habitability (that is, providing the occupants with adequate space and protecting them from cold, damp, heat, rain, etc.);
- Accessibility (for example, to the needy, elderly, etc.);
- Location (so that housing is close to place of work, schools, etc.); and
- Cultural adequacy (so that housing design, etc., reflects the cultural traditions of the occupants).

In 1999 in Comment No. 12, the Committee issued its guidelines on the right to food, which, it said, is not merely.a minimum package of calories, proteins and other specific nutrients.. It defined the right to adequate food as consisting of the availability of food in a quantity and quality sufficient to satisfy the dietary needs of individuals, free from adverse substances and acceptable within a given culture; and the accessibility of such food in ways that are sustainable and that do not interfere with the enjoyment of other rights.

The Committee also provided useful guidance on the obligations of states for the provision of social and economic rights, and the ways in which these obligations may be discharged. The state of country's development is not an excuse for not providing these rights; a state must do what it can within its means, and must justify any lack of priority given to its legal obligations.

It must also adopt appropriate development strategies for the different sectors to which these rights pertain. Measures can be legislative, administrative or facilitative, and may include a mix of public and private initiatives. Similarly, remedies can be judicial as well as administrative. An essential step towards progressive implementation is monitoring, with reference to standards and benchmarks. The Committee has also drawn attention to the role of the international community helping states without adequate resources to ensure that their basic needs are met; this role is stipulated in article 56 of the United Nations Charter and article 23 of the Covenant.

These initiatives and developments augur well for the realization of social and economic rights. However, it must be recognized that the dominant economic force of our times globalization runs counter to them and will probably undermine them. It is therefore important, in concluding this section, to turn to the nature of globalization and to its impact on these rights.

## GLOBALIZATION

Globalization is a compendium of ideas, practices, institutions, directions of change and ideologies. Some of these diminish rights, others promote them, and some do both simultaneously: for example, the Internet and other forms of technology provide more opportunities for both freedom of expression and access to information, and uncover new possibilities for networking, but, at the same time, they greatly increase the influence of corporations and the opportunities for hate speech, pornography and sexual trafficking.

That makes it particularly difficult to distinguish between the positive and negative consequences of globalization for rights. However, even though they are intertwined, it may be possible to distinguish the economic processes of globalization from the more political and social processes. This document focuses on the negative consequences for rights, which I believe are dominant, but it would be unwise to ignore the positive potential of globalization.

The economic processes are connected with the development of national market economies and their integration globally on market principles. The market system is driven by the search for profits, which replace older values of reciprocity and social solidarity by the morality of profits. In order to increase profits, more and more objects, which previously were communal or in other ways inalienable, are brought within the domain of the market as commodities? Historically, this has had the effect of converting commons into private property and breaking up the cohesion of communities.

This is all too evident in areas where the market frontier has moved in recent decades, such as in Africa and Asia: migration to cities, the anomie of urban life, the collapse of the extended family, and the replacement of sentiment by money as the basis for human motivation. Throughout history, societies have tried to combat or moderate the natural consequences of the market. The development of trade unions and their politics and the democratization of the state have provided a counterbalance to the predatory tendencies of the market. In the West, the balance between the market and democratic politics produced the welfare state.

Global capitalism is relatively unfettered by regulations. On the contrary, it enjoys the support of powerful capitalist states, most notably of course the United States and the member countries of the EU. A number of international economic institutions especially the IMF, the World Bank and the World Trade Organization share and reinforce the ideology of global capitalism.

These states and institutions have taken it upon themselves to create the political and legal conditions for the global market they favour: removal of barriers to international trade and services, the movement of capital, the global protection of property rights, the privatization of state companies, the deregulation of business activities and the phasing out of welfare services.

All these developments have diminished the capacity of states to provide essential social services to the people. The effects of structural adjustment policies in Africa and the South Pacific, imposed by the IMF and the World Bank, have been little short of disastrous; they have reduced the access of all but the most privileged groups to education, health and nutrition.

Even in Europe, where the welfare state was born, there have been severe cutbacks. In East Asia, where welfare was often provided by commercial corporations, benefits have been phased out allegedly because of the corporation's inability to compete in the international economy if they have to absorb the costs of welfare.

Several of the negative social and political consequences of globalization are to do with its asymmetries. The obvious asymmetry is that between capital and labour.the former may move freely, but not the latter. It is therefore possible for capitalists to move, or threaten to move, their enterprises as a way to negotiate economic concessions from the host state, or to negotiate with workers for low wages and no unionization. Labour is at a considerable disadvantage in what is clearly an unequal situation. Likewise, capital is entitled to national treatment wherever it chooses to go, but not migrant workers, who are subject to considerable legal and practical discrimination in host countries.

Global capital relies increasingly on part-time or informal forms of labour, which means that workers have little security of employment, and that wages and rates of unionization are low. The result is also that the workforce consists increasingly of women who are more prepared, able or compelled to accept these terms. To a significant extent, several states are also becoming captives of global capitalism. They dare not impose high taxes for fear of scaring away foreign as well as domestic capital. In some countries there has been little attempt to enforce industrial safety standards for the same reason. In free economic zones that many countries have established to attract foreign capital, large portions of the national legal and fiscal systems are suspended. States that wish to engage with the international economic system and few think that they can afford not to have to accept complex legal and administrative regimes, granting extensive rights to foreign capital and prohibiting discrimination to support domestic entrepreneurs.

The result is that these states are unable to provide basic welfare services to their people. China's experience is a good illustration of what happens to social and economic rights when the market becomes the dominant matrix of economy. Despite its general economic backwardness, China used to ensure its people equal and decent standards of education, health and shelter. With the spread of market practices and ideology, these services are being phased out, and becoming commodities that must be purchased on the market.

The result is that basic needs are beyond the capacity of millions of people. South Africa is finding that, despite pressures from the historically disadvantaged groups for the satisfaction of basic needs and the constitutional requirements to do so its social policies are effectively governed by its commitment to engage fully with the international economic system.

## GLOBALIZATION AND HUMAN RIGHTS

The effects of globalization enable us to gain fresh insights into the nature of rights. Certain kinds of rights are important for globalization property, association, independent judiciary and the rule of law. But globalization does not conceive of social and economic rights it thinks in terms of social and economic benefits as outcomes of markets, not as any kind of preconditions.

It points to various weaknesses of the regime of rights: in an age of mass migrations many rights are restricted to citizens; the human rights regime provides no redress against the violation of rights by non-state institutions, despite the overwhelming power of transnational corporations to determine our life chances; and the basic framework for the protection and enforcement of rights is still the state, while the obligations to protect human rights are international. The international system is vigorous in elaborating norms, but lacks the jurisdictional basis and often the political will to enforce them. However, most states lack resources to protect human rights, especially economic and social rights. Globalization has sharpened the distinction between civil and political rights, which it needs, and economic, social and cultural rights, which threaten its dominance. Clearly, rhetoric is less powerful than material forces.

## CONCLUSION AND RECOMMENDATIONS

### ANALYSIS

The World Summit for Social Development adopted a human rights framework as part of its strategy to eradicate poverty. The observance of human rights facilitates peaceful coexistence and consequently social and political stability. A democratic society is predicated on respect for human rights. This much is generally recognized. Somewhat more controversial is the third proposition underlying the Social Summit strategy that a society that wants to achieve social justice also has to implement social and economic rights. There is a powerful school of thought that argues that social justice is the outcome of the market economic system, and not a contrivance of the state. This school of thought, associated with globalization and the hegemony of the United States, is a principal obstacle to the implementation of social justice. But there are other obstacles too.

Although human rights norms covering key areas of human existence have been negotiated through international collaboration, the machinery for their enforcement at the international level is rudimentary and grossly under resourced. In most states as well, the system for the enforcement of rights is highly inadequate. Even though a majority of states profess a primary commitment to human rights, in practice their governments do not wish to encumber their diplomatic relations with the inconvenience of holding other governments accountable for human rights violations the more so if their own economy might suffer from demanding such accountability.

For the most part, the so-called human rights and governance conditionalities are little more than blackmail to force states to develop and open their markets to outside investors. At home, many governments are reluctant to rule by the logic of human rights, and their police and security forces are often implicated in serious violations of rights. Despite the ideology and rhetoric of human rights, human rights activists are looked upon as troublemakers and subjected to harassment and persecution. The truth is that human rights too often threaten powerful vested interests.

### RECOMMENDATIONS

If human rights are to become the framework for social development, fundamental reforms in and strengthening of the human rights regime are necessary. The first and the hardest is to accept the implications of the universality of human rights. The concept of universality has been discussed largely in terms of the relevance of a common core of human rights to all societies. But it also has another dimension the responsibility of the world community to ensure that all people, wherever they might be, are guaranteed their rights.

Similarly, the concept of the interdependence or indivisibility of rights has to be placed in the context of global responsibility for the promotion of rights. The West has insisted on the indivisibility of rights because it is suspicious of many governments that have argued that civil and political rights should be postponed until there is a higher level of economic development.

If the West is serious about the indivisibility of rights, then it is obliged to ensure that sufficient funds are transferred to poorer countries for the satisfaction of the basic needs of their people. However, it has so far refused to accept the logic of this position, and has shown a marked reluctance to engage in serious negotiations on the implementation of the Declaration on the Right to Development; foreign aid has fallen to 0.22 per cent of gross national product, despite the formula agreed to long ago of 0.77 per cent.

In order to make human rights the framework for social and economic policies, it is necessary to build a genuine international consensus on their value and importance which is hard to do. The more concrete the issues such as child labour, environment, terms of international trade, intellectual property rights where rights really matter, the more differences seem to divide West and the rest.

Many international differences are played out in the language of rights; paradoxically this delegitimizes rights, as was the case in Kosovo and East Timor intervention became possible only when President Clinton criticized Indonesia. Both the West and the East are guilty of double standards. Consensus requires both intellectual effort in uncovering values that unite different religions and cultural traditions, and a willingness to incorporate values that have animated non-Western societies in the international regime of rights. It also requires political will, which is harder to establish for reasons already discussed.

Mainstreaming human rights in development, which should be a special responsibility of multilateral financial and development institutions, in conjunction with state policies and initiatives, is a prerequisite of the Copenhagen Programme of Action. Mainstreaming means that the elimination of poverty should be the principal aim of development projects and, before a project is undertaken, there should be a study of human rights implications.

United Nations agencies have shown some interest in mainstreaming human rights, but it is the Bretton Woods institutions, which wield greater economic clout, that need to be persuaded of the value of social and economic rights. Consideration should be given to establishing a.world development fund for social and economic rights., to be financed directly from tax revenues worldwide on specified luxury products. Social and economic rights must be given the priority that has been denied them. Considerable research and imagination are needed to provide the practical underpinnings of economic and social rights, the modalities for enforcement, and standards and benchmarks for monitoring progress. This will require more funding for this enterprise, the establishment of networks and the commitment of governments.

Together with regional organizations, the United Nations must devote more resources to human rights work more human rights experts should be trained and recruited, more human rights missions should be organized, and more field offices of the OHCHR should be established. The international machinery for the supervision of the observance of human rights should be strengthened. All states should sign protocols that give their nationals the right of direct access to international committees and tribunals this aspect of their work has proved more fruitful than periodic reports by governments.

Furthermore, the United Nations and other international organizations should increase their capacity for dealing with civil conflicts and wars, which today are a major source of suffering and oppression. This suggests the need for better protection of minorities, and a mechanism for swift response to mass violations of rights. The regime of human rights should be extended to cover the policies and conduct of large private economic corporations. They have power without responsibility.

The human rights of millions of people depend on the policies of these corporations. Neither the state nor the international system is likely to support the struggles of the oppressed which are essentially attacks on the present state and international systems.

Therefore the revolutionary potential of rights is likely to remain dormant for the foreseeable future. Popular support for human rights will not be secured so long as poverty is not seen as a concern of the rights regime. But this in turn will not happen until the concept of rights is used to mobilize society to demand greater equity.

Unless there are pressures from civil society, in both the rich and the poor countries, for social justice and respect for human dignity, little progress will be made. A major weakness of the human rights movement has been the inability to involve the masses as subjects rather than objects of rights. In this lies the most fundamental challenge to human rights scholars and activists. The agenda of the World Summit for Social Development has little prospect for success unless there is this transformation in the regime of rights.

# 5

# Vulnerable Groups

## VULNERABLE GROUPS; THEIR HEALTH AND HUMAN RIGHTS

Human right applies universally to all. The process of identifying vulnerable groups within the health and human right generated from the pressing reality on the ground that stemed from the fact that there are certain groups who are vulnerable and marginalized lacking full enjoyment of a wide range of human rights, including rights to political participation, health and education. Vulnerability within the right to health framework means deprivation of certain individuals and groups whose rights have been violated from the exercising agency. Certain groups in the society often encounter discriminatory treatment and need special attention to avoid potential exploitation.

This population constitutes what is referred to as Vulnerable Groups. Vulnerable groups are disadvantaged as compared to others mainly on account of their reduced access to medical services and the underlying determinants of health such as safe and potable drinking water, nutrition, housing, sanitation etc. For example, persons with disabilities often don't get employment or adequate treatment or people living with HIV/AIDS, face various forms of discrimination that affects their health and reduces their access to health services.

The issue of participation and prevention of violation is important for understanding the vulnerable groups; their health and human rights. The United Nations Economic, Social and Cultural Rights Committee mentions that an important aspect of implementing the right to health "is the improvement and furtherance of participation of the population in the provisions of preventive and curative health services, such as the organization of the health sector, the insurance system and, in particular in political decisions relating to the right to health taken at both the community and national levels". The General Comment 14 of the Article 12 also proscribes any discrimination in access to health care and underlying determinants of health, as well as to means and entitlements for their procurement, on the grounds of race, colour, sex, language, religion, political or other opinion, national or social origin, property, birth, physical or mental disability, health status, sexual orientation and civil, political, social or other status, which has the intention or effect of nullifying or impairing the equal enjoyment or exercise of the right to health.

The Committee stresses that measures, such as the strategies and programmes designed to eliminate health-related discrimination, can be pursued with minimum resource implications through the adoption, modification or abrogation of legislation or the dissemination of information. The Committee recalls General Comment No.3, Paragraph 12, which states that even in times of severe resource constraints, the vulnerable members of society must be protected. Protecting and fulfilling the rights of the vulnerable groups constitutes the immediate state obligations under the Covenant for Economic Cultural and Social Rights.

There are many and complex linkages between health and human rights of the vulnerable groups. Violations or lack of attention to human rights can have serious health consequences for certain groups. The manner in which health policies and programmes are designed can either protect or violate human rights of certain groups.

The chances of enjoying good health must not be unfairly disadvantaged because of sex, class, religion, age, sexual orientation, ethnic identity, perhaps their recognition of the vital role of societal environment to both health and realization of human rights. Both the approaches recognize the fact that there is a complex relation between the individual and the society that impacts their health. For example, the health of an individual or groups may depend on the conditions such as sufficient income, living conditions, access to safe drinking water, etc., and all the factors are heavily influenced by whether or not an individual belongs to a group that suffers discrimination.

Public health is assumed to seek the greatest good for the greatest number of people. Application of human rights principles to public health strategies has expanded the scope of the latter by going beyond averages and focusing attention also on those population groups in society which are considered most vulnerable. The focused attention on vulnerable and disadvantaged groups in the international human rights instruments reinforces the principle of equity.

An ideal public health strategy would be the one which addresses the concerns for equity and justice in every society but in practical terms there are limitations of every health system. This necessitates the need to focus on the immediate service delivery by prioritizing the needs. Human rights norms and standards form a strong basis for health systems to prioritize the health needs of vulnerable and marginalized population groups. Focus on the vulnerable group is very useful for human rights documentation.

It allows review of context specific violations, identify the challenges faced by the specific groups and their access to healthcare, gather information on group-specific risk factors, cultural and social differences among groups and its impact on health and health-seeking behaviour, document the negative attitude of the health system resulting in denial, draws attention to how national legislation and development policies impact upon the status of such groups.

This facilitates advocacy for Right to Health and empowers the disadvantaged groups by raising awareness about their rights and potential violations. Different societies have different conditions/situations that generate and perpetrate vulnerability among certain individuals and groups. Hence identifying vulnerable groups within the right to health framework is an ongoing process.

## VULNERABLE GROUPS IN INDIA

In India there are multiple socio-economic disadvantages that members of particular groups experience which limits their access to health and healthcare. The task of identifying the vulnerable groups is not an easy one. Besides there are multiple and complex factors of vulnerability with different layers and more often than once it cannot be analysed in isolation. The present document is based on some of the prominent factors on the basis of which individuals or members of groups are discriminated in India, *i.e.*, structural factors, age, disability, mobility, stigma and discrimination that act as barriers to health and healthcare.

The vulnerable groups that face discrimination include Women, Scheduled Castes, Scheduled Tribes, Children, Aged, Disabled, Poor migrants, People living with HIV/AIDS and Sexual Minorities. Sometimes each group faces multiple barriers due to their multiple identities. For example, in a patriarchal society, disabled women face double discrimination of being a women and being disabled.

## VULNERABLE GROUPS FACING STRUCTURAL DISCRIMINATION

Structural norms are attached to the different relationships between the subordinate and the dominant group in every society. A group's status may for example, be determined on the basis of gender, ethnic origin, skin colour, etc. The norms act as structural barriers giving rise to various forms of inequality. Access to health and healthcare for the subordinate groups is reduced due to the structural barriers. In India, members of gender, caste, class, and ethnic identity experience structural discrimination that impact their health and access to healthcare.

Women face double discrimination being members of specific caste, class or ethnic group apart from experiencing gendered vulnerabilities. Women have low status as compared to men in Indian society. They have little control on the resources and on important decisions related to their lives. In India, early marriage and childbearing affects women's health adversely. About 28 per cent of girls in India, get married below the legal age and experience pregnancy. These have serious repercussions on the health of women. Maternal mortality is very high in India. The average maternal mortality ratio at the national level is 540 deaths per 100,000 live births. It varies between states and regions, *i.e.*, rural-urban. The rural Maternal Mortality Rate is 617 deaths of women age between 15-49 years per one lakh live births as compared to 267 maternal deaths per one lakh live births among the urban population.

In most cases the deaths occur from preventable causes. A large proportion of women is reported to have received no antenatal care. In India, institutional delivery is lowest among women from the lower economic class as against those from the higher class. Women face violence and it has an impact on their health. During infancy and growing years a girl child faces different forms of violence like infanticide, neglect of nutrition needs, education and healthcare. As adults they face violence due to unwanted pregnancies, domestic violence, sexual abuse at the workplace and sexual violence including marital rape and honour killings.

The experience of violence and its impact on health varies just as to the women's caste, class and ethnic identity. Caste also perpetrates inequality. Caste in Indian society is a particular form of social inequality that involves a hierarchy of groups ranked in terms of ritual purity where members who belong to a particular group or stratum share some awareness of common interest and a common identity. The caste system is linked to the possession of natural resources, livelihood resources and in the Indian context also to land economy and land based power relations.

Traditionally, caste relations were based on the hierarchy of occupations where work related to leather, cleaning dead cattle from village grounds, work related to funeral ceremonies, etc were placed at the bottom. People or castes who were performing the task of eliminating the polluted elements from society were considered 'untouchables' vis-à-vis the Brahmins who were highest in the order based on the purity-impurity principle. Structurally the lower castes were economically dependent on the higher castes for existence. The Scheduled Caste remained economically dependent, politically powerless and culturally subjugated to the upper caste. This impacted their overall lifestyle and access to food, education and health.

A major proportion of the lower castes and Dalits are still dependent on others for their livelihood. Dalits does not refer to a caste but suggests a group who are in a state of oppression, social disability and who are helpless and poor. They were earlier referred as 'untouchables' mainly due to their low occupations *i.e.*, cobbler, scavenger, sweeper. In a caste-dominated country like India, Dalits who comprises more than one-sixth of the Indian population, stand as a community whose human rights have been severely violated. Literacy rates among Dalits are only about 24 per cent.

They have meager purchasing power; have poor housing conditions; lack or have low access to resources and entitlements. In rural India they are landless poor agricultural labourers attached to rich landowners from generations or poor casual labourers doing all kinds of available work. In the city they are the urban poor employed as wage labourers at several work sites, beggars, vendors, small service providers, domestic help, etc., living in slums and other temporary shelters without any kind of social security.

The members of these groups face systemic violence in the form of denial of access to land, good housing, education and employment. Structural discrimination against these groups takes place in the form of physical, psychological, emotional and cultural abuse which receives legitimacy from the social structure and the social system. Physical segregation of their settlements is common in the villages forcing them to live in the most unhygienic and inhabitable conditions.

All these factors affect their health status, access to healthcare, and quality of health service received. There are high rates of malnutrition reported among the marginalized groups resulting in mortality, morbidity and anaemia. Access to and utilization of healthcare among the marginalized groups is influenced by their socio-economic status within the society. Structural discrimination directly impedes equal access to health services by way of exclusion.

The negative attitude of the health professionals towards these groups also acts as a barrier to receiving quality healthcare from the health system. In the case of women, discrimination increases by the complex mix of two factors-being a women and being a member of the marginalized community. A large proportion of Dalit girls drop out of primary school inspite of reservations and academic aptitude, because of poverty, humiliation, isolation or bullying by teachers and classmates and punishment for scoring good grades.

The scavenger community among the Dalits is vulnerable to stress and diseases with reduced access to healthcare. The Scheduled Tribes like the Scheduled Castes face structural discrimination within the Indian society. Unlike the Scheduled Castes, the Scheduled Tribes are a product of marginalization based on ethnicity. In India, the Scheduled Tribes population is around 84.3 million and is considered to be socially and economically disadvantaged. Their percentages in the population and numbers however vary from State to State. They are mainly landless with little control over resources such as land, forest and water.

They constitute a large proportion of agricultural labourers, casual labourers, plantation labourers, industrial labourers etc. This has resulted in poverty among them, low levels of education, poor health and reduced access to healthcare services. They belong to the poorest strata of the society and have severe health problems. They are less likely to afford and get access to healthcare services when required. The health outcomes among the Scheduled Tribes are very poor even as compared to the Scheduled Castes.

The Infant Mortality Rate among Scheduled Castes is 83 per 1000 live births while it is 84.2 per 1000 per live births among the Scheduled Tribes. Among the Scheduled Castes and the Scheduled Tribes the most vulnerable are women, children, aged, those living with HIV/AIDS, mental illness and disability. These groups face severe forms of discrimination that denies them access to treatment and prevents them from achieving a better health status. Gender based violence and domestic violence is high among women in general in India.

Girl child and women from the marginalized groups are more vulnerable to violence. The dropout and illiteracy rates among them are high. Early marriage, trafficking, forced prostitution and other forms of exploitation are also reportedly high among them. In situations of caste conflict, women from marginalized groups face sexual violence from men of upper caste i.e, rape and other forms of mental torture and humiliation.

## VULNERABILITY OF CHILDREN AND AGED

Children and the elderly population face different kind of vulnerability. Mortality and morbidity among children are caused and compounded by poverty, their sex and caste position in society. All these have consequences on their nutrition intake, access to healthcare, environment and education. These factors directly impacts food security, education of parents and their access to correct health information and access to health care facilities. Malnutrition and chronic hunger are the important causes of death among children from poor families. Diarrhoea, acute respiratory diseases, malaria and measles are some of the main causes of death among children, most of which are either preventable or treatable with low-cost interventions.

Tetanus in newborns remain a problem in at least five states: Uttar Pradesh, Madhya Pradesh, Rajasthan, West Bengal, and Assam. Poverty has a direct impact on the mortality and morbidity among children. Neo-natal mortality is about two times higher among people with low standard of living while Under-5 mortality among children from lower economic class is five times than that of households with high standard of living. 73.4 per cent of children have some form of anemia. In India, a girl child faces discrimination and differential access to nutritious food and gender based violence is evident from the falling sex ratio and the use of technologies to eliminate the girl child. Among children the health indicators vary between the different social groups. High mortality and morbidity is reported among children from Scheduled Castes, Scheduled Tribes and Other Backward Classes as compared to the general population.

Infant morality is higher among the rural population. The vaccination coverage is very poor among children who live in rural India. Vaccination coverage among children between 12-23 months who have received the recommended vaccines is only 39 per cent in rural India as compared to 58 per cent in urban India. In India, children's vulnerabilities and exposure to violations of their protection rights remain spread and multiple in nature.

The manifestations of these violations are various, ranging from child labour, child trafficking, to commercial sexual exploitation and many other forms of violence and abuse. With an estimated 12.6 million children engaged in hazardous occupations, for instance, India has the largest number of child labourers under the age of 14 in the world. Child labour in the agriculture sector accounts for 80 per cent of child labour in India and 70 per cent of working children globally.

In, Sivakasi, an estimated 1, 25,000 children make the child labour force, comprising 30 per cent of the entire labour force. Those children working in the brick kilns, stone quarries, mines, carpet and zari industry suffer from occupation related diseases. In India, however there is a huge gap in the industry-specific and exposure-specific epidemiological evidence. Most of the studies are small-scale and community-based studies.

There is a large proportion of children in India who are living with HIV/ AIDS. The most common sources of infection among children is the Mother-to-Child Transmission, sexual abuse, blood transfusion, unsterilised syringes, including injectable drug use. Among children, there are some groups like street children and children of sex workers who face additional forms of discrimination. A large number of children are reportedly trafficked to the neighbouring countries. Trafficking of children also continues to be a serious problem in India. The nature and scope of trafficking range from industrial and domestic labour, to forced early marriages and commercial sexual exploitation. Moreover, for children who have been trafficked and rescued, opportunities for rehabilitation remains scarce and reintegration process arduous.

While systematic data and information on child protection issues are still not always available, evidence suggests that children in need of special protection belong to communities suffering disadvantage and social exclusion such as scheduled casts and tribes, and the poor. In India, the population of the elderly is growing rapidly and is emerging as a serious area of concern for the government and the policy planners. Data on the age of India's population, in Census 2001, there are a little over 76.6 million people above 60 years, constituting 7.2 per cent of the population.

The number of people over 60 years in 1991 was 6.8 per cent of the country's population. The vulnerability among the elderly is not only due to an increased incidence of illness and disability, but also due to their economic dependency upon their spouses, children and other younger family members. The 2001 census, 33.1 per cent of the elderly in India live without their spouses. The widowers among older men form 14.9 per cent as against 50.1 per cent widows among elderly women. Among the elderly, 71.1 per cent of women were widows while widowers formed only 28.9 per cent of men. Vulnerability among the elderly also depends on their living arrangement since the elderly are less capable of taking care of themselves compared to younger persons and need the care and support of others in several aspects.

About 2.9 per cent of elderly in India live alone. More elderly women live alone compared to elderly men. The significance of the living arrangement among the elderly becomes evident when seen in the context of their level of economic dependence. Lack of economic dependence has an impact on their access to food, clothing and healthcare. Among the basic needs of the elderly, medicine features as the highest unmet need. Healthcare of the elderly is a major concern for the society as ageing is often accompanied by multiple illnesses and physical ailments. Pain in the joints, followed by cough and blood pressure, piles, heart diseases, urinary problems, diabetics and cancer are the common ailments reported among elderly.. One out of two elderly in India suffers from at least one chronic disease which requires life-long medications. Providing healthcare to elderly is a burden for especially poor households.

About 29 per cent of the elderly populations in India are reported to have received no medical attention before death. Among the elderly, the widows, poor and disabled constitute those who are more disadvantaged. Widows face structural disadvantages associated with gender and marital status. There is striking gender differential that exists in the ownership of property and assets and in the participation of their management. At all India level, aged women like those in other age groups suffer from lack of ownership of property and financial assets and participation in their management compared to aged men in both urban and rural India. Lack of property ownership affects their access to resources like food, housing, health etc. Visual impairment, hearing problem, locomotor problem and problems in speech are common forms of disability among elderly. Senility and neurosis are common mental illness reported among elderly.

## VULNERABILITY DUE TO DISABILITY

Disability poses greater challenges in obtaining the needed range of services. Persons with disabilities face several forms of discrimination and has reduced access to education, employment and other socioeconomic opportunities. In India, there is an increase of proportion of disabled population. The proportion of disabled population in India is about 21.9 million. The percentage of disabled population to the total population is about 2.13 per cent. There are two broad categories of disability, one is acquired which means disability acquired because of accidents and medical reasons the other is disability since the onset of birth.

The National Sample Survey Organisation Report, about one-third of the disabled population have disability since their birth. There are interstate and interregional differences in the disabled population. The disabled face various types of barriers while seeking access to health and health services. There are different types of disability and the needs of the disabled differ accordingly. Among those who are disabled women, children and aged are more vulnerable and need attention. Mental illness is a prominent form of disability. Five out of ten leading causes of disability and premature death worldwide are due to psychiatric conditions.

Depression and anxiety are the most common mental disorders. Psychotic disorders such as schizophrenia and bipolar disorder, although less common are profoundly disabling. The other area of concern is the mental health of women and the elderly. Neurotic and stress related cases are reportedly higher among women than men though among men there is reporting of higher number of cases of serious illness. Dementia and major depression are two of the leading contributors to mental diseases in older people. But inspite of such proportion of mental illness, the health care provisions for persons with mental illness are very poor in India.

People with mental illness face severe forms of human rights violations. In Special Homes, Hospitals and Asylums, they are kept in chains, denied basic needs like food, clothing and face different forms of abuse. There is social stigma attached to mental illness. Women with mental illness are subjected to physical and sexual abuse both within families and the institutions.

There are 42 mental hospitals in the country with bed availability of 20,893 in the government sector and another 5096 in the private sector hospital settings to take care of an estimated 1,02,70,165 people with severe mental illness and 5,12,51,625 people with common mental disorders. Psychiatric medicines are supplied only in a few primary health centers, community centers and district hospitals. Services like child guidance and rehabilitative services are also available only in mental hospitals and in big cities.

Several states do not have mental hospitals. The Persons with Disabilities Act 1995, commonly referred as the PWD Act came into force on Feb. 7, 1996. Mental illness has been considered in the Act, but there is no reference to any provision within the Act to be given or set aside for people with mental illness. The Act also does not assure the right to treatment.

## VULNERABILITY DUE TO MIGRATION

Migrants and their denial of rights have to be understood from the existing contradictions within and across countries—from skilled and voluntary migrants at one end of the spectrum to the poor and unskilled migrant population on the other end destined to be excluded from the fabric of the host nation/areas. For the latter, the intersection of human rights and migration is a negative one, with bad experiences throughout the migratory 'life cycle', in areas of origin, journey or transit and destination. The intersection of health and human rights becomes even more complex when irregular or illegal migration clashes with the interest of the area of destination. Cases of exploitation of migrants by employers, smugglers or traffickers in such cases never meet justice. All these directly impact the rights of individual migrants. India has a large number of international migrants. About 5.1 million persons are migrants by last residence from across the international border in India. Neighbouring countries are the main sources of origin of the international migrants to India with the bulk of these migrants coming from Bangladesh, followed by Pakistan and Nepal. But these are migrants who have entered the country legally.

There are many who enter the country illegally. Those are the one who are most vulnerable to abuse and exploitation by employers, migration agents, corrupt bureaucrats and criminal gangs. In many situations, migrants do not know what rights they are entitled to and still less how to claim them, hence the cases of abuse go unrecorded. Another area where exploitation is rampant is forced labour which takes place in the illicit underground economy and hence tends to escape national statistics. Illegal migrants often live on the margins of society, trying to avoid contact with authorities and have little or no legal access to prevention and healthcare services. They face higher risks of exposure to unsafe working conditions. Many often they do not approach the health system of the host countries for fear of their status being discovered. Internal migration of poor labourers has also been on the rise in India. The poor migrants usually end up as casual labourers within the informal sector. This population is at high risk for diseases and faces reduced access to health services. In India, 14.4 million people migrated within the country for work purposes either to cities or areas with higher expected economic gains during the 2001 census period. Large number of migrants are employed in cultivation and plantations, brick-kilns, quarries, construction sites and fish processing. Large numbers of migrants also work in the urban informal manufacturing construction, services or transport sectors and are employed as casual labourers, head loaders, rickshaw pullers and hawkers.

The rapid change of residence due to the casual nature of work excludes them from the preventive care and their working conditions in the informal work arrangements in the city debars them from access to adequate curative care. Among the migrants who are vulnerable, the Internally Displaced People deserve mention. In India, the Internally Displaced People are estimated to be around 6 lakhs. Internal displacement arises out of ethnic conflicts, religious conflicts, political reasons, development projects, natural disaster etc. The Internally Displaced People are vulnerable to health risks and access to treatment.

The emotional stress of displacement and the toll that this takes does have a great impact on physical as well as mental health. Large number of mental health problems are reported among Internally Displaced People. Stress disorder leads to cardio-vascular stress, psycho-trauma, endocrine stress, musculo-skeletal stress, stress-belly and cranial stress. Hypertension, reactive depression and nervous breakdown are common even among the youth who are Internally Displaced People. There are reports of lack of basic facilities like food, medical supplies and sanitation in the State government organized relief camps for the internally displaced people in case of a political conflict. Women and child migrants are the most vulnerable. In the case of internal migration in India, women and children mostly migrate as associated migrants with the main decision to migrate being taken by the male of the household. As associated migrants, they suffer greater vulnerability due to reduced economic choices and lack of social support in the new area of destination. In the case of semi-skilled, low-skilled or unskilled women migrants, this can translate into their entry into the low paying, unorganized sector with high exposure to exploitation and abuse. International migration of women for employment has also increased.

In India, there are a large number of international women migrants. Female migration to India constitutes 48 per cent of the total inmigration from other countries. Migration among women has been high from Bangladesh and Nepal as compared to other neighbouring countries. Low/skilled or semi-skilled migration has an impact on their choice of occupation and the conditions of work. Many of the low/semi-skilled female migrants work in the unorganized sector, in hazardous conditions, live in shanty arrangements and are denied access to health and healthcare. Trafficking also contributes to the cross-border movement of a large proportion of women and children into other countries. There are established routes of trafficking in India, used to facilitate the movement of women and children from across the borders in order to sustain the underground economy. Women and children in an irregular situation are doubly vulnerable owing to their lack of proper legal status and high risk of sexual exploitation and suffer from poor antenatal care coverage, prevalence of anemia, prevalence of reproductive tract infections experience high incidences of violence. Children of poor migrant parents suffer from malnutrition and low immunization due to their parents' perpetual low-income uncertain jobs that necessitate frequent shifts based on concentration and are more susceptible to HIV/AIDS infection.

## VULNERABILITY DUE TO STIGMA AND DISCRIMINATION

There are certain attitudes and perceptions towards certain kinds of illnesses and sexual orientation which results in discrimination against individuals/groups. This section deals with the stigma and discrimination faced by the People living with HIV/AIDS and Sexual Minorities. These groups face various kinds of discrimination and have reduced access to healthcare. Stigma is the greatest barrier of health and healthcare in their context. Negative responses and attitude of the society towards these groups are strongly linked to people's perception of the causes of HIV/ AIDS and sexual orientation.

The rights of People living with HIV/AIDS are violated when they are denied access to health, education, and services. They suffer when their close or extended families and friends fail to provide them the support that they need. India's National AIDS Control Organization estimated in 2005 that there were 5.206 million HIV infections in India, of which 38.4 per cent occurred in women and 57 per cent occurred in rural areas. Many experts argue that the current figures are gross underestimations and that a significant number of AIDS cases go unreported or untracked.

Prevalence estimates are based primarily on sentinel surveillance conducted at public sites. The national information system for collecting HIV testing information from the private sector is very weak. Vulnerability to HIV is also increased by the lack of power of individuals and communities to minimize or modulate their risk of exposure to HIV infection and once infected, to receive adequate care and support.

Some individuals are more vulnerable to the infection than others. Low status of woman may force a monogamous woman to engage in unprotected sex with her spouse even if he is engaging in sex with others. Similarly adolescent girls and boys may be vulnerable to HIV by being denied access to preventive information, education, and services. Sex workers may have greater vulnerability to HIV if they cannot access services to prevent, diagnose, and treat sexually transmitted infections, particularly if they are afraid to come forward because of the stigma associated with their occupation. There are strong perceptions of the causes of AIDS, routes of transmission, and their level of knowledge about the illness. These are compounded by the marginalization and stigmatization on the basis of such attributes as gender, migrant status or behaviours that may be perceived as risk factors for HIV infection. For example, women whose husbands have died of AIDS are rejected by their own and their husband's families and they are denied property inheritance of their husbands.

The available provisions of care are inadequate. Since April 1, 2004, anti-retroviral treatment is provided free of cost in India, at government hospitals in the six high prevalence states of Tamil Nadu, Andhra Pradesh, Maharashtra, Karnakata, Manipur, and Nagaland. However, of the estimated 5.1 million people living with HIV/AIDS in 2005, 600,000 people needed antiretroviral therapy, but only 7,000 adults were receiving such treatment through the government programme. Besides anti-retroviral drugs there is shortage of several other drugs in the public facilities which are needed by persons living with HIV/ AIDS.

People living with HIV/AIDS face discrimination even from the health providers who deny them quality of care. Negative attitudes from health professionals generate anxiety and fear among people living with HIV/AIDS, and as a result many do not reveal or seek treatment for their HIV status. Another group that faces stigma and discrimination are the sexual minorities.

Those identified as gay, lesbian, transgender, bisexual, kothi and hijra, experience various forms of discrimination within the society and the health system. Due to the dominance of heteronomous sexual relations as the only form of normal acceptable relations within the society, individuals who are identified as having same-sex sexual preferences are ridiculed and ostracized by their own family and are left with very limited support structures and networks of community that provide them conditions of care and support. Their needs and concerns are excluded from the various health policies and programmes. Only the National AIDS Prevention and Control Policy recognize sexual minority and homosex in the context of identifying 'high risk behaviour'. But pervasive discrimination from the health providers delays or deters their health seeking.

Hence they remain excluded from the process of government surveillance carried among the high risk population in the context of HIV/AIDS. The surveillance amongst 'MSM' or men who have sex with men, is usually carried out by NGOs and through 'support groups', *i.e.* amongst males who are accessible to NGOs and who are willing to identify with categories, such as kothi, around which support groups are structured. They also undergo considerable amount of psychological stress.

## CONSTITUTES VIOLATION OF RIGHT FOR VULNERABLE GROUPS

The violation of the right to health of vulnerable groups may result from direct government action, from failure of the government to fulfill its minimum core obligations and from the patterns of systematic discrimination.

*The specific examples of violations of right to health of vulnerable groups would be:*

- Deliberate withholding or misrepresentation of information on the health status of disadvantaged groups that may have been essential for the prevention and treatment of illness or disability.
- Imposing discriminatory practices affecting the group's health status and needs.
- Adopting laws and policies that interfere with the rights of the groups, for example, women's reproductive rights.
- Failure to protect women against violence; violence against women is often systematic and serious enough to require women to seek hospital treatment for injuries and involve other health complication related to violence. When governments fail to take preemptive steps to prevent and treat victims of violence it is tantamount to violation of right.
- Failure of government to provide adequate public health measures against infectious diseases that affect the disadvantaged groups.
- Failure to cover the eligible population with child immunization packages.
- Failure to provide adequate obstetric and family planning services
- Failure to provide adequate primary healthcare, basic healthcare service to disadvantaged group.
- Inappropriate health resource allocation including disproportionate investment of public resources in ways that benefit the health of only a narrow section of the population, *i.e.*, when government spends in expensive diagnostic and curative health services and equipment that limited number of privileged people can afford and on the other hand primary and preventive health services which

large section of people use, suffer due to lack of adequate funds. Such a pattern of financing is a form of indirect discrimination affecting the health and healthcare of vulnerable groups.

- Government policies and practices creating imbalances in providing health services, *i.e.,* poor infrastructure in rural areas or predominantly tribal areas.
- Systematic discrimination in access to medicines and essential drugs for particular groups, *i.e.,* HIV/AIDS drugs, reproductive health services for particular groups like women living in poverty, in rural areas, belonging to marginalized communities.

## ADVOCACY ON HEALTH AND HUMAN RIGHTS OF VULNERABLE GROUPS IN INDIA

- Identify disadvantaged/marginalized groups; their health status and needs in different situations
- Review the health information and services that are available to protect the health of the poor, vulnerable, or otherwise disadvantaged groups, including their quality, accessibility, affordability and acceptability.
- Collect disaggregated information on the health disparities among the marginalized groups. Identify the unmet need, particularly those resulting from adverse discrimination
- Assess the relevance of public health messages and determine whether they are accessible and meaningful.
- Assess whether the vulnerable group's dignity is preserved by the health services made available to them; whether they have the necessary health information and services that they require; whether they are allowed freedom for the choice of treatment; whether their full, free and informed consent was obtained during specific interventions; and whether confidentiality has been a part of the treatment where it was necessary.
- Identify barriers to the implementation of relevant laws, obligations and commitments; this could mean lack of political will; weak infrastructure or mechanisms for effective administration of policies and programmes; harmful traditional practices; cultural norms or policies imposed by and as a result of adverse reforms of the health sector to funding health services
- Promote capacity-building among health professionals to ensure conformity with the right to health in service delivery.
- Examine the curricula of medical and other health professional training schools and advocate for the inclusion of health and human rights of vulnerable groups in Medical Education.

- Increase public awareness on the right to health of the vulnerable groups and engage in community education and mobilization.
- Assess government compliance with specific obligations; whether government is meeting minimum essential level of health rights; whether there is systematic discrimination associated with the treatment of poor, vulnerable and otherwise disadvantaged groups.
- Undertake advocacy to facilitate change by identifying violations to right to health; familiarize yourself with the nature of the state obligations arising from the right to health and the common ways in which government violates them; document any identified violations and use it as a basis for monitoring and advocacy.
- Work on national enforcement procedures to ensure state accountability.
- Prepare parallel reports.

## ADVOCACY FOR RIGHT TO HEALTH INTERNATIONALLY

Advocacy for right to health of vulnerable groups involves identifying the barriers to health and healthcare of the vulnerable and disadvantaged groups and lobbying for their rights with the government nationally and internationally. The rights of the vulnerable groups are recognized in numerous international instruments. The International Covenant on Economic, Social and Cultural Rights which provides the most comprehensive article on the right to health in the international human rights law recognizes the health needs of the vulnerable groups and explains by illustrations a number of steps to be taken by the State parties to achieve the full realization of the right to health of general population and vulnerable groups in particular.

The signatories of the Treaty of International Covenant on Economic, Social and Cultural Rights representing nearly 155 governments of the world made an international commitment to protect and respect, Right to Health of the population of the respective nations as Parties while another 66 governments are Signatory Parties of the Covenant. The Treaty came into force on the 3rd January 1976. By ratifying international human rights treaties that affirm the right to health, a state agrees to be accountable to the international community, as well as to the people living within its jurisdiction, for the fulfillment of its obligations. State parties to an international human rights treaty are required to adopt legislative measures and to employ all appropriate means to ensure that the population can enjoy the rights conferred by the treaty.

This means that international treaty provisions must be incorporated into the domestic legislation. Individuals and communities can access effective judicial or other appropriate remedies in the face of violations of their rights. A central advocacy principle for NGOs using a human rights approach to health hence should be that governments are accountable for their obligations under international law, regional law, and within the framework of national constitutions and legislation. Monitoring and state compliance with universal norms of human rights related to health is an essential component of the Treaty of Economic Social and Cultural Rights.

There are three forms of monitoring rights: investigative reports prepared by the special rapporteurs or working groups; individual complaint procedures by which nationals and other residents of a state can complain to international bodies for alleged violations of their human rights; and reports prepared by states which have ratified international human rights conventions and which therefore are parties to the convention. Such reports are submitted periodically to the international expert bodies set in conformity with the convention.

The periodic reports are examined in the presence of representatives from the state concerned. Reporting obligations are built into the convention as a mechanism for monitoring the human right. NGOs involved in monitoring the right to health must ensure that the governments send periodic reports to the Committee on Economic Social and Cultural Rights. They can also send parallel reports to the committee.

## SCOPE AND LIMITATIONS OF THE INDIAN STATE VIS-A-VIS RIGHT TO HEALTH

The Constitution of India and the laws do not accord health and healthcare as rights to the population in general. While civil and political rights are enshrined as fundamental rights that are justiciable, social and economic rights like health, education, livelihoods etc. exist as Directive Principles for the State and are hence not justiciable.

There are however instances in which cases have been filed in the various High Courts of states and Supreme Court of India on the right to life, Article 21 of the Indian Constitution, or on the various directive principles to demand access to healthcare, especially in emergency situations. International protection of human rights is only effective when they are made viable by national protection.

National-level legislation, policies and enforcement mechanisms are the key factors in rights being operationalized for individuals and groups within a nation. National laws offer variable degrees of protection against human rights violation and enables national bodies to hear cases of denial and enforce the norms.

At present there is a problem of justiciability of the Right to health in Indian Constitution since the same is not protected by national legislation. Though India has ratified the Treaty on the Economic Social and Cultural Right which covers Right to Health, that cannot be effectively used to advocate for right to health in India. The Courts or petitioners can merely derive inspiration from the treaties on the cases on denial/violation on right to health but may not be able to use it effectively to deliver justice. The international treaties have only an evocative significance unless protected by national legislation. Absence of national legislation on right to health in India is the main reason why it cannot be realised. Health and human rights advocacy in India needs to intensify the attempts towards transforming the critical principles of the Directive principles on health and work into independent rights through rigorous judicial activism, *i.e.,* filing Public Interest Litigations, gathering testimonials for denial on right to health, etc. There needs to be a concerted move towards making a national legislation on right to health.

# 6

# Human Rights Violations

## INTRODUCTION

### HUMAN RIGHTS AND SEXUALITY MINORITIES

The founding document on which most human rights organizations base their advocacy is the Universal Declaration on Human Rights. From this initial document has emerged a whole series of human rights declarations, conventions and treaties pertaining to the rights of various marginalized groups and communities such as children, women, indigenous people, disabled people, prisoners, religious and ethnic minorities, refugees, etc. However, one significant absence in international human rights law has been an express articulation of the specific interests of sexuality minorities.

This silence is dismaying, for the focus on human rights is often justified by invoking the Nazi holocaust and resolving to prevent another such genocide. What is forgotten in this invocation of history is that the Nazis not only systematically persecuted Jews, communists and disabled people, but also went about eliminating homosexuals. In fact thousands of homosexuals lost their lives in Nazi concentration camps. It is only in the final decade of the 20th century that the gay/ lesbian/ bisexual/ transgender movement brought to the fore the rights of those discriminated against because of their sexuality. In 1991, Amnesty International for the first time came out with a policy to support the rights of people imprisoned because of their sexual orientation or because of engaging in homosexual activity in private. In the mid 1990's, the Human Rights Committee held that the anti sodomy law of Tasmania violated the right to privacy and the right to non discrimination guaranteed to all persons under the International Covenant on Civil and Political Rights.

In Scandinavia, the provision of equal rights for sexuality minorities, including marriage rights, was an important breakthrough. The other major development has been the South African Constitution, which for the first time expressly prohibited discrimination on grounds of sexual orientation. But while the scope of human rights has been extended to include hitherto marginalized communities at the global level, a similar movement is yet to take place in India.

In fact, most human rights organizations in India have not begun to address the question of rights of gays, lesbians, bisexuals, transgender, hijras and others who are oppressed due to their sexuality. Sexuality is sometimes viewed even in liberal and radical circles as a frivolous, bourgeois issue. In such a context, homosexuality is seen implicitly as something deviant and unnatural that is at best defended as an individual freedom but not a matter of priority for the human rights movement. Generally, issues of poverty and gender, class and caste oppression are seen as more important than that of sexuality. But this ignores the fact that sexuality is integrally linked to ideologies and structures of social oppression such as patriarchy, capitalism, the caste system and religious fundamentalism. Hence, the struggle for sexuality rights cannot be separated from the broader human rights struggle for economic, political and social liberation.

## THE STATUS OF SEXUALITY MINORITIES IN INDIA

As reported in various studies, homosexual orientation is common in almost every culture and every society. However, homophobia is chiefly the product of a Judeo Christian morality spread to various parts of the world through European colonialism, which exported its laws and its morality into other local contexts. It has to be noted that homosexuality also finds a mention in the various precolonial laws. Homosexuality is seen as an offence in Manusmrithi, which however can be expiated. Lesbianism by contrast merits more serious punishment. Islamic Shariat law treats homosexual conduct as a serious offence, though it is being argued by some recently formed gay Muslim organizations that Islamic law can be interpreted in a nonhomophobic fashion. It was with the enactment of uniform criminal laws in India, in 1860 that there was a uniform proscription of homosexual behaviour. Though sexuality minorities have always existed in India sometimes in forms, which are culturally sanctioned and at other times in invisibility and silence, their issues have never seriously been articulated.

It is only recently that the rights of sexuality minorities as an issue have been taken seriously in India by various civil society organizations. With the founding of India's first gay magazine Bombay Dost in the late 1980's and the starting of a lesbian collective in Delhi called Sakhi, lesbian, gay and bisexual issues were first articulated in a public forum. Since those early beginnings, the fledgling sexuality minority rights movement has grown increasingly vocal and articulate. Today there are organizations, helplines, publications/newsletters, health resources, social spaces and drop-in centers in most of the major cities in India like Delhi, Mumbai, Calcutta, Bangalore, Hyderabad, Pune, Chennai, Patna and Lucknow. There has also been a branching out into smaller cities and towns like Akola, Trichi and Gulbarga.

In spite of this, the support structures provided are painfully inadequate with few or no such organizations for lesbians, bisexuals and hijras. What is more, many of the newly emerging organizations die out silently while even the more established ones have been able to reach out in concrete terms only to a small section of the sexuality minority population due to lack of resources, personnel, government support and extreme societal/state discrimination.

## CONTEXT AND METHODOLOGY

It is in these twin contexts of the global movement for recognition of sexuality minority rights and the increasing assertiveness of sexuality minority voices at the local level that the present report is located. PUCL-K has been receiving reports that there has been a sharp increase in attacks on sexuality minorities in Bangalore, including harassment and illegal detentions by the police of gay and bisexual men in public recreational areas. All sexuality minorities, *i.e.* gays, bisexuals, lesbians, transgender, transvestites, hijras and other homosexual men and women, suffer in different degrees social and political marginalisation due to their sexuality and/ or gender.

To mobilize against these police violations, the Coalition for Sexuality Minorities' Rights, comprising sexuality minority organizations, lawyers, women's organizations and social activists, was formed. This coalition approached PUCL-K to investigate reports of human rights abuses against sexuality minorities, and to help mobilize public opinion against such abuses. The PUCL-K invited ALF, Manasa and PDF to join in the investigation.

A team was formed for the purpose comprising Arvind Narrain, Sharada, Venkatesh, Ramdas Rao, and Laxminarayana. This team met on 2nd July 2000 to investigate reports of widespread police harassment of sexuality minorities in Bangalore. It was able to meet representatives of various organizations supporting rights of sexuality minorities such as Sabrang; Sangama; Good As You; Swabhava and Snehashraya. However, as the team sat to hear the testimony of members of the affected communities, it became apparent that it was impossible to discuss police harassment without understanding the deeper structural roots of homophobia.

For example, police harassment builds on and is reinforced by the fact that society looks at sexuality minorities with disgust and hatred and values them as less than human beings. It is felt quite acceptable to violate the human rights of people who the majority has never really considered as human beings worthy of the same respect as 'normal individuals'. Hence in order to understand the oppression of sexuality minorities one needs to examine the various forms of oppression, both societal and state. It is only within this larger framework that one can comprehend the kinds of violence that sexuality minorities are subject to in our culture and society. Due to the law, societal values and mainstream culture being unfavorable towards sexuality minorities, very few can afford to be open about their 'illicit' sexual orientations. Therefore, we would like to thank those who came forward and testified before the team. This report is a record of such testimonies and conveys something of the pain, anxieties and hopes of the people we met.

It is an attempt to break through the invisibility and the silence that society has tried to throw over people simply because of their sexual orientation. In spite of our best efforts we could speak to only gays, bisexuals and one hijra person. However we were able to remedy the lack of an adequate hijra voice by having an extended meeting with some hijra people on 8 October, 2000.

The absence of lesbians in the hearing is itself an indication of the kind of oppression that they face, both as women and as non-heterosexual people and the infinitely greater silence that surrounds many issues pertaining to lesbians. We tried to make up for this absence by meeting a small group of lesbians separately on 16 December 2000.

We also circulated a questionnaire on issues, which emerged in the course of the testimony to gays, bisexuals and lesbians. Apart from members of the community, the team also met Dr. Shekhar Seshadri of NIMHANS and other prominent physicians, as well as a reputed homeopathic doctor. We also met the ACP Cubbon Park circle, Mr. Santosh Hegde and Mr. Mariswamy Gowda, Inspector of Upparpet Police Station.

In this report, we have put together the testimonies of at least 25 people we met both in the office of Sangama and in other public spaces, as well as the information we gathered through questionnaires, interviews and a review of existing documentation. The names of those who testified at the hearings have been changed to protect their confidentiality because of fears expressed about police and societal victimization. We would also like to apologize for the relative sketchiness of certain sections of the report, such as the ones on the workspaces, household spaces and impact on the self — areas in respect of which information is not readily forthcoming. We hope that the next organization, which takes up this issue, will fill in these gaps and produce a more comprehensive report.

## FOCUS OF THE REPORT

This report examines the human rights violations suffered by sexuality minorities in India under two broad heads, namely the state and society, as two sites from which violence against sexuality minorities is perpetrated. The violations by the state can be further subdivided into violations by the law and by the police. Societal violence is inflicted through the various sites like the family, the medical establishment, workspaces, household spaces, public spaces and popular culture. Both societal and state violence impinge strongly on the individual person's dignity. The report then goes on to document issues of further marginalization among sexuality minorities, namely the position of lesbians, bisexuals and sexuality minorities from low income/non English-speaking backgrounds and hijras. Finally, we conclude by putting forth a series of recommendations on how both state and societal violations of the basic human rights of sexuality minorities can be combated.

## DISCRIMINATION BY THE STATE

The state is one of the powerful institutions through which discrimination against sexuality minorities is encoded, institutionalized and enforced. The prime means through which discrimination becomes a structural feature of everyday living of sexuality minority populations is through use of the law and the police.

### THE LAW

Legal discrimination against sexuality minorities operates through the criminal and civil law systems. The regime of discrimination can be analysed under the following heads:

#### Sec 377 of the Indian Penal Code

Legal Discrimination against the sexuality minorities takes many forms, the most notorious being Section 377 of the Indian Penal Code, a British colonial legislation criminalizing homosexual behaviour, that continues to be in the Indian statute book although it has long since been removed from the British statute book.

- *Section 377 Reads*: Of unnatural offences: Whoever voluntarily has carnal intercourse against the order of nature with any man, woman, or animal, shall be punished with imprisonment of either description for a term which may extend to 10 years and also be liable to fine.
- *Explanation*: Penetration is sufficient to constitute the carnal intercourse necessary to the offense described in this section.

*Section 377 is repugnant on a number of counts, the main ones being:*

- It does not distinguish between consensual and coercive sex. Thus cases of abuse and voluntary sex between two consenting adults can be prosecuted under this provision. This would violate the constitutionally protected right to privacy under the expanded definition of right to life.
- The definition of "unnatural offences" is obsolete. It invites questions such as what is "the order of nature"? As conceived by whom? Previously, it was considered that the order of nature was that the sexual act be performed only for the sake of reproduction. But today it would not be considered "against the order of nature" if people have sex mainly for pleasure. Moreover, empirical evidence easily shows that homosexuality and bisexuality is widespread in the Indian society covering a large section of people belonging to different regional, linguistic, and religious backgrounds and social strata. Section 377 denies these people a right to their sexuality.

- It is also important to note that this section does not prohibit homosexuality, but only prohibits certain sexual acts, which both homosexuals and heterosexuals, married and unmarried people, might engage in. However this section is almost always used to target sexuality minority populations as they are erroneously seen as the only ones to perform 'carnal intercourse against the order of nature'.
- It serves to legislate into being a new morality, a morality that condemns many forms of sex between two consenting adults including oral sex and anal sex and other kinds of sex, which the judges might decide, fall within the definition of "carnal intercourse against the order of nature".
- In the entire history of the statute from 1860 to 1992, there have been very few reported cases under 377 in the higher courts, with most of the persecutions being for non-consensual acts of sodomy. In fact, currently Section 377 exists only to be used by the police mostly to victimize gay and bisexual men whom they catch in public areas to extort money and blackmail, despite the fact that blackmail and extortion are criminal offences. Section 377 has also been used to intimidate lesbian women, particularly in the cases of women who have run away together, or if they make their relationship known..

However, since Section 377 has also been used to prosecute cases of child sexual abuse, any demand for its repeal will have to go hand in hand with the enactment of a law on child sexual abuse.

**Other forms of Legal Discrimination**

- Section 46 of the Army Act notes that "Any person subject to this act who is guilty of disgraceful conduct of a cruel, indecent or unnatural kind… can be removed from service". There are similar provisions in the Navy Act that subjects all employees of the Indian Navy to the disciplinary requirements under a similar enactment.
- The legal provisions relating to obscenity, the concept of moral turpitude as a ground for dismissal from service, and provisions in the various state Police Acts can also be used to target same sex behaviours and identities. Thus, the only way homosexuality figures in Indian law is as a conduct to be prohibited.
- There is no recognition of the rights of sexuality minorities in law. For instance, same sex unions do not even have legal recognition, let alone any of the economic and legal rights/benefits available to heterosexual marriage contracts. Same-sex couples are deprived of, among other things, the right to common property and inheritance, "next of kin" privileges in the event of illness or death of their partner, and custody maintenance and adoption rights. Given the

fact that all cases of same-sex union in India that have appeared in the media are those of women from smaller towns, their economic and social vulnerability makes the legal and social acceptance of their relationship vital..

- Homosexual relationships are not recognized when it comes to defining the family for the purposes of insurance claims, compensation under the workman's compensation act, gratuity benefits and for the purposes of nomination.
- The constitution, while it contains certain prohibited grounds of discrimination such as race, caste, creed, sex, etc, does not specifically include sexual orientation. Thus the position of the law includes aspects which both empower the police to harass and reduce sexuality minorities to non-entities in the eyes of the law. In other words, sexuality minorities are subjects who have become fit to be harassed, but are invisible when it comes to themselves being right holders.

## THE POLICE

In the testimonies we heard, oppression by the police turned out to be one of the major concerns of the gay, bisexual and transgender people. The oppression took the following forms.

### Extortion

This appeared to be one of the most common forms of oppression. The police often stop gay/bisexual men in the cruising areas, threaten them saying we know what you are doing, take their names and addresses and extort money from them. It is difficult to estimate the number of cases of extortion suffered by the community, as there are obviously no police records. Since FIRs are almost never recorded it appears to be one of the easiest ways for the police to make easy money as the gay/bisexual men are so scared of being 'outed' to wider society that they will part with whatever they have with them.

### Illegal Detention

Another technique used by the police is illegal detention. The police in this case take people in for questioning and detain them in the lock up for periods of time varying from overnight to a few days. They do not file a First Information Report and keep no documentary evidence of the person's detention. Due to the lack of such evidence, these cases do not come to the attention of the public.

### Abuse

Members of the community spoke about police abuse as another form that oppression took. The police often abuse the men using filthy language, beat them up and even subject them to sexual abuse. When this happens there is no recourse for the largely underground population of male gays/bisexuals as any reporting would mean that the anonymity is shattered. The systematic abuse suffered by sexuality minorities is brought out in a revealing remark like "the police were very nice they beat me only once". Such a remark shows the degree of internalization of self-hatred wherein the person believes that he actually deserved to be beaten up. This is a serious psychological consequence of abuse.

**Outing**

The police have also on occasions outed gay/bisexual men to their families. In the recent testimony we came to know about a recent case when the police got to know about the sexual behaviour of a gay/bisexual person and revealed the same to the family. In an environment wherein not only is homosexuality/bisexuality as an orientation a matter of deep public ridicule, but also a matter of private shame, outing by the police is a definite form of oppression.

*The following incidents document the forms of police oppression:*

- Recently there have been a number of reports of the police in Bangalore targeting people who are presumed to be homosexual in public recreational areas such as Cubbon Park and Krishna Rao Park.
- On 23 February 2000, 3 men in Cubbon Park were taken to the local police station and illegally detained for a day after being forced to pay Rs.100/- each as extortion.
- On 27 March 2000, 3 men who were chatting in front of the High Court building were taken to an isolated place in the park, verbally abused, harassed and warned against visiting the place again. In all these four instances, FIRs were not filed against these men and no receipts given for the money taken.
- On 22 April, 2000, 10 men were picked up in the same area and taken to Vidhana Soudha police station where they were verbally abused, some badly beaten up, all their money taken, and their addresses were taken with threats to inform their families and embarrass them.
- In another incident at Coles Park, a policeman beat up and chased away a number of people on the mere suspicion of being homosexual; when a bystander protested, he was told to mind his business.
- On 8 June 2000, the police arrested Narayana, a self-identified kothi on suspicion of theft. He was not informed of the charge against him, neither was there any implicating prima facie evidence. He spoke to members of the team about the abuse meted out by the police. "I kept pleading that I was innocent, but was kept in the lockup was then taken by a public bus to Hubli for investigation and shamefully handcuffed to the seat. Even after the real thief was arrested on the third day and the goods recovered, I was still not

> released. The activists who came to demand my release were informed that I was not under arrest but was co-operating with the police investigation. The police then seized my diary, which contained the addresses of my kothi friends. Subsequently I was taken handcuffed to the cruising areas and told to identify the other kothis. When I complained to the Station House Officer about my continued detention I was told that I would be released only if I provided information about other kothis. I was finally released after eight days of verbal abuse and public humiliation and was threatened with serious consequences if I did not frequently report to the police station."

These are just a few examples of a widespread pattern of police extortion, physical, verbal, and sexual abuse, and blackmail perpetrated on gays/ bisexuals by Hoysala teams and the beat constables in parks and other recreational areas. Since gay/bisexual men have no acceptance and no social space in society, these cruising areas are the few spaces available to them to informally network and socialize with other gay/bisexual men. Ironically, these public areas, lacking the privacy and protection of a home, are also places where gays/bisexuals are most prone to attack not only by the police but also by goondas and hustlers who take advantage of their vulnerability and stigmatized existence, to freely hound and rob them. Given their social invisibility, information about such attacks does not easily become public and hence is difficult to investigate and act upon.

Nevertheless, the documented cases of police highhandedness towards gays/ bisexuals are serious enough to warrant a thorough investigation into such charges. It appears that instead of protecting the citizens and upholding the law, the police themselves are violating laws relating to extortion, assault, wrongful confinement and wrongful restraint.

## Emergence of Sexuality Minority Activism

One welcome development is the formation in April 2000 of a coalition of sexuality minorities to resist these increasing police violations against gay/ bisexual men in parks and other recreational areas. The coalition has been able to bring about some public awareness and support for the issue, leading in turn to the admittedly minimal empowerment of a hitherto powerless minority to be able to at least report instances of police harassment to a sensitive group.

The coalition comprises several Bangalore-based organizations, such as ALF, Good As You, Manasa, Sabrang, Sangama, Snehashraya, and Swabhava, which are involved with the rights of sexuality minorities. The members of the coalition, police atrocities on the homo/bisexual and transgender people have increased alarmingly in the months spanning February to April 2000. "They are actively harassing, blackmailing, physically and verbally abusing the gay and homosexual group of people," alleged members of the Coalition.

"There have been several such instances of abuse. A week ago, we saw a person being beaten up in a public area under the Fraser Town Police Station by cops belonging to the Hoysala team No. 36. Similarly two weeks ago 11 persons were beaten up in two separate incidents in Cubbon Park."

**The Police Response**

- In the last week of April, members of CSMR met the Police Commissioner T. Madiyal on this issue and he assured them he would look into the matter. In the second week of May, the coalition was invited for a discussion by the Cubbon Park police inspector and sub-inspector. They thanked the coalition for reporting cases of police excesses to them. The group was told that the cops in Hoysala team No.36 had been changed.
- When the Joint Commissioner of Police Dr. Ajai Kumar Singh was asked what the police view was on the subject of gay rights, he said: "Homosexuality is an offence under Section 3 of The Indian Penal Code and it is the duty of the police to prevent any kind of offence from happening. If the cop on duty questions or prevents any form of crime, he is only doing his job. Where is the question of harassment or atrocity? These are not cases of human rights violation because these groups are not legally recognized. Let them repeal the IPC Act, which bans homosexuality. Even if the Act were changed, people would still be penalized if they continued to attract or encourage obscenity in public places. They can carry on with their activities in their homes, but not outside". Singh also added that the police was under tremendous pressure from the general public for taking money from gay groups and turning public spaces, particularly Cubbon Park, into a park for people with alternative sexuality. "The allegation is from both the sides. The police will obviously have to take the side of law and make sure that public places were not misused. So far we have not received any notice from the National Human Rights Commission on police atrocities on gay and transgender people." About the complaint of the coalition that the police are guilty of extortion, abuse and illegal detention of sexuality minorities, his response was: "If the allegation is against extortion, physical abuse or illegal detention, then the aggrieved should immediately lodge a formal complaint in the said police station and as suggested, look into the matter. Justice will be done.".
- The PUCL team met the Assistant Commissioner of Police of the Cubbon Park Circle, Mr. Santosh Hegde, on 29 November 2000 to find out if the police having jurisdiction over Cubbon Park are following any specific policy with respect to sexuality minorities. Denying that there was any such policy, he said that in his entire career there was not a single case booked under Section 377. He

maintained that the police do not normally arrest men on the suspicion of being homosexual in a public park, which is frequented by people from all sections of society. Hence it is not possible to arrest someone merely on suspicion of being homosexual, because a defence lawyer could easily shoot it down. However if a homosexual act did take place, and proof was available the police would definitely arrest the perpetrator. About extortion, Mr. Hegde admitted that policemen are not all 'Satya Harishchandras' and it was possible that some of them do extort money from homosexuals but the problem was that homosexuals do not come forward to lodge a complaint due to social stigma. As regards the nature of homosexuality, Mr. Hegde was quite clear that it was an animal-like behaviour.

- Mr. Mariswamy Gowda's comments to our team were guarded and cautious but sufficiently revealing about how the police deal with sexuality minorities. He admitted the difficulty in booking cases under Section 377 of the IPC; unless one of the sexual partners complains that he was coerced into a homosexual act it is almost impossible to book a case against a homosexual. In fact, just as to the officer, to the best of his knowledge not a single case has been booked against homosexuals in Bangalore, at least in the last 20 years. Like other officers, this officer believed that homosexuality is an unnatural offence under Section 377, although it was clear from his account that he was referring not to homosexuality *per se* but to homosexual acts. When asked about if the police go on clean up drives against sexuality minorities, he guardedly admitted that the police did on occasions chase away hijras and those suspected of 'indulging' in homosexual acts as it amounted to a public nuisance.

**Concluding Comments**

It is clear that police regard homosexuality as an aberration and an instance of animal-like behaviour. Despite these prejudices regarding homosexuality, they still have to adhere to a certain rule of law framework laid down in the Indian Penal Code and the Criminal Procedure Code. Thus as Mr. Hegde noted, it was not possible to arrest merely on the suspicion that someone was a homosexual.

In cases of extortion, illegal detention and physical abuse, the police are obliged to look into the matter if a complaint was lodged. This however is easier said than done due to the fear on the part of sexuality minorities of being 'outed' to their families, fellow employees and wider society. Hence unless further steps are taken to guarantee the confidentiality of the complainant, it is unlikely that sexuality minorities would be able to lodge FIR's in the police station.

The existence of a rule of law framework can also be a space that human rights organizations and sexuality minority organizations should claim in order to protect the basic human rights of sexuality minorities. However the extent of ignorance among the top levels of the police with respect to Section 377 is shocking and inexcusable.

As noted before, what is penalized in Indian law is homosexual acts and not homosexuality, which is a wider concept and can be defined as 'same sex attraction'. Further Mr. Singh is wrong in asserting that groups that support gay rights are illegal. This convenient elision from sexual behaviour to sexual orientation serves the police well during the so-called "clean-up drives" against the sexual minorities. Despite the Police Commissioner's explicit denial, Mr. Mariswamy Gowda asserted that the police under his jurisdiction periodically round up a number of people whom they identify as gays and release these people only after ensuring that they don't reappear in the area; hijras whose sex work makes them "a public nuisance" face a similar eviction.

During these "clean-up drives," no charges are pressed, no legal procedures are followed by the police; obviously, the police are aware that their actions are untenable as it violates the rights of free association and assembly guaranteed to all citizens under the constitution of India. In operating entirely outside the ambit of law, the police are confident that they have the support of the dominant culture. This makes it well nigh impossible for sexuality minorities to emerge from the pall of invisibility.

While Sec 377 provides the legal sanction to arrest people who engage in the sexual acts forbidden by law, cases under this provision rarely come to court. Thus what is clear is that the police have no clear policy on sexuality minorities. The law is more often used by the constables to extract money and favours from the affected people. While the police officers at the top-level claim that they follow the norms with regard to sexuality minorities, the average constable feels at liberty to misuse Section 377 to extort, harass and abuse sexuality minorities. Organizations dealing with sexuality minorities should use this gap between the claim and the practice to hold the police force accountable for the violations of the rights of sexuality minorities.

## SOCIETAL DISCRIMINATION

Underpinning intimidation by organs of the state is an insidious and pervasive culture of silence and intolerance practiced by different sections and institutions of society. Many people deny the existence of sexuality minorities in India, dismissing same-sex behaviour as a Western, upper-class phenomenon. Many others label it as a disease to be cured, an abnormality to be set right or a crime to be punished. While there are no organized hate groups in India as in the West, the persecution of sexuality minorities in India is more insidious. Often, sexuality minorities themselves don't want to admit the fact of persecution because it intensifies their fear, guilt and shame.

Social stigma casts a pall of invisibility over the life of sexuality minorities, which makes them frequent targets of harassment, violence, extortion, and often, sexual abuse from relations, acquaintances, hustlers, goondas, and the police. All this denial and rejection by society under various pretexts backed by an enforced invisibility, exposes sexuality minorities to constant abuse and discrimination.

Social discrimination against sexuality minorities manifests itself in the production of the ideology of heterosexism which establishes the male-female sexual relationship as the only valid/ possible lifestyle and renders invalid the lives and culture of those who do not fit in. The ideology of heterosexism pervades all dominant societal institutions such as the family, the medical establishment, popular culture, public spaces, workspaces and household spaces. As suggested, examine each of these sites thorough which sexuality minorities are silenced and oppressed individually.

## THE FAMILY

Most Indian families socialize children into the inevitability of heterosexual marriage and the pressure to marry begins to be applied slowly but inexorably. Both men and women experience the pressure, but undoubtedly the pressure is greater on women, who in the Indian context have far less independence. There is no space within the family to express a non-heterosexual alternative. In this conservative context some sexuality minorities have chosen to 'come out' to their families as having an alternative sexual orientation. The reaction to this particular disclosure has ranged from acceptance to violent rejection.

The family may completely disown their son or daughter and refuse to accept that he or she is homosexual and forces the child to undergo psychiatric treatment in a vain attempt to convert them into heterosexuality or to push them into an unhappy marriage where the wife suffers equally, bearing the burden of an unworkable marriage, and her sexual freedom curbed. In one reported case of a boy studying in a prestigious college in Bangalore, when he came out to his parents, they chose to disown him.

They stopped paying his college fees forcing him to discontinue his studies for one year. However after a year had passed they were mollified enough to finally accept him. In another reported case of a young man whose mother found out he was gay, she threatened to take legal action against him. The most tragic case pertains to a newly married gay man who could not bear the vicious verbal abuse of his domineering brother and he and his wife are rumored to have committed suicide. Often, as in this case, the suicide is deflected by friends and family and attributed to a family quarrel or some other cause.

In fact, such a suicide, brought about by social persecution, is nothing short of social murder. However there are some families who have taken time to adjust to a new reality, going through phases of denial, hatred, bitterness and finally acceptance. In one recent case, a retired police officer and his wife came to the group Sabrang to find out more about homosexuality as his son had come out to him as being gay.

The parents after going through initial shock were learning to cope with the new reality. What also needs to be understood is that nothing prepares parents for such a disclosure considering the absolute lack of non-judgmental information. Since there are few mechanisms, which can help parents to understand and cope with such disclosures, violence and hostility are understandable responses to coming out in a cultural context of homophobia.

## THE MEDICAL ESTABLISHMENT

The medical establishment is in itself complex and involves different systems of medicine which span ayurveda, homeopathy and allopathy. It includes various kinds of medical practitioners such as quacks, hakims and popular psychiatrists. This section will examine the attitudes to sexual minorities of allopathic and homeopathic systems as well as analyse the columns of one popular psychologist.

### The Allopathic System

The discipline of medicine was the first to classify homosexuality as one of the sexual perversions. However, after a sustained struggle by the gay and lesbian movement, the American Psychiatric Association finally removed homosexuality off the list of diseases in 1973. The WHO has also recommended that homosexuality should not be treated as a disorder in its classification system called ICD-10.

In India the medical establishment has adopted the WHO system of classification of mental and behavioural disorders known as ICD-10. It distinguishes between "ego syntonic" and "ego dystonic" homosexuality and categorises ego dystonic homosexuality, bisexuality and heterosexuality as psychiatric disorders. In ego dystonic homosexuality, bisexuality or homosexuality, the gender identity or sexual preference is not in doubt, but the individual wishes it were different and seeks treatment.

In ego syntonic homosexuality, by contrast, the individual is comfortable with his or her sexual preference or gender identity. Psychiatric treatment to change the patient's identity or sexual preference is warranted in the case of ego dystonic sexuality of any kind. Ego syntonic homosexuality warrants treatment if the individual experiences anxiety about coming out and other issues of self-esteem but is not considered a disorder.

Apart from the ego syntonic-dystonic distinction, if a person faces problems in maintaining a sexual relationship due to the person's sexual preference or gender identity then ICD-10 classifies it as a sexual relationship disorder, which also warrants treatment. In order to determine whether the patient's experience is either ego syntonic or ego dystonic, medical professionals are expected to carry out an evaluative process in which sexuality is looked at in all its dimensions such as sexual desire, sexual fantasy, sexual arousal and orgasm. If the patient is ego dystonic, then doctors have various options, including prescription of drugs, cognitive behavioural therapy and aversion therapy. This type of therapy exposes the person to visual images of the disorder he/she is dealing with, followed by a mild electric current so that the image is associated with discomfort.

For example, if a person with homosexual fantasies is shown a picture of an attractive man and simultaneously administered a mild shock the frequency of the homosexual desire comes down. Prior to the prescription of treatment such as behavioural therapy, the doctors are expected to get the consent of the patient to the prescribed treatment.

**The Allopathic System and Human Rights**

*When it comes to the procedures the human rights of sexuality minorities are violated in the following ways:*

- The classification system of ego dystonic homosexuality, bisexuality and heterosexuality adopted by ICD-10 has been seen as problematic. Though ICD- 10 clearly includes even ego dystonic heterosexuality as a disorder, that is eyewash, as the majority of cases happen to be ego dystonic homosexuality or bisexuality. Further as Halpert argues, "to even suggest that it is the responsibility of gay and lesbian clients to change their sexual orientation in order to be happier and more well adjusted is to ignore the negative stigma society attaches to homosexual behaviour. To attempt to cure is to reinforce bigotry."
- There is enormous scope for rights violation, because doctors carry social prejudices against sexuality minorities into the treatment. The doctor is expected to carry out an evaluative process to determine whether the patient does have ego dystonic homosexuality. However whether the doctor goes through the process or not, there still remains enormous scope for the societal biases and prejudices carried by the doctor to play a role in diagnosis. As an interview with a behavioural therapist in a prominent Bangalore based hospital revealed, ego dystonic homosexuality is seen as a condition when the patient is distressed about his homosexuality. As the doctor himself admitted, the distress could be due to different factors such as pressure to get married or need to conform to culturally appropriate sexual practices. In spite of these social pressures playing such a strong role in causing the patient distress, the doctor determines that any patient who comes to him suffers from ego dystonic homosexuality and merits treatment. The doctor also drew a linkage between drug use and gays, as well as HIV/AIDS and

gays, noting that both were more common in the gay community. These unsubstantiated prejudices about sexuality minorities undoubtedly lead the doctor to prescribe treatment to all people who came to him for treatment as all of them are perceived as suffering from a medical illness.

- As Dr. Shekhar Seshadri pointed out, even if the doctor is well meaning and sympathetic towards the cause of sexuality minorities, the enormous social pressure put upon the doctor to make the patient normal by the family, society and sometimes the patient himself or herself becomes difficult to resist and the doctor ends up prescribing treatment options which do enormous harm to the patient.
- The doctor has no prescribed procedures to follow when a patient is diagnosed as having ego dystonic homosexuality. There is an absence of concrete norms with respect to when and under what circumstances treatment options can be prescribed for ego dystonic disorders and a complete absence of any meaningful understanding of what informed consent actually means. That is doctors can prescribe aversion therapy or any other treatment without providing the patient with information on the normalcy of homosexuality/ bisexuality or the existence of support groups. Thus the patient makes a 'choice' to go in for treatment in a context of little information and much prejudice. The treatment choice made by the patient would not be an informed choice. By contrast, the resolution of the American Psychological Association notes that 'conversion therapy requires all psychologists to disseminate accurate information about sexual orientation, provide informed consent and alternative treatment information in a non discriminatory manner in a value neutral environment.' In an environment where there is little information about sexuality minorities, and very little support for sexuality minorities to lead their lives as sexuality minorities, it becomes incumbent upon the doctor to provide accurate information on sexuality minority rights, the existence of support groups, and other information which would help the patient make an informed choice about whether to go in for treatment or not.'
- The PUCL team asked the behaviour therapist mentioned above about the treatment options prescribed for a person diagnosed as suffering from ego dystonic homosexuality. Though reluctant to answer the question at first, he noted that one kind of treatment was to change the gender inappropriate behaviour of the patient, thus for example 'sissy behaviour'. Since the patient lacked gender appropriate skills he would be taught to walk, talk and interact in a gender appropriate manner. Further there were masturbatory

techniques, which they prescribed as well as aversion therapy, which was practiced. All these techniques are aimed at coercing sexuality minorities into the socially sanctioned heterosexual behaviour. While prescribed treatment was subject to the 'informed consent' of the patient, this was obtained without informing the patient about homosexuality in a nonjudgmental fashion and without intimating the patient about the existence of organizations working for the rights of sexuality minorities.

**The Homeopathic System**

Apart from the influential system of Allopathy, other systems of medicine such as ayurveda and homeopathy also see homosexuality categorically and un-problematically as a disease and perversion for which they offer various cures. In a revealing interview with a reputed homeopathic doctor, the PUCL team was able to glean the mindset operating in many such doctors. Since homosexuality doesn't involve chemical imbalance, Allopathy is unable to diagnose it as a disease whereas homeopathy can, since it focuses on the individual as a whole, in terms of a unique personal history.

While there were many homosexual activists who tried to establish it as a normal condition, the doctor warned us that it was not only a pathological disease but also a criminal offence meriting punishment under the law. Given the gravity of this medico-legal aberration, the parents should unilaterally take measures to get it cured irrespective of the wishes of their ward. He assured us that there were certain drugs which homeopathy does prescribe to cure homosexuality and that he himself had cured a few such people.

He however added that such medicine should be prescribed only after counseling the patient. As for its genesis, homosexuality, just as to this doctor, could invariably be linked to a dysfunctional family or a history of sexual abuse or boyhood homosexual behaviour. In all the above cases there was every chance that inevitably the boy could turn into a homosexual adult. What was evident from the above interview was that homeopathy associated homosexuality with disease, perversion and an 'abnormal' personal history. Homeopathic doctors like their other counterparts are also steeped in a pervasive heterosexism, which offers itself as a sound medical science.

**Popular Psychology**

Catering to mass newspaper audience, popular psychology with its reassuring expertise reflects back to the dominant culture images of its own normality as well as censuring practices, which are beyond the pale of social morality. This is to be seen in the regular columns contributed by family counselors on issues pertaining to sexuality. A very good example is Saul Perreira whose column entitled "Saul's Solutions" appeared in Times of India during 1997-98. In his column of 22 February 1997, Saul Perreira warns young people seeking advice on matters related to homosexuality that "it is an avoidable indulgence and has several dangers associated with it: the risk of infection, the guilt, the pressure of remaining in the relationship by compulsion, the social stigma and the social withdrawal that will ensue." Perreira's persistent anxiety in his columns is to reinforce the idea that the only healthy sexual relationship is a romantic heterosexual one leading to a presumed monogamous happy marriage.

Hence, a past homosexual relationship should be hushed up. If it persists it should be firmly put down through exposure and punishment. Homosexuality springs from "lack of meaningful exposure to girls", but Perreira reassures his young male readers: "give yourself a reasonable chance to sort this matter".

In this case, the boy's problem is a common one besetting a young homosexual pushed into a marriage not of his choosing, but not wishing to spoil his bride's life either. Saul sidesteps the boy's problem and advises him on how to turn into a 'normal' heterosexual through therapy. Such anxieties and evasions reflect the dilemmas of Indian mainstream society being increasingly forced to acknowledge people of different sexualities in its midst.

## POPULAR CULTURE

Popular culture today - comprising organs of mass media such as the press, television and films - does not offer any positive role models for relationships between sexuality minorities. As in other societal institutions, there is a resounding silence on the issue of lesbian, gay, bisexual or transgender relationships, lives and culture. Sexuality minorities figure in popular culture, if at all, only as objects of fun and derision replaying stereotypes of gay men as effeminate and lesbians as manly.

### Films and Books in English

The last decade has seen a spurt of films on issues relating to sexuality minorities, such as 'Fire' and 'Bomgay' and the recent documentary by the young Delhi-based film maker, Nishit Saran on coming out to his mother, called 'Summer in my veins' As for writing about sexuality minorities, some prominent studies are: Shakuntala Devi's The World of Homosexuals; the path breaking survey, Less than Gay; Arvind Kala's somewhat sensational and prejudiced account, Invisible Minority; Giti Thadani's important study of lesbianism in the Indian tradition, Sakhiyani; and Ruth Vanita and Saleem Kidwai's Same Sex Love in India.

Suniti Namjoshi, Shyam Selvadurai, and Firdaus Kanga are some of the noted fiction writers exploring issues of different sexualities. In 1999, Penguin published anthologies of gay and lesbian writing in India edited by Hoshang Merchant and Ashwini Sukthankar respectively, which had a good reception, on the whole.

## English Language Press

The portrayal of sexuality minorities in the English language press has become more and more positive in the last decade, especially after the publication of Bombay Dost, the first gay magazine in India, which started in June 1990, and major media coverage given to the marriage of two policewomen Leela and Urmila in 1988. A typical article of English language press is Parvati Nair's 'Gay... and happy' which gives a sympathetic account of gay men, one of whom is quoted as saying: "The two most common misconceptions about gay men seem to be that they are either impotent and are threfore a failure with women or that they are sex-crazed and casually rape every young boy they come across. This is a ridiculous generalization; it's like believing that every 'straight' single male is celibate or that all married women are unhappy.

Nobody is perfect and there are decent gays and perverts just as there are among straight people". Newspapers and news magazines such as Times of India, India Today, Sunday, The Week, Bangalore Monthly and Asian Age have been carrying articles with a positive slant. Some newspapers such as Asian Age and Times of India support gay rights more than others. However many articles still play on stereotypes and spread misinformation. One common stereotype sees homosexuality as a form of sex work and gays as people who are pushed into homosexuality for economic reasons. "They made me a gay". S. Seetalakshmi also plays on the same stereotype: "Though many people deny the existence of homosexuality in India, a large number of young boys and girls are lured into it for various reasons including money and jobs".

Another article titled, 'Students take to the gay way to make money' replays the same stereotypes and notes that young students pick up elderly men to make money. Often the stark illustrations accompanying these articles are quite revealing of how the dominant culture constructs gays: depressed, lonely, fragmented and dwelling in the depths of a gloomy and perverse underworld. The suggestion is that gays have created their own private little hells and have put themselves out of reach of humanity.

## Regional Language Press

The regional press moves beyond mild expression of stereotypes and is often viciously homophobic characterizing homosexuality as a disease, perversion and disorder; it is also a Western disease, which those who are influenced by western values succumb to. It's not something that exists locally.

*Here are some representative instances:*

- In an article in Kannada by Ravi Belligere titled, 'Bangalore's secret sex society', Bangalore's gay group is described as a sex-obsessed group, which meets regularly as a group to have sex.
- The Kannada magazine Grihashoba reported the Sydney gay pride festival with a photo of 3 Australian drag queens, thereby constructing homosexuality as exotic, Western and other.

- In an article in Sapthahik Pahadi Lahar, Rajiv Dikshit, a reputed social activist, announces that Bangalore is now 'A City Drowning in the Gutter of Homosexuality'. It attracts young men from all over the country who come to study but flock to its numerous pubs and are initiated into the prevailing homosexual culture and end up in male sex work. Like many others, Dikshit equates homosexual behaviour with male sex work. Homosexuality is also seen as the latest perversion coming from a jaded and hedonist Western society that is constantly in search of more decadent pleasures; an exploitative society that sets up a regime of sexual pleasure in order to push further its agenda of globalization. Dikshit's progressive rhetoric can barely conceal its sensationalism and its rigid sexual morality.
- One of the worst examples is a piece in Telugu by Dr. Pattabhiram, a wellknown hypnotist in Hyderabad who contributes a regular column in the popular magazine on hypnotism as a therapy. Answering the question as to why no cure has been found for AIDS so far, Dr. Pattabhiram attributes the rise of the disease solely to homosexual behaviour, which, just as to him, even animals like rats and dogs find abominable and resist being subjected to, in laboratory experiments. This, he thinks, is the reason why a vaccine has not been developed for AIDS so far. Despite its degrading nature, homosexuality remains an irresistible addiction for many humans who however can be cured of it through hypnotism. This article betrays all the stigmas usually attached to homosexuality, *i.e.* that it's a disease to be treated medically, that it leads directly to AIDS, that it is too revolting even for animals and so on. Such blatantly unscientific medical advice that feeds into the lurid popular characterization of homosexuality only serves to uphold the conventional heterosexist social order.

**Other Media**

Apart from books and newspapers, other forms of media construct dominant images of sexuality minorities. English satellite channels provide considerable news and information on sexuality minorities and show many films about them. Star TV, for example, has given a lot of visibility to the issue. The Internet has become the easiest medium to get information on issues relating to same sex relationships; e-mail groups link hundreds of Indian lesbians, gays and bisexuals.

Here again regional media stand out in contributing to the stereotypical portraits of homosexuals as effeminate and abnormal. Some examples are "Daayra", "Darmiyan" and "Tamanna" on hijras. However, there are exceptions too: a popular Sun TV serial in Tamil is reported to have portrayed gay characters very positively.

## PUBLIC SPACES

Public spaces are not only gendered but also heterosexist. Men have more access to public spaces than women. The kind of oppression men face in the public parks has already been documented. Apart from the police, society too oppresses sexuality minorities. Especially for lesbians there is no safe access to public spaces, no space where they can meet other lesbians. Even gay, bisexual and transgender people spoke to us about the 'un-safeness' of cruising areas.

## WORKSPACES

Most sexuality minorities dare not be open about their sexuality at their work space for fear of ostracism at best and termination of employment at worst. Thus what is normal heterosexual social interaction becomes impossible as sexuality minorities try and disguise the 'he' for the 'she' and vice versa. In addition to this hidden psychological violence, which most sexuality minorities suffer, some have suffered direct discrimination too. Activists spoke about one young boy from Thiruvananthapuram who was dismissed from his dance troupe on his employer finding out that he was gay.

## HOUSEHOLD SPACES

Most of the time when people of the same sex live together, there might not be an 'unnatural' connotation put to it. However when the couple is found out to be lesbian or gay, discrimination does ensue. When a Bombay-based activist came out, she quickly found out that she had to find a new place to live in as her landlord asked her and her partner to move out.

Activists also spoke about the huge barriers hijra populations faced in getting accommodation due to what can be called hijra-phobia, which is deeply ingrained in the dominant culture.

# IMPACT OF DISCRIMINATION ON THE SELF

The combined operation of the various societal institutions and mechanisms which bear down upon the affected person constructs a mindset wherein the person begins to think of himself as dirty, worthless, unclean and vulgar. The invisibility and silence which surrounds the existence of sexuality minority lives and worlds produces its own order of oppression, creating in many the impression that they are the only ones 'cursed' with such desires in the world. In one particularly poignant incident that emerged in the testimony the team came to know of a person from Dharwad who came to know that there were other people in the world with desires similar to his own only when he was sixty years old. There is an enormous erosion of self-esteem, which is perpetuated by the way dominant society operates, what it believes in and what it says. It is a process of selfabuse wherein the person believes that what society says about sexuality minorities is true for herself.

*As Elavarti Manohar reflected in his personal account of coming out:*

- "I began to dislike myself for being a homosexual and felt ashamed that I had to hide my sexuality all the time. Many questions haunted me. 'Why did I become a homosexual? Am I not man enough? What if someone discovers that I am gay? Would I be able to live the rest of my life with shame.?' I could own my sexuality under the cover of darkness, in a world peopled by anonymous individuals; everywhere else I had to suppress it. Leading a double life was tearing me apart. Suppressing my sexuality did not help either."

This process of self-abuse in some people leads to cycles of depression and selfrejection, leading to attempts at suicide and sometimes-actual suicide. This is especially true for an adolescent gay/lesbian/bisexual for whom there is confusion about one's sexuality and sexual identity. Many who testified at the hearing spoke about having contemplated suicide at one time or another in their life. Recently, in Kerala about 5 or 6 couples of lesbian women were reported to have attempted suicide because of their lesbianism. Subsequently, some of the survivors are being persecuted for being lesbian.

## ISSUES OF FURTHER MARGINALIZATION

So far, the report has dwelt on the problems faced by sexuality minorities in general. However, they are not a monolithic community any more than other social minorities are; the problems of discrimination and abuse appear different for each section of sexuality minorities. Since in India discrimination against male gays is more overt and has already been touched upon in this report, as suggested, now focus successively on how lesbians, bisexuals and hijras are treated in Indian society and how the position of sexuality minorities is bound up with issues of class, caste and gender. Our purpose is to show that social and economic marginalisation for sexuality minorities is accentuated even further as one moves from one group to another.

### LESBIANS

Even more than gay/bisexual men, lesbians are a largely silent and invisible people and often said to be non-existent in India. For this reason, they rarely face police harassment through Section 377. But this hidden, invisible space forces them to live an anonymous and secretive life, in shame and guilt. There are a number of reasons for this closet existence.

The most important reason has to do with Indian society, which is constructed on the norms of heterosexuality, monogamous marriage, and the control/denial of women's sexuality. These norms stigmatize lesbian and bisexual women just as they perpetrate violence against heterosexual women and keep them in a subordinate position in the family. Thus gender discrimination and discrimination against lesbians and bisexual women go together. Another reason is that public space in Indian society is predominantly male; unlike gay/bisexual men who are able to find public places, albeit risky and restricted, lesbians and bisexual women have no such spaces.

Often they are confined to the home, which though defined as the woman's space, is hardly the place where woman's sexuality, least of all lesbian and bisexual women's sexuality, can find expression. Patriarchy forces all women, heterosexual or lesbian, into marriage, and pushes them into obligatory roles of mother and wife. This is one of the reasons why even the various organizations which have been formed by sexuality minorities have had limited lesbian participation. In the meeting the team had with a small group of lesbians on 16 December, 2000, the team realised that though there are commonalties that lesbians share with other sexuality minorities, the way oppression operates among them is significantly different. Thus, for instance, about the incidence of police harassment, Lakshmi pointed out that the issue might be more relevant for gay men than for lesbians.

Similarly, the struggle for lifting Section 377, she felt, would help mostly gay/bisexual men. The more important issue was the right of all homosexual people to marry those of their own gender. The most critical problem facing lesbians in India was the way society simply refused to recognize them and was trying to silence their existence. This was ensured through the family, which, they all agreed, was the most oppressive and the least supportive for lesbian relationships. In fact, single women who rejected marriage are safer and more tolerated by society than lesbian couples who want to be in a relationship. Even close friendships between women are frowned upon by the family due to some unexpressed suspicion. If their parents found out about their daughter being in a lesbian relationship, some might even complain to the police that she had been kidnapped and bring her back into the family and get her married off. Conversely, if their family supported them, Sheela felt that they could do anything in society. Everybody in Indian society thinks that the only security for women is obtained from a marital relationship with a man. This becomes inevitable, as close relatives will ask the parents if your daughter has not yet got married and this pressurizes parents too. Everybody thinks that only if a girl gets married to a man will she be secure. Lakshmi was of the opinion that in our society there is no space for individuality for women who have to live entirely just as to social norms and parental demands.

"In all circumstances, we have to do what our parents say regardless of our desires. If they say sit we have to sit, if they say stand we have to stand." Even where parents are broadminded, they are afraid of society and tend to conform to social norms. Speaking about their personal experiences, the two couples said that they had met each other at college and decided to enter into stable relationships.

It was difficult to get to know other lesbians, as there were no spaces where one could meet other lesbians. Once one got into a lesbian relationship, one could not confide in anyone else and kept it a secret as far as possible. When Sheela called up Devaki, the latter would ensure that her mother did not know about it. But Devaki was lucky to have a sister who knew about their relationship and would help her by clearing the ground; however if her brother came to know about it he would not be as supportive. Sensing similar support, Devaki had approached her aunt who, quite to her surprise, revealed to her that she too had been a lesbian but she had been forced to get married. "At least that gave me some consolation. Only a lesbian will understand the problems of another." Her aunt told her that she should not make the mistake she did and yield to pressure and get married.

Nevertheless, many lesbians are able to continue their relationship even after their marriage. What also emerged during the course of the discussion was that becoming a lesbian was a process of self discovery: As Nandini noted, at first she felt that she was doing something wrong and she prayed to God to forgive her. But now she had accepted her identity. Lakshmi and Nandini pointed out that their families regarded their relationships as frivolous and temporary, which they would get over the moment they got married.

Whereas for them the relationship was long lasting and the recurrent nightmare they had was that the relationship would be broken up and that they would be separated. About the media, they felt that while it is overwhelmingly heterosexual in focus, there was increasing coverage of homosexuality and lesbianism in publications like Femina and in a film like Fire, which had increased the awareness of their identity and their situation in society.

In conclusion, they felt that for sexuality rights activists, the first priority is to push for same sex marriage. As Devaki said: "if it becomes legal, our parents will fall silent, they will have to give us support." Only when homosexuality is treated on par with heterosexuality in all respects can lesbianism flourish in our society.

## BISEXUALS

Bisexuals are people who are attracted to persons of both genders. Bisexuality decentres our binary notions about homosexual/heterosexual. For many bisexuals, the gender of their partner is not very important. Many of the oppressions documented in the report are common to all sexuality minorities including bisexuals such as police oppression, oppression by the medical establishment, family and society. However, there are concerns centering on bisexual identity/ orientation, which are specific to bisexuals. In India, as in other parts of the world, sexuality minority activism is led by gay men. So the problems and issues of bisexual men and women tend to get sidelined.

A dominant strand of opinion in both mainstream society and gay/lesbian groups, bisexuals are unstable and confused people who wear the mask of bisexuality in order to get wider acceptance in society. Further, bisexuality as an issue is rarely discussed in gay/lesbian groups though there are exceptions. There are also no groups/organizations which take up bisexual issues exclusively. From the responses to a questionnaire we circulated among a few bisexuals, it was evident that many bisexuals experience a denial of their sexuality as they face reactions from gay and straight people that range from perplexity to outright hostility.

One of our respondents cited a remark of a gay activist during a meeting that "there were no true bisexual males, only behaviourally bisexual males". To the question as to whether bisexuals experience any denial of their identity, the response was: "Yes, many times. Both from heterosexuals and homosexuals. Male homosexuals were particularly very bi-phobic."

A lot of the bisexual concerns that emerged in the responses centered around lack of social spaces, lack of support organizations and lack of a cohesive community in India. Lack of any bisexuality activism in India was also felt to be a serious problem. However, it must be understood that gays, lesbians, bisexuals, and hijras are not mutually exclusive identities or for that matter exhaustive. As our survey of different sexuality minorities suggests, sexuality is not a monochrome issue, and sometimes needs to be understood in terms of ambiguities, fluidities and continuities which move beyond the dichotomies of male versus female, gay versus heterosexual, and so on.

## HIJRAS

Hijras as a community express a feminine gender identity, coming closest experientially to what would be called in the West a transsexual, that is "a female trapped in a male body." It is a socio-religious construct marked by extreme gender nonconformity in the sense that there is no correlation between their anatomical sex and gender identity. For most heterosexuals and many homosexuals, if their anatomical sex is male, their gender identity is male. For hijras, though their anatomical sex is male, their gender identity is female.

The hijra role attracts persons with a wide range of cross gender characteristics and accommodates different personalities, sexual preferences, needs and behaviours. Many of them undergo sex reassignment surgery, while some of the hijris are born hermaphrodites. While hijras are despised, punished and pushed beyond the pale in most societies, they are supposed to have a sanctioned place in Hindu society as a viable and recognized 'third gender', accommodating gender variation, ambiguity and contradictions.

It could also be argued that hijras are generally visible, 'out' and part of an organized community unlike other sexuality minorities who still remain closeted. But this presumed cultural status can barely conceal the stark reality of the hijra existence in Indian cities where their transgressive sexuality - which is violative of heterosexist norms of society - is circumscribed by experiences of shame, dishonor and violence. In Bangalore, as in South India generally, the hijras do not have the cultural role that they do in North India, and take up sex work as the only way to earn a living. They usually run 'hamams' frequented by working class men. It is a demeaning and dangerous profession, as they are often subjected to the depredations of brutal customers, many of them 'rowdies' and the unscrupulous police. The following account of the abuses suffered by hijras under various aspects is based on our discussions with them on 8 October 2000.

**Workspaces/Household Spaces**

Hijras normally live in working class areas where they find relative acceptance in their chosen profession of running hamams. Due to societal intolerance it is very difficult for hijras to get suitable housing. As a result, most of them end up staying in localities where they have traditionally been staying.

If they do try getting accommodation in other localities, they are turned away. They live in the hamam, which, entirely devoid of the privacy of a home, serves as both workspace and household space. The hijras we spoke to felt that their neighbors were accepting of them, as they knew them at a personal level.

However, though there might be a certain safety in the locality, they reported a number of abuses committed in the hamam. Asha related to us her painful experiences in dealing with customers after undergoing sensitive and imperfect sex reassignment surgery. In spite of being in extreme pain and repeatedly asserting that she did not want to have sex, she was forced to entertain customers by the madam of the hamam. Though she pleaded with the customers to treat her gently, she was forced to undergo anal and oral sex. Hijras reported that the police not only regularly raid the hamams to collect their hafta but abuse their official authority by having non-consensual sex with them.

They related an incident when two constables and one inspector raided the hamam late at night on the suspicion that the hamam was employing female prostitutes. They were stripped and made to stand naked in a line to show that they were not female. Finally, the policemen insisted on having sex with them individually, while the others were made to wait outside. Apart from the police and the customers, 'goondas' also regularly raid the hamams in search of easy money and sex.

During one such raid, they threw stones at the hamam, and forced the doors open in order to compel the hijras inside to have sex with them. They spoke about a goonda who would come to the hamam and force them into degrading behaviour such as using the same condom first for anal and then for oral sex. He would also insist on making them eat his pan straight out of his mouth.

If at any point they refused to cooperate they were warned that their faces would be slashed by a knife or disfigured by acid; in quite a few cases, they bore marks showing that their faces had been actually slashed and disfigured. In such cases, the hijras cannot seek help from the police whose protection favours those with economic and social power.

**Public Spaces**

Sexual harassment in the hijra's workspace is repeated on a greater scale in the public spaces where the hijras are often subjected to abuse, sexual and physical, by the police, goondas, and the public.

- In one incident, two hijras who were talking to their friends in Cubbon Park were picked up by the police, beaten up and taken to the police station. There they were subjected to a spectacle of public humiliation by being asked lewd questions,, derisive laughter and even sexual molestation.
- There are other reports of hijras being forced to clean up the police station, electric shocks being administered to their private parts and even raped in the Hoysala vans if they refused to give money.
- Hijras are often harassed and abused on the street with the police and the general public as amused bystanders. In one case, a passenger in a bus was harassing a hijra who turned to a policeman for help whose response was typical: "If you are like this who can help you?" In another case goondas were harassing Manorama opposite Sangam Theatre in Majestic while the public gathered around and watched in amused tolerance. Manorama angrily turned on the public: "If your brother is like me will you keep staring?" As she observed to us, "Even if it's dogs people show pity, but when they see us they start abusing and throwing stones. Why don't they see us as human beings?"
- On another occasion, a "kothi" who had accompanied some hijras to buy medicines was caught hold of by two men who were soon joined by two others, all of whom gang raped her and had oral sex with her as well. She was threatened with a knife when she sought to resist.
- Another incident involved a gang of twenty goondas who followed three hijras and forced them on to their motorbikes and took them to Kanteerva Stadium where they were raped.

What is evident from the above narratives is that hijras have to live with an ever-present fear of serious physical and sexual abuse and hence prefer to go out as a group rather than alone.

**The Family**

The moment a person decides to assert their gender identity as a hijra, the family casts them out of the house. The family's rejection is often conditioned by the wider societal intolerance towards gender non-conformity. Ayesha reported that her family told her not to come back as it would affect their social standing when their son reappeared as a hijra in the family. When she decided to go in for sex reassignment surgery, at first she could not talk about it with her family. When she did reveal her plans, they were so outraged that she had no choice but to run away from the family in order to carry out her plans. After her operation, she heard that her father had broken his leg and wanted to see her again. But he would see her only on the condition that she would revert to her male attire. Ayesha refused to go saying that it involved her self-respect; if her father wanted to see her, he would have to accept her as a woman dressed in a woman's clothes. It had taken her a long time to accept the "feeling in her heart" that she was a woman, though earlier she did not have the social support or personal courage to express it openly as now.

**Discrimination in Employment/Education**

Hijras find it extremely difficult to get suitable employment of their choice. Due to social discrimination in employment most of them are forced into sex work. Rani was employed in Kemp Fort as a sales assistant, but could not go back to the job after her sex reassignment surgery. She was now looking for employment in a place, which would respect her identity as a hijra.

Unfortunately, there are very few places where hijras can find employment and are yet treated with dignity. A similar discrimination operates when it comes to educational opportunity, as in the case of Ayesha who could not pursue her studies at an engineering college after her sex reassignment surgery. Apart from the fact of social discrimination, the low levels of literacy in the community also ensure the social, economic and political powerlessness of the community.

There are, however, a few people who are able to overcome these formidable barriers and occupy positions of some authority. The three examples that can be cited are those of the Madhya Pradesh MLA, Shabnam Mausi, the recently elected mayor of Ghorakpur, Asha Devi, and the local example of Dolly, who is a school teacher at a government school.

**Discrimination by the Medical Establishment**

Hijras face discrimination by the medical establishment at two levels, both when they go in for treatment for STD's/HIV/AIDS and when they go in for sex reassignment surgery. In some Western countries, there are stringent regulations governing such surgery, with the surgery being permitted only after extensive psychological counseling, but in India there is no legal framework governing such surgery. Often, such surgery is undertaken by poorly qualified doctors in hazardous and unsanitary conditions. When Manorama and her two friends decided to have the surgery, they found that they did not have enough money, and had to do sex work for a while to earn the amount. A fellow hijra took them on payment of a commission to a doctor in Dindigul who was known to do such surgeries for a fee of ₹ 5000, which did not include nursing care. The doctor's clinic was a tiny airless room with a toilet consisting of three benches, which served as an operation table.

The surgery was so painful that Manorama wondered whether it was worth going through the pain in order to become a hijra. The surgery turned out to be defective, leading to a severe infection, loss of urine control and other painful complications. The surgery was not followed by a urine and blood check up.

Since the surgery was defective, they have had to keep visiting other doctors to deal with the infections resulting from the surgery. The hazards faced by hijras in undergoing risky sex reassignment surgeries are an aspect of their poverty, which puts good medical care out of their reach as well as their social position as a despised underclass, which makes their lives cheap and dispensable.

## LOW-INCOME GROUPS AND/OR NON-ENGLISH BACKGROUND

Thus, different sections of the sexuality minorities' community face varying degrees of rejection and discrimination. However, Indian society is also a deeply stratified one where barriers of class, caste and religion, language, education cut across these different sexualities and create further, deeper oppressions. Among sexuality minorities, male gays have been the most assertive, in being able to come out and struggle for their rights. But most of these gays are from the urban, educated middle class and are not always able to recognize and articulate the grievances of constituencies other than their own.

For sexuality minorities from small towns or rural areas and from lower socio-economic backgrounds, their deprivations are often felt in terms of language, education, and social and economic status. Not having the benefit of an English education, they lack access to information about their legal rights and protection, lifestyle choices and so on, which is available only in English.

For example, there are no sufficient role models available in regional language media for poorer, non-urban sexuality minorities to draw upon, so that they go through life suffering the social stigma of homosexuality in silence and shame. All this provides their middleclass siblings in the cities a comparative advantage. Thus, when the police go on one of their periodical so-called "clean-up drives", its brunt is especially felt among the poorer sections - casual laborers, coolies, hawkers, etc. - who can't afford the protection and privacy of their own homes and are driven to making furtive sexual contacts and having sex in filthy public toilets where they are easy prey to the police, hustlers and goondas.

It is also a fact that they are treated by the police far worse than those from a more privileged background. Like class, caste and religion create their own exclusions within the sexuality minorities' community. Sexuality minorities from lower castes sometimes feel a double bind where they have to hide their lower caste status along with their sexuality minority status; just as many Muslim lesbian women who are poor and illiterate have to cope with the repressive family ties of their community in addition to the social alienation experienced due to their sexuality. Recently, two sexuality groups have been formed in Kannada to overcome these social disabilities.

## CONCLUSIONS AND RECOMMENDATIONS

What became apparent in the course of our study is that discrimination against sexuality minorities is embedded in both state and civil society. Any proposal for social change would have to take into account this complex reality. A greater respect for sexuality minorities as people would depend upon a variety of factors, including a change in gender relations and class relations. Change would also crucially hinge upon overturning the existing regime of sexuality that enforces its own hierarchies,, exclusions and oppressions. Despite the importance of social change, one still has to redress the ongoing human rights violations against sexuality minorities. In this context, our team suggests the following measures.

### LEGAL MEASURES

- Section 377 of the IPC and other discriminatory legislations that single out same-sexual acts between consenting adults should be repealed.
- Section 375 of the IPC should be amended to punish all kinds of sexual violence, including sexual abuse of children. A comprehensive sexual assault law should be enacted applying to all men, women and others irrespective of their sexual orientation and marital status.
- Comprehensive civil rights legislation should be enacted to offer sexuality minorities the same protection and rights now guaranteed to others on the basis of sex, caste, creed and colour. The constitution should be amended to include sexual orientation as a ground of non-discrimination.
- Same-sex marriages should be recognized as legal and valid; all legal benefits, including property rights that accrue to heterosexual married people should be made available to same-sex unions.
- Every person must have the right to decide their gender identity, including transgender, transvestites and hijras.

### POLICE REFORMS

- The police administration should appoint a standing committee comprising Station House Officers and human rights and social activists to promptly investigate reports of gross abuses by the police against gay/bisexual men in public areas and police stations, and the guilty policeman immediately punished.
- The police administration should adopt transparency in their dealings with sexuality minorities; make available all information relating to procedures and penalties used in detaining gay people in public places.
- The police at all levels should undergo sensitization workshops to break down their social prejudices and to train them to accord

sexuality minorities the same courteous and humane treatment, as they should towards the general public.

## REFORMING THE MEDICAL ESTABLISHMENT

- The classification system adopted by ICD-10, wherein ego dystonic homosexuality, bisexuality and heterosexuality are classified as disorders, should be reconsidered in the light of mounting evidence as to how this system is biased against sexuality minorities.
- The Medical Council of India should adopt guidelines specifying what doctors need to do in cases when the patient has a problem with her sexual orientation. The guidelines should require the doctor to mandatorily provide for the right of the patient to have non-judgmental information on sexuality minorities and on the existence of support groups. The guidelines should further require that treatment to change sexual orientation should be considered only as a measure of the last resort.
- The Medical Council of India should issue guidelines to ensure that discrimination in medical treatment of sexuality minorities, which would include refusal to treat a person on the basis of his/her sexual orientation, is treated as professional misconduct.
- Bring medical curricula in schools and medical colleges in line with current medical thinking that moves beyond seeing homosexuality as a disease and a deviance.

## INTERVENTIONS BY CIVIL SOCIETY

- Human rights and social action organizations should take up the issues of sexuality minorities as a part of their mandate for social change. Socialist and Marxist organizations, Gandhian organizations, environmental organizations, dalit organizations and women's organizations, among others, which have played a key role in initiating social change, should integrate the concerns of sexuality minorities as part of their mandate.
- A comprehensive sex-education programme should be included as part of the school curricula that alters the heterosexist bias in education and provides judgment-free information and fosters a liberal outlook with regard to matters of sexuality, including orientation, identity and behaviour of all sexualities.
- The Press Council of India and other watchdog institutions of various popular media should issue guidelines to ensure sensitive and respectful treatment of these issues.

# 7

# Regional Systems of Protection and Promotion

In addition to the universal instruments of human rights protection several regional systems of human rights have developed, which usually provide a higher standard of rights and their implementation.

The advantage of regional systems is their capacity to address complaints more efficiently. In the case of courts, binding decisions with compensation can be given and also the recommendations of the Commissions on Human Rights are generally taken seriously by states.

They may result not only in "lead cases" to interpret and clarify provisions of human rights instruments, but also in changes of national law in order to bring it into conformity with international human rights obligations. In addition, regional systems tend to be more sensitive to cultural and religious concerns, if there are valid reasons for them.

## EUROPE

The European human rights system has three layers, namely the system of the Council of Europe (presently 46 members), of the Organization for Security and Cooperation in Europe (55 members) and of the European Union (presently 25 members). The European system of human rights is the most elaborate regional system. It has developed as a reaction to the massive human rights violations during World War II. Human rights, the rule of law and pluralistic democracy are the cornerstones of the European legal order.

*European Human Rights Instruments*:

- Charter of Fundamental Rights of the European Union (2000)
- Convention for the Protection of Human Rights and Fundamental Freedoms (1950) and 14 additional protocols
- European Charter for Regional or Minority Languages (1992)
- European Convention for the Prevention of Torture and other Inhuman and Degrading Treatment (1987)
- European Social Charter (1961), as revised in 1991 and 1996 and Additional Protocols 1988 and 1995.

- Final Act of Helsinki (1975) and follow- up process of CSCE/OSCE with Charter of Paris for new Europe (1990)
- Framework Convention for the Protection of National Minorities (1994)

## THE HUMAN RIGHTS SYSTEM OF THE COUNCIL OF EUROPE

### An Overview

The main instrument is the European Convention on Human Rights (ECHR) of 1950 and its 13 additional protocols. Of particular importance are protocols No. 6 and 13 (not yet in force) on the abolition of the death penalty, which distinguish the European human rights approach from that of the United States, and protocol No. 11, which replaced the European Commission on Human Rights and the European Court of Human Rights by one permanent European Court of Human Rights. The ECHR mainly contains civil and political rights.

The European Social Charter of 1961 set out to add economic and social rights, but never gained the same importance as the ECHR. From the beginning it suffered from a weak and inefficient system of implementation. However, parallel to the growing attention to economic and social rights on the universal level since the late 1980s, new attention has been given also to the European Social Charter which was amended twice in 1988 and 1995 and now also offers the possibility of collective complaints based on an additional protocol. A major innovation has been introduced by the European Convention for the Prevention of Torture and Inhuman or Degrading Treatment or Punishment of 1987, which established a European Committee for the Prevention of Torture and Inhuman or Degrading Treatment or Punishment.

The Committee sends delegations to all member states of the Convention to undertake regular or special visits to all places of detention. The logic of the system is its preventive effect as opposed to ex post facto protection, which is still taken care of by the ECHR and its court. In December 2002, the UN General Assembly adopted an additional protocol to the UN Convention against Torture which foresees a similar mechanism to operate worldwide.

The European Framework Convention for the Protection of National Minorities (1995) was elaborated after the summit meeting of the Council of Europe in Vienna 1993 as a reaction to the increasing problems with minority rights in Europe. These problems are the result of the dissolution of the Soviet Union and the Socialist Republic of Yugoslavia and more generally of the process of self-determination in Europe in the 1990s. States have to protect the individual rights of members of national minorities, but also to provide conditions which allow minorities to maintain and develop their culture and identity.

The enforcement mechanism however is limited to a reporting system and an Advisory Committee of Experts in charge of reviewing the reports.

The Council of Europe in 1999 also established a "Commissioner on Human Rights", who gives information about his or her activities in an annual report.

Furthermore, there is a confidential monitoring system of the performance of members in different areas of human rights, which is the responsibility of the Council of Ministers on the basis of reports prepared by the Secretariat.

*European Human Rights Institutions and Bodies Council of Europe*:

- European Court of Human Rights (single court 1998)
- European Committee on Social Rights (as revised 1999)
- European Committee for the Prevention of Torture or Other Inhuman or Degrading Treatment (CPT, 1989)
- Advisory Committee of the Framework Convention on National Minorities (1998)
- European Commission on Racism and Intolerance (ECRI, 1993)
- European Commissioner for Human Rights (1999)
- Committee of Ministers of the Council of Europe

*OSCE*:

- Office for Democratic Institutions and Human Rights (ODIHR, 1990)
- High Commissioner on National Minorities (OSCE, 1992)
- Representative for the Freedom of the Media (OSCE, 1997)

*European Union*:

- European Court of Justice
- European Monitoring Centre on Racism and Xenophobia (EUMC, 1998)
- European Agency for Fundamental Rights (2007)

**The European Court of Human Rights**

The main instrument of protection of human rights in Europe is the European Court of Human Rights in Strasbourg, the obligatory jurisdiction of which today is recognised by all member states of the Council of Europe. The number of judges is equal to the number of member states of the Council of Europe.

In each case a so-called "national judge" is involved in order to facilitate the understanding of the national legislation. However, judges once appointed serve only in their personal capacity.

*In order for a complaint to be admissible, four major pre-conditions have to be fulfilled*:

- Violation of a right protected by the ECHR and its additional protocols
- Complainant(s) being a victim of the violation
- Exhaustion of all effective domestic remedies
- Complaint to be made less than 6 months after exhaustion of domestic remedies

If considered admissible, a chamber of 7 judges decides about the merits of the case. Their judgment is final if the case is not considered as being of particular importance or representing a new line of jurisdiction, in which case a grand chamber of 17 judges serves in an appeal function.

The judgments are binding and may also provide compensation for damages. The supervision of the execution of the judgments is the task of the Committee of Ministers. The main problem of this system at present is the large number of complaints received which has increased from about 1.000 in 1989 to more than 44.000 in 2004, resulting in an overloading of the system. The Protocol No. 14 to the ECHR of 2004 has been adopted to address this problem.

## HUMAN RIGHTS SYSTEM OF THE ORGANIZATION OF SECURITY AND COOPERATION IN EUROPE (OSCE)

The OSCE, which replaced the Conference on Security and Cooperation in Europe in 1994, is a very particular organisation. It neither has a legal charter nor international legal personality and its declarations and recommendations are only of a political nature and not legally binding on states. Nonetheless, the often very detailed catalogues of obligations adopted in various follow-up conferences or expert meetings and monitored by the Council of representatives of member states and regularly organized follow-up conferences is a rather successful monitoring mechanism.

The "Helsinki Process" played a major role in building cooperation between East and West during the Cold War and providing a basis for cooperation in the wider Europe of 55 countries. Under the title of "human dimension", the OSCE undertakes a number of activities in the field of human rights and minority rights in particular. These also play a major role in the various field missions as in the case of Bosnia and Herzegovina or Serbia and Montenegro as well as Kosovo. For this purpose OSCE missions have a human rights department and human rights officers are deployed throughout the country to monitor and report on the human rights situation, but also to promote human rights and to assist in certain cases of protection.

The OSCE also supports national institutions of human rights in the countries where it maintains a mission like the ombudspersons in Bosnia and Herzegovina or in Kosovo. Special mechanisms have been developed in the form of the High Commissioner for Minorities and the Representative for the Freedom of the Media (Freedom of Expression and Freedom of the Media), which have their offices in The Hague and Vienna, respectively. The High Commissioner on National Minorities is an instrument of conflict prevention with the mandate to deal with ethnic tensions at the earliest possible stage.

The OSCE also had a major role in monitoring democratic elections in a number of countries in Europe transforming into pluralist democracies. The democratisation process and the promotion of human rights is supported by the Office of Democratic Institutions and Human Rights (ODIHR) located in Warsaw. The OSCE also plays a major role in conflict resolution and post-conflict reconstruction in Europe.

## HUMAN RIGHTS POLICY OF THE EUROPEAN UNION

Whereas the European Economic Community created in 1957 originally did not concern itself with political issues like human rights, the political integration of Europe towards a European Union since the 1980s has enabled human rights and democracy to become key-concepts of the common European legal order. A major role was played by the European Court of Justice which developed a human rights jurisdiction derived from "common constitutional traditions of member states" and international treaties to which those member states were parties, notably the European Convention on Human Rights. Several human rights were constructed as general principles of community law, like the right to property, freedom of association and religion or the principle of equality, which is of particular importance in European community law. Since the 1980s the European Community also developed a human rights policy in its relations with third countries, which is also reflected in the so-called Copenhagen criteria for the recognition of new states in South- Eastern Europe.

Art. 6 and 7 of the 1995 Treaty on European Union explicitly refer to the European Convention of 1950 and it is foreseen that the European Union will accede to that convention as a member. In 2000 a Convention was convened to draft the Charter of Fundamental Rights of the EU, adopted by the Nice summit in 2000. Presently this Charter is the most modern human rights document in Europe and includes civil and political as well as economic, social and cultural rights similar to the UDHR.

So far, it has no legally binding status. However, as it enshrines a number of human rights obligations which also form part of various international treaties of which the European Union member states are parties, the Charter can be understood as an interpretation and clarification of those binding obligations. Since 1995 the EU includes human rights clauses in its bilateral agreements, such as the "Stability and Association Agreements", the Cotonou Agreement or the Euromed Agreement.

Although a new European constitution, which should have given the European Charter on Fundamental Human Rights a binding status has not (yet) come into force, a stronger focus on human rights might be achieved in other ways. The European Union has developed a human rights policy both for its internal relations as well as its international relations, where it forms part of its Common Foreign and Security Policy. The Annual Report on Human Rights published by the Council of the European Union reflects the importance of this human rights policy for the European Union in general. The Council makes public statements, but is also active behind the scenes in a case-oriented "human rights diplomacy" and together with the European Commission pursues "human rights dialogues" with several countries like China and Iran. The European Parliament has taken a lead in keeping human rights high on the EU agenda and also issues annual reports on human rights.

On its initiative financial support for projects of NGOs in the field of human rights and democracy is available from the European Initiative for Democracy and Human Rights, operated by Europe Aid on behalf of the European Commission, which defines the political strategy. Special emphasis is given to the struggle against torture and the death penalty, or the campaign for the International Criminal Court. The European Union Monitoring Centre on Racism and Xenophobia (EUMC), created by the European Union to address the growing problem of racism and xenophobia in Europe and established in Vienna in 1998, monitors the situation in Europe and promotes activities against racism and xenophobia.

A European Agency for Fundamental Rights will be established in Vienna in 2007 to monitor the human rights treated in the European Charter. Based on the work of EUMC, it will collect data and provide reports on Human Rights situations on request and thus support European Union Human Rights policies. In 1998, Art. 13 was introduced into the on the European Community Treaty empowering the Community to combat discrimination on the grounds of racial or ethnic origin, religion or belief, age, disability or sexual orientation.

In 2000, the Council adopted directive 2000/43/ EC on the implementation of the principle of equal treatment irrespective of racial or ethnic origin, in particular, in the fields of employment, access to education and training, and social advantages, which applies both to public and private sectors within the EU. Similarly, the European Union has a particular focus on equality. The European Community Treaty member states have to apply the principle of "equal payment for men and women" and to adopt measures providing equality of opportunity. Additionally, this principle has been further developed in regulations and directives like the updated equal treatment directive 2002/73/EC.

## THE AMERICAS

The Inter-American system of Human Rights started with the American Declaration of the Rights and Duties of Man, which was adopted in 1948, together with the Charter of the Organization of American States (OAS). The Inter-American Commission on Human Rights, created by OAS in 1959 and consisting of 7 members, is the main body of the system. In 1978, the American Convention on Human Rights, adopted in 1969, came into force, and since has been complemented by two additional protocols, one on economic, social and cultural rights and one on the abolition of the death penalty. The United States is not a member of the Convention, although the seat of the Commission is in Washington. The Convention also provided for the Inter-American Court on Human Rights, which was established in 1979 with its seat in Costa Rica, where the "Inter-American Institute of Human Rights" is also located. There are several legal instruments granting rights to women, but the Inter-American Convention on the Prevention, Punishment and Eradication of Violence against Women (Convention of Belém do Pará), which came into force in 1995, deserves special mentioning. It has already been ratified by 31 of the 34 member-states of OAS. This Convention regular national reports are to be submitted to the Inter-American Commission of Women, established already in 1928. There is also a Special Rapporteur on the Rights of Women (since 1994).

*Inter-American System of Human Rights*:

- American Declaration on the Rights and Duties of Man (1948)
- Inter-American Commission on Human Rights (1959)
- American Convention on Human Rights (1969/1978)
- Additional Protocol on Economic, Social and Cultural Rights (1988)
- Additional Protocol on the Abolition of the Death Penalty (1990)
- Inter-American Court on Human Rights (1979/1984)
- Inter-American Commission on Women (1928)
- American Convention on the Prevention, Punishment and Eradication of Violence against Women (1994)

Individuals, groups or NGOs can make complaints, called "petitions" to the Inter-American Commission on Human Rights, which may also request information on human rights measures taken. The Inter-American Court cannot be addressed directly, but only through the Commission, which can decide which cases are to transfer to the Court. In this way, in the past, the Court did not get many cases, which now seems to have changed. The Court can also give advisory opinions, *i.e.* on the interpretation of the Convention.

Like the Commission it has seven members and works on a non-permanent basis. The Commission can also undertake on-site investigations and issues special reports on particular issues of concern. There are several NGOs, which assist victims of human rights violations to take cases to the Inter- American Commission on Human Rights and the Court.

## AFRICA

The African system of human rights was created in 1981 with the adoption by the then OAU of the African Charter on Human and Peoples' Rights, which came into force in 1986. It provides for the African Commission on Human and Peoples' Rights, consisting of 11 members, which has its seat in Banjul, the Gambia.

Today, all 53 member states of the African Union (AU), which succeeded the OAU in 2001, have ratified the African Charter, which follows the approach of the Universal Declaration of Human Rights uniting all categories of human rights in one document.

Its preamble refers to the "values of African civilization", which is intended to inspire the African concept of human and peoples' rights. Besides individual rights it also enunciates peoples' rights. Furthermore, it spells out duties of individuals, for example towards the family and society, which, however, have little relevance in practice.

*African System of Human Rights*:

- African Charter on Human and Peoples' Rights (1981, in force 1986)
- African Commission on Human and Peoples' Rights (1987)
- Protocol on the Establishment of an African Court on Human and People's Rights (1997, in force 2003)
- Protocol on the Rights of Women (2003, in force 2005)
- African Charter on the Rights and Welfare of the Child (1990, in force 1999)

The Commission has a large mandate in the field of promotion of human rights, but can also receive complaints from states (which has never happened so far) and individuals or groups. Admissibility criteria are wide and also allow for communications from NGOs or individuals on behalf of victims of violations. However, the Commission cannot issue legally binding decisions, which is one reason why a protocol to the Charter on the establishment of the African Court on Human and Peoples' Rights has been adopted, which came into force in 2003. It can receive complaints only through the Commission as in the Inter- American System.

The Court can be directly addressed by individuals only if states make a special declaration in that respect, which is the exception so far. However, in 2004, the Assembly of Heads of State and Government decided to merge the Court with the Court of the African Union on the basis of a new legal instrument, while all necessary measures for the functioning of the Human Rights Court can already be taken. A regular monitoring of the national situation of human rights is to take place on the basis of the examination of state reports by the Commission, which, however, are often irregular and unsatisfactory. Following the UN practice, the Commission has appointed special rapporteurs on extra-judicial, summary and arbitrary executions, on prisons and conditions of detention, on the rights of women, on human rights defenders and on freedom of expression. The Commission also sends fact-finding missions and promotional missions organises extraordinary sessions in particular cases, such as after the execution of nine members of the Movement for the Survival of the Ogoni People in 1995 and their unfair trial. An important part of the momentum of the Commission comes from Non-Governmental Organizations from Africa and beyond, which are allowed to participate in all public meetings of the Commission.

They often bring cases of violations and support the work of the Commission and its special rapporteurs. It is also important that governments make the Charter directly applicable in their national legal systems. This has happened, for example, in the case of Nigeria with the result that Nigerian NGOs as, for example, "Constitutional Rights Project" successfully brought cases of violations of the Charter before Nigerian Courts.

Following the adoption of the UN-Convention on the Rights of the Child in 1989 an African Charter on the Rights and Welfare of the Child was adopted in 1990. However, it only came into force in 1999 and in 2005 had been ratified by only 35 AU-states. The Charter foresees the establishment of an African Committee of Experts on the Rights and Welfare of the Child which has to meet at least once a year. In view of the slow ratification process it remains to be seen whether this convention and its committee will produce good results.

## OTHER REGIONS

For the Islamic countries, the "Cairo Declaration on Human Rights in Islam" of 1990 needs to be mentioned, which was drawn up by the Foreign Ministers of the Organization of the Islamic Conference, but never adopted officially? All rights stipulated in this Declaration are subject to the Islamic Sharia. Furthermore, an Arab Charter on Human Rights has been elaborated by Arab human rights experts and adopted by the Council of the League of Arab States in 1994 but has never entered into force for lack of ratifications. In Asia, in spite of several attempts, it has not yet been possible to adopt a regional Human Rights instrument or to establish an Asian Human Rights Commission, mainly because of the diversity within the region. However, there are efforts within regional integration areas like ASEAN, which may finally also lead to an Asian Commission on Human Rights in the future. On the level of civil society, more than 200 Asian NGOs under the leadership of Asian Legal Resources Centre in Hong Kong, on the occasion of the 50th Anniversary of the UDHR in 1998, elaborated an "Asian Human Rights Charter" as a "Peoples' charter".

There is also a Euro-Asian Dialogue between the European Union and 10 ASEM states on human rights, which has already had four sessions. A similar dialogue exists between the European Union and China. As an inter-regional agreement, the Cotonou Partnership Agreement between 78 African, Caribbean and Pacific (ACP) States and the 15 members of the European Union of 2000, in Art. 9 (2) recalls that "respect for human rights, democratic principles and the rule of law constitute the essential elements of this agreement."

# 8

# Freedom from Poverty

## INTRODUCTION

Although poverty has been seen as a historical phenomenon, the forms in which it manifests itself today are becoming increasingly complex. This complexity is a result of many factors, including the changing nature of relationships between humans, the relationship between society and factors and processes of production, and the outlook of governments and international institutions like the World Bank, the International Monetary Fund, or the United Nations on various dimensions of poverty. The concept of poverty has evolved over time. Poverty, which used to be seen as income-related only, is now viewed as a multi-dimensional concept that derives from and is closely linked to politics, geography, history, culture and societal specificities.

In developing countries, poverty is pervasive and is characterised by hunger, lack of land and livelihood resources, inefficient redistribution policies, unemployment, illiteracy, epidemics, lack of health services and safe water. In developed countries, poverty manifests itself in the form of social exclusion, in rising unemployment and low wages. In both cases, poverty exists because of lack of equity, equality, human security and peace.

Poverty means a drought of access in a world of plentiful opportunity. The poor are not able to change their situation as they are denied the means of that capability due to lack of political freedom, inability to participate in decision-making processes, lack of personal security, inability to participate in the life of a community and threats to sustainable and intergenerational equity. Poverty is the denial of economic, social and political power and resources that keeps the poor immersed in poverty.

## DEFINITION AND DESCRIPTION OF THE ISSUE DEFINING POVERTY

*There are various definitions of poverty and its manifestations*:

- From the income perspective, poverty defines a person as poor if, and only if, their income level is below the defined poverty line. Many countries have adopted income poverty lines to monitor the progress in reducing the incidence of poverty. The cut-off poverty line is defined in terms of having enough income for a specified amount of food. The UNDP Human Development Report (HDR) 1997, "poverty means that opportunities and choices most basic to human development are denied - to lead a long, healthy, creative life and to enjoy a decent standard of living, freedom, dignity, self-respect and the respect of others."

- The Human Poverty Index (UNDP, HDR 1997) uses indicators of the most basic dimensions of deprivation - a short life, a lack of basic education and a lack of access to public and private resources, thereby acknowledging that human poverty is more than income poverty.
- From a human rights perspective, the Office of the High Commissioner for Human Rights views poverty as "a human condition characterized by the sustained or chronic deprivation of the resources, capabilities, choices, security and power necessary for the enjoyment of an adequate standard of living and other fundamental civil, cultural, economic, political and social rights."
- In the Draft Guidelines: A Human Rights Approach to Poverty Reduction Strategies by the Office of the High Commissioner for Human Rights, September 2002, poverty is viewed as an "extreme form of deprivation". The Report suggests that only those capability failures should count as poverty that are deemed to be basic in some order of priority. While these may differ from one society to another, the common set of needs considered basic in most societies include the need of being adequately nourished, avoiding preventable morbidity and premature mortality, being adequately sheltered, having basic education, being able to ensure the security of the person, having equitable access to justice, being able to appear in public without shame, being able to earn a livelihood and taking part in the life of a community.

Debates on how to index and measure poverty persist, but the complexity of human life means that poverty will always remain in search of a definition. Vulnerability and deprivation, being essentially subjective, cannot be narrowed to a rigid framework that is universally applicable.

## DIMENSIONS OF POVERTY

The phenomenon of poverty is understood and articulated differently depending on the specific economic, social, cultural and political context. Going a step forward, we shall now try to relate the words included in definitions of poverty (*e.g.* justice, vulnerability, dignity, security, opportunities etc.) to real-life issues, which would help explain the different dimensions of poverty.

**Livelihoods**

Denial of access to land, forests, water, *e.g.* in rural areas, state forest laws do not allow indigenous people to collect food and fodder that rightfully belong to them. In the urban context, the city wants rural migrants for their labour, but does not take responsibility for their shelter, health and educational needs, pushing them further into vulnerability and insecurity. Discrimination based on caste, ethnicity and race have also been critical factors for denying communities and groups access to natural resources vital for their livelihoods and therefore their human right to live in dignity.

**Basic Needs**

Denial of food, education, healthy living and housing, *e.g.* the commercialisation of water, electricity, school and hospital services pushes the prices of essential services beyond the reach of the poor, forcing them to sell their meagre assets and live a sub-human existence, which ultimately robs them of the right to living in dignity.

**Justice**

Denial of justice *per se* or timely justice, *e.g.* the poor in many countries cannot access the judicial system due to the high costs associated with it. Youngsters from slums, ethnic, racial or religious minorities are the first to be rounded up as easy suspects for crimes not even committed by them, or women who seek intervention by the police in matters of domestic violence are disregarded on the pretext of the issue being a private matter. Often, due to pressure from the state and other powerful lobbies, courts are seen to delay judicial matters relating to workers' compensation or the rehabilitation of displaced people, which costs the poor their livelihoods.

**Organisation**

Denial of the right to organise, assume power and to resist injustice, *e.g.* poverty interferes with the freedom of workers to organise themselves for better working conditions.

**Participation**

Denial of the right to participate in and influence decisions that affect life, *e.g.* growing collusion of political and corporate interests usurps the space of citizens to effectively participate in public matters such as the provision of basic services. Illiteracy and lack of information due to displacement deny refugees the right to determine their future. Most Roma, due to their migratory nature, are often not even listed on electoral registers and therefore cannot vote.

**Human Dignity**

Denial of the right to live a life in respect and dignity, *e.g.* in rural areas, caste, ethnic, racial and other minority groups who form a large part of the landless or marginal landowners are forced to compromise their dignity for earning meagre wages. Children, instead of being at school, are forced into exploitative labour such as waste recycling, leather tanning or agriculture.

**Groups Susceptible to Poverty**

Though poverty is a widely spread phenomenon and affects people all over the world, it is particularly acute for women and children. Feminisation of poverty has become a significant problem in countries with economies in transition due to the increase in male migration, unemployment and due to the proliferation of household export-oriented economies that are underpaid for their labour.

Most female labour is undocumented and unpaid. Women are preferred to men as workers in many sectors of economy as they are seen as a 'docile workforce.' In many communities, women do not possess and do not have control over land, water, property and other resources and face social and cultural barriers in realising their human rights.

Poverty denies children the opportunity to fulfil their potential as human beings and makes them vulnerable to violence, trafficking, exploitation and abuse. Higher infant and child mortality is often caused by malnutrition; high child/adult ratios are an additional cause for income poverty. With the rapid rise of urbanisation, the number of children living on the streets is increasing.

Around 113 million children all over the world (97% of which are in developing countries) have never been to school and fall easy prey to different forms of exploitation or child labour. Furthermore, increasing commercialisation of education and health services deprives children of their basic constitutional rights in many countries.

**Why Poverty Persists**

Northern governments which control the governance of the world economy are content to tolerate and maintain trade and financial structures which concentrate wealth in the industrialised world and exclude the poorest countries and people from a share in global prosperity, resulting in inequality among nations of the North and South.

Interestingly enough, both within developed and developing countries there is a widening gap between the rich and the poor. The structural adjustment programmes (SAPs) of the World Bank and the stabilisation packages of the International Monetary Fund came with the promise of generating expanded opportunities of employment, income, wealth and economic development by integrating national economies into a global economic system.

SAPs that seek to eradicate poverty through fiscal discipline without addressing the inequities in the distributive systems may intensify poverty, as countries spend money paying off debts, thereby however neglecting expenditure on basic services like health, education and shelter.

The neo-liberal globalisation puts emphasis on production for exports and ignores the basic rights of people to fulfil their own needs and earn a livelihood with dignity. The rollback of the state from its welfare responsibilities of health, education, food and shelter and the absence of safety nets impact the poor. Inflation, contraction of employment and erosion of real wages brought out by liberalisation and privatisation of assets also affect the poor.

The UNDP Human Development Report 2002 points out that rapid economic growth in already rich countries of Western Europe, North America and Oceania combined with slow growth on the Indian Subcontinent and consistent slow growth in Africa contributed to the increase in global inequality in the second half of the 20th century. Even in the OECD (Organization for Economic Cooperation and Development) countries, the gains have been captured by the richest people, with the incomes of the top 1% of families growing 140%, three times the average, resulting in a dramatic increase in income inequality and the emergence of the "new poor".

- The richest 5% of the world's people have incomes 114 times larger than those of the poorest 5%.
- The income of the richest 25 million Americans is equal to that of almost 2 billion of the world's poorest people.

Today, a quarter of the world's people live in severe poverty confined to the margins of society.

The Human Development Report 2002 of UNDP, an estimated 1.2 billion people survive on less than the equivalent of $1,— a day. Interestingly, the Human Development Report 2005 states that this measurement method does not enjoy full recognition anymore, instead more specified data is needed in order to monitor the progress on the way to achieving the Millennium Development Goals. Consequently, the examination of developments in this process also leads to highly alarming data, such as the prediction that in case the present policies are kept, the goal to reduce child mortality will be missed and the goal to ensure primary education will not be met, leaving 47 million children out of school by 2015.

While there has been progress as far as access to safe drinking water and the provision of basic vaccinations are concerned, some goals, like the achievement of literacy, still lack proper implementation. The Human Development Report 2005, 800 million people remain illiterate worldwide. Another issue to be considered remains the pledge to combat child mortality, a challenge highlighted by the 2005 Human Development Report just as to which in 2002 every three seconds a child under 5 years of age died. More needs to be done, for example, in the fight against HIV/AIDS, and the policy of some of the worst-affected countries to deny and neglect the topic or even emphasise stereotypes will certainly not add to the achievement of the relevant MDG.

## INTERCULTURAL PERSPECTIVES AND CONTROVERSIAL ISSUES

### RELATIVE POVERTY AND ABSOLUTE POVERTY

Relative Poverty denotes that a person or group of people is poor in relation to others or in relation to what is considered to be a fair standard of living/level of consumption in a particular society. Absolute Poverty denotes that people are poor in relation to what is held to be the standard of minimum requirement.

An individual who is categorised as absolutely poor by American standards may be considered relatively poor, say, in the African context. Although Jim's basic economic needs are taken care of, he experiences exclusion and stagnation and is unhappy with his atomised existence and powerlessness. The latter indeed shows how Jim is relatively poor in comparison to others from his society who are socially and politically active.

#### Social Exclusion

Social Exclusion is often used synonymously with 'relative poverty', but the concepts are not identical. Social exclusion may lead to poverty and at the same time, social exclusion may be the outcome of poverty.

In the case of Jim, social exclusion has resulted in paralysing his political existence, whereas in the case of the Sahariya community of Rajasthan, their economic poverty and destitution have been instrumental for their social exclusion.

## IMPLEMENTATION AND MONITORING

During the UN Millennium Assembly session in 2000, heads of states and governments acknowledged their collective responsibility to uphold the principles of human dignity, equality and equity at the global level. They set eight goals for development and poverty eradication to be achieved by 2015. These include: to eradicate extreme poverty and hunger, achieve universal primary education, promote gender equity and empower women, reduce child mortality, improve maternal health, ensure environmental sustainability and develop a global partnership for development. The decade of 1997–2006 has been declared the First United Nations Decade for the Eradication of Poverty.

Each year, 17 October is celebrated as the UN International Day for the Eradication of Poverty. Globalisation and its controversial implications are generating new forms of poverty.

Moreover, these new forms are manifested in societies that are at different levels of socio-political and economic development, comprising people of different faiths, beliefs and cultures. For example, the impact of globalisation on Africa is quite unlike that on India mainly due to the different socio-political and economic conditions in Africa as compared to India.

These distinct differences between cultures and geographic regions have also had an impact on how people have perceived threats emerging from impoverishment and social marginalisation. The critical issue, therefore, is to further develop the framework that monitors these different forms of poverty at the global and local levels and also to empower people to strengthen their resistance and struggle against exploitative forces.

The UN Charter and the Universal Declaration of Human Rights sought to provide the moral framework for constructing a new system of rights and obligations, placing highest emphasis on guaranteeing human dignity, peace and human security for all people in the period after the second World War.

It is the holistic approach to human rights that enables a response to the multi-dimensional nature of poverty. This approach goes beyond charity, recognising that freedom from poverty is only possible when the poor are empowered through human rights education. It affirms that the poor have legal entitlements and that state and non-state actors have legal obligations to fulfil. While individual states have the main responsibility for realising the human rights of its citizens, other states and non-state actors also have an obligation to contribute to and support this process.

This is of utmost importance for establishing equitable, just and non-protectionist systems of multilateral trade, an adequate flow of financial assistance, and for ensuring that the poor have a stake in the development process in this globalising world.

These values find expression in political statements such as the Rio Declaration, Agenda 21, the Copenhagen Declaration, the Beijing Platform for Action and the Habitat Agenda, designed by states as an international developmental architecture to eradicate poverty and make an indispensable requirement for sustainable development.

## Treaty Bodies Monitoring Poverty

The monitoring bodies examine the state reports at regular intervals, may accept complaints, and make observations and recommendations to states, economic institutions, UN agencies and others to take steps to improve their human rights record, including poverty alleviation.

The Concluding Observations on various State Party Reports by the Committee on Economic, Social and Cultural Rights show that lack of clarity of the status of the Covenant in domestic law, lack of enforcement of laws based on international human rights commitments and lack of information on the treaty instrument are impeding factors.

Reports observe that debt burden, the absence of disaggre-gated data, widespread corruption in state authorities, military regimes undermining judiciary, and entrenched conservative religious influences imposing discrimination get in the way of implementing poverty reduction strategies. Though the number of countries ratifying the conventions has increased dramatically since 1990, there is a huge gap between commitments, policy intentions and actual implementation. The lack of political will of governments, conflicting commitments made on international platforms like the WTO (*e.g.* TRIPS which could result in increasing the costs of medicines to satisfy corporate greed, and thus denying individuals their basic human right to a healthy life and living in dignity) and inadequate resource allocation for realising various commitments are major threats.

## SPECIAL RAPPORTEURS AND INDEPENDENT EXPERTS

The Commission on Human Rights has appointed two Independent Experts – one has the mandate to report to a special working group on the implementation of the right to development (Resolution 1998/72) while the other has the responsibility for investigating and making recommendations regarding the effect extreme poverty has on human rights (Resolution 1998/25).

The Independent Expert on Human Rights and Extreme Poverty evaluates the measures taken at the national and international levels to promote the full enjoyment of human rights by people living in extreme poverty, examines the obstacles encountered and the progress made by women and men living in extreme poverty, and also makes recommendations and proposals in the sphere of technical assistance and other areas for the reduction and eventual elimination of poverty.

In her Report to the Commission on Human Rights, the Independent Expert presented essential findings on how the situation of the poor can be changed. To fulfil those requirements, human rights education is necessary to empower the poor and help them change their destiny. The human rights education process promotes and enhances critical analysis of all the circumstances and realities that confront the poor.

It provides appropriate knowledge, skills and capacities to deal with the forces that keep them poor. It enables the building of organisations and the creation of self-help networks so that they can claim and pursue the progressive realisation of all human rights and fully eradicate poverty. In her 2004 report, the Independent Expert on human rights and extreme poverty, Ms. A.-Z. Lizin of Belgium, pointed out that "The total world military budget for 2003 alone would cover the cost of building all the schools that Africa needs for young people aged from 0 to 18 years and pay their teachers for 15 years".

# 9

# Human Rights by Issue

## ADULTISM

Adultism is a predisposition towards adults, defined as "behaviours and attitudes based on the assumptions that adults are better than young people, and entitled to act upon young people without agreement".

It is also seen as, "an addiction to the attitudes, ideas, beliefs, and actions of adults." Adultism is popularly used to describe any discrimination against young people and is distinguished from ageism, which is simply prejudice on the grounds of age; not specifically against youth. Adultism is ostensibly caused by fear of children and youth.

### ETYMOLOGY AND USAGE

#### Coinage

The word adultism first appears in psychology literature in 1933, when it was defined as a condition wherein a child possessed adult-like "physique and spirit".

*It was exemplified by*:

- A boy of 12 and a girl of 13 who had the spirit and personality of adults.... They were placed in institutions because of stealing and prostitution. These forms of precocity lead the individual into difficulties and should be recognized early in the development of the individual.

This definition has been superseded by another from a late 1970s journal article proposing that adultism is the abuse of the power that adults have over children. The author identified examples of adultism not only in parents but in teachers, psychotherapists, the clergy, police, judges, and juries. Co-Counseling adopted the term in the late 1980s to describe "the oppression of and discrimination against people who are young." Since then the term has come to describe any mistreatment or silencing of children and/or youth. In 1996, Jenny Sazama, an adultism expert with an organization called Youth On Board, explained that,

- Young people are systemically mistreated and disrespected by society, with adults as the agents of the oppression. The basis of young people's oppression is disrespect. Manifestations of the oppression include: systematic invalidation, denial of voice or respectful attention, physical abuse, lack of information, misinformation, denial of any power, economic dependency, lack of rights, and any combination of the above.

This definition is now used widely by youth-serving organizations and education institutions seeking to counter the effects of adultism. The Child Welfare League of America writes,

- "[Adultism is] an adult practice of forming certain beliefs about young people and practicing certain behaviours towards them because of societal views, usually negative, that are based on their age. Adultism happens when this prejudice is combined with the ability of adults to exert control over the lives of young people. When adults practice adultism, young people are viewed as objects instead of resources. The end result is that young people become disempowered and disenfranchised.

While not meeting universal acceptance, one national media organization promotes the notion that "adultism is the foundation for all forms of oppression," due to the commonality of every person's having experienced said discrimination. Illustrating the commonality of this problem, local youth-serving organizations increasingly address adultism. A programme in Oakland, California, describes the impact of adultism, which "hinders the development of youth, in particular, their self-esteem and self-worth, ability to form positive relationships with caring adults, or even see adults as allies." The Texas Network of Youth Services offers a list of traits associated with adultism.

**Similar Terms**

Adultism is a generalization of paternalism, allowing for the broad force of adulthood beyond males, and may be witnessed in the infantalization of children and youth. It has been proposed pedophobia (the fear of children) and ephebiphobia (the fear of youth) are antecedents to adultism. Tokophobia, the fear of childbirth, may also be a precursor; gerontophobia, or its antonym, gerontocracy, may be extensions of adultism. Similar terms such as adult privilege, adultarchy, and adultcentrism/adultocentrism have been proposed as alternatives which are more morphologically parallel. Some activists alternatively call adultism "youthism," equating it to sexism and heterosexism.

The dilemma inherent in this term is present in other activist circles, where "youthism" is employed to indicate "one form of ageism which describes people who hold beliefs or take actions advocating unfavourable balance of power or resources towards the 'younger' generations." At least one prominent organization describes discrimination against youth as ageism, which is any form of discrimination against anyone due to their age. The National Youth Rights Association argues that ageism is a more natural and understandable term than adultism and thus is more commonly used among the young people affected by this discrimination.

Advocates of using 'ageism' also believe it makes common cause with older people fighting against their own form of age discrimination. However, a national organization called Youth On Board counters this, arguing that "addressing adultist behaviour by calling it ageism is discrimination against youth in itself." The opposite of adultism is jeunism, which is defined as the preference of young people and adolescents over adults.

## CAUSES

In his seminal 1978 article, Flasher explained that adultism is born of the belief that children are inferior, professing that adultism can be manifested as excessive nurturing, possessiveness, or over-restrictiveness, all of which are consciously or unconsciously geared towards excessive control of a child. Recently, theologians Heather Eaton and Matthew Fox proposed, "Adultism derives from adults repressing the inner child." John Holt stated, "An understanding of adultism might begin to explain what I mean when I say that much of what is known as children's art is an adult invention."

*That perspective is seemingly supported by Maya Angelou, who remarked*:

- We are all creative, but by the time we are three or four years old, someone has knocked the creativity out of us. Some people shut up the kids who start to tell stories. Kids dance in their cribs, but someone will insist they sit still. By the time the creative people are ten or twelve, they want to be like everyone else.

## EVIDENCE OF ADULTISM

A 2006/2007 survey conducted by the Children's Rights Alliance for England and the National Children's Bureau asked 4,060 children and young people whether they have ever been treated unfairly based on various criteria (race, age, sex, sexual orientation, etc). A total of 43% of British youth surveyed reported experiencing discrimination based on their age, far eclipsing other categories of discrimination like sex (27%), race (11%), or sexual orientation (6%).

## CLASSIFICATION OF ADULTISM

Experts have identified multiple forms of adultism, offering a typology that includes internalized adultism, institutionalized adultism, cultural adultism, and other forms.

### Internalized Adultism

University of Michigan professor Barry Checkoway asserts that internalized adultism causes youth to "question their own legitimacy, doubt their ability to make a difference" and perpetuate a "culture of silence" among young people. "Adultism convinces us as children that children don't really count," reports an investigative study, and it "becomes extremely important to us [children] to have the approval of adults and be 'in good' with them, even if it means betraying our fellow children.

This aspect of internalized adultism leads to such phenomena as tattling on our siblings or being the 'teacher's pet,' to name just two examples." Other examples of internalized adultism include many forms of violence imposed upon children and youth by adults who are reliving the violence they faced as young people, such as corporal punishment, sexual abuse, verbal abuse, and community incidents that include store policies prohibiting youth from visiting shops without adults, and police, teachers, or parents chasing young people from areas without just cause.

**Institutional Adultism**

Institutional adultism may be apparent in any instance of systemic bias, where formalized limitations or demands are placed on people simply because of their young age. Policies, laws, rules, organizational structures, and systematic procedures each serve as mechanisms to leverage, perpetuate, and instill adultism throughout society. These limitations are often reinforced through physical force, coercion or police actions and are often seen as double-standards. This treatment is increasingly seen as a form of gerontocracy.

Institutions perpetuating adultism may include the fiduciary, legal, educational, communal, religious, and governmental sectors of a community.

*For examples see*:

- Access to contraceptives
- Access to healthcare
- adoption of new parents
- Age of candidacy
- Age of consent
- Child soldiers
- Cohabitation with relatives/close friends
- Compulsory education
- Criminalization
- Curfews
- Drinking age
- Emancipation laws in each state/country
- Freedom of religion
- Mosquito sound devices
- Over-medicating children
- Policing
- Public school choice
- The Draft (Men's rights)

- Voluntary employment when legal or approved by parent/the state
- Voting age

## Cultural Adultism

Cultural adultism is a much more ambiguous, yet much more prevalent, form of discrimination or intolerance towards youth. Any restriction or exploitation of people because of their young age, as opposed to their ability, comprehension, or capacity, may be said to be adultist.

These restrictions are often attributed to euphemisms afforded to adults on the basis of age alone, such as "better judgment" or "the wisdom of age." A parenting magazine editor comments, "Most of the time people talk differently to kids than to adults, and often they act differently, too." This summarizes cultural adultism.

*For examples*:

- Academic misconceptions of youth
- Child abuse
- Child labour
- Child prostitution
- Commercialization
- Controversy over sagging
- Corporal punishment
- Drinking age
- Generation gap
- Literature
- Mass marketing to youth
- Mental illness
- Moralism
- Online filters
- Peer pressure
- poverty
- Runaways
- Scapegoating
- Stereotypes about Youth subculture
- Teen sex
- Unemployment gaps in ages 18 to 25

## RESULTS

## Social Stratification

Discrimination against age is increasingly recognized as a form of bigotry in social and cultural settings around the world. An increasing number of social institutions are acknowledging the positions of children and youth as an oppressed minority group. Many youth are rallying against the adultist myths spread through mass media from the 1970s through the 1990s. Research compiled from two sources (a Cornell University nation-wide study, and a Harvard University study on youth) has shown that social stratification between age groups causes stereotyping and generalization; for instance, the media-perpetuated myth that all adolescents are immature, violent and rebellious.

Opponents of adultism contend that this has led to growing number of youth, academics, researchers, and other adults rallying against adultism and ageism, such as organizing education programmes, protesting statements, and creating organizations devoted to publicizing the concept and addressing it. Simultaneously, research shows that young people who struggle against adultism within community organizations have a high rate of impact upon said agencies, as well as their peers, the adults who work with them, and the larger community to which the organization belongs.

### Cultural Responses

There may be many negative effects of adultism, including ephebiphobia and a growing generation gap. A reactive social response to adultism takes the form of the children's rights movement, led by young people who strike against being exploited for their labour. Numerous popular outlets are employed to strike out against adultism, particularly music and movies. Additionally, many youth-led social change efforts have inherently responded to adultism, particularly those associated with youth activism and student activism, each of which in their own respects have struggled with the effects of institutionalized and cultural adultism.

### Academic Developments

A growing number of governmental, academic, and educational institutions around the globe have created policy, conducted studies, and created publications that respond to many of the insinuations and implications of adultism. Much of popular researcher Margaret Mead's work can be said to be a response to adultism. Current researchers whose work analyses the effects of adultism include sociologist Mike Males and critical theorist Henry Giroux.

## ADDRESSING ADULTISM

Any inanimate or animate exhibition of adultism is said to be "adultist". This may include behaviours, policies, practices, institutions, or individuals. Educator John Holt proposed that teaching adults about adultism is a vital step to addressing the effects of adultism, and at least one organization and one curriculum do just that. Several educators have created curricula that seek to teach youth about adultism, as well. Currently, organizations responding to the negative effects of adultism include the United Nations, which has conducted a great deal of research in addition to recognizing the need to counter adultism through policy and programmes. The CRC has particular

Articles (5 and 12) which are specifically committed to combating adultism. The international organization Human Rights Watch has done the same. Common practice accepts the engagement of youth voice and the formation of youth-adult partnerships as essential steps to resisting adultism. In the USA, adultism hasn't yet became a major political issue or seen to interfere with the American concept of equality, but if it were, it would be equally as divisive and controversial like the historic issues of racism and classism, and current-day issues like combating homophobia and ageism against the elderly.

## CULTURAL RIGHTS

The cultural rights movement has provoked attention to protect the rights of groups of people, or their culture, in similar fashion to the manner in which the human rights movement has brought attention to the needs of individuals throughout the world. Cultural rights are different from human rights specifically because they are vested in groups of people, whereas human rights deal with individuals.

### PROTECTING A CULTURE

Cultural rights focus on groups such as religious and ethnic minorities and indigenous societies that are in danger of disappearing. Cultural rights include a group's ability to preserve its way of life, such as child rearing, continuation of language, and security of its economic base in the nation, which it is located.

The related notion of indigenous intellectual property rights has arisen in attempt to conserve each society's culture base and essentially prevent ethnocide. The cultural rights movement has been popularized because much traditional cultural knowledge has commercial value, like ethno-medicine, cosmetics, cultivated plants, foods, folklore, arts, crafts, songs, dances, costumes, and rituals.

Studying ancient cultures may reveal evidence about the history of the human race and shed more light on our origin and successive cultural development. However, the study, sharing and commercialization of such cultural aspects can be hard to achieve without infringing upon the cultural rights of those who are a part of that culture.

### CULTURAL BIGOTRY

The notion of cultural rights is not too cultural. Cultural rights has many ways that it can be looked upon. "Cultural rights are vested not in individuals but in groups, such as religious and ethnic minorities and indigenous societies." All cultures are brought up differently, therefore cultural rights include a group's ability to preserve its culture, to raise its children in the ways its forebears, to continue its language, and to not be deprived of its economic base by the nation in which it is located." Anthropologist sometimes choose not to study some cultures beliefs and rights, because they believe that it may cause misbehaviour, and they choose not to turn against different diversities of cultures. Although anthropologist sometimes do turn away from studying different cultures they still depend a lot on what they study at different archaeological sites.

## AGEISM

Ageism is a form of discrimination which is based on someone's chronological age. Many people use this term specifically to refer to discrimination against older people, but ageism can strike people of all ages. Like other forms of discrimination, ageism can be extremely harmful, especially when it is viewed as culturally normal and acceptable. In some regions of the world, campaigns to fight ageism have been initiated in an attempt to educate people and stamp out ageism. The term was coined in 1969 by Robert Butler, who likened discrimination against the elderly to discrimination on the basis of gender, creed, or ethnic identity.

He hoped that by creating a specific term to discuss age discrimination, he could bring such a discussion out into the open, making people more aware of it. By defining ageism, he also made it possible to create legislation which is designed to make it illegal. Like other "-isms" such as racism and sexism, ageism often involves heavy stereotyping. For example, someone may think that older people make poor employees because of their perceived fragility, or that a young person would not make a good employee because he or she would be irresponsible. Often, such stereotypes are heavily reinforced in the community at large, with people internalizing values, beliefs, and norms which support age discrimination. Ageism in the workplace is a serious issue for many elderly and youth activists. Seniors often face hiring discrimination because employers think that they are not worth training, or not fit to perform a job, while young people often find themselves marginalized when they seek employment. Some people refer to ageism in employment as "adultism," referencing the preference for "adults" in the workplace. However, "jeunism," discrimination in favour of the young, can also strike; some workplaces, for example, want to have younger staffs because they think young people are easier to control, more attractive, or because they think that a young staff will appeal to their target demographic.

Both seniors and children are marginalized in many societies. Seniors, for example, are presumed to be incapable of making decisions because of their advanced age, while children are not allowed to make choices because they are perceived as too young. Some regions of the world have laws which are considered ageist by activists, such as laws limiting the drinking age, or laws mandating retirement at a specific age. Ageism can be difficult to fight. Recognizing and combating ageism in yourself is an important first step, as is discussing the issue with the people around you. By making people more aware of ageism as an issue, you can help to reduce the amount of ageism in your community and society at large.

## FUNCTION

Ageism functions to strip individuals of their rights or worth solely based on their age. This is unfair to senior citizens because it trivializes their wisdom and experience that they have gained over the course of a lifetime. This is also unfair to teenagers and children because it assumes that their opinions and ideas do not hold any value simply because they have not been alive long enough to gain the experiences that would properly educate their beliefs.

## IDENTIFICATION

Ageism is identified in a lot of ways. It can be seen in simply the formation of generalizations that postulate that members of a certain age group act a particular way. These generalizations can then be extended to prompt prejudice and discriminatory behaviours against individuals simply because of the age of an individual. It is often seen in the workplace, as senior citizens are often denied jobs due to their age. Such cases have been brought to lawsuits over discrimination.

## MISCONCEPTIONS

There is a common misconception that only young people can exhibit ageist outlooks. This is not the case, simply because the idea of "aging" is so subjective depending on who is defining the concept. The word "old" can be defined as any number, depending on who is using the word. There is also the misconception that the elderly never exhibit ageist tendencies towards the young. This is also not the case, as often the inexperience of youth will lead people to trivialize the interest and behaviours of the youth.

## PREVENTION/SOLUTION

Prevention is the best option to battling ageism. Those who are made aware of the dangers of ageist outlooks are less likely to exhibit ageist views that can cause discrimination in the workplace and the rest of society. By encouraging others to practice acceptance and tolerance of other people and cultures, things like discrimination and hate become easier to fight.

## CONSIDERATIONS

The world is become an increasingly more litigious place. Following an ageist outlook and applying that outlook to discrimination within the workplace and greater society is a dangerous way to behave as it may lead to legal issues being filed by those who feel they have been treated unjustly. On a moral level, ageism trivializes the abilities of individuals based on their age. On a personal and financial level, ageism can lead to upheaval and devastation.

# DEMOCRACY

Human rights and democracy have historically been viewed as separate, albeit parallel, concepts. However, understandings of both human rights and democracy are dynamic and varied, and recent re-conceptualizations of both ideas have led to the emergence of a discourse that recognizes their interdependence. Specifically, definitions of democracy have expanded from the traditional procedural democracy to encompass the ideals of a substantive, liberal democracy. Likewise, the human rights framework has begun to further develop conceptions of social, economic, and cultural rights, in addition to civil and political rights, thus expanding the notion of human rights to include human security, and extending human rights to the collective as well as the individual level.

These renewed definitions present opportunities for recognizing the convergence of the theories and fields related to human rights and democracy. The necessity of acknowledging the interdependence of democracy and human rights is becoming especially important in emerging democracies such as Palestine. In these cases, in which the development and reform of democratic institutions is starting to take place, it is imperative to ensure that such institutions are built on foundations of both human rights and democracy if they are to be sustainable.

To be sure, previous attempts at democracy by the Palestinian Authority in the 1990s proved to be ephemeral, largely due to the absence of protection for human rights. Likewise, human rights advocates have found it difficult to affect systemic change in the absence of a legitimate democracy. Thus, as Palestine looks ahead to new opportunities for democracy in the future, it is necessary to integrate the broadened human rights framework, including human security, with the ideals and institutions of a liberal, participatory democracy. This document begins with a theoretical discussion of the principles of democracy, distinguishing between substantive and procedural democracy and identifying key elements and institutions inherent in a liberal democracy. The next part examines the emerging re-conceptualization of the human rights framework, including the human security perspective, which has enhanced the complementarity between human rights and democracy. The following part discusses the convergence of the democracy and human rights fields and theories, and concludes that the two concepts are not only complementary, but are indeed interdependent. The second half of the document focuses on the application of this theory in the case of Palestine by analysing past and present experiences with democracy and human rights in the Occupied Territories, including obstacles and points of progress, and discussing recommendations for future implementation.

## THEORETICAL ANALYSIS

### Defining Democracy: Principles and Institutions

The idea of democracy has been understood and applied in different ways, both temporally and culturally, with democracy taking various forms in different societies. From a historical perspective, the direct democracy of ancient Athens has been transformed into the representative democracy that is common today. Likewise, former restrictions on the political participation of women and other marginalized groups have been challenged in modern times to allow for more inclusive democracies.

Most recently, both theorists and practitioners of democracy are starting to further articulate differences between procedural democracies and substantive, liberal democracies. However, all of these forms of democracy are based to some extent on the original Greek notion of demokratia, that is, "government by the people," from the words demos and kratos.

This core concept still forms the crux of modern definitions of democracy, including the 1993 Vienna Declaration's statement that "democracy is based on the freely expressed will of the people to determine their own political, economic, social and cultural systems and their full participation in all aspects of their lives." From this starting point, it is possible to identify several key principles and institutions that are inherent to a sustainable democracy. While historically there has been more emphasis on the political institutions and procedures that comprise democracy, namely elections, political parties, and governmental bodies, increased attention has recently been given to the ideals and principles that underscore those mechanisms. As stated by David Beetham, Director of the Centre for Democratization Studies at the University of Leeds, "to define democracy simply in institutional terms is to elevate means into ends, and to concentrate on the forms without the substance." Jack Donnelly, Professor of International Studies at the University of Denver, agrees, noting that "pure procedural democracy can easily denigrate into non-democratic or even anti-democratic formalism," thus, "substantive conceptions rightly insist that we not lose sight of the core values of popular authority and control over government."

However, Donnelly also notes that purely substantive approaches fail to recognize the "idea of the people ruling rather than just benefiting... The term 'democratic' easily slides into an essentially superfluous synonym for 'egalitarian.'" That is, government for the people is not synonymous with government by the people, and therefore may or may not be democratic. To be sure, substantive conceptions risk being susceptible to normative associations that identify any positive sociopolitical elements as indicators of democracy. This document takes the position that neither "substantive" nor "procedural" conceptions of democracy should be considered more important than the other; indeed, it is questionable if the two notions can even be separated.

Instead, substantive and procedural elements should be viewed as complementary and in fact essential to each other. The principles that underscore substantive democracy will only remain theoretical ideals unless mechanisms are present for translating those ideals into reality, while procedural institutions, however democratic in form, are meaningless if they do not yield ends that reflect democratic values. For the remainder of this document, the term "substantive democracy" will refer to democracies that embody both the principles and the institutions that form the foundation of democracy, in contrast to "electoral democracies," which may be democratic in name and form but not in practice. The basic elements of a substantive democracy, just as to Beetham, "are that the people have a right to a controlling influence over public decisions and decision makers, and that they should be treated with equal respect and as of equal worth in the context of such decisions."

Beetham refers to these concepts as popular control and popular equality, both of which contribute to the foundation of the principles and institutions that inform democracy. These primary elements, in conjunction with the rule of law, open government, and public participation, form the core of substantive democracies, as reflected in their mechanisms and institutions, and the presence of civil society and citizen rights.

**Mechanisms**

The primary indicator of democracy is the presence of popular elections. Beetham, "popular authorization is achieved through regular competitive elections just as to universal secret ballot, which ensures voters a choice of candidates and policies and gives them the opportunity to dismiss politicians who no longer command their confidence." As Shadrack Gutto, Director of the Centre for Applied Legal Studies at the University of Witwatersrand in Johannesburg, states however, "for elections to be substantially 'free and fair,' it is imperative that enabling principles and rights be observed," including "the rights to or freedom of association, opinion, expression, and assembly."

Gutto also notes the importance of available and adequate material and human resources to educate voters, register voters, monitor the voting process, count election results, and reconcile disputes. Indeed, the democratic nature of an electoral process should be assessed by "the reach, inclusiveness, independence, integrity, and impartiality of elections, as well as how equally the electoral process treats citizens, how much effective choice it offers them, how far the government actually fulfills the electoral choices made, and how many people in practice exercise the right to vote." In addition, political parties function as a mechanism within electoral systems by organizing different policies into cohesive programmes, nominating appropriate candidates, and advocating for the implementation of decisions supported by the electorate.

**Institutions**

As Beetham articulates, "although elections form a key mechanism for the popular control of government, they are of limited effectiveness on their own without institutions that secure a government's continuous accountability to the public." Gutto agrees, noting how "elected representatives can play a democratic role only to the extent that enabling institutions of governance with clear systems and procedures that are secured by a normative framework and laws exist." Open and accountable political institutions depend primarily on the decentralization of governance and the separation of powers between the executive, legislative, and judiciary spheres.

These branches should be monitored through a system of checks and balances by each other, through horizontal accountability, and also be answerable to the people as a whole through vertical accountability. These institutions' specific roles and functions can be best understood and implemented when articulated in a constitution or equivalent "rule of law." The constitution should also articulate the financial responsibilities of the legislature, as well as allow for a system of regional and local government.

**Civil Society**

As Gutto notes, "however effective public institutions and accountability processes may be in any society aspiring to democracy, their effectiveness and impact would nevertheless be diminished in the absence of a vibrant and activist civil society." Civil society, sometimes referred to as "democratic society," creates opportunities for active citizenship and direct involvement in the functioning of a democracy. The key elements of civil society include an independent media, sources of policy expertise independent of the state, and associations that may include organizations dedicated to social services, development, health, education, human rights, women's empowerment, or other issues. An active civil society has the additional benefit of fostering respect for the rights of other citizens by creating environments of diversity and dialogue.

**Citizen Rights**

Democracy also includes the presence of political and civil rights for citizens, especially freedom of expression, association, and assembly, which require the guarantee of due legal process and liberty and security of person to be effective. There has been recent debate on the necessity of economic, social, and cultural rights as conditions of democracy, however, it is becoming more widely accepted that "for civil and political rights and freedoms to have any value, citizens must possess the capacity to exercise them." The majority of political, civil, economic, social, and cultural rights at the national level relate directly or indirectly to the international human rights framework, as will be discussed further.

**The Dynamism of Democracy**

It should be noted that, despite these common elements, democracy can take a variety of forms; there is no "one size fits all" democracy. As Beetham explains, "different societies and diverse circumstances require different arrangements if democratic principles are to be effectively realised."

Abdul Aziz Said, Professor of International Peace and Conflict Resolution at American University, agrees, noting that "the form of democracy is always cast in the mold of the culture of a people;" he thus urges a "more democratic theory of democracy" that recognizes its potential for variation and dynamism. Relatedly, Said specifically emphasizes that "democracy is not a western product." As noted above, the principles and institutions that inform substantive democracy are based on tenets that transcend national and political ideologies; thus, democracy is not exclusive to the West. This point has several implications. First, it implies that there is no fundamental incompatibility between democracy and the Arab world, nor between democracy and Islam. As Said notes, "the lack of democracy in the Middle East is due more to a lack of preparation for it than to a lack of religious and cultural foundations."

Secondly, the idea that democracy is not exclusive to the West can serve to caution superpowers to avoid imposing their models of democracy on other societies, and encourage them to instead assume a supportive role in developing democracy in local contexts. Likewise, superpowers should be cautious of pursuing national interests under the guise of democracy to prevent the association of democracy with western imperialism. At the same time, local democracy advocates are called upon to consider how their social mechanisms, values, and contexts can inform culturally sustainable democracies.

**Defining Human Rights: The Human Security Perspective**

As Donnelly summarizes, "human rights are, literally, the rights that one has simply as a human being. As such they are equal rights, because we are all equally human beings. They are also inalienable rights, because no matter how inhumanely we act or are treated we cannot become other than human beings." Human rights are defined in several key documents, namely, the Universal Declaration of Human Rights, adopted by the United Nations General Assembly in 1948; the International Covenant on Civil and Political Rights, adopted in 1966; and the International Covenant on Economic, Social, and Cultural Rights, also adopted in 1966.

The Vienna Declaration, adopted at the World Conference on Human Rights in 1993, further expanded the meaning of human rights. Originally, human rights were developed to outline a set of individual rights that states were required to respect or provide for their citizens. The framework not only included the prohibition of certain acts, but also the "imposition of the duty to perform certain obligations in order to promote and protect the enjoyment of certain rights." In other words, abuse of human rights can take the form of both violations and denials. While the full realisation of human rights is still an ideal, much has been achieved in the name of human rights.

Anthony Langlois, Professor of International Relations at Flinders University in Adelaide, Australia, achievements include "international recognition of human rights as the basic set of norms of human behaviour, the internationalization of human rights institutions of various types, and the development of International Human Rights Law." The notion of human rights has begun to be broadened in recent years. First, the responsibility of ensuring human rights has been expanded beyond only state governments to include individuals, groups of people, and other non-state actors. Secondly, the common association of human rights law with peacetime has given way to the widespread recognition that human rights law applies in conflict situations, just as it does in periods of stability.

Finally, and perhaps most importantly for the context of this document, the past ten years have seen increased acknowledgment of the interdependence and indivisibility of human rights. While this has always been true in theory, in the past the two separate Covenants suggested divisions between political and civil rights and economic, social, and cultural rights. While some divisions still exist, the gaps between the two fields of rights were largely bridged in 1993 at Vienna, where it was declared that "human rights are universal, indivisible and interdependent and interrelated" and that the international community "must treat human rights globally in a fair and equal manner."

In other words, the notion of human rights is expanding to include the concept of human security in a more conscious and deliberate manner. The United Nations Development Report of 1994, "human security can be said to have two main aspects. It means, first, safety from such chronic threats as hunger, disease and repression. And second, it means protection from sudden and hurtful disruptions in the patterns of daily life—whether in homes, in jobs or in communities." This renewed interest in human security and development has accordingly placed increased emphasis on economic and social rights, thus contributing to the re-conceptualization of the human rights framework.

As Beetham summarizes: The idea of economic and social rights as human rights expresses the moral intuition that, in a world rich in resources and the accumulation of human knowledge, everyone ought to be guaranteed the basic means for sustaining life, and that those denied these are victims of a fundamental injustice. Expressing this intuition in the form of human rights both gives the deprived the strongest possible claim to that of which they are deprived and emphasizes the duty of responsible parties to uphold or help them meet their entitlement.

## Democracy and Human Rights

Democracy and human rights are clearly different notions; "they are distinct enough for them to be viewed as discreet and differentiated political concepts." Whereas democracy aims to empower "the people" collectively, human rights aims to empower individuals. Similarly, human rights is directly associated with the how of ruling, and not just the who, which may be the case in an electoral democracy, though not in a substantive democracy. Thus, "democracies" exist that do not necessarily protect human rights, while some non-democratic states are able to ensure some, though not all, human rights. On another level, the international acceptance, institutionalization, and legal aspects of human rights mentioned above do not apply to democracy.

These distinctions have influenced the traditional separation of the theories and fields of human rights and democracy. From the human rights perspective, many have adhered to the separationist theory, which argues that "democracy is not immediately needed for the observation of human rights and that the maintenance of an essential link between human rights and democracy may well have the effect of delaying the implementation of human rights norms in various states." A recent corollary of the separationist theory is the "democracy as neo-imperialism" notion that charges that "democracy is a 'Western-centric' approach to government that is not found indigenously in all societies and is not desirable for all peoples." These arguments are subject to several key counter arguments that show the interdependence of human rights and democracy.

First, in terms of the neo-imperialist argument, it is certainly true that Western superpowers should not impose their particular forms of democracy on other societies and expect them to be accepted and sustainable, as noted above. However, it is equally culturally insensitive to claim that democracy is only an option in the West, or that it is incompatible with other cultures. Secondly, in reference to the separationist theory, while it would be unwise to "wait" for democracy to start promoting human rights, it must also be recognized that some human rights are intrinsically linked with institutions and principles of democracy.

Furthermore, separating human rights from democracy undermines opportunities for implementation, in that it reduces human rights to standards or norms; as Langlois states, "human rights amount to little more than charity if they are not functioning in a democratic framework." Essentially, the inclination to separate human rights from democracy is rooted in the acceptance of their traditional definitions. An electoral democracy that lacks the other institutions and principles of a substantive democracy can function without necessarily guaranteeing human rights, just as some narrowly defined human rights can still be realised in the absence of democracy.

However, the re-conceptualization of democracy as substantive, and of human rights as being more far-reaching and inclusive, underscores the necessity of linking the two. This interdependence occurs on the levels of principle, enforcement, and specific rights. On the conceptual level, as Langlois notes, "both contemporary liberal democracy and human rights are derived from and express the assumptions of liberalism," which include individualism, egalitarianism, and universalism. Furthermore, both democracy and human rights pursue a common agenda, and it is "only within a democracy [that] human rights standards or norms transcended such that the values articulated by these norms or standards are genuine rights."

In addition, it is only in a well-functioning democracy that individual citizens have access to mechanisms to ensure the implementation of their rights. The relationship between human rights and democracy is perhaps most clear through an examination of civil and political rights, especially those articulated in Article 21 of the UDHR and Article 25 of the ICCPR, both of which ensure citizen participation in government through free and fair elections and through direct service and participation.

These rights are related to the rights of expression, association, assembly, and movement, which are also interdependent with democracy, as well as the rights to liberty, security of person, and the guarantee of due process of the law. Economic, social, and cultural rights are also being increasingly recognized as being mutually dependent, if not integral, with democracy. As Gutto writes, "the pursuit of the right to development and socio-economic rights is strongly associated with the social democracy vision of poverty eradication and the equitable distribution of ownership, control, and the benefits of wealth."

Indeed, political and civil rights can best be realised by citizens who meet a basic level of physical security in terms of access to shelter, water, sanitation, and food, as well as education, healthcare, and employment or income. Socially, democracy is interrelated with rights to equality and non-discrimination, especially for marginalized groups including women and minorities. Culturally, the respect for diversity and pluralism inherent to democracy is linked to the protection of rights related to language, religion, or ethnicity. It is thus clear that human rights and democracy are interdependent, especially when defined in the broader conceptualizations of democracy as substantive democracy, and human rights as civil, political, economic, social, and cultural rights. These different kinds of rights cannot be realised in a non-democratic system, and likewise, no democracy is sustainable without the presence of these rights. While this relationship is evident in theory, it is perhaps more useful to consider the inter-dependence of human rights and democracy through the case study of an emerging democracy.

## HUMAN RIGHTS AND DEMOCRACY IN PALESTINE

The status of democracy in Palestine is somewhat open to interpretation. Many democracy advocates agree that Palestine is moving in the direction of becoming a substantive democracy, but that it still has ways to go. Specifically, the will of the people reflects a keen desire for democracy, but that has yet to translate into viable democratic institutions and principles. As Nathan J. Brown of the Carnegie Endowment for International Peace states, "Palestine is... a model liberal democracy.

Its most significant flaw is that it does not exist." That is, democracy in Palestine is evident in theory, but it has not been able to fully manifest itself in practice. Obstacles to realising both human rights and democracy are rooted in both external and internal factors. In terms of external factors, the Israeli occupation and the protracted Israeli-Palestinian conflict have posed obvious challenges to the development of democracy and human rights in Palestine.

To start with democracy, political reform is difficult in the midst of any ongoing violent conflict. In the case of Israel-Palestine, the challenge of political reform is further exacerbated by the nature of the occupation, which creates a complicated system of dual authority between Israel and the PA. Indeed, just as to democracy advocates interviewed for this report, the occupation remains the most prominent obstacle to Palestinian democracy. Challenges resulting from the external influence of the occupation are interrelated with internal factors as well, most notably corruption in the executive branch of the PA under Arafat and the failure of the security services to be effective. Indeed, the Oslo Accords "were predicated on the ability of the PA to enhance Israeli security and thus focused on enabling the executive and placing few fetters on the security services in internal matters." In addition to, and perhaps, because of the fact that the PA lacked sovereignty, it also lacked legitimacy. This problem emerged not only from the external fact of the occupation however, but also from internal shortcomings such as centralization of power, lack of accountability and transparency, corruption, and human rights violations. To be sure, human rights, like democracy, have suffered from both internal and external factors.

On the one hand, numerous human rights violations by Israel against Palestinians have been cited, including targeted assassinations, restrictions on movement, collective punishment, and home demolitions. On the other hand, Palestinian security forces under the PA have also been guilty of numerous human rights violations, including detention without trial and/or specific charges, improper trials, torture, maltreatment, and use of the death penalty.

Both human rights and democracy have also been hindered by poverty and the lack of human security in many communities in Palestine. As George Giacaman of Muwatin stated, "the democratic system is not sustainable with rampant poverty. Democracy requires a more equitable economic system based on a fair distribution of wealth." Khalid Nassif of the Civic Forum Institute agreed, noting that democracy regresses in the absence of economic and social rights that ensure human security. Nassif, "when the economy improves, people have a greater sense of freedom and safety, and they can give more time and attention to joining parties and organizations and taking an interest in democracy."

Clearly then, both human rights and democracy in Palestine have been hindered by both internal and external factors, primarily, the conflict with

Israel and the limitations of the PA, and also by regional and international influences. Nevertheless, the will for both democracy and human rights in Palestine is strong on both individual and collective levels, and in fact, both exist to some extent in theory and on document. The current key issue before Palestinians at this time is to translate those conceptualizations into realised practices and institutions, which can only be possible through an integrative approach that recognizes the interdependence of human rights and democracy.

At the same time, Israel and the international community must acknowledge that a democratic state in Palestine requires the existence of a state, as well as democracy. The next part of this document examines the institutions and elements of a substantive democracy that are necessary for bringing the ideals of human rights and democracy in Palestine to fruition.

**Elections**

The presidential elections of January 2005 were a major step towards procedural democracy. The elections followed the death of president Yasser Arafat, who had been elected in January 1996, and provided an opportunity for new leaders and parties to emerge. Though the election of Mahmoud Abbas was predicted, the elections saw widespread participation, with 71 per cent of registered voters casting ballots, and were declared free and fair by local and international monitors.

To refer to Beetham's standards for democratic electoral processes, the January elections were deemed successful in terms of their reach, inclusiveness, independence, integrity, and impartiality. The Central Elections Commission was credited with making laudable efforts in registering voters, coordinating the monitoring of the voting process, and counting and implementing results. While the process was far from flawless, it was considered to be an overall success, and resulted in a smooth transfer of power and authority. The success of the election was largely made possible by pressure on both Israeli and Palestinian officials to protect rights to association, assembly, and expression, and the process itself underscored the procedural rights defined in Article 21 of the UDHR and Article 25 of the ICCPR. The municipal elections of May 2005 were likewise considered to be successful overall. In addition to being another step towards procedural democracy, these elections also affirmed support in the electoral system and thus contributed to the strengthening of substantive democracy. As journalist Bakr Abu Bakr wrote in the Palestinian daily Al-Hayat Al-Jadidah: It is important...to point out what these elections represent to a Palestinian people still struggling to be free, still fighting Israeli occupation, and exercising democracy... They represent: first, an assertion of a course and a way of life chosen by the Palestinian people exemplified by freedom, dignity, dialogue, responsibility, and respect for the will of the people; second, the will and aspiration of many popular leaderships to serve the people...; third, a demonstration of Palestinian solidarity...; fourth, the continuity of Palestinian political struggle towards common goals; fifth, a renewal of societal leaderships.

Clearly, the elections represented more than simply a procedure; they were a tangible expression of democratic ideals and principles. These ideals were intertwined with human rights, including the rights to dignity, freedom, and political participation. Furthermore, the electoral process, while reflecting human rights, also served to facilitate human rights by functioning as an expression of Palestinian unity. The next phase of elections, for the Palestinian Legislative Council, were originally scheduled for July 2005 but were postponed to allow more time to formalize amendments to the proposed new electoral law.

While most democracy advocates support the adoption of the new law and recognize the need for giving ample time for its passage, most view the indefinite postponement as a setback to democratic processes and momentum. Furthermore, the postponement was interpreted by many as an attempt by Fatah to consolidate its support to secure a victory over Hamas in particular. This widely accepted theory, regardless of its veracity, has unfortunately undermined the apparent commitment to democratic procedures established in the presidential and municipal elections.

**Political Parties**

Political parties are a mechanism that can facilitate free and fair elections, and thus contribute significantly to a sustainable procedural democracy. Likewise they provide opportunities for citizen participation and expression, and thus contribute to the development of a substantive, liberal democracy as well. As Giacaman stated, "a multi-party system is essential for establishing a sustainable democracy."

In Palestine, there exists some foundation for a pluralist party structure. Although Fatah has remained the dominant party for some time, and has at times been difficult to distinguish from the PLO and the PA, other political parties have always remained in existence, and Islamist parties like Hamas in particular have gained considerable support in the past ten years. Thus, it is clear that "there is a plurality of parties; the parties are based on ideological differences but still operate within a national consensus; and they generally accept one another's legitimacy.

Missing, of course, are the democratic institutions that would induce existing parties to channel their energies towards electioneering and governance." That is, while various groups have long existed in Palestine, until recently they have lacked the electoral processes within which to operate. To be sure, the majority of parties in Palestine have traditionally considered themselves "movements" or "fronts," and thus focus their attention on activities not necessarily related to electoral processes.

In addition, the historical dominance of Fatah, and more recently, Hamas, have created challenges for the development of electoral parties in that "Fatah is too indistinguishable from the PA and Hamas too removed from it." Indeed, while Fatah has traditionally identified itself as the primary force for Palestinian liberation, its loose cohesion has suffered from various fractions, due both to its position as the central party of the PA and to its handling of the second intifada.

In contrast, Hamas has distanced itself from the PA, identifying itself as an "alternative to the status quo" and "the main opposition to Fatah and the PA." This contrast was not only established on the conceptual level but on the direct level as well, as Hamas provided numerous social services to communities that Fatah and the PA had been unable to supply. Also, Hamas has distinguished itself from Fatah by intentionally using religious rhetoric, in contrast to Fatah's secular nature. In the past six months however, the nature of Hamas's political involvement has been shifting from that of an independent movement to a perhaps viable party in that members participated for the first time in municipal elections and plan to participate in PLC elections. Many democracy advocates are now calling for a "third movement" that would provide an alternative to the so-called "old guard" of Fatah and the PA, and to fundamentalist groups like Hamas.

As Mustafa Barghouthi, Director of the Health, Development, Information, and Policy Institute on Palestine commented, "Palestinians do not have to choose between autocracy and fundamentalism. There is a democratic alternative. Palestine could be a state that is independent and sovereign." Dr. Lily Feidy of MIFTAH agreed, advocating for a third movement that is secular and democratic.

Nassif, who has observed numerous town meetings through the work of the Civic Forum Institute, it is evident that "people want change, and want more participation by political parties. They want real democracy, and they want political parties to function as a fundamental part of that democracy." It should be noted that electoral party systems can take many forms, and in fact, a strictly organized party system could actually be detrimental in Palestine since many active reformists in the PLC have functioned essentially as independents, in practice at least if not in name. However, it is clear that the development of institutions to support electoral parties is becoming a necessity.

Brown suggests three minimal steps to further democratic transition in the area of electoral parties. First, Fatah must be disentangled from the PA, for "when politicization of official positions runs deeply throughout the bureaucracy, and where there is a conflation of roles and ruling bodies... mechanisms of horizontal and vertical accountability begin to break down." Secondly, parties need to develop clear structures of internal governance and take "significant organizational steps, such as determining their membership, internal procedures, selection of candidates, and decision-making structures." Third, organizations need to re-orient themselves to function in electoral competition, that is, groups need to consciously decide if they are primarily violent movements or if they are electoral parties.

In order for these steps to take place, certain human rights must be ensured. The rights to assembly and movement are inherent to political party organization, and the rights to opinion and expression are necessary for allowing diverse parties to develop and mature. These rights must be protected by both the PA and by Israel. As Barghouthi stated, "[Israeli] suppression of secular democratic forces in Palestine will lead to a polarization... between Hamas fundamentalists and the PA." Indeed, the protection of human rights are essential for the emergence of a third movement.

**Separation of Powers**

As Hussein Sirriyeh, Professor of Arabic and Middle Eastern Studies at the University of Leeds, writes, "the definition of democracy should not merely be restricted to the narrower sense of free elections and a multi-party system. It should also encompass a broader spectrum of ingredients, including government by consent and accountability..." To be sure, in order for political parties to function in effective institutions, especially the legislature, there needs to be a clear separation of power between the executive, legislative, and judiciary branches, with a viable system of checks and balances between them, articulated in a Constitution.

This is necessary for ensuring transparency and accountability, and for enabling the different branches to fulfill their respective duties. In Palestine, power was largely concentrated in the executive branch under the leadership of Arafat, who developed a highly personalized system of authority. Under this system, Arafat managed to bypass the majority of institutions to extend his personal influence. While this strategy was arguably motivated by Arafat's attempt to unite various factions of Palestinians with different opinions and interests, and to bolster his status as the unifying symbol of Palestine, the centralization of power proved detrimental and only further crippled the already limited legitimacy of the PA. This centralization manifested itself in various ways. The most measurable indication was evident in the PA budget, in which over one quarter of the PA revenues were placed under the direct and unaccountable control of Arafat by 1997.

The executive's domination was also felt strongly by the legislative and judiciary branches. While the PLC had the authority to draft and pass laws, it had no mechanism to ensure that the president would approve them. Thus, numerous bills and laws that were passed by the PLC, including the Basic Law, were subject to interminable waiting for Arafat's approval. Similarly, the executive responded to many court orders from the judiciary by simply ignoring them. Sirriyeh proposes several theses to explain the authoritarian nature of the PA under Arafat.

Some of these reasons include the desire of the PA to make an impression on the Israelis by suppressing anti-Oslo opposition, the issue of internalized PNA insecurity, the "outsider" status of the original PA leadership, the lack of political experience of the PA, and the desire to promote national unity by subordinating divisions within Palestine. Whatever the reason, the failure to separate powers, compounded by widespread corruption within the PA, resulted in a system that lacked transparency, accountability, and ultimately, legitimacy. This crippled the development of democratic institutions in their early stages, and it is only recently that the new PA leadership under Abu Mazen has begun to confront the process of de-centralizing authority.

**Judiciary**

The branch of government that perhaps requires the most immediate attention is the judiciary. The judiciary was virtually nonexistent during the majority of the post-Oslo period, and it was only in 2002 with the passing of the judicial organizational law that the judiciary began to be managed by an independent judicial council. However, to date the council has consisted of judges who, while inexperienced in administrative matters, are intent on preserving their autonomy, thus causing them to lose the support of the bar association. The judiciary has also been embroiled in rivalries with the PLC and the executive branch's Ministry of Justice, with disputes occurring most recently over a draft judicial law for reform introduced by a special committee under Abu Mazen and currently referred to the legislature.

Despite these challenges, the fact that an independent judiciary council does exist provides a foundation for starting judicial reform. Although building a strong judiciary is a long, complex process, it is imperative for several reasons. On the conceptual level, judicial reform is symbolically significant because it can address the general lawlessness that directly affected many Palestinian communities during the second intifada and can thus restore confidence in the PA.

To be sure, an effective court system has the potential to restore order and thus serve as an indicator to Palestinians of the authenticity of reforms. Furthermore, "judicial reform is a logical priority because it can be a genuine tool—not simply a symbolic one—in addressing the corruption that is perhaps one of the most corrosive issues for Palestinian governance." Although laws exist regarding hiring for government positions, disclosing personal finances, and monitoring public funds, there have been no mechanisms for implementing them or prosecuting corrupt officials.

This problem can be addressed by focusing initial reform efforts on the office of public prosecution. A strong judiciary can serve other important functions as well, including being a leading force in constitutional reform and the development and application of the Basic Law. It also can function as a key body for placing checks and balances on the executive and legislative branches.

Indeed, just as to Hamdi Shaqqura of the Palestinian Centre for Human Rights, the empowerment of a strong and independent judiciary can alleviate current debates regarding concern over the popularity of Hamas as a political party. Shaqqura suggests that any hypothetical attempts by elected Hamas officials to "Islamicize" the system or re-introduce violence as an acceptable policy would be countered by the judiciary. Finally, a strong, independent judiciary is necessary for preserving human rights. First, it would provide a legitimate institution for prosecuting cases of human rights abuses.

Lamis Alami of the Palestinian Independent Commission for Citizens' Rights, ombudsmen and monitoring groups like PICCR can document human rights violations, but they currently lack effective institutions for addressing them. Furthermore, an effective judiciary branch is necessary for protecting rights to fair and public hearings and trials, as articulated in Articles 10 and 11 of the UDHR.

**Security**

Closely related to the topic of judicial reform is the issue of security. Indeed, in order to ensure due process and avoid violations such as arbitrary arrests or torture, it is necessary that an effective security apparatus, including a police force, operates with legitimacy. Viable security services are necessary for preserving the rule of law, which is essential in a sustainable democracy.

The issue of security is particularly important in Palestine, as security continues to play a vital role in many aspects of the Israeli-Palestinian conflict. To be sure, "for some external actors—especially Israel—security forms the basic logic of the reform process," and many of Israel's actions and policies are justified by concern for security. In the post-Oslo period however, many Palestinians perceived that the thrust of the so-called security reforms in the Occupied Territories was to protect Israeli security at the expense of Palestinian security. Inside Palestine, security concerns were not only associated with Israel but with internal elements as well, as the security services came to be associated with authoritarianism, corruption, and human rights violations against fellow Palestinians, including illegal detentions, improper trials, torture, and executions. The failure of the Palestinian security services after Oslo is largely attributable to other flaws within the PA. Primarily, "the absence of an effective control by an identifiable institution led to the excessive manipulation of responsibilities by members and leaders of these organizations." To be sure, "the security services effectively answered to the president regardless of the content of the Basic Law. When Arafat was president, he encouraged multiple security services but declined to draw clear divisions of responsibilities among them."

This resulted in a lack of order and organization, lack of mandate, lack of professionalism, and consequently, lack of legitimacy. Indeed, over a dozen security organizations were operating under Arafat, and none of them proved effective in providing either internal or external security. As Brown suggests, "the myriad layers of overlapping forces and command structures need to be replaced with a consolidated and transparent organization with clear lines of command to a democratically accountable official or set of officials."

The president should still have some involvement, but other executive branch officials should include members of the Ministry of the Interior. Furthermore, the PLC should be involved by finishing the draft of the legal framework for the security services' operation, as well as by examining the security budget. In addition to these top-down measures, reforms need to occur directly within the security services, first through consolidation and re-organization, and also through improved trainings.

Specifically, security personnel trainings should be infused with human rights training, and ideally, should take place in conjunction with local human rights organizations. This model is helpful for facilitating a professional ethos within the security services; that is, "their training should focus not only on developing technical expertise but also on fostering a sense of what security services should not do."

*Steps should also be taken to establish a multi-level system of monitoring and accountability, including*:

- A system for security personnel and officers to report human rights abuses and violations;
- A procedure for families to appeal for investigations;
- A joint investigative body at the local level consisting of senior and junior security officers, human rights activists, and jurists to review cases of abuse allegations;
- A stronger Committee on Human Rights within the PLC;
- A stronger PICCR or similar ombudsman institution. Some reforms have already taken place under Abu Mazen, but the process of security reform will inevitably be long and complex. Nevertheless, "Palestinian reform will clearly be moving forward if the Ministry of Interior exercises real oversight, if the PLC passes a set of laws governing security forces, and if the regular reporting of human rights groups and other NGOs suggests that the security forces are more respectful of the limits to their authority."

**Civil Society**

As discussed above, democracy depends largely on the presence of a vibrant civil society. In Palestine, the presence of a strong civil society can be considered one of the most promising assets for the development of a sustainable democracy. Numerous civil organizations have existed since the early years of the occupation, essentially "keeping the country going before the PA, and still very active" after Oslo and during the present period.

Dajani notes that, in Palestine, "in the absence of a state and central government, and without any formal, centrally organized political socialization via schools, the media, religion, friends or family, people began to organize themselves in civil groups—which subsequently became known as NGOs—and took over the role of a government."

These organizations have assumed a variety of roles and duties, including the provision of social services, political activism, human rights monitoring, education and advocacy, media and outreach, and others. Civil society groups have thus taken a number of forms, such as women's groups, media outlets, trade unions, human rights groups, religious groups, etc. While duplication, and at times, competition, are inevitable, many civil society organizations collaborate with each other and complement each others' work, and over 90 organizations belong to the Palestinian NGO Network, an umbrella group that seeks to support, strengthen, and consolidate Palestinian civil society.

Organizations that focus on women's rights and empowerment are especially important for ensuring the viability of a sustainable democracy. As Feidy explains, a strong Palestinian women's movement has existed since the 1920s, and women have been active in civil society throughout Palestinian history. However, women have been largely marginalized under the PA, with the old guard seeking to limit the participation of both women and youth.

Alami, the women's agenda has lagged at times because many active women believe that political activism against the occupation deserves more attention than the women's movement, although one cannot really separate one agenda from the other. Indeed, if women are to have an impact politically, they need to have the rights and access to participation. As Giacaman stated, "Equality is central to democracy."

In addition to political marginalization, women also face challenges related to employment, education, violence, early marriage, and inheritance rights. Many Palestinian Muslim women also confront unique issues related to certain interpretations of Islam. The range of challenges related to women has resulted in a variety of responses by different civil society groups. Some focus on advocating for legal reform, such as the establishment of a quota to ensure a certain percentage of local or PLC seats are reserved for women, while others focus more on assisting female candidates and encouraging women to run for office or to vote for candidates who are female or who support women's rights.

Other groups focus on making women aware of their civil and political rights through trainings, workshops, and conferences. As Musalim explains of his work with PCPD, "We are not speaking for people; rather, we empower people to speak on behalf of themselves. People have listened too long. They need to use their own voices now." This approach is especially important for women's empowerment. An obvious institution for channeling these voices is the media, and indeed, newspapers and media outlets are important institutions within Palestinian civil society. A strong foundation exists in Palestine for a free press; just as to Brown, "the basis for independent media that can facilitate reform [in Palestine] is solid." To be sure, the majority of media outlets in Palestine are privately owned, in contrast to the state-controlled media that dominates in some other parts of the Arab world and elsewhere.

Similarly, despite noted attempts by some PA officials to constrict discourse on certain topics such as Islamist parties, or certain stories, such as internal discord, the PA never fully stifled public expression. Nevertheless, there is still much room for improvement. Palestinian journalists should thus continue to build on their sound foundation of free media institutions to ensure that the media can function as a viable institution in a substantive democracy. Journalists and media outlets are not the only groups focusing on media concerns. Many organizations that advocate for democracy and reform are embracing media issues, as well as women's rights, as key areas of concentration for their work, under the larger goal of promoting democracy and working towards the development of sustainable institutions.

Some of the leading democracy organizations include MIFTAH, which focuses on democracy, human rights, gender equity, and participatory governance; Muwatin, which initiates intellectual debate on democratic issues and options; PCPD, which promotes human rights, tolerance, participation, accountability, empowerment, and rule of law; and Civic Forum Institute, which aims to increase citizens' awareness of democratic concepts and institutions and develop civil society institutions. This list is not intended to be exhaustive, but rather is meant to provide brief insight into the types of organizations that currently exist in the area of democracy advocacy. Civil society is just one vital aspect of a participatory democracy, in which citizens are active participants in their government and communities, rather than just passive recipients. It should be noted that democratic participation can take many forms, including voting, holding public office, volunteering a service, writing letters to officials and/or newspapers, participating in marches, protests, and other forms of direct activism, and countless others. It is not the objective of this document to evaluate the impact of various forms of participation; rather, it is to recognize the importance of citizen agency. Perhaps the best indication of the potential for participatory democracy in Palestine was the early years of the first intifada, which saw widespread popular participation of different forms.

Though the nonviolent "people power" strategies employed during that time have yet to be duplicated on the same scale, the spirit of that period is evident in the willingness of the people to express their opinions and voice their criticisms of both the PA and Israel. Participatory democracy, and thus civil society, are both inputs and outputs of human rights. First of all, as an output, the emergence of civil society depends on the rights to freedom of thought, opinion, and expression, the right to assembly and association, and the right to participation and service in government or country.

As an input, many civil society groups adopt missions that help to ensure economic, social, and cultural rights such as access to social services like food, clothing, housing, and medical care, education, and human security and others focus on securing civil and political rights. In addition, human rights organizations in particular, as a part of civil society, play an important role in monitoring and documenting human rights violations and advocating for the protection of rights.

**Assessment of Democracy and Human Rights in Palestine**

Foundations clearly exist in Palestine for the emergence of a substantive democracy, but the process still has far to go. A helpful way of conceptualizing Palestine's current level of democracy is the transition theory, advocated by Dankwart Rustow. This theory, democratic development occurs in four main stages: "a stage when a national unity is being established; a preparatory phase of prolonged and inconclusive political struggle; a decision phase when a historical movement of choosing a democratic path is taken; and a habituation phase witnessing a consolidation of democracy."

In the case of Palestine, a national unity has long been established, and one might consider the post-Oslo period and second intifada to be periods of prolonged struggle. It is possible that, at present, Palestine is transitioning into the third stage, embarking upon a path of decision to work deliberately towards democracy. Most democracy advocates interviewed agreed, suggesting that Palestine is in a middle stage, on the way to democracy. It is thus important at this stage to identify obstacles that prevent Palestine from fully realising a substantive democracy.

First, it should be noted that any transition to democracy is a long, slow process. In the case of Palestine, there have also been additional setbacks in the form of clashes in reform visions, both internally and between internal and external actors. Another obstacle is the persistence of the old guard, who continue to occupy many key positions. The past six months have seen hope for progress in both of these areas however, with the election of Abu Mazen. The new president has committed himself to reform, and in doing so has reconciled differences between international and domestic agendas, and has opened up the PA and Fatah to be more transparent and accountable.

As Brown notes however, "the primary obstacle to further Palestinian reform lies in the international context: Political reform is difficult in the midst of an ongoing conflict." Specifically, it is not possible to establish a substantive democracy under occupation. Unfortunately, international actors like the United States have to date have "approached diplomacy and reform as sequential rather than interdependent... [though] it is precisely the mutual dependence of reform and peace that make both so difficult achieve." To be sure, the "peace now, democracy later" philosophy of Oslo proved to be ineffectual and perhaps even detrimental, and it is doubtful that the current logic of "democracy now, peace later" will be any different. As Brown notes, it is futile to build "public institutions that are expected to establish authority and accountability while placing them in a context of extremely limited autonomy."

Perhaps a better way to conceptualize the peace and democracy equation is to integrate the variable of human rights. As has been discussed in this document, democracy is necessary for human rights, and human rights are necessary for democracy.

Likewise, a real just peace cannot exist unless peace is integrated with the protection of human rights. Because human rights is thus a common variable to both peace and democracy, it makes sense to focus on the human rights framework when pursuing both diplomacy and institution-building. Only when human rights and democracy are pursued simultaneously will either be achieved, and it is only then that a just peace will be possible.

Human rights and liberal democracy are not merely complementary, rather, they are interdependent. A democracy that is substantive as well as procedural cannot function without human rights, just as human rights, meaning civil, political, economic, social, and cultural rights, cannot be ensured in the absence of democracy. In the case of Palestine, a foundation exists for both the realisation of human rights and the development of a substantive democracy, but both internal and external factors have hindered the building of viable institutions to actualize those ideals.

Greater attention thus needs to be given to the development of mechanisms such as elections, political parties, and separation of powers, and the restructuring of institutions including the judiciary branch and security sector. Despite the absence of these institutions to date, the will and perseverance of the Palestinian people, through both civil society and direct participation, has continued to push forward the democracy and human rights movements. Thus, attention must be given to these bottom-up efforts of popular participation, in addition to the top-down efforts of institution-building, if a liberal democracy is to be established. To be sure, no amount of institutional reform will be sustainable if it does not develop in tandem with popular will and public participation. For this reason, it is necessary for civil society organizations and actors to continue to facilitate political participation and raise public awareness, and it is imperative that individuals and communities seize opportunities to demonstrate their will. Media institutions in particular can play a key role in this process by serving as a means of popular communication, education, and mobilization. The human rights framework can be helpful for developing direction and coordination for these efforts, and can integrate the distinct yet interdependent ideals of peace and justice, and human rights and democracy.

## EDUCATION

The right to education is recognized as a human right by the United Nations and is understood to establish an entitlement to free, compulsory primary education for all children, an obligation to develop secondary education accessible to all children, as well as equitable access to higher education, and a responsibility to provide basic education for individuals who have not completed primary education. In addition to these access to education provisions the right to education encompasses also the obligation to eliminate discrimination at all levels of the educational system, to set minimum standards and to improve quality.

The right to education is enshrined in Article 26 of the Universal Declaration of Human Rights and Article 14 of the International Covenant on Economic, Social and Cultural Rights. The right to education has also been reaffirmed in the 1960 UNESCO Convention against Discrimination in Education, 1st Protocol of ECHR and the 1981 Convention on the Elimination of All Forms of Discrimination Against Women. The right to education may also include the right to freedom of education. Education narrowly refers to formal institutional instructions. Generally, international instruments use the term in this sense and the right to education, as protected by international human rights instruments, refers primarily to education in a narrow sense.

The 1960 UNESCO Convention against Discrimination in Education defines education in Article 1(2) as: "all types and levels of education, (including) access to education, the standard and quality of education, and the conditions under which it is given." In a wider sense education may describe "all activities by which a human group transmits to its descendants a body of knowledge and skills and a moral code which enable the group to subsist".

In this sense education refers to the transmission to a subsequent generation of those skills needed to perform tasks of daily living, and further passing on the social, cultural, spiritual and philosophical values of the particular community. The wider meaning of education has been recognised in Article 1(a) of UNESCO's 1974 Recommendation concerning Education for International Understanding, Co-operation and Peace and Education relating to Human Rights and Fundamental Freedoms. The article states that education implies: "the entire process of social life by means of which individuals and social groups learn to develop consciously within, and for the benefit of, the national and international communities, the whole of their personal capabilities, attitudes, aptitudes and knowledge."

The European Court of Human Rights has defined education in a narrow sense as "teaching or instructions... in particular to the transmission of knowledge and to intellectual development" and in a wider sense as "the whole process whereby, in any society, adults endeavour to transmit their beliefs, culture and other values to the young."

## FULFILLING THE RIGHT TO EDUCATION

The fulfilment of the right to education can be assessed using the 4 As framework, which asserts that for education to be a meaningful right it must be available, accessible, acceptable and adaptable. The 4 As framework was developed by the former UN Special Rapporteur on the Right to Education, Katarina Tomasevski, but is not necessarily the standard used in every international human rights instrument and hence not a generic guide to how the right to education is treated under national law.

The 4 As framework proposes that governments, as the prime duty-bearer, has to respect, protect and fulfil the right to education by making education available, accessible, acceptable and adaptable. The framework also places duties on other stakeholders in the education process: the child, which as the privileged subject of the right to education has the duty to comply with compulsory education requirements, the parents as the 'first educators', and professional educators, namely teachers.

*The 4 As have been further elaborated as follows*:

- *Availability*: Education is free and government-funded and there is adequate infrastructure and trained teachers able to support education delivery.
- *Accessibility*: The system is non-discriminatory and accessible to all, and positive steps are taken to include the most marginalised.
- *Acceptability*: The content of education is relevant, non-discriminatory and culturally appropriate, and of quality. The school itself is safe and teachers are professional.
- *Adaptability*: Education can evolve with the changing needs of society and contribute to challenging inequalities, such as gender discrimination, and can be adapted locally to suit specific contexts.

A number of international NGOs and charities work to realise the right to education using a rights-based approach to development.

## DEVELOPMENT OF THE RIGHT TO EDUCATION

In Europe, before the Enlightenment of the eighteenth and nineteenth century, education was the responsibility of parents and the church. With the French and American Revolution education was established also as a public function. It was thought that the state, by assuming a more active role in the sphere of education, could help to make education available and accessible to all. Education had thus far been primarily available to the upper social classes and public education was perceived as a means of realising the egalitarian ideals underlining both revolutions. However, neither the

American Declaration of Independence (1776) nor the French Declaration of the Rights of Man (1789) protected the right to education as the liberal concepts of human rights in the nineteenth century envisaged that parents retained the primary duty for providing education to their children. It was the states obligation to ensure that parents complied with this duty, and many states enacted legislation making school attendance compulsory.

Furthermore child labour laws were enacted to limit the number of hours per day children could be employed, to ensure children would attend school. States also became involved in the legal regulation of curricula and established minimum educational standards. In On Liberty John Stuart Mill wrote that an "education established and controlled by the State should only exist, if it exists at all, as one among many competing experiments, carried on for the purpose of example and stimulus to keep the others up to a certain standard of excellence."

Liberal thinkers of the nineteenth century pointed to the dangers to too much state involvement in the sphere of education, but relied on state intervention to reduce the dominance of the church, and to protect the right to education of children against their own parents. In the latter half of the nineteenth century, educational rights were included in domestic bills of rights. The 1849 Paulskirchenverfassung, the constitution of the German Empire, strongly influenced subsequent European constitutions and devoted Article 152 to 158 of its bill of rights to education. The constitution recognised education as a function of the state, independent of the church. Remarkable at the time, the constitution proclaimed the right to free education for the poor, but the constitution did not explicitly require the state to set up educational institutions. Instead the constitution protected the rights of citizens to found and operate schools and to provide home education. The constitution also provided for freedom of science and teaching, and it guaranteed the right of everybody to choose a vocation and train for it.

The nineteenth century also saw the development of socialist theory, which held that the primary task of the state was to ensure the economic and social well-being of the community through government intervention and regulation. Socialist theory recognised that individuals had claims to basic welfare services against the state and education was viewed as one of these welfare entitlements. This was in contrast to liberal theory at the time, which regarded non-state actors as the prime providers of education.

Socialist ideals were enshrined in the 1936 Soviet Constitution, which was the first constitution to recognise the right to education with a corresponding obligation of the state to provide such education. The constitution guaranteed free and compulsory education at all levels, a system of state scholarships and vocational training in state enterprises. Subsequently the right to education featured strongly in the constitutions of socialist states. As a political goal, right to education was declared in F. D. Roosevelt's 1944 speech on the Second Bill of Rights.

## IMPLEMENTATION

International law does not protect the right to pre-primary education and international documents generally omit references to education at this level. The Universal Declaration of Human Rights states that "everybody" has the right to education, hence the right accures to all individuals, although children are understood as the main beneficiaries.

*The rights to education are separated into three levels*:

- Primary (Elemental or Fundamental) Education. This shall be compulsory and free for any child regardless of their nationality, gender, place of birth, or any other discrimination. Upon ratifying the International Covenant on Economic, Social and Cultural Rights States must provide free primary education within two years.
- Secondary Education must be generally available and accessible.
- Higher Education (at the University Level) should be provided just as to capacity. That is, anyone who meets the necessary education standards should be able to go to university.

Both secondary and higher education shall be made accessible "by every appropriate means, and in particular by the progressive introduction of free education". The only country that has declared reservations about introducing free secondary or higher education is Japan.

### Role of the State

Today education is considered an important public function and the state is seen as the chief provider of education through the allocation of substantial budgetary resources and regulating the provision of education. The pre-eminent role of the state in fulfilling the right to education is enshrined in the 1966 International Covenant on Economic, Social and Cultural Rights. Traditionally, education has been the duty of a child's parents, however with the rise of systems of education, the role of parents has diminished. With regards to realising the right to education the World Declaration on Education for All, adopted at the 1990 World Conference on Education for All states that "partnerships between government and non-governmental organisations, the private sector, local communities, religious groups, and families" are necessary.

### Compulsory Education

The realisation of the right to education on a national level may be achieved through compulsory education, or more specifically free compulsory primary education, as stated in both the Universal Declaration of Human Rights and the International Covenant on Economic, Social and Cultural Rights.

## ANTI-HOMELESSNESS LEGISLATION

Anti-homelessness legislation can take two forms; legislation that aims to help and re-house homeless people, and legislation that is intended to criminalize homelessness and/or send the homeless to homeless shelters compulsively.

## INTERNATIONAL LAW

Since the publication of the Universal Declaration of Human Rights (Charter of the United Nations — UN) in 1948, the public perception has been increasingly changing to a focus on the human right to housing, travel and migration as a part of individual self-determination rather than the human condition.

The Declaration, an international law reinforcement of the Nuremberg Trial Judgements, upholds the rights of one nation to intervene in the affairs of another if said nation is abusing its citizens, and rose out of a 1939–1945 World War II Atlantic environment of extreme split between "haves" and "have nots." The modern study of homeless phenomena is most frequently seen in this historical context.

## LAWS SUPPORTING THE HOMELESS

Laws supporting homeless people generally place obligations on the state to support or house homeless people.

### Scotland

The Scottish parliament passed the Homelessness Etc (Scotland) Act 2003 which has an aim of ensuring that by 2012 everyone assessed as being unintentionally homeless will be entitled to permanent accommodation. In addition, the Homeless Persons (Unsuitable Accommodation) (Scotland) Order came into force in December 2004 and requires councils to ensure that pregnant women and households with children are not placed in unsuitable temporary accommodation, unless there are exceptional circumstances.

### United States

The charter of the McKinney-Vento Homeless Assistance Act of 1986 (Stewart B. McKinney Homeless Assistance Act) is to "coordinate the Federal response to homelessness and to create partnerships between the Federal agencies addressing homelessness and every level of government and every element of the private sector".

## LAWS CRIMINALIZING THE HOMELESS

*Use of the law that criminalizes the homeless generally takes on one of four forms*:

- Restricting the public areas in which sitting or sleeping are allowed.
- Removing the homeless from particular areas.
- Prohibiting begging.
- Enforcing laws on the homeless and not on those who are not homeless. (The French novelist Anatole France noted this

phenomenon as long ago as 1894, famously observing that "the law, in its majestic equality, forbids the rich as well as the poor to sleep under bridges".)

**England and Wales**

The Vagrancy Act 1824 makes it an offence to sleep on the streets or to beg. In essence, therefore, it is a crime in England and Wales to be homeless or to cadge subsistence money. When the Act was passed, criticism of it centred on the fact that it created a catch-all offence. To sleep on the streets or to beg subsistence became a crime, whatever reason an individual might have had for being in such a predicament. That provision still pertains today in England and Wales. So far as it extended to Scotland, it was repealed by the Civic Government (Scotland) Act 1982.

## COMMUNICATION RIGHTS

Rights relating to communication have been central to the concept of universal human rights emerging in the mid-20th century, and its consolidation in the United Nations Charter and the Universal Declaration of Human Rights (UDHR). But Jean d'Arcy is generally credited with being the first to explicitly make the case for a "right to communicate" In 1969, then Director of Radio and Visual Services in the UN Office of Public Information, he wrote: "The time will come when the (UDHR) will have to encompass a more extensive right than man's right to information, first laid down 21 years ago in Article 19. This is the right of man to communicate. It is the angle from which the future development of communications will have to be considered if it is to be fully understood".

### INTERGOVERNMENTAL PLATFORMS: NWICO, UNESCO, AND THE MACBRIDE COMMISSION

The issue was catapulted to the forefront of geopolitics soon after. Soon the idea of a "right to communicate"was at the centre of an international diplomatic row that lasted several years the debate over what became known as a New World Information and Communication Order - NWICO. Against a backdrop of the emergent role of media and communication, many countries became seriously concerned at the impact on national identity, ¬cultural ¬integrity, and political and economic sovereignty. NWICO, spearheaded by the Non-Aligned Movement (NAM) of UN countries focused on:

- The "free flow" doctrine of information flow, which was reinforcing the dominance of western media and news content;
- The growing concentration of the media and communication industry translating into more foreign ownership of media in smaller and poorer countries;
- How the growing importance of western-controlled technologies to media production and dissemination was making it difficult for others to keep up.

As the only UN body equipped to debate in a coherent manner the range of issues raised, the battle would primarily be staged at UNESCO, where it would stay for a decade. From 1973, the NAM was developing a much more sophisticated plan for a New World Information Order. At the 1976 UNESCO General Assembly, the wide gulf between NAM and western countries (USA, UK and others) became apparent. A showdown was avoided only by the creation of an International Commission for the Study of Communication Problems, generally called the MacBride Commission after its Chair, Seán MacBride. The MacBride Commission's report to the 1980 General Assembly, "Many Voices One World", bore the hallmarks of a fractious political process, fudging many issues and containing numerous caveats. But it was comprehensive (with a notable weakness in relation to gender) and wide-ranging, and came with concrete recommendations, including: "Communication needs in a democratic society should be met by the extension of specific rights such as the right to be informed, the right to inform, the right to privacy, the right to participate in public communication - all elements of a new concept, the right to communicate.

In developing what might be called a new era of social rights, we suggest all the implications of the right to communicate be further explored." For the first time, the NWICO had a general framework, a detailed justification, a set of proposals, and a unifying concept - the "right to communicate". Eventually the Commission's findings were endorsed-a defining moment for NWICO, but one which was short-lived. The veneer of agreement was thin; instead of bringing the sides together, the process merely exposed the gulf between them and entrenched the positions, especially of West governments mired within Cold War geo-politics. The USA led a "counter-offensive" on UNESCO, supported strongly by the private media industry and lobbies. The main charge was that less developed countries were attempting to impose government control of media, and to suppress freedom of the press - despite the fact that press freedom was strongly endorsed at every turn by NWICO. The US (in 1984) and UK (in 1985) eventually withdrew from UNESCO, partly due to NWICO.

While the newly politicised "information society" was becoming ascendant, NWICO in its original form had declined. It did manage to stay on the UNESCO agenda, though with little action, until 1987. With the "New Communication Strategy" under new UNESCO Director-General Federico Mayor in 1989, it basically died out. Yet the arguments that animated the NWICO movement continued, and even in some respects became sharper. The arguments continued to surface in new calls-outside of governments this time - for "communication rights".

## BEYOND NWICO: CIVIL SOCIETY ENGAGEMENTS

For many, the main session from NWICO was that the way forward would have to be through the democratization of media and communication, rather than through state - or industry - led efforts to create new global orders. In practice, a major shift was needed towards civil society, which had so far been largely excluded. Those that had been involved - mainly journalists' organizations and some academics -continued debating in the form of the MacBride Round Table, which met annually from 1989 to 1999, and brought new civil society actors into the discussion. A growing number of NGOs, some quite independent of previous debates and largely unaware of them (and often of each other), also began to question trends in media, knowledge, and communication.

These included community media associations, faith-based organizations, international trade unions, emerging Internet NGOs, and advocacy groups springing up to address diverse issues (*e.g.*, internet surveillance, concentration of media ownership, commercial censorship, copyright and patent excesses). These were now set alongside more traditional concerns of government censorship and controls. The growing significance of digital technologies and the emergence of the Internet also provided new arguments for democratization, as existing social contradictions manifested themselves in so-called "digital divides". New arenas opened up where traditional and emerging advocacies could converge. As was its strength, civil society let its praxis on the ground and advocacies on national and regional arenas dictate the discourse, although initiatives were not labelled "communication rights" work at the time. However, a history of the Communication Rights movement "from below", would probably include various threads of activism: the telecentre movement, Free/Open Source Software (FOSS) communities, independent media centres, gender-based organizations in communications, local content/local language advocates, nonprofit ISPs - all empowered by new networking tools and technologies. These formations - supported by sympathetic donor institutions and academics - evolved independently and sharpened critiques of new information/communication hierarchies.

By the 1990s, various coalitions were formed and initiatives taken to address the larger picture underlying many of these concerns, among them the People's Communication Charter and the Platform for Democratization of Communication. Many broad-based conferences and meetings were held to pull the threads together and exchange understanding internationally. Gradually a new civil society-based constituency was emerging, but now from a different perspective and benefiting from historical experience and on-the-ground praxis. Many of these coalesced in October 2001 into the Campaign for Communication Rights in the Information Society (CRIS Campaign), at the ¬onset of another global governance arena of struggle - the World Summit on the Information Society (WSIS).

## THE "RIGHT TO COMMUNICATE" AND "COMMUNI CATION RIGHTS"

The terms "right to communicate" and "communication rights" are not synonymous, and history, principle and tactics are bound in their usage by different groups. As we have seen, the term "right to communicate" became associated with a (mis)reading of the NWICO promoted by its opponents. Even today, in the context of the WSIS, some claim that attempts to promote a "right to communicate" are merely veiled efforts to revive the NWICO.

For these opponents, the idea of "communication rights" as distinct from a "right to communicate", is more difficult to criticize since it leaves behind the connotations of NWICO. At the political level, there also have been calls for the creation of a new right under international law. This would build on the existing international legal framework, establishing a "right to communicate" as an unambiguous right of all people. This position clearly recognizes that many existing human rights are key components of this, but that an explicit "right to communicate" would both bolster these, conceptually and on the ground. However, the specifics of this right, its precise wording, in what legal form it would be incorporated and so forth, have not been fully teased out. On the other hand, the term "communication rights", in a plural form, implicitly points towards existing rights that relate to communication. The emphasis shifts subtly to realising the existing communication rights on the ground, not on establishing a new global covenant. Calling for the realisation of communication rights, and reaffirming that everyone has - or should have - a right to communicate, are entirely complementary.

The "right to communicate" can be used as an informal rallying cry for advocacy, while it can also be used in a formal legal sense, in which it should take its place alongside other fundamental rights enshrined in international law. "Communication rights" relates immediately to a set of existing human rights, that are denied many people, and whose full meaning can only be realised when they are considered together as an interrelated group. The CRIS Campaign is the most articulated global civil society alliance that seeks to promote the concept and praxis of communication rights. But beyond this formation, many others have adopted the term in various platforms.

A "right to communicate" was strongly endorsed at several points by influential actors during the WSIS process. The issue gained some prominence, although efforts to discredit it, and the fear of controversy, were probably responsible for its exclusion from the final text. UN Secretary-General Kofi Annan stated that: "millions of people in the poorest countries are still excluded from the "right to communicate", increasingly seen as a fundamental human right." And the European Commission noted: "The Summit should reinforce the right to communicate and to access information and knowledge." Other key NGOs not members of the CRIS Campaign have also endorsed it. Article 19, in its overview of the right to communicate, describes it as: "an umbrella term, encompassing within it a group of related, existing rights. This means that any elaboration of the right to communicate must take place within the framework of existing rights."

## COMMUNICATION RIGHTS VIZ. "FREEDOM OF EXPRESSION"

"Freedom of expression" ranks among the sacrosanct foundations of all human rights. It is contained in numerous international Treaties and Conventions, and enshrined in varying formulations in virtually all national constitutions and legislation. The most frequently cited reference is to Article 19 of the UDHR:

- "Everyone has the right to freedom of opinion and expression; this right includes the freedom to hold opinions without interference and to seek, receive and impart information and ideas through any media and regardless of frontiers."

### Is Freedom of Expression Enough?

The question facing communication rights advocates is why anything more than "freedom of expression" is needed. Furthermore, given that such a basic right is still denied to many in practice, surely our energies should focus on securing freedom of expression for all? Would securing freedom of expression in effect secure communication rights? The ideal from which freedom of expression draws its legitimacy assumes a group of communicating individuals, each with an equal right to conceive, impart and receive ideas from others, and thereby to rationally arrive at decisions of mutual benefit. The trouble with this is that we do not live as a group of equally empowered individuals.

We live in a society of hugely varying levels of access to power, a society in which most communication between people is heavily mediated and filtered - with mass media, governments, commercial corporations, special interest groups and many others all vying for attention, seeking to influence and control the content and flow of communications. An exclusive insistence on freedom of expression says nothing about the process by which society's means of expression - newspapers, television, radio, films, music and educational material - are controlled, and in whose interests they operate.

In this context, freedom of expression - in the sense of laws to prevent direct government interference and to defend free speech - can do little to prevent the domination of the loudest voices, *i.e.*, those who can most strongly influence the means of communication within society, whether they are the government, newspaper proprietors and media owners, or powerful interest groups. In this example, how real is the "freedom to receive and impart information" if one can hardly read nor write, or cannot speak the official language of the country? Or how real is freedom to "seek and receive information" if governments and corporations are not obliged to provide it? Or if you cannot afford to pay for educational materials, or access key means of communication such as telephony or (increasingly) the Internet? If you know your communications means are being spied on? These are symptoms of unequal access to power, of a world in which communication is possible only increasingly through complex and contested media and mechanisms. Thus a key challenge for freedom of expression advocates is the conceptual shift from the idea of equal individuals, to a complex and variegated society with heavily mediated communication and various and differential configurations of power. Tackling this requires an additional set of concepts and instruments, which is at the core of "communication rights" discourse.

## FRAMING "COMMUNICATION RIGHTS"

Communication rights can be seen as providing the conditions for the full exercise of freedom of expression in a complex and mediated society in which power and control of resources are distributed very unevenly. freedom of expression is indeed at the heart of Communication rights. However, the advocacy for Communication rights goes further in that it creates the environment in which freedom of expression may be fully consummated at the level of society. Communication rights are premised on communicating, the completion of an interaction between people; it maintains that freedom to interact with others is ultimately about generating a cycle of communication, from which learning, understanding and cooperation may ensue.

An initial approximation of the goal of Communication Rights is thus: to secure the generation of a considered, creative and respectful cycle of interaction between people and groups in society, that in practice endorses the right of all equally to have their ideas expressed, heard, listened to, considered and responded to.

## ENABLING RIGHTS

Communication Rights draw on aspects of other key human rights - "flanking" or "enabling" rights - contained in the International Bill of Rights and supplementary treaties and legal documents.

*For example*:

- A right to participate in one's own culture, and use one's mother language, including ethnic, religious or linguistic minorities;
- A right to information regarding governance and matters of public interest (freedom of information);
- A right to information regarding governance and matters of public interest (freedom of information);
- A right to the protection of the moral and material interests of authorship;
- A right to one's honour and reputation, and to protection against attacks;
- A right to privacy;
- A right to peaceful assembly and association;
- A right to free primary education and progressive introduction of free secondary education.

A dimension of each of these bears strongly on the process of communication in society (all could be suffixed with "in relation to media and communication"). These might be termed "top-level" communication rights. However, they are further specified and sometimes additional dimensions added. For example: the right to a diverse and independent media and to access to media, has been recognized in various fora as diverse as the European Court of Human Rights, Supreme Court of Sri Lanka, the German Federal Constitutional Court, UNESCO, and Resolutions of the Council of the European Union. The promotion of communication rights attempts to strip away layers of social, historical, economic, and psychological barriers to communication, to reinforce an environment of mutual respect, and to build the capacities of all in communication and interaction.

**The Added Value of Communication Rights**

This interpretation of communication rights has a number of implications. First, the whole set of communication rights yields something more than the sum of its parts. Communication rights bring together relevant dimensions from a set of component enabling rights, and can be realised only through them. However, Communication rights can also be seen as meta rights, which gives new and additional meaning to those enabling rights. Second, the emergence of communication rights in practice is the creation of a climate of mutual respect and tolerance not just between individuals which hold these rights, but between diverse communities and cultures, ethnic groups and nationalities.

Calling for communication rights at the same time endorses and supports the notion and value of diversity. Third, communication rights unavoidably implicate social processes and dynamics. Communication rights by their very nature question whether social structures differentially constrain and enable the capacity of different individuals and groups to communicate effectively within societies. The concept of communication rights forces us to engage much more comprehensively the spirit of "freedom of expression" towards the elimination of constraints on whole parts of society, and building the access and capacities of those who are excluded.

## COMMUNICATION RIGHTS: WHY NOW?

Why is it that "communication rights" as a concept is especially relevant now more than it was in the past? What justifies a movement at this time to attempt to enforce and deepen our communication rights?

Communication rights have greatly grown in relevance in the last decades, due to a number of factors and trends in the sphere of global information and communications, including:

- Corporate media dominance and media concentration;
- Emergence of "copyright" regimes and the erosion of the public domain of global knowledge;

- Erosion of civil rights in the digital environment, especially post 9-11 (*e.g.*, stronger comprehensive and globally-framed and enforced frameworks for electronic surveillance).
- Limitations of market-driven initiatives in telecommunications and ICTs;
- Negative effects of media systems on identity/ies and culture/s;

All of these concerns can be analysed and understood, and integral solutions designed, using the concept of communi-cation rights. Together, these dynamics hugely influence each step of the communication process in society. These trends can fundamentally shape the outcomes of social communication and who benefits from it, through controlling the creation and ownership of knowledge, the processes and media of dissemination and communication, and its use to solve political, economic, and social goals.

The imminent danger is that each moment in the cycle is becoming harnessed to the needs of capital and the market. The ultimate danger is that the cycle of society's social communication process is interrupted, the process of social learning becomes ever more feeble, and in the end the process of creativity is transformed and reduced to short-term, unsustainable, generation of profits for a small minority. Society may find itself having virtually lost the capacity for creativity, for an inclusive and equitable sharing of knowledge, for democratic participation in political structures, for diverse cultural expression and expression of identity, even the capacity to learn from past and present generations. "Communication rights", as a concept and as praxis, potentially have the depth and breadth to analyse and understand these dangers, and design integral solutions designed to tackle them.

## RIGHT TO COMMUNICATE VS. COMMUNICATION RIGHTS

A 'right to communicate' and 'communication rights' are closely related, but not identical, in their history and usage. In the Cold War tensions of the 1970s and 80s, the former became associated with the New World Information and Communication Order (NWICO) debate, thus, efforts within UNESCO to formulate such a right were abandoned. The latter emphasizes the fact that an array of international rights underpinning communication already exists, but many are too often ignored and require active mobilisation and assertion. While some, especially within the mass media sector, still see the right to communicate as a "code word" for state censorship, the technological innovations in interactive electronic, global communication of recent decades are seen by others as challenging the tradtional mass media structures and formulations of communication rights values arising from them, thereby renewing the need to re-consider the need for a right to communicate. These issues are explored more fully in Raboy's and Shtern,s Media Divides: Communication rights and the right to communicate in Canada (2010).

## CONSUMER/SURVIVOR/EX-PATIENT MOVEMENT

The Consumer/Survivor/Ex-Patient Movement, also known as the User/Survivor Movement, is a diverse association of individuals (and organizations representing them) who are either currently "consumers" (clients) of mental health services, or who consider themselves survivors of psychiatry or mental health services, or who simply identify as "ex-patients" of mental health services. The movement typically campaigns for more choice and improved services, and/or empowerment and user-led alternatives, and against prejudice in society more generally. Common themes are "talking back to the power of psychiatry", rights protection and advocacy, and self-determination.

While activists in this movement may share a collective identity, individuals can be seen as enacting their concerns along a continuum from conservative to radical, just as to their position in relation to psychiatric treatment and their relative levels of resistance and patienthood. This can in turn relate to an individual's experiences of the mental health system, particularly if subject to forced detention and/or forced medication, electroshock or other practice. The modern self-help and advocacy movement in the field of mental health services developed in the 1970s, but former psychiatric patients have been campaigning for centuries to change laws, treatments, services and public policies.

"The most persistent critics of psychiatry have always been former mental hospital patients", although few were able to tell their stories publicly or to openly confront the psychiatric establishment, and those who did so were commonly considered so extreme in their charges that they could seldom gain credibility. In 1620 in England, patients of the notoriously harsh Bethlem Hospital banded together and sent a "Petition of the Poor Distracted People in the House of Bedlam (concerned with conditions for inmates)" to the House of Lords. A number of ex-patients published pamphlets against the system in the 18th century, such as Samuel Bruckshaw (1774), on the "iniquitous abuse of private madhouses", and William Belcher (1796) with his "Address to humanity, Containing a letter to Dr Munro, a receipt to make a lunatic, and a sketch of a true smiling hyena".

Such reformist efforts were generally opposed by madhouse keepers and medics. In the late 18th century, moral treatment reforms developed which were originally based in part on the approach of French ex-patient turned hospital-superintendent Jean-Baptiste Pussin and his wife Margueritte. From 1848 in England, the Alleged Lunatics' Friend Society campaigned for sweeping reforms to the asylum system and abuses of the moral treatment approach. In the United States, The Opal (1851-1860) was a ten volume Journal produced by patients of Utica State Lunatic Asylum in New York, which has been viewed in part as an early liberation movement. Beginning in 1868, Elizabeth Packard, founder of the Anti-Insane Asylum Society, published a series of books and pamphlets describing her experiences in the Illinois insane asylum to which her husband had had her committed. A few decades later, another former psychiatric patient, Clifford W. Beers, founded the National Committee on Mental Hygiene, which eventually became the National Mental Health Association. Beers sought to improve the plight of individuals receiving public psychiatric care, particularly those committed to state institutions. His book, A Mind that Found Itself (1908), described his experience with mental illness and the treatment he encountered in mental hospitals.

Beers' work stimulated public interest in more responsible care and treatment. However, while Beers initially damned psychiatrists for tolerating mistreatment of patients, and envisioned more ex-patient involvement in the movement, he was influenced by Adolf Meyer and the psychiatric establishment, and toned down his hostility as he needed their support for reforms. His reliance on rich donors and his need for approval from experts led him to hand over to psychiatrists the organization he helped establish. In the UK, the National Society for Lunacy Law Reform was established in 1920 by angry ex-patients sick of their experiences and complaints being patronisingly discounted by the authorities who were using medical "window dressing" for essentially custodial and punitive practices.

In 1922, ex-patient Rachel Grant-Smith added to calls for reform of the system of neglect and abuse she had suffered by publishing "The Experiences of an Asylum Patient".We Are Not Alone (WANA) was founded by a group of patients at Rockland State Hospital in New York in the mid to late 1940s, and continued to meet as an ex-patient group. Their goal was to provide support and advice and help others make the difficult transition from hospital to community. By the early 1950s WANA dissolved after it was taken over by mental health professionals who transformed it into Fountain House, a psychosocial rehabilitation service for people leaving state mental institutions.

The founders of WANA found themselves pushed aside by professionals with money and influence, who made them "members" of the new organization. During that period, people who received psychiatric treatment identified themselves as patients, and this term was generally unchallenged as a self-description until the 1970s. A perceived patronizing attitude by health care workers led to resentment among some current and former patients, which eventually found expression in more militant groups beginning in the early 1970s. Originated by crusaders in periods of liberal social change, and appealing not so much to other sufferers as to elite groups with power, when the early reformer's energy or influence waned, mental patients were again mostly friendless and forgotten.

The 1950s saw the advent and widespread use of lobotomy and shock therapy. These were associated with grave concerns and much opposition on grounds of basic morality, harmful effects, or misuse. Towards the 1960s, psychiatric medications came in to widespread use and also caused controversy relating to adverse effects and misuse. There were also associated moves away from large psychiatric institutions to community-based services (later to become a full-scale deinstitutionalization), which sometimes empowered service users, although community-based services were often deficient.

Coming to the fore in the 1960s, an anti-psychiatry movement vocally challenged the fundamental claims and practices of mainstream psychiatry. The ex-patient movement of this time contributed to, and derived much from, antipsychiatry ideology, but has also been described as having its own agenda, described as humanistic socialism. For a time, the movement shared aims and practices with "radical therapists", who tended to be Marxist and equally keen on challenging the social structures that kept people oppressed and boxed. However, the consumer/survivor/ex-patients gradually felt that the radical therapists did not necessarily share the same goals and were taking over, and they broke away from them in order to maintain independence. By the 1970s, the women's movement, gay rights movement, and disability rights movements had emerged.

It was in this context that former mental patients began to organize groups with the common goals of fighting for patients' rights and against forced treatment, stigma and discrimination, and often to promote peer-run services as an alternative to the traditional mental health system. Unlike professional mental health services, which were usually based on the medical model, peer-run services were based on the principle that individuals who have shared similar experiences can help themselves and each other through self-help and mutual support.

Many of the individuals who organized these early groups identified themselves as psychiatric survivors. Their groups had names such as Insane Liberation Front and the Network Against Psychiatric Assault. They saw the mental health system as destructive and disempowering. With more people out of mental hospitals, there was a larger number of people who could now make links with one another for progressive causes. Dorothy Weiner and about 10 others, including Tom Wittick, established the Insane Liberation Front in the spring of 1970 in Portland, Oregon.

Though it only lasted 6 months, it had a notable influence in the history of North American ex-patients groups. News that former inmates of mental institutions were organizing was carried to other parts of North America. Individuals such as Howard Geld, known as Howie the Harp for his harmonica playing, left Portland where he been involved in ILF to return to his native New York to help found the Mental Patients Liberation Project in 1971. During the early 1970s, groups spread to California, New York, and Boston, which were primarily antipsychiatry, opposed to forced treatment including forced drugging, shock treatment and involuntary committal. In 1972, the first organized group in Canada, the Mental Patients Association, started to publish In A Nutshell, while in the US the first edition of the first national publication by ex-mental patients, Madness Network News, was published in Oakland, continuing until 1986.

A well-known book of the time by an ex-patient was Judi Chamberlin's 1978 "On Our Own: Patient-Controlled Alternatives to the Mental Health System." Chamberlin publicized the concept of mentalism, a form of stereotyping and oppression of those associated with psychiatric treatment and diagnosis. The major spokespeople of the movement have been described in generalities as largely white, middle-class and well-educated. It has been suggested that other activists were often more anarchistic and anti-capitalist, felt more cut-off from society and more like a minority with more in common with the poor, ethnic minorities, feminists, prisoners and gay rights than with the white middle classes.

The leaders were sometimes considered to be merely reformist and, because of their "stratified position" within society, to be uncomprehending of the problems of the poor. The "radicals" saw no sense in seeking solutions within a capitalist system that creates mental problems. However, they were united in considering society and psychiatric domination to be the problem, rather than people designated mentally ill. Some activists condemned psychiatry under any conditions, voluntary or involuntary, while others, usually the more middle-class, conceded the right of people to undergo psychiatric treatment on a voluntary basis. Voluntary psychotherapy, at the time mainly psychoanalysis, did not therefore come under the same severe attack as the somatic therapies. But it was valued, if at all, only as a possibly helpful technique if applied by laypersons including ex-patients themselves.

The ex-patients emphasized individual support from other patients; they espoused assertiveness, liberation, and equality; and they advocated user-controlled services as part of a totally voluntary continuum. However, although the movement espoused egalitarianism and opposed the concept of leadership, it is said to have developed a cadre of known, articulate, and literate men and women who did the writing, talking, organizing, and contacting.

Very much the product of the rebellious, populist, anti-elitist mood of the 1960s, they strived above all for self-determination and self-reliance. In generally, the work of some psychiatrists, as well as the lack of criticism by the psychiatric establishment, was interpreted as an abandonment of a moral commitment to do no harm. There was a deep anger and resentment towards a profession that had the authority to label them as mentally disabled and was perceived as infantilizing them and disregarding their wishes.

By the 1980s, individuals who considered themselves "consumers" of mental health services rather than passive "patients" had begun to organize self-help/advocacy groups and peer-run services. While sharing some of the goals of the earlier movement, consumer groups did not seek to abolish the traditional mental health system, which they believed was necessary. Instead, they wanted to reform it and have more choice. Consumer groups encouraged their members to learn as much as possible about the mental health system so that they could gain access to the best services and treatments available.

In 1985, the National Mental Health Consumers' Association was formed in the United States. A 1986 report on developments in the United States noted that "there are now three national organizations... The 'conservatives' have created the National Mental Health Consumers' Association... The 'moderates' have formed the National Alliance of Mental Patients... The 'radical' group is called the Network to Abolish Psychiatry". Many, however, felt that they had survived the psychiatric system and its "treatments" and resented being called consumers. The National Association of Mental Patients in the United States became the National Association of Psychiatric Survivors. "Phoenix Rising: The Voice of the Psychiatrized" was published by ex-inmates (of psychiatric hospitals) in Toronto from 1980 to 1990, known across Canada for its antipsychiatry stance. In late 1988, leaders from several of the main national and grassroots psychiatric survivor groups decided an independent coalition was needed, and Support Coalition International (SCI) was formed in 1988, later to become MindFreedom International.

In addition, the World Network of Users and Survivors of Psychiatry (WNUSP), was founded in 1991 as the World Federation of Psychiatric Users (WFPU), an international organisation of recipients of mental health services. An emphasis on voluntary involvement in services is said to have presented problems to the movement since, especially in the wake of deinstitutionalization, community services were fragmented and many individuals in distressed states of mind were being put in prisons or re-institutionalized in community services, or became homeless, often distrusting and resisting any help.

Patients rights groups have been speaking out against psychiatric abuses for decades but have been censored and denied by the psychiatric establishment. Reading about the experiences they suffered through has been described as comparable to reading the stories of Holocaust survivors. Recipients of mental health services demanded control over their own treatment and began to have an influence on the public mental health system. They often promoted a recovery model. Whether they considered themselves consumers or survivors, activists demanded a voice and a choice.

## THE MOVEMENT TODAY

In the United States, the number of mental health mutual support groups (MSG), self-help organizations (SHO) (run by and for mental health consumers and/or family members) and consumer-operated services (COS) was recently estimated to be 7,467. The movement may express a preference for the "survivor" label over the "consumer" label, with more than 60 per cent of ex-patient groups reported to support anti-psychiatry beliefs and considering themselves to be "psychiatric survivors." There is some variation between the perspective on the consumer/survivor movement coming from psychiatry, anti-psychiatry or consumers/survivors themselves. The most common terms in Germany are "Psychiatrie-Betroffene" (people afflicted by/confronted with psychiatry) and "Psychiatrie-Erfahrene" (people who have experienced psychiatry). Sometimes the terms are considered as synonymous but sometimes the former emphasizes the violence and negative aspects of psychiatry.

The German national association of (ex-)users and survivors of psychiatry is called the Bundesverband Psychiatrie-Erfahrener (BPE). There are many grassroots self-help groups of consumers/survivors, local and national, all over the world, which are an important cornerstone of empowerment. A considerable obstacle to realising more consumer/survivor alternatives is lack of funding. Alternative consumer/survivor groups like the National Empowerment Centre in the US which receive public funds but question orthodox psychiatric treatment, have often come under attack for receiving public funding and been subject to funding cuts. As well as advocacy and reform campaigns, the development of self-help and user/survivor controlled services is a central issue. The Runaway-House in Berlin, Germany, is an example. Run by the Organisation for the Protection from Psychiatric Violence, it is an antipsychiatric crisis centre for homeless survivors of psychiatry where the residents can live for a limited amount of time and where half the staff members are survivors of psychiatry themselves.

In Helsingborg, Sweden, the Hotel Magnus Stenbock is run by a user/survivor organization "RSMH" that gives users/survivors a possibility to live in their own apartments. It is financed by the Swedish government and run entirely by users. Voice of Soul is a user/survivor organization in Hungary. Creative Routes is a user/survivor organization in London, England, that among other support and advocacy activities puts on an annual "Bonkersfest".WNUSP is a consultant organization for the United Nations. After a "long and difficult discussion", ENUSP and WNUSP (European and World Networks of Users and Survivors of Psychiatry) decided to employ the term (ex-)users and survivors of psychiatry in order to include the identities of the different groups and positions represented in these international NGOs. WNUSP contributed to the development of the UN's Convention on the Rights of Persons with Disabilities and produced a manual to help people use it called "Implementing the Disability Rights Treaty, for Users, Survivors of Psychiatry" and ENUSP is consulted by the European Union and World Health Organization. In 2007 at a Conference held in Dresden on "Coercive Treatment in Psychiatry: A Comprehensive Review", the president and other leaders of the World Psychiatric Association met, following a formal request from the World Health Organization, with four representatives from leading consumer/survivor groups.

The National Coalition of Mental Health Consumer/Survivor Organizations campaigns in the United States to ensure that consumer/survivors have a major voice in the development and implementation of health care, mental health, and social policies at the state and national levels, empowering people to recover and lead a full life in the community. The

United States Massachusetts-based Freedom Centre provides and promotes alternative and holistic approaches and takes a stand for greater choice and options in treatments and care. The centre and the New York-based Icarus Project (which does not self-identify as a consumer/survivor organization but has participants that identify as such) have published a Harm Reduction Guide To Coming Off Psychiatric Drugs and were recently a featured charity in Forbes business magazine.

Mad pride events, organized by loosely connected groups in at least seven countries including Australia, South Africa, the United States, Canada, the United Kingdom and Ghana, draw thousands of participants. For some, the objective is to continue the destigmatization of mental illness. Another wing rejects the need to treat mental afflictions with psychotropic drugs and seeks alternatives to the "care" of the medical establishment. Many members of the movement say they are publicly discussing their own struggles to help those with similar conditions and to inform the general public. Survivor David Oakes, Director of MindFreedom, hosts a monthly radio show and the Freedom Centre initiated a weekly FM radio show now syndicated on the Pacifica Network, Madness Radio, hosted by Freedom Centre co-founder Will Hall. A new International Coalition of National Consumer/User Organizations was launched in Canada in 2007, called Interrelate.

**IMPACT**

There has been some substantial research into consumer/survivor initiatives (CSIs). Many of the studies have been cross-sectional or retrospective and have not used comparison groups, which limits the firm conclusions that can be drawn. However, the findings suggest that CSIs can help with social support, empowerment, mental wellbeing, self-management and reduced service use, identity transformation and enhanced quality of life. However, studies have focused on the support and self-help aspects of CSIs, neglecting that many organizations locate the causes of members' problems in political and social institutions and are involved in activities to address issues of social justice.

A recent series of studies in Canada compared individuals who participated in CSIs with those who did not. The two groups were comparable at baseline on a wide range of demographic variables, self-reported psychiatric diagnosis, service use, and outcome measures. After a year and a half, those who had participated in CSIs showed significant improvement in social support and quality of life (daily activities), less days of psychiatric hospitalization, and more were likely to have stayed in employment (paid or volunteer) and/or education.

There was no significant difference on measures of community integration and personal empowerment, however. There were some limitations to the findings; although the active and nonactive groups did not differ significantly at baseline on measures of distress or hospitalization, the active group did have a higher mean score and there may have been a natural pattern of recovery over time for that group (regression to the mean). The authors noted that the apparent positive impacts of consumer-run organizations were achieved at a fraction of the cost of professional community programmes. Further qualitative studies indicated that CSIs can provide: safe environments that are a positive, welcoming place to go; social arenas that provide opportunities to meet and talk with peers; an alternative worldview that provides opportunities for members to participate and contribute; and effective facilitators of community integration that provide opportunities to connect members to the community at large.

System-level activism was perceived to result in changes in perceptions by the public and mental health professionals (about mental health or mental illness, the lived experience of consumer/survivors, the legitimacy of their opinions, and the perceived value of CSIs) and in concrete changes in service delivery practice, service planning, public policy, or funding allocations. The authors noted that the evidence indicated that the work benefits other consumers/survivors (present and future), other service providers, the general public, and communities. They also noted that there were various barriers to this, most notably lack of funding, and also that the range of views represented by the CSIs appeared less narrow and more nuanced and complex than previously, and that perhaps the consumer/survivor social movement is at a different place than it was 25 years ago. There has also been criticism of the movement.

Well-positioned forces in the USA, led by figures such as psychiatrists E. Fuller Torrey and Sally Satel, and some leaders of the National Alliance for the Mentally Ill, have lobbied against the funding of consumer/survivor groups that promote antipsychiatry views or promote social and experiential recovery rather than a biomedical model, or who protest against outpatient commitment. Torrey has said the term "psychiatric survivor" used by ex-patients to describe themselves is just political correctness and has blamed them, along with civil rights lawyers, for the deaths of half a million people due to suicides and deaths on the street. Such claims have been controverted by recent publications such as U.S.A. Today which published an article indicating that the medical model and the way persons with mental illness are treated today cause people to die 25 years early on average. There is great need for further development of the recovery model whose outcome is to support people in regaining their wellness instead of a life sentence of psychiatry which has been found to cause early death.

His accusations have been described as inflammatory and completely unsubstantiated, however, and issues of self-determination and self-identity said to be more complex than that. More generally, organized psychiatry often views radical consumerist groups as extremist, as having little scientific foundation and no defined leadership, as trying to restrict "the work of psychiatrists and care for the seriously mentally ill", and as promoting disinformation on the use of involuntary commitment, electroconvulsive therapy, stimulants and antidepressants among children, and neuroleptics among adults.

## EQUAL PAY FOR EQUAL WORK

Equal pay for equal work is the concept that individuals doing the same work should receive the same remuneration. It is most commonly used in a context of sexual discrimination, as equal pay for women.

Equal pay does not simply relate to basic salary but also to the full range of benefits, non salary payments, bonuses and allowances that are paid. The U.S. Democratic Party has historically supported legislating equal pay for equal work. Its 2008 party platform reads: "When women still earn 76 cents for every dollar that a man earns, it doesn't just hurt women; it hurts families and children.

As suggested, pass the 'Lilly Ledbetter' Act, which will make it easier to combat pay discrimination; as suggested, pass the Fair Pay Act; and as suggested, modernize the Equal Pay Act." The Lilly Ledbetter Fair Pay Act was signed into law in January 2009. Free market supporters believe that government actions to correct gender pay disparity serve to interfere with the system of voluntary exchange. They see the fundamental issue is that the employer is the owner of the job, not the government or the employee. The employer negotiates the job and pays just as to performance, not just as to job duties. A private business would not want to lose its best performers by compensating them less and can ill afford paying its lower performers higher because the overall productivity will decline. There are also specific affirmative defences to the criticism above that government is forcing employers to pay less qualified workers the same as superior workers. The EPA's four affirmative defences allows unequal pay for equal work when the wages are set "pursuant to, a seniority system; a merit system; a system which measures earnings by quantity or quality of production; or ... any other factor other than sex" If an employer can prove that a pay differential exists because of one of these factors, there is no liability.

## FETAL RIGHTS

Fetal rights are the legal or ethical rights of fetuses. The term is used most often in the context of the abortion debate, as the basis for an argument in support of the pro-life stance. Some laws seek to protect or otherwise recognize the fetus. Some of these grant recognition under specific conditions: the fetus can legally be a victim of a crime such as feticide, a beneficiary of insurance or social assistance, or an inheritor of property.

- The American Convention on Human Rights (1969) is a treaty signed by 24 Latin American countries, which states that from the moment of conception, human beings have rights.

- The Unborn Victims of Violence Act is a United States law which defines violent assault committed against pregnant women as being a crime against two victims: the woman and the fetus she carries. This law was passed in 2004 after the murder of Laci Peterson and the fetus she was carrying.
- In 2002, U.S. President George W. Bush announced a plan to ensure health care coverage for fetuses under the State Children's Health Insurance Programme (SCHIP).
- Iranian law holds that anyone who brings about a miscarriage must pay a monetary fine, which varies depending upon the stage of development and/or sex of the fetus, in compensation.

Legislative measures sometimes seek to establish the right to life of the fetus from the moment of fertilization.

*Such laws regard the fetus as a person whose legal status is on par with that of any other member of the species homo sapiens*:

- The 1978 American Convention on Human Rights states, in Article 4.1, "Every person has the right to have his life respected. This right shall be protected by law and, in general, from the moment of conception." The Convention is considered binding only for the 24 of 35 member nations of the Organization of American States who ratified it.
- In 1983, the Eighth Amendment of the Constitution of Ireland, also known as the "Pro-Life Amendment," was added to the Constitution of The Republic of Ireland by popular referendum. It recognizes "the right to life of the unborn".
- In 1993, the Federal Constitutional Court of Germany held that the constitution guaranteed the right to life from conception, but that it is within the discretion of parliament not to punish abortion in the first trimester, providing that women agreed to undergo special counselling designed to discourage termination and "protect unborn life". The intermediate decision was the result of an attempt to join East Germany's abortion law to that of West Germany after reunification in 1990.

*Other governments have laws in place that state that fetuses are not legally recognized persons*:

- In Canadian law, under section 223 of the Criminal Code of Canada, a fetus is a "human being... when it has completely proceeded, in a living state, from the body of its mother whether or not it has completely breathed, it has an independent circulation or the navel string is severed."

Much opposition to legal abortion in the West is based on a concern for fetal rights. Similarly many pro-choice groups oppose fetal rights, even when they do not impinge directly on the abortion issue, because they perceive this as a slippery slope strategy to restricting abortions. Various initiatives, prompted by concern for the ill effects which might be posed to the health or development of a fetus, seek to restrict or discourage women from engaging in certain behaviours while pregnant. Also, in some countries, laws have been passed to restrict the practice of abortion based upon the gender of the fetus.

- Many jurisdictions actively warn against the consumption of alcoholic beverages by pregnant women, recommending a maximum intake or total abstinence, due to its association with Fetal alcohol syndrome. Countries that encourage those who are pregnant to avoid alcohol either entirely or partially include Australia, Canada, France, Iceland, Israel, the Netherlands, Norway, New Zealand, Spain, the United Kingdom, and the United States.
- Many national and international agencies recommend dietary guidelines for pregnant women due to the health risks posed by the consumption of fish contaminated with methylmercury through industrial pollution. Studies have linked exposure to various levels of methylmercury in utero to neurological disorders in children.
- The use of tobacco products or exposure to secondhand smoke during pregnancy has been linked to low birth weight. Governor Mike Huckabee of Arkansas, citing studies which attribute 10% of infant deaths to tobacco-smoking mothers, considered adopting a smoking ban for pregnant women in 2006 with the aim of reducing infant mortality.
- No U.S. state has enacted a law which criminalizes specific behaviour during pregnancy, but, nonetheless, it has been estimated that at least 200 American women have been criminally prosecuted or arrested under existing child abuse statutes for allegedly bringing about harm in-utero through their conduct during pregnancy. Reasons for pressing charges included use of illicit drugs, consumption of alcohol, and failure to comply with a doctor's order of bedrest or caesarean part. Drug addicts have been accused of "supplying drugs to a minor" through unintentional chemical subjection via the umbilical cord. Others have been charged with assault with a deadly weapon with the "deadly weapon" in question being an illegal drug. Minnesota, Wisconsin and South Dakota allow women who continue to use substances while pregnant to be civilly committed. Some states require that medical providers report any infant who is born with a physical dependency, or who tests positive for residual traces of alcohol or drugs, to child welfare authorities.
- Cultural preferences for male children in some parts of Asia, such as Mainland China, India, South Korea, and Taiwan, have sometimes led to sex-selective abortion of female fetuses. This phenomenon might be partially responsible for the disparity between male-to-female birth rates which is observed in some places. India banned the practice of abortion for reasons of fetal sex in 1994.

# CHILDREN'S RIGHTS

Children's rights are the human rights of children with particular attention to the rights of special protection and care afforded to the young, including their right to association with both biological parents, human identity as well as the basic needs for food, universal state-paid education, health care and criminal laws appropriate for the age and development of the child. Interpretations of children's rights range from allowing children the capacity for autonomous action to the enforcement of children being physically, mentally and emotionally free from abuse, though what constitutes "abuse" is a matter of debate. Other definitions include the rights to care and nurturing. "A child is any human being below the age of eighteen years, unless under the law applicable to the child, majority is attained earlier." Cornell University, a child is a person, not a subperson, and the parent has absolute interest and possession of the child, but this is very much an American view.

The term "child" does not necessarily mean minor but can include adult children as well as adult nondependent children. There are no definitions of other terms used to describe young people such as "adolescents", "teenagers," or "youth" in international law, but the children's rights movement is considered distinct from the youth rights movement. The field of children's rights spans the fields of law, politics, religion, and morality.

## RATIONALE

As minors by law children do not have autonomy or the right to make decisions on their own for themselves in any known jurisdiction of the world. Instead their adult caregivers, including parents, social workers, teachers, youth workers and others, are vested with that authority, depending on the circumstances. Some believe that this state of affairs gives children insufficient control over their own lives and causes them to be vulnerable.

Louis Althusser has gone so far as describe this legal machinery, as it applies to children, as "repressive state apparatuses".Structures such as government policy have been held by some commentators to mask the ways adults abuse and exploit children, resulting in child poverty, lack of educational opportunities, and child labour. On this view, children are to be regarded as a minority group towards whom society needs to reconsider the way it behaves. However, there is no evidence that such views are widely shared in society. Researchers have identified children as needing to be recognized as participants in society whose rights and responsibilities need to be recognized at all ages.

## HISTORIC DEFINITIONS OF CHILDREN'S RIGHTS

Consensus on defining children's rights has become clearer in the last fifty years. A 1973 publication by Hillary Clinton stated that children's rights were a "slogan in need of a definition".

Some researchers, the notion of children's rights is still not well defined, with at least one proposing that there is no singularly accepted definition or theory of the rights held by children. Children's rights law is defined as the point where the law intersects with a child's life.

That includes juvenile delinquency, due process for children involved in the criminal justice system, appropriate representation, and effective rehabilitative services; care and protection for children in state care; ensuring education for all children regardless of their origin, race, gender, disabilities, or abilities, and; health care and advocacy.

## TYPES OF RIGHTS

Children's rights are defined in numerous ways, including a wide spectrum of civil, cultural, economic, social and political rights. Rights tend to be of two general types: those advocating for children as autonomous persons under the law and those placing a claim on society for protection from harms perpetrated on children because of their dependency. These have been labeled as the right of *empowerment and as the right to protection.*

*One Canadian organization categorizes children's rights into three categories*:

- *Provision*: Children have the right to an adequate standard of living, health care, education and services, and to play. These include a balanced diet, a warm bed to sleep in, and access to schooling.
- *Protection*: Children have the right to protection from abuse, neglect, exploitation and discrimination. This includes the right to safe places for children to play; constructive child rearing behaviour, and acknowledgment of the evolving capacities of children.
- *Participation*: Children have the right to participate in communities and have programmes and services for themselves. This includes children's involvement in libraries and community programmes, youth voice activities, and involving children as decision-makers.

In a similar fashion, the Child Rights Information Network, or CRIN for short, categorizes rights into two groups:

- Economic, social and cultural rights, related to the conditions necessary to meet basic human needs such as food, shelter, education, health care, and gainful employment. Included are rights to education, adequate housing, food, water, the highest attainable standard of health, the right to work and rights at work, as well as the cultural rights of minorities and indigenous peoples.
- Environmental, cultural and developmental rights, which are sometimes called "third generation rights," and including the right to live in safe and healthy environments and that groups of people have the right to cultural, political, and economic development.

Amnesty International openly advocates four particular children's rights, including the end to juvenile incarceration without parole, an end to the recruitment of military use of children, ending the death penalty for people under 21, and raising awareness of human rights in the classroom. Human Rights Watch, an international advocacy organization, includes child labour, juvenile justice, orphans and abandoned children, refugees, street children and corporal punishment. Scholarly study generally focuses children's rights by identifying individual rights.

*The following rights "allow children to grow up healthy and free"*:

- Freedom of speech
- Freedom of thought
- Freedom from fear
- Freedom of choice and the right to make decisions
- Ownership over one's body

Other issues affecting children's rights include the sale of children, child prostitution and child pornography.

**Difference Between Children's Rights and Youth Rights**

"In the majority of jurisdictions, for instance, children are not allowed to vote, to marry, to buy alcohol, to have sex, or to engage in paid employment." Within the youth rights movement, it is believed that the key difference between children's rights and youth rights is that children's rights supporters generally advocate the establishment and enforcement of protection for children and youths, while youth rights generally advocates the expansion of freedom for children and/or youths and of rights such as suffrage. Also, many people who support youth rights, are concerned with adolescents and not children.

**Parental Rights**

Parents affect the lives of children in a unique way, and as such their role in children's rights has to be distinguished in a particular way. Particular issues in the child-parent relationship include child neglect, child abuse, freedom of choice, corporal punishment and child custody. There have been theories offered that provide parents with rights-based practices that resolve the tension between "commonsense parenting" and children's rights.

The issue is particularly relevant in legal proceedings that affect the potential emancipation of minors, and in cases where children sue their parents. A child's rights to a relationship with both their parents is increasingly recognized as an important factor for determining the best interests of the child in divorce and child custody proceedings. Some governments have enacted laws creating a rebuttable presumption that shared parenting is in the best interests of children.

## MOVEMENT

The Children's Rights Movement is a historical and modern movement committed to the acknowledgment, expansion, and/or regression of the rights of children around the world. While the historical definition of child has varied, the United Nations Convention on the Rights of the Child explains, "A child is any human being below the age of eighteen years, unless under the law applicable to the child, majority is attained earlier." There are no definitions of other terms used to describe young people such as "adolescents", "teenagers" or "youth" in international law. Thomas Spence's The Rights of Infants is an early English-language assertion of the natural rights of children.

In the USA, the Children's Rights Movement was born in the 1800s with the orphan train. In the big cities, when a child's parents died or were extremely poor, the child frequently had to go to work to support himself and/or his family. Boys generally became factory or coal workers, and girls became prostitutes or saloon girls, or else went to work in a sweat shop. All of these jobs paid only starvation wages.

In 1852, Massachusetts required children to attend school. In 1853, Charles Brace founded the Children's Aid Society, which worked hard to take street children in. The following year, the children were placed on a train headed for the West, where they were adopted, and often given work. By 1929, the orphan train stopped running altogether, but its principles lived on. The National Child Labour Committee, an organization dedicated to the abolition of all child labour, was formed in the 1890s. It managed to pass one law, which was struck down by the Supreme Court two years later for violating a child's right to contract his work. In 1924, Congress attempted to pass a constitutional amendment that would authorize a national child labour law.

This measure was blocked, and the bill was eventually dropped. It took the Great Depression to end child labour nationwide; adults had become so desperate for jobs that they would work for the same wage as children. In 1938, President Franklin D. Roosevelt signed the Fair Labour Standards Act which, amongst other things, placed limits on many forms of child labour. Now that child labour had been effectively eradicated in parts of the world, the movement turned to other things, but it again stalled when World War II broke out and children and women began to enter the work force once more. With millions of adults at war, the children were needed to help keep the country running. In Europe, children served as couriers, intelligence collectors, and other underground resistance workers in opposition to Hitler's regime. In the early twentieth century, moves began to promote the idea of children's rights as distinct from those of adults and as requiring explicit recognition.

The Polish educationalist Janusz Korczak wrote of the rights of children in his book How to Love a Child; a later book was entitled The Child's Right to Respect. In 1917, following the Russian Revolution, the Moscow branch of the organization Proletkult produced a Declaration of Children's Rights. However, the first effective attempt to promote children's rights was the Declaration of the Rights of the Child, drafted by Eglantyne Jebb in 1923 and adopted by the League of Nations in 1924.

This was accepted by the United Nations on its formation and updated in 1959, and replaced with a more extensive UN Convention on the Rights of the Child in 1989. From the formation of the United Nations in the 1940s and extending to present day, the Children's Rights Movement has become global in focus. While the situation of children in the United States has become grave, children around the world have increasingly become engaged in illegal, forced child labour, genital mutilation, military service, and sex trafficking. Several international organizations have rallied to the assistance of children.

They include Save the Children, Free the Children, and the Children's Defence Fund. The Child Rights Information Network, or CRIN, formed in 1983, is the group of 1,600 non-governmental organizations from around the world which advocate for the implementation of the Convention on the Rights of the Child. Organization's report on their countries' progress towards implementation, as do governments that have ratified the Convention. Every 5 years reporting to the United Nations Committee on the Rights of the Child is required for governments. While there is a long history of children's rights in the U.S., scholars contend that there is no "golden age". Many children's rights advocates in the U.S. today advocate for a smaller agenda than their international peers. Groups predominately focus on child abuse and neglect, child fatalities, foster care, youth aging out of foster care, preventing foster care placement, and adoption. A long standing movement promoting youth rights in the United States has made substantial gains in the past.Anti-Children's Rights propagandists often raise the spectre of Rights without Responsibilities.

The Children's Rights Movement assert that it is rather the case that children have rights which adults, states and government have a responsibility to uphold. The UK maintains a position that UNCRC is not legally enforceable and is hence 'aspirational' only - albeit a 2003 ECHR ruling states: "The human rights of children and the standards to which all governments must aspire in realising these rights for all children are set out in the Convention on the Rights of the Child."

18 years after ratification, the four Children's Commissioners in the devolved administrations have united in calling for adoption of the Convention into domestic legislation, making children's rights legally enforceable. Several countries have created an institute of children's rights ombudsman, most notably Sweden, Finland and Ukraine, which is first country worldwide to install children at that post. In Ukraine Ivan Cherevko and Julia Kruk became first children's rights ombudsmen in late 2005

The United Nations Convention on the Rights of the Child has outlined a standard premise for the children's rights movement and has been ratified by all but two nations - the United States and Somalia. Somalia's inability to sign the Convention is attributed to their lack of governmental structure. The US administration under Bush has opposed ratifying the Convention because of "serious political and legal concerns that it conflicts with U.S. policies on the central role of parents, sovereignty, and state and local law." However, the new administration may be taking another look at it.

## INTERNATIONAL LAW

The Universal Declaration of Human Rights is seen as a basis for all international legal standards for children's rights today. There are several conventions and laws that address children's rights around the world.

A number of current and historical documents affect those rights, including the 1923 Declaration of the Rights of the Child, drafted by Eglantyne Jebb and her sister Dorothy Buxton in London, England in 1919, endorsed by the League of Nations and adopted by the United Nations in 1946. It later served as the basis for the Convention on the Rights of the Child.

### Convention on the Rights of the Child

The United Nations' 1989 Convention on the Rights of the Child, or CRC, is the first legally binding international instrument to incorporate the full range of human rights—civil, cultural, economic, political and social rights. Its implementa-tion is monitored by the Committee on the Rights of the Child. National governments that ratify it commit themselves to protecting and ensuring children's rights, and agree to hold themselves accountable for this commitment before the international community.

The CRC is the most widely ratified human rights treaty with 190 ratifications. Somalia and USA are the only two countries which have not agreed to the CRC. The CRC is based on four core principles, namely the principle of non discrimination, the best interests of the child, the right to life, survival and development, and considering the views of the child in decisions which affect them.

The CRC, along with international criminal accountability mechanisms such as the International Criminal Court, the Yugoslavia and Rwanda Tribunals, and the Special Court for Sierra Leone, is said to have significantly increased the profile of children's rights worldwide.

### Enforcement

A variety of enforcement organizations and mechanisms exist to ensure children's rights and the successful implementation of the Union. They include the Child Rights Caucus for the United Nations General Assembly Special Session on Children.

It was set up to promote full implementation and compliance with the Convention on the Rights of the Child, and to ensure that child rights were given priority during the UN General Assembly Special Session on Children and its Preparatory process. The United Nations Human Rights Council was created "with the hope that it could be more objective, credible and efficient in denouncing human rights violations worldwide than the highly politicised Commission on Human Rights."

The NGO Group for the Convention on the Rights of the Child is a coalition of international non-governmental organisations originally formed in 1983 to facilitate the implementation of the United Nations Convention on the Rights of the Child. Many countries around the world have children's rights ombudspeople or children's commissioners whose official, governmental duty is to represent the interests of the public by investigating and addressing complaints reported by individual citizens regarding children's rights. Children's ombudspeople can also work for a corporation, a newspaper, an NGO, or even for the general public.

**United States Law**

Children are generally afforded the basic rights embodied by the Constitution, as enshrined by the Fourteenth Amendment to the United States Constitution. The Equal Protection Clause of that amendment is to apply to children, born within a marriage or not, but excludes children not yet born. This was reinforced by the landmark US Supreme Court decision of In re Gault.

In this trial 15-year-old Gerald Gault of Arizona was taken into custody by local police after being accused of making an obscene telephone call. He was detained and committed to the Arizona State Industrial School until he reached the age of 21 for making an obscene phone call to an adult neighbour. In an 8–1 decision, the Court ruled that in hearings which could result in commitment to an institution, people under the age of 18 have the right to notice and counsel, to question witnesses, and to protection against self-incrimination. The Court found that the procedures used in Gault's hearing met none of these requirements.

There are other concerns in the United States regarding children's rights. The American Academy of Adoption Attorneys is concerned with children's rights to a safe, supportive and stable family structure. Their position on children's rights in adoption cases states that, "children have a constitutionally based liberty interest in the protection of their established families, rights which are at least equal to, and we believe outweigh, the rights of others who would claim a 'possessory' interest in these children." Other issues raised in American children's rights advocacy include children's rights to inheritance in same-sex marriages and particular rights for youth.

## CIVIL RIGHTS

In contemporary political thought, the term 'civil rights' is indissolubly linked to the struggle for equality of American blacks during the 1950s and 60s. The aim of that struggle was to secure the status of equal citizenship in a liberal democratic state. Civil rights are the basic legal rights a person must possess in order to have such a status. They are the rights that constitute free and equal citizenship and include personal, political, and economic rights. No contemporary thinker of significance holds that such rights can be legitimately denied to a person on the basis of race, colour, sex, religion, national origin, or disability.

Antidiscrimination principles are thus a common ground in contemporary political discussion. However, there is much disagreement in the scholarly literature over the basis and scope of these principles and the ways in which they ought to be implemented in law and policy. In addition, debate exists over the legitimacy of including sexual orientation among the other categories traditionally protected by civil rights law, and there is an emerging literature examining issues of how best to understand discrimination based on disability.

## RIGHTS

### The Civil-Political Distinction

Until the middle of the 20th century, civil rights were usually distinguished from 'political rights'. The former included the rights to own property, make and enforce contracts, receive due process of law, and worship one's religion. Civil rights also covered freedom of speech and the press. But they did not include the right to hold public office, vote, or to testify in court. The latter were political rights, reserved to adult males. The civil-political distinction was conceptually and morally unstable insofar as it was used to sort citizens into different categories.

It was part of an ideology that classified women as citizens who were entitled to certain rights but not to the full panoply to which men were entitled. As that ideology broke down, the civil-political distinction began to unravel. The idea that a certain segment of the adult citizenry could legitimately possess one bundle of rights, while another segment would have to make do with an inferior bundle, became increasingly implausible. In the end, the civil-political distinction could not survive the cogency of the principle that all citizens of a liberal democracy were entitled, in Rawls's words, to "a fully adequate scheme of equal basic liberties". It may be possible to retain the distinction strictly as one for sorting rights, rather than sorting citizens. But it is difficult to give a convincing account of the principles by which the sorting is done.

It seems neater and cleaner simply to think of civil rights as the general category of basic rights needed for free and equal citizenship. Yet, it remains a matter of contention which claims are properly conceived as belonging to the category of civil rights. Analysts have distinguished among "three generations" of civil rights claims and have argued over which claims ought to be treated as true matters of civil rights.

### Three Generations of Rights

The claims for which the American civil rights movement initially fought belong to the first generation of civil rights claims. Those claims included the pre-20th century set of civil rights — such as the rights to receive due process and to make and enforce contracts — but covered political rights as well. However, many thinkers and activists argued that these first-generation claims were too narrow to define the scope of free and equal citizenship. They contended that such citizenship could be realised only by honouring an additional set of claims, including rights to food, shelter, medical care, and employment.

This second generation of economic "welfare rights," the argument went, helped to ensure that the political, economic, and legal rights belonging to the first generation could be made effective in protecting the vital interests of citizens and were not simply document guarantees. Yet, some scholars have argued that these second-generation rights should not be subsumed under the category of civil rights. Thus, Cranston writes, "The traditional 'political and civil rights' can...be readily secured by legislation.

Since the rights are for the most part rights against government interference...the legislation needed had to do no more than restrain the executive's own arm. This is no longer the case when we turn to the 'right to work', the 'right to social security' and so forth". However, Cranston fails to recognize that such first-generation rights as due process and the right to vote also require substantial government action and the investment of considerable public resources. Holmes and Sunstein have made the case that all of the first-generation civil rights require government to do more than simply "restrain the executive's own arm."

It seems problematic to think that a significant distinction can be drawn between first and second-generation rights on the ground that the former, but not the latter, simply require that government refrain from interfering with the actions of persons. Moreover, even if some viable distinction could be drawn along those lines, it would not follow that second-generation rights should be excluded from the category of civil rights. The reason is that the relevant standard for inclusion as a civil right is whether a claim is part of the package of rights constitutive of free and equal citizenship. There is no reason to think that only those claims that can be "readily secured by legislation" belong to that package. And the increasingly dominant view is that welfare rights are essential to adequately satisfying the conditions of free and equal citizenship. In the United States, however, the law does not treat issues of economic well-being *per se* as civil rights matters. Only insofar as economic inequality or deprivation is linked to race, gender or some other traditional category of antidiscrimination law is it considered to be a question of civil rights.

In legal terms, poverty is not a "suspect classification." On the other hand, welfare rights are protected as a matter of constitutional principle in other democracies. For example, section 75 of the Danish Constitution provides that "any person unable to support himself or his dependents shall, where no other person is responsible for his or their maintenance, be entitled to receive public assistance." And the International Covenant on Economic, Social, and Cultural Rights provides that the state parties to the agreement "recognize the right of everyone to an adequate standard of living for himself and his family, including adequate food, clothing and housing, and to the continuous improvement of living conditions." A third generation of claims has received considerable attention in recent years, what may be broadly termed "rights of cultural membership."

These include language rights for members of cultural minorities and the rights of indigenous peoples to preserve their cultural institutions and practices and to exercise some measure of political autonomy. There is some overlap with the first-generation rights, such as that of religious liberty, but rights of cultural membership are broader and more controversial. Article 27 of the International Covenant on Civil and Political Rights declares that third-generation rights ought to be protected: In those States in which ethnic, religious or linguistic minorities exist, persons belonging to such minorities shall not be denied the right, in community with the other members of their group, to enjoy their own culture, to profess and practice their own religion, or to use their own language. Similarly, the Canadian Charter of Rights and Freedoms protects the language rights of minorities and section 27 provides that "This Charter shall be interpreted in a manner consistent with the preservation and enhancement of the multicultural heritage of Canadians."

In the United States, there is no analogous protection of language rights or multiculturalism, although constitutional doctrine does recognize native Indian tribes as "domestic dependent nations" with some attributes of political self-rule, such as sovereign immunity. There is substantial philosophical controversy over the legitimacy and scope of rights of cultural membership. Kymlicka has argued that the liberal commitment to protect the equal rights of individuals requires society to protect such rights.

He argues that "granting special representational rights, land claims, or language rights to a minority....can be seen as putting the various groups on a more equal footing, by reducing the extent to which the smaller group is vulnerable to the larger". Such special rights do not amount to "group rights," in the sense of granting the group any power or priority over the individual. Rather, the rights "compensate for unequal circumstances which put the members of minority cultures at a systemic disadvantage in the cultural marketplace". Waldron criticizes Kymlicka for exaggerating the importance for the individual of membership in her particular culture and for underestimating the mutability and interpenetration of cultures.

Individual freedom requires some cultural context of choice, but it does not require the preservation of the particular context in which the individual finds herself. Liberal individuals must be free to evaluate their culture and to distance themselves from it. Kukathas criticizes Kymlicka for implying that the liberal commitment to the protection of individual rights is insufficient to treat the interests of minorities with equal consideration. Kukathas contends that "we need to reassert the importance of individual liberty or individual rights and question the idea that cultural minorities have collective rights".

But the system of uniform legal rules that he endorses would keep the state from intervening even when a minority culture inflicts significant harm on its more vulnerable members, *e.g.*, when cultural norms strongly discourage females from seeking the same educational and career opportunities as males. Barry asserts that "there are certain rights against oppression, exploitation, and injury, to which every single human being is entitled to lay claim, and…appeals to cultural diversity and pluralism under no circumstances trump the value of basic liberal rights". The legal system should protect those rights by impartially imposing the same rules on all persons, regardless of their cultural or religious membership.

Barry allows for a few exceptions, such as the accommodation of a Sikh boy whose turban violated school dress regulations, but thinks that the conditions under which such exceptions will be justified "are rarely satisfied". Barry's position reflects and elaborates Gitlin's earlier condemnation of views advocating distinctive rights for cultural and ethnic minorities. Gitlin condemned such views on the ground that they represent a "swerve from civil rights, emphasizing a universal condition and universalizable rights, to cultural separatism, emphasizing difference and distinct needs". At the other end of the spectrum, Taylor argues for a form of communitarianism that attaches intrinsic importance to the survival of cultures. In his view, differential treatment under the law for certain practices is sometimes justifiable on the ground that such treatment is important for keeping a culture alive.

Taylor goes as far as to claim that cultural survival can sometimes trump basic individual rights, such as freedom of speech. Accordingly, he defends legal restrictions on the use of English in Quebec, invoking the survival of Quebec's French culture. However, it is unclear why intrinsic value should attach to cultural survival as such. Following John Dewey, Kymlicka rightly emphasizes that liberty would have little or no value to the individual apart from the life-options and meaningful choices provided by culture. But both thinkers also reasonably contend that human interests are ultimately the interests of individual human beings. In light of that contention, it would seem that a culture that could not gain the uncoerced and undeceived adherence of enough individuals to survive would have no moral claim to its continuation. Legal restrictions on basic liberties that are designed to perpetuate a given culture have the cart before the horse: persons should have their basic liberties protected first, as those protections serve the most important human interests. Only when those interests are protected can we then say that a culture should survive, not because the culture is intrinsically valuable, but rather because it has the uncoerced adherence of a sufficient number of persons.

**Blacks and Native Americans**

The treatment of blacks under slavery and Jim Crow presents a history of injustice and cultural annihilation that is similar in some respects to the treatment of Native Americans. However, civil rights principles played a very different role in the struggle of Native Americans against the injustices perpetrated against them by whites. Civil rights principles demand inclusion of the individuals from a disadvantaged group in the major institutions of society on an equal basis with the individuals who are already treated as full citizens. The principles do not require that the disadvantaged group be given a right to govern its own affairs.

A right of political self-determination, in contrast, demands that a group have the freedom to order its affairs at it sees fit and, to that extent, political self-determination has a separatist aspect, even if something less than complete sovereignty is involved. The pursuit of civil rights by American blacks overshadowed the pursuit of political self-determination.

The fact that American blacks lacked any territory of their own on which they could rule themselves favoured the civil rights strategy. Moreover, the civil war amendments, and the civil rights laws that accompanied them, were meant to incorporate black Americans into the body politic as free and equal citizens. Although this effort was defeated by Jim Crow, the principle of citizenship for blacks had been enshrined in law. And so, in their struggle to defeat Jim Crow, blacks could and did repeatedly demand that white Americans live up to their constitutional promise of equality. In contrast, for Native Americans, the pursuit of political-self-determination, in the form of tribal sovereignty, overshadowed the pursuit of civil rights. Even after the coerced tribal removals and federal efforts to impose regimes of individual land ownership, tribes still retained some territorial basis on which a measure of self-rule was possible.

Moreover, a line of Supreme Court decisions dating to the early 1800's held that Indian tribes possessed some — albeit very limited — inherent powers of sovereignty. Accordingly, pursuit of political self-determination rather than civil-rights protections seemed, in the eyes of many Indians, to be the most reasonable strategy for counteracting white oppression. During the civil rights movement of the 1950's and 60's, there was some tension between Native Americans and blacks due to their different attitudes towards self-determination and civil rights. Some Native Americans looked askance at the desire of blacks for inclusion and thought the desire hopelessly naïve. And activists emerged from the black power movement who had a similar view of the effort at racial inclusion and who called for a form of political self-determination. Such a call was part of a tradition of black nationalism that can still be found today in the United States.

Nonetheless, in the United States, unlike civil rights principles, black nationalist principles have not become part of the law. In 1968, Congress enacted an Indian Civil Rights Act. The act extended the reach of certain individual constitutional rights against government to intratribal affairs. Tribal governments would for the first time be bound by constitutional principles concerning free speech, due process, cruel and unusual punishment, and equal protection, among others. Freedom of religion was omitted from the law as a result of the protests of the Pueblo, whose political arrangements were theocratic, but the law was a major incursion on tribal self-determination, nonetheless. A married pueblo woman brought suit in federal court, claiming that the tribe's marriage ordinances constituted sex discrimination against her and other women of the tribe, thus violating the ICRA. The ordinances excluded from tribal membership the children of a Pueblo woman who married outside of the tribe, while the children of men who married outsiders were counted as members.

Martinez had initially sought relief in tribal forums, to no avail, before turning to the federal courts. The Supreme Court held that federal courts did not have jurisdiction to hear the case: the substantive provisions of the ICRA did apply to the Pueblo, but the inherent sovereign powers of the tribe meant that the tribal government had exclusive jurisdiction in the case. The ruling has been both questioned and defended by feminist legal scholars. In contrast to the United States, the Canadian Indian Act provides that men and women are to be treated equally when it comes to the band membership of their children.

This law and the Santa Clara case raise the general issue of whether and when it is justifiable for a liberal state to impose liberal principles on illiberal political communities that had been involuntary incorporated into the larger state. Addressing this issue, Kymlicka argues that "there is relatively little scope for legitimate coercive interference" because efforts to impose liberal principles tend to be counterproductive, provoking the charge that they amount to "paternalistic colonialism." Moreover, "liberal institutions can only really work if liberal beliefs have been internalized."

Kymlicka concludes, then, that liberals on the outside of an illiberal culture should support the efforts of those insiders who seek reform but should generally stop short of coercively imposing liberal principles. At the same time, Kymlicka acknowledges that there are cases in which a liberal state is clearly permitted to impose its laws, citing with approval the decision in a case that involved the application of Canadian law to a tribe that had kidnapped a member and forced him to undergo an initiation ceremony. Applying Kymlicka's general line of thinking might prove contentious in many cases. Consider Santa Clara. His arguments could be used to support the decision in that case: the exercise of jurisdiction might be deemed "paternalistic colonialism."

But one might argue, instead, that jurisdiction is needed to vindicate the basic liberal right of gender equality. However, it does seem that, if a wrong akin to kidnapping or worse is required before federal courts can legitimately step in, then the Santa Clara case falls short of meeting such a requirement. The argument might then shift to whether the requirement imposes an excessively high hurdle for the exercise of federal jurisdiction.

Accordingly, Kymlicka's approach might not settle the disagreement over Santa Clara, but it does provide a very reasonable normative framework in terms of which liberal thought can address the difficult issues presented by the case and, more generally, by the problem of extending liberal principles to Native American tribes.

## FREE AND EQUAL CITIZENSHIP

Civil rights are those rights that constitute free and equal citizenship in a liberal democracy. Such citizenship has two main dimensions, both tied to the idea of autonomy. Accordingly, civil rights are essentially connected to securing the autonomy of the citizen.

### Public and Private Autonomy

To be a free and equal citizen is, in part, to have those legal guarantees that are essential to fully adequate participation in public discussion and decisionmaking. A citizen has a right to an equal voice and an equal vote. In addition, she has the rights needed to protect her "moral independence," that is, her ability to decide for herself what gives meaning and value to her life and to take responsibility for living in conformity with her values. Accordingly, equal citizenship has two main dimensions: "public autonomy," *i.e.*, the individual's freedom to participate in the formation of public opinion and society's collective decisions; and "private autonomy," *i.e.*, the individual's freedom to decide what way of life is most worth pursuing. The importance of these two dimensions of citizenship stem from what Rawls calls the "two moral powers" of personhood: the capacity for a sense of justice and the capacity for a conception of the good. A person stands as an equal citizen when society and its political system give equal and due weight to the interest each citizen has in the development and exercise of those capacities.

### Ancient and Modern Citizenship

The idea of equal citizenship can be traced back to Aristotle's political philosophy and his claim that true citizens take turns ruling and being ruled. In modern society, the idea has been transformed, in part by the development of representative government and its system of elections. For modern liberal thought, by contrast, citizenship is no longer a matter of having a direct and equal share in governance, but rather consists in a legal status that confers a certain package of rights that guarantee to an individual a voice, a vote, and a zone of private autonomy.

The other crucial differences between modern liberalism and earlier political theories concern the range of human beings who are regarded as having the capacity for citizenship and the scope of private autonomy to which each citizen is entitled as a matter of basic right. Modern liberal theory is more expansive on both counts than its ancient and medieval forerunners. It is true that racist and sexist assumptions plagued liberal theory well into the twentieth-century. However, two crucial liberal ideas have made possible an internal critique of racism, sexism, and other illegitimate forms of hierarchy.

The first is that society is constructed by humans, a product of human will, and not some preordained natural or God-given order. The second is that social arrangements need to be justified before the court of reason to each individual who lives under them and who is capable of reasoning. The conjunction of these ideas made possible an egalitarianism that was not available to ancient and medieval political thought, although this liberal egalitarianism emerged slowly out of the racist and sexist presuppositions that infused much liberal thinking until recent decades. Many contemporary theorists have argued that taking liberal egalitarianism to its logical conclusion requires the liberal state to pursue a programme of deliberately reconstructing informal social norms and cultural meanings.

They contend that social stigma and denigration still operate powerfully to deny equal citizenship to groups such as blacks, women, and gays. Accordingly, Kernohan has argued that "the egalitarian liberal state should play an activist role in cultural reform", and Koppelman has taken a similar position: "the antidiscrimination project seeks to reconstruct social reality to eliminate or marginalize the shared meanings, practices and institutions that unjustifiably single out certain groups of citizens for stigma and disadvantage".

This position is deeply at odds with at least some of the ideas that lie behind the advocacy of third-generation civil rights. Those rights ground claims of cultural survival, whether or not a culture's meanings, practices and institutions stigmatize and disadvantage the members of some ascriptively-defined group. The egalitarian proponents of cultural reconstruction can be understood as advocating a different kind of "third-generation" for the civil rights movement: one in which the state, having attacked legal, political and economic barriers to equal citizenship, now takes on cultural obstacles.

A cultural-reconstruction phase of the civil rights movement would run contrary to Kukathas's argument that it is too dangerous to license the state to intervene against cultures that engage in social tyranny. It also raises questions about whether state-supported cultural reconstruction would violate basic liberties, such as freedom of private association. The efforts of New Jersey to apply antidiscrimination law to the Boy Scouts, a group which discriminates against gays, shows the potential problems. The Supreme Court invalidated those efforts on grounds of free association. Nonetheless, it may be necessary to reconceive the scope and limits of some basic liberties if the principle of free and equal citizenship is followed through to its logical conclusions.

## DISCRIMINATION

In liberal democracies, civil rights claims are typically conceptualized in terms of the idea of discrimination. Persons who make such claims assert that they are the victims of discrimination. In order to gain an understanding of current discussion and debate regarding civil rights, it is important to disentangle the various descriptive and normative senses of 'discrimination'.

## The Idea of Discrimination

In one of its central descriptive senses, 'discrimination' means the differential treatment of persons, however justifiable or unjustifiable the treatment may be. In a distinct but still primarily descriptive sense, it means the disadvantageous treatment of some persons relative to others. This sense is not purely descriptive in that an evaluative judgment is involved in determining what counts as a disadvantage. But the sense is descriptive insofar as no evaluative judgment is made regarding the justifiability of the disadvantageous treatment. In addition to its descriptive senses, there are two normative senses of 'discrimination'.

In the first, it means any differential treatment of the individual that is morally objectionable. In the second sense, 'discrimination' means the wrongful denial or abridgement of the civil rights of some persons in a context where others enjoy their full set of rights. The two normative senses are distinct because there can be morally objectionable forms of differential treatment that do not involve the wrongful denial or abridgement of civil rights. If I treat one waiter rudely and another nicely, because one is a New York Yankees fan and the other is a Boston Red Sox fan, then we have acted in a morally objectionable way but have not violated anyone's civil rights. Discrimination that does deny civil rights is a double wrong against its victims. The denial of civil rights is by itself a wrong, whether or not others have such rights. When others do have such rights, the denial of civil rights to persons who are entitled to them involves the additional wrong of unjustified differential treatment. On the other hand, if everyone is denied his civil rights, then the idea of discrimination would be misapplied to the situation. A despot who oppresses everyone equally is not guilty of discrimination in any of its senses. In contrast, discrimination is a kind of wrong that is found in systems that are liberal democratic but imperfectly so: it is the characteristic injustice of liberal democracy.

The first civil rights law, enacted in 1866, embodied the idea of discrimination as wrongful denial of civil rights to some while others enjoyed their full set of rights. It declared that "all persons" in the United States were to have "the same right…to make and enforce contracts…and to the full and equal benefit of all laws…as is enjoyed by white citizens". The premise was that whites enjoyed a fully adequate scheme of civil rights and that everyone else who was entitled to citizenship was to be legally guaranteed that same set of rights. It is a notable feature of civil rights law that its prohibitions do not protect only citizens.

Any person within a given jurisdiction, citizen or not, can claim the protection of the law, at least within certain limits. Thus, noncitizens are protected by fair housing and equal employment statutes, among other antidiscrimination laws. Noncitizens can also claim the legal protections of due process if charged with a crime. Even illegal aliens have limited due process rights if they are within the legal jurisdiction of the country. On the other hand, noncitizens cannot claim under U.S. law that the denial of political rights amounts to wrongful discrimination.

Noncitizens can vote in local and regional elections in certain countries, but the denial of equal political rights would seem to be central to the very status of noncitizen. The application of much of civil rights law to noncitizens indicates that many of the rights in question are deeper than simply the rights that constitute citizenship. They are genuine human rights to which every person is entitled, whether she is in a location where she has a right to citizenship or not. And civil rights issues are, for that reason, regarded as broader in scope than issues regarding the treatment of citizens.

## Why Discrimination is Unjust

Given the principle of equal citizenship, discrimination in the sense of the denial of civil rights is an injustice that denies certain citizens the rights to which they are entitled. But it is not obvious that the principle entails that discrimination in the sense of differential treatment is unjust, even if the differential treatment disadvantages persons based on their race, sex, or another paradigmatic civil rights category.

The common view is that such differential treatment is an injustice that violates the basic rights of the individual. In other words, the view is that it is a civil right to not be treated disadvantageously on account of one's race or sex. An argument for the soundness of the common view cannot simply invoke existing laws that ban discrimination based on race, sex, and similar categories.

The point of the common view is that the injustice of racial and gender discrimination explains why there ought to be those laws. What is required is an account that shows why such discrimination is an injustice. There are two main approaches to providing an account of the injustice of discrimination based on race and sex. The first is "individualistic" in that it seeks to explain the injustice in a way that abstracts from the broader social and political context in which the differential treatment occurs. The second is "systemic" in that it seeks to explain the injustice in a way that links the differential treatment to social patterns that reduce, or threaten to reduce, the members of certain groups to second-class citizenship.

### *Individualistic Accounts*

Kahlenberg asserts the popular view that race discrimination is unjust because it treats a person on the basis of a characteristic that is immutable or beyond her control. But Boxill rejects such a view, arguing that there are many instances in which it is justifiable to treat persons based on features that are beyond their control. Denying blind people a driver's license or persons with little athletic ability a place on the basketball team is not an injustice to such individuals. Moreover, Boxill notes that, if scientists developed a drug that could change a person's skin colour, it would still be unjust to discriminate against people because of their skin colour. Flew argues that racism is unjust because it treats differently persons who "are *in all relevant respects* the same".

The defining characteristics of a race "are strictly superficial and properly irrelevant to all, or almost all, questions of social status and employability". But if 'relevant' means 'rationally related', then it does not appear to be a requirement of justice that a person always treat others only on the basis of relevant characteristics.

The idea that it is such a requirement rests on the false premise that all morally bad treatment is a violation of justice and rights. If I give a waiter a poor tip because he is not a fan of my favourite sports team, then we have behaved badly but have not violated the waiter's rights or committed an injustice against him. And it is unclear, on Flew's account, why giving a poor tip because of a waiter's race is any different than doing so because of his preferences in sports. Often people will insist that the injustice of racial or sex discrimination stems from the connection between those forms of discrimination and the reliance on stereotypes. It is not just that race is irrelevant but that those who act on race-based grounds are using inaccurate stereotypes instead of treating a person "as an individual," as the phrase goes.

However, if "being treated as an individual" means that others must take into account all of the potentially relevant information about the person in their behaviour towards her, then there is no plausibility to the claim that anyone has a right to such treatment. Life's scarcity of time and resources undermines the idea that there is such a right. Moreover, in some cases, stereotypical beliefs reflect reliable generalizations about a group. The term 'statistical discrimination' refers to the use of such reliable generalizations. Consider the case of a pregnant job applicant: as a statistical matter, there is a higher antecedent likelihood that she will take more sick days than a nonpregnant applicant during the first year of employment. Yet, an employer who relies on statistical discrimination in excluding the pregnant applicant is acting illegally under the Pregnancy Discrimination Act.

The act was passed because many people quite reasonably thought that it was unjust for a pregnant applicant to be treated in that way. But if the treatment is unjust, then one cannot explain why that is so by invoking the un reliability of the generalization on which the treatment is based. Garcia provides an account of racial discrimination that loosens the link between it and injustice, but still preserves some connection. On his account, such discrimination against others expresses a character defect, *viz.*, the failure to care enough, or in the right way, for their interests.

Accordingly, such discrimination is a matter of what is "in the heart" of the racist individual: "racially focused ill-will or disregard. This echoes the claim made by Gunnar Myrdal in his classic work, *An American Dilemma*, that "the American Negro problem is a problem in the heart of Americans". Garcia's account weakens the link between racial discrimination and injustice because not every act expressing racial ill-will or disregard will be an injustice.

Garcia writes that racial discrimination against a person "will often offend against justice," but he does not argue that it always so offends. He points out that discrimination against a person based on race may amount to a failure of benevolence, rather than a violation of rights. For example, racial disregard may lead a person to refuse to contribute to a charity organization that works with inner-city youth. In such a case, the person has failed to show benevolence for morally discreditable reasons, and so has behaved badly. But no injustice has been committed. On the other hand racial ill-will is often expressed in violations of the rights of persons: hate crimes that harm the property or person of an individual on account of race; efforts to prevent members of certain racial groups from voting; charging racial minorities higher prices for the same product than the prices charged to similarly situated whites; denying persons equality of opportunity in the job and housing markets on account of their race. Such actions would count as injustices, not simply failures of benevolence.

Thus, Garcia's approach preserves some link between discrimination and injustice, but it is much more attenuated than the link posited by the popular view that disadvantageous treatment on the basis of race is *ipso facto* an injustice to the person so treated.

***Systemic Accounts***

Many thinkers reject the idea that the injustice of discrimination stems fundamentally from what is in the mind or heart of the individual. Crespi criticized Myrdal on the ground that the latter's individualistic understanding of racial discrimination entailed that "ethical exhortation" was the remedy for racial injustice. Crespi argued that what really needed remedy were the social and economic structures that advantage whites. More recently, Steinberg and Bonilla-Silva, among others, have argued that racial discrimination should not be understood as a "moral problem," *i.e.*, as a problem with individual attitudes or actions, but rather as a problem of persistent structural inequality.

And MacKinnon has made a parallel argument when it comes to sex discrimination. For example, she contends that pornography is "not a moral problem" but rather a political one, meaning that it does not pose a problem of the virtue and vice of individuals and their behaviour but rather one concerning relations of power that subordinate women to men. On the systemic account of racial and sex discrimination, the injustice of discriminatory acts lies in their connection to broader patterns in society that reduce the members of certain groups to second-class citizenship, or worse. Considered in abstraction from these broader patterns, refusing employment to someone on account of her race might be morally objectionable insofar as it treated a person arbitrarily when some important interest of hers was at stake. But the objectionable treatment amounts to an injustice because such acts are not sporadic but rather systemic and add up to a system in which persons have their entire lives substantially diminished on account of their race or sex. And such a system is what violates the right to equality — the basic civil right. Individual acts of racial or gender discrimination do so only derivatively, by reinforcing the systemic violation.

There are different ways in which a systemic account can be elaborated. For example, in MacKinnon's account of sex discrimination, the system of gender inequality revolves around the sexual subordination of women. Butler, Brown and other feminists provide accounts which do not share MacKinnon's focus on sexual subordination. On the matter of racial discrimination, Cox focuses on the ways in which racial conflict is rooted in class conflict, while Omi and Winant emphasize "the specificity of race as an autonomous field of social conflict, political organization, and cultural/ideological meaning".

In whatever way the details are elaborated, all systemic accounts rest on the premise that women, racial minorities, and other groups are second-class citizens and that they are so because of their group membership. The advocates of systemic accounts typically represent their views as incompatible with individualistic ones. They do so by insisting that discrimination is "not a moral problem" of the individual's heart or mind, but one concerning group power relations and social patterns of disadvantage. But their insistence rests on a false dichotomy. Discrimination based on race, sex and other categories can be a problem of the individual's heart and mind, as well as an issue that concerns systemic patterns of disadvantage in society.

As Wasserstrom pointed out, discrimination can operate at both the individual and systemic levels. It is not necessary to deny the existence of patterns of discriminatory treatment that reduce, or threaten to reduce, some persons to second-class citizenship in order to affirm that it is an injustice to deny a person a job because of her sex. And it is not necessary to deny that, apart from social patterns of disadvantage, the individual who is denied a job for such reasons has been treated in an unjust way, in order to affirm that there are such patterns that reduce some to second-class status.

**Justifying Antidiscrimination Law**

Antidiscrimination laws typically pick out certain categories such as race and sex for legal protection, define certain spheres such as employment and public accommo-dations in which discrimination based on the protected categories is prohibited, and establish special government agencies, such as the Equal Employment Opportunity Commission, to assist in the laws' enforcement.

There are many questions that can be raised concerning the justifiability of such laws. Some of the central philosophical questions derive from the fact that the laws restrict freedom of association, including the liberty of employers to decide whom they will hire. Some have argued that the liberal commitment to free association requires the rejection of antidiscrimination laws, including those that ban employment discrimination such as the Civil Rights Act of 1964. Most liberals thinkers reject this view, but any liberal defence of antidiscrimination laws must cite considerations sufficiently strong to override the infringements on freedom of association that the laws involve. There are two different approaches within liberal thought to the justification of antidiscrimination laws. Both approaches regard as very important the interests people have in the areas protected by the laws, such as employment and public accommodations.

And both approaches agree that the disadvantageous treatment of a person in those areas on the basis of race, sex, and the other traditional civil rights categories is morally arbitrary. However, on the first approach, the key to the justification of antidiscrimination laws rests squarely on the fact that the conduct prohibited by the laws is morally arbitrary. In contrast, the second approach holds that it is not the morally arbitrary conduct as such that justifies the laws but rather the fact that conduct based on those categories has had systemic effects reducing the members of certain groups to second-class citizenship. Thus, the difference between the two approaches tracks the distinction between the individualistic and systemic accounts of why discrimination is wrong. Although many legal theorists endorse the systemic approach to the justification of antidiscrimination law, the U.S. Supreme Court seems to have adopted the individualistic one.

**The Existence of Discrimination**

Many debates over civil rights issues turn on assumptions about the scope and effects of existing discrimination against particular groups. For example, some thinkers hold that systemic discrimination based on race and gender is largely a thing of the past in contemporary liberal democracies and that the current situation allows persons to participate in society as free and equal citizens, regardless of race or gender. Many others reject that view, arguing that white skin privilege and patriarchy persist and operate to substantially and unjustifiably diminish the life-prospects of nonwhites and women.

These differences drive debates over affirmative action, race-conscious electoral districting, and pornography, among other issues. Questions about the scope and effects of discrimination are largely but not entirely empirical in character. Such questions concern the degree to which participation in society as a free and equal citizen is hampered by one's race or sex. And addressing that concern presupposes some normative criteria for determining what is needed to possess the status of such a citizen.

Moreover, there are subtle aspects of discrimination that are not captured by thinking strictly in terms of categories such as race, sex, religion, sexual orientation, and so on. Piper analyses "higher-order" forms of discrimination in which certain traits, such as speaking style, come to be arbitrarily disvalued on account of their association with a disvalued race or sex. Determining the presence and effects of such forms of discrimination in society at large would be a very complicated conceptual and empirical task. Additional complications stem from the fact that different categories of discrimination might intersect in ways that produce distinctive forms of unjust disadvantage.

Thus, some thinkers have asserted that the intersection of race and sex creates a form of discrimination against black women which has not been adequately recognized or addressed by judges or liberal legal theorists. And other thinkers have begun to argue that our understanding of discrimination must be expanded beyond the white-black paradigm to include the distinctive ways in which Asian-Americans and other minority groups are subjected to discriminatory attitudes and treatment.

Among the most careful empirical studies of discrimination have been those conducted by Ayers. He found evidence of "pervasive discrimination" in several types of markets, including retail car sales, bail-bonding, and kidney-transplantation. Yet, his assessment is that "we still do not know the current ambit of race and gender discrimination in America".

## SEXUAL ORIENTATION

Some civil rights laws in the United States include the category of sexual orientation, but many people contest the legitimacy of the laws. The state of Colorado went so far as to ratify an amendment to its constitution that would prohibit any jurisdiction within the state from enacting a civil rights law that would protect homosexuals. The amendment was eventually invalidated by the U.S. Supreme Court on the ground that it was the product of simple prejudice and served no legitimate state purpose, thus violating the Equal Protection Clause.

But federal courts have upheld the military's "don't ask, don't tell" policy and the U.S. Congress enacted the Defence of Marriage Act, which prohibits courts from ruling that same-sex marriages must be recognized on equal protection grounds. On the other hand, same-sex marriages are legally recognized in Massachusetts, though there are efforts to rescind the recognition, and marriage laws have also been extended to same-sex couples in the Netherlands, Belgium, Canada and Spain. In addition, several jurisdictions have recognized same-sex partnerships with many, though not all, of the legal rights of marriage. Opponents of same-sex marriage have claimed that it would weaken the commitment of heterosexuals to marriage, but some advocates have presented empirical data that appears to undercut any such claim. Much of the discussion of "gay rights" involves the question of whether sexual orientation is genetically determined, socially determined, or the product of individual choice.

However, it is not clear why the question is relevant. The discussion appears to assume that genetic determination would vindicate the civil rights claims of gays, because sexual orientation would then be like race or sex insofar as it would be biologically fixed and immutable. But it is a mistake to think that racial or sex discrimination is morally objectionable because of the biological fixity or unchosen nature of race and sex. It is objectionable because it expresses ill-will or indifference, and it is unjust because it treats an individual in a morally arbitrary manner and, under current conditions, reinforces social patterns of disadvantage that seriously diminish the life prospects of many persons.

The view that sexual orientation is like race or sex in a morally relevant way should focus on the analogous features of discrimination based on sexual orientation. Wintermute and Koppelman assert that discrimination based on sexual orientation is not just analogous to sex discrimination but that it is a form of sex discrimination.

If it is legally permissible for Jane to have sex with John, then banning Joe's having sex with John would seem to amount to discrimination against Joe on grounds of his sex. If Joe were a woman, his having sex with John would be permitted, so he is being treated differently because of his sex. However, Koppelman contends that this formal argument should be supplemented by more substantive ones referring to the systemic patterns of social disadvantage from which gays and lesbians suffer. In fact, one can argue that the treatment of gays and lesbians is an injustice to them as individuals and amounts to a systemic pattern of unjust disadvantage. The individual injustice arises from the arbitrary nature of denying persons valuable life-opportunities, such as employment and marriage, on the basis of their sexual orientation. The systemic injustice arises from the repeated and widespread acts of individual injustice. The most controversial civil rights issues regarding sexual orientation concern the principle of equal treatment for same-sex and heterosexual couples.

Most scholars endorse such a principle and argue that equal treatment requires that same-sex marriages be legalized. Moreover, it is often argued in the literature that a person's choice of sex partner is central to her life and protected under a right of privacy. In Bowers v. Hardwick, the United States Supreme Court rejected this argument, upholding the criminalization of homosexual sodomy. The decision was condemned by legal and political thinkers and was overturned by the Court in Lawrence v. Texas. The Court invoked the right of privacy in declaring the state's criminal ban on sodomy between same-sex partners. Nonetheless, some scholars who argue for the equal legal treatment of same-sex relations contend that privacy-based arguments are inadequate. They point out that one can hold the view that adults have a right to engage in same-sex intimacies even as one contends that such intimacies are morally abominable and ought not to receive any encouragement from government. Such a view would reject equal legal treatment for those in intimate same-sex relationships. Finnis takes such a view, arguing that same-sex relations are "manifestly unworthy of the human being and immoral" and should not be encouraged by the state, but finding that criminalizing same-sex relations violates rights of individual privacy. Lee and George also find such relations to be morally defective and unworthy of equal treatment by the state; though George does not think that any sound *a priori* principle prohibits criminalization. Finnis, Lee and George argue for their condemnation of same-sex relations on the ground of natural law theory. However, unlike traditional versions of natural law theory, their version does not rest on any explicit theological or metaphysical claims. Rather, it invokes independent principles of practical reasoning that articulate the basic reasons for action. Such reasons are the fundamental goods that action is capable of realising and, for Finnis, Lee and George, include "marriage, the *conjuntio* of man and woman". Homosexual conduct, masturbation, and all extra-marital sex aim strictly at "individual gratification" and can be no part of any "common good." Such actions "harm the character" of those voluntarily choosing them. In taking the actions, a person becomes a slave to his passions, allowing his reason to be overridden by his raw desire for sensuous pleasure.

On Finnis's account, when consensual sexual conduct is private, government may not outlaw it, but government "can rightly judge that it has a compelling interest in denying that 'gay lifestyles' are a valid and humanly acceptable choice and form of life". And for Finnis, Lee and George, equal treatment of same-sex and heterosexual relations is out of the question due to the morally defective character of same-sex relations. Macedo responds to Finnis by arguing that "all of the goods that can be shared by sterile heterosexual couples can also be shared by committed homosexual couples".

Macedo points out that Finnis does not condemn sexual intercourse by sterile heterosexual couples. But Finnis replies that there is a relevant difference between homosexual couples and sterile heterosexual ones: the latter but not the former are united "biologically" when they have intercourse. Lee and George make essentially the same point: only heterosexual couples can "truly become one body, one organism". But Macedo points out that, biologically, it is not the man and woman who unite but the sperm and the egg. It can be added that the "biological unity" argument seems to run contrary to Finnis's claim that his position "does not seek to infer normative conclusions from non-normative premises".

More importantly, Macedo and Koppelman make the key point that the human good possible through intimate relations is a function of "mutual commitment and stable engagement" and that same-sex couples can achieve "the precise kind of human good" that is available to heterosexual ones. Accordingly, equal treatment under the law for same-sex couples, including the recognition of same-sex marriage, would remove unjustifiable obstacles faced by same-sex couples to the achievement of that human good.

## DISABILITY

During the 1970's and 80's, persons with disabilities increasingly argued that they were second-class citizens. They organized into a civil rights movement that pressed for legislation that would help secure for them the status of equal citizens.

Protection against discrimination based on disability was written into the Canadian Charter of Rights and Freedoms and The Charter of Fundamental Rights of the European Union. The disability rights movement in the U.S. culminated with the passage of the Americans With Disabilities Act of 1990. The ADA has served as a model for legislation in countries such as Australia, India and Israel

**The Medical and Social Models**

The traditional model for understanding disability is called the "medical model." It is reflected in many pre-ADA laws and in some philosophical discussions of disability which treat it as an issue of the just distribution of health care. The medical model, a disabled person is one who falls below some baseline level that defines normal human functioning. That level is a natural one, on this view, in that it is determined by biological facts about the human species.

Thus, the medical model supposes that the question of who counts as disabled can be answered in a way that is value-free and that abstracts from existing social practices and the physical environment those practices have constructed. It also gives the medical profession a privileged position in determining who is disabled, as the study and treatment of normal and subnormal human functioning is the specialty of that profession. The consensus among current disability theorists is that the medical model should be rejected. Any determination that a certain level of function is normal for the species will presuppose judgments that do not simply describe biological reality but impose on them some system of evaluation. Moreover, the level of functioning a person can achieve does not depend solely on her own individual abilities: it depends as well on the social practices and the physical environment those practices have shaped. Disability theorists thus posit an important analogy between the categories of 'race' and 'disability'.

As they understand it, neither category refers to any real distinctions in nature. Just as there is variation in skin colour, there is variation in acuity of vision, physical strength, ability to walk and run and so on. And just as there is no natural line dividing one "race" from another, there is no natural line dividing those who are functionally "abnormal" from those who are not so. The rejection of the medical model has led to a "social model," just as to which certain physical or biological properties are turned into dysfunctions by social practices and the socially-constructed physical environment. For example, lack of mobility for those who are unable to walk is not simply a function of their physical characteristics: it is also a function of building practices that employ stairs instead of ramps and by automotive design practices that require the use of one's legs to drive a car. There is nothing necessary about such practices. Accordingly, the social model conceives of disability as socially-imposed dysfunction.

The social model brings attention to how engineering and design practices can work to the disadvantage of persons with certain physical characteristics. And the idea of dysfunction is certainly a value-laden one. But it seems no more accurate to think that dysfunction is entirely imposed by society than it is to think that it is entirely the product of an individual's physical or mental characteristics. Individual characteristics in the context of the socially-constructed environment determine the level of functioning that a person can achieve. And some individual characteristics would impair a person's functioning under all or almost all practicable alternatives to current social practices. Moreover, despite the fact that "normal human functioning" is a value-laden concept, it does not follow that it is entirely subjective or that reasonable efforts to specify the elements of some morally acceptable level of human functioning are misguided.

Indeed, some defensible understanding of what counts as better or worse human functioning would seem to be necessary to determine when some social practice has turned a physical characteristic into a significant disadvantage for a person. In addition, the social model's conception of what it is to be a disabled person seems overbroad. The social practice of requiring students to pass courses in order to receive a degree creates a barrier that some persons cannot surmount. It does not seem that such people are, *ipso facto*, disabled. Such examples of "exclusionary" social practices could be multiplied indefinitely.

Some thinkers may not be troubled by the implication that everyone is disabled in every respect in which she is excluded or otherwise disadvantaged by some social practice. But it is difficult to see how the idea of disability would then be of much use.

**Race, Disability, and Discrimination**

The disability rights movement began with the idea that discrimination on the basis of disability was not different in any morally important way from discrimination based on race. The aim of the movement was to enshrine in law the same kind of antidiscrimination principle that protected persons based on their race. But some theorists have questioned how well the analogy holds. They point out that applying the antidiscrimination norm to disability requires taking account of physical or mental differences among people. This seems to be treatment based on a person's physical features, apparently the exact opposite of the ideal of "colour blindness" behind the traditional antidiscrimination principle.

Even race-based affirmative action does not really seem to be parallel to antidiscrimination policies that take account of disability. Advocates of affirmative action assert that the social ideal is for persons not to be treated on the basis of their race or colour at all. Race-conscious policies are seen as instruments that will move society towards that ideal. In contrast, policies designed to counter discrimination based on disability are not sensibly understood as temporary measures or steps towards a goal in which people are not treated based on their disabilities. The policies permanently enshrine the idea that in designing buildings or buses or constructing some other aspect of our physical-social environment, we must be responsive to the disabilities people have in order for the disabled to have "fair equality of opportunity". The need for a permanent "accommodation" of persons with disabilities seems to mark an important difference in how the antidiscrimination norm should be understood in the context of disability, as opposed to the context of race.

However, it is important to recognize that, at the level of fundamental principle, the reasons why disability-based discrimination is morally objectionable and even unjust are essentially the same as the reasons why racial discrimination is so. At the individual level, disadvantageous treatment of the disabled is often rooted in ill-will, disregard, and moral arbitrariness. At the systemic level, such treatment creates a social pattern of disadvantage that reduces the disabled to second-class status. In those two respects, the grounds of civil rights law are no different when it comes to the disabled.

Another way in which disability is thought to be fundamentally different from race concerns the special needs that the disabled often have that make life more costly for them. These extra costs would exist even if the socially-constructed physical environment were built to provide the disabled with fair equality of opportunity and their basic civil and political liberties were secured. In order to function effectively, disabled persons may need to buy medications or therapies or other forms of assistance that the able-bodied do not need for their functioning. And there does not seem to be any parallel in matters of race to the special needs of some of those who are disabled. The driving idea of the civil rights movement was that blacks did not have any special needs: all they needed was to have the burdens of racism lifted from them and, once that was accomplished, they would flourish or fail like everyone else in society. However, Silvers argues that the parallel between race and disability still holds: all the disabled may claim from society as a matter of justice is that they have fair equality of opportunity and the same basic civil rights as everyone else. Any special needs that the disabled may have do not provide the grounds of any legitimate claims of justice. On the other hand, Kittay argues that the special needs of the disabled are a matter of basic justice. She focuses on the severely mentally disabled, for whom fair opportunity in the labour markets and political rights in the public sphere will have no significance, and on the families which have the responsibility of caring for the severely disabled.

Pogge also questions Silvers' view, suggesting that it is implausible to deny that justice requires that society provide resources for meeting the needs of the severely disabled. Still, it may be the case that some version of Silvers' approach may be justifiable when it comes to disabled persons who have the capacity "to participate fully in the political and civic institutions of the society and, more broadly, in its public life". In the case of such persons, the basic civil right to equal citizenship would require that they have the equal opportunity to participate in such institutions, regardless of their disability. Although there may be some aspects of the racial model that cannot be applied to persons with severe forms of mental disability, the principles behind the American civil rights struggles of the 1950's and 60's remain crucial normative resources for understanding and combating forms of unjust discrimination that have only more recently been addressed by philosophers and by society more broadly.

**Contractarianism and the Disabled**

The emergence of the issue of disability rights has posed an important challenge for versions of liberalism inspired by the social contract tradition. One of the putative advantages of such forms of liberalism is that they better reflect strong and widely held intuitions about justice and individual rights than does utilitarianism. As Rawls famously wrote, "Each person possesses an inviolability founded on justice that even the welfare of society as a whole cannot override". However, several thinkers have argued that Rawls's own contractarian theory does not make adequate room for the severely disabled. These arguments are not about the rights of the severely disabled, but rather begin from the assumption that those who are so disabled do have robust moral rights and then proceed to the question whether contractarianism can account for those rights.

The problem for Rawls derives from the conception of personhood that accompanies his idea that society should be conceived as a fair system of cooperation among free and equal persons, extending over generations. On that conception, "a person is someone who can be a citizen, that is, a normal and fully cooperating member of society over a complete life." Additionally, persons are represented as having two "moral powers," the capacities for a sense of justice and for a conception of the good. The parties to Rawls's original position choose principles of justice with such a conception of the person in mind. Critics have argued that Rawls's principles of justice fail to take adequate account of the legitimate claims of the severely disabled and that the heart of the problem is Rawls's contractarianism.

Nussbaum claims that Rawls goes astray in following traditional contractarianism and conceiving of society as a scheme of cooperation for mutual advantage. Yet, Becker defends mutual-advantage theories, arguing that they can incorporate a conception of reciprocity sufficiently rich to underwrite principles that truly do justice to the disabled. Stark and Brighouse argue that Rawls's theory, in particular, can be extended or modified to take account of disabled, without repudiating its contractarian core. Kittay agrees with the liberal idea that justice must not be sacrificed for other values, but she doubts that any form of liberalism can make adequate room for the claims of justice made on behalf of the severely disabled. In contrast, Silvers and Francis defend a form of contract theory in which the parties seek to build mutual trust. They argue that the interests of disabled would not be discounted in such a contract.

## LEGAL CASES AND STATUTES

- Americans With Disabilities Act. 42 U.S.C. §§12101-12213.
- Bowers v. Hardwick 478 U.S. 186.
- Boy Scouts v. Dale, No. 99-699.
- Civil Rights Act of 1866. 42 U.S.C §1981.
- Civil Rights Act of 1964. 42 U.S.C. §§2000e et seq.
- Defence of Marriage Act 28 U.S.C. §1738c.
- Ex Parte Crow Dog 109 U.S. 556.
- Indian Civil Rights Act of 1968. 28 U.S.C. §§1301-1303.
- Oklahoma Tax Commission v. Citizen Band, Potawatomi Indian Tribe 498 U.S. 505.
- Pregnancy Discrimination Act 42 U.S.C. §2000 (e)(k).
- Romer v. Evans 517 U.S. 620.
- Santa Clara Pueblo v. Martinez 436 U.S. 49.
- Thomasson v. Perry 80 F.3d 915

## BUSINESS AND HUMAN RIGHTS

Non-state actors, particularly multinational or trans-national corporations have become important players throughout the world. As the influence and reach of corporations has grown as a result of globalization and other global developments, there is an increasing debate about the roles and responsibilities of corporate actors with regard to human rights.

International human rights standards have traditionally been the responsibility of governments, aimed at regulating relations between the state and individuals/groups. In view of the increased role played by corporate actors at both the national and international level, the United Nations human rights machinery is considering the scope of business' human rights responsibilities and exploring ways for corporate actors to be accountable for the impact of their activities on human rights. However, the practical meaning of the link between business and human rights remains unclear for many and substantial debates over which human rights can and should apply to business, and in what way are ongoing.

*OHCHR's work on the issue of business and human rights is focused on three areas*:

- Advocacy by the High Commissioner;
- Support to the Special Representative of the Secretary-General on the issue of transnational corporations and other business enterprises;
- Active involvement in the United Nations Global Compact;

The High Commissioners has expressed support for the development of human right standards applicable to the business sector, while at the same time advocating the implementation of voluntary initiatives towards corporate social responsibility.

OHCHR is providing ongoing support and advice to the work of the Special Representative of the Secretary-General on the issue of transnational corporations and other business enterprises with regard to human rights. The mandate was established by the United Nations Commission on Human Rights in 2005 by resolution 2005/69 and was extended by the Human Rights Council. In resolution 2005/69, the Commission on Human Rights mandated the High Commissioner, in collaboration with the SRSG, to convene annually a consultation with executives from a particular business sector to discuss the human rights challenges faced by that sector.

In November 2005, the High Commissioner convened a consultation with representatives from the extractive sector. In January 2007, the High Commissioner convened a consultation with representatives from the finance sector. The UN Global Compact is certainly the most prominent voluntary initiative in the field of business and human rights. It is a personal initiative of the United Nations Secretary-General dating from 2000, aimed at getting business leaders to voluntarily promote and apply within their corporate domains 10 principles relating to human rights, labour standards, the environment, and anti-corruption. At present, thousands of companies, many of them large transnational companies, from all continents have signed on to the Global Compact. OHCHR is one of now 6 UN agencies which work in partnership with the Secretary-General's Global Compact office. Since the launch of the Global Compact, OHCHR has been requested by the United Nations Secretary-General to serve as "guardian" of the human rights principles and to contribute to efforts made to encourage companies to implement these principles in their core operations and business model.

OHCHR activities have been grouped around the themes of learning and dialogue. OHCHR is involved in Global Compact governance through its membership of the Global Compact Inter-Agency Team which is responsible for ensuring coherent support for the internalization of the principles within the United Nations and among all participants.

OHCHR has joined the Global Compact Office and other partners in publishing tools for companies participating in the Global Compact on how to understand and implement the human rights principles of the Global Compact. The 18th of June 2008 the Human Rights Council was unanimous in "welcoming" the policy framework for business and human rights the SRSG proposed in his final report under the 2005 mandate.

The policy framework comprises three core principles: the State duty to protect against human rights abuses by third parties, including business; the corporate responsibility to respect human rights; and the need for greater access by victims to effective remedies. The Human Rights Council has renewed the mandate for a period of 3 years with the new resolution A/HRC/8/L.8 that requests the Special Representative of the Secretary General to operationalize the framework elaborated and specifically:

- To provide views and recommendations on ways to strengthen the fulfillment of the duty of the State to protect all human rights from abuses by transnational corporations and other business enterprises, including through international cooperation;
- To elaborate further on the scope and content of the corporate responsibility to respect all human rights and to provide concrete guidance to business and other stakeholders;
- To explore options and make recommendations, at the national, regional and international levels, for enhancing access to effective remedies available to those whose human rights are impacted by corporate activities;
- To integrate a gender perspective throughout his work and to give special attention to persons belonging to vulnerable groups, in particular children;
- To liaise closely with the efforts of the human rights working group of the Global Compact in order to identify, exchange and promote best practices and sessions learned on the issue of transnational corporations and other business enterprises;
- To work in close coordination with United Nations and other relevant international bodies, offices, departments and specialized agencies, and in particular with other special procedures of the Council;
- To continue to consult on the issues covered by the mandate on an ongoing basis with all stakeholders, including States, national human rights institutions, international and regional organizations, transnational corporations and other business enterprises, and civil society, including academics, employers' organizations, workers' organizations, indigenous and other affected communities and non-governmental organizations, including through joint meetings;
- To report annually to the Council and the General Assembly;

In Resolution 2005/69 The Commission on Human Rights requested the Secretary-General to appoint a special representative on the issue of human rights and transnational corporations and other business enterprises, for an initial period of two years, with the following mandate:

- To identify and clarify standards of corporate responsibility and accountability for transnational corporations and other business enterprises with regard to human rights;
- To elaborate on the role of States in effectively regulating and adjudicating the role of transnational corporations and other business enterprises with regard to human rights, including through international cooperation;

- To research and clarify the implications for transnational corporations and other business enterprises of concepts such as "complicity" and "sphere of influence";
- To develop materials and methodologies for undertaking human rights impact assessments of the activities of transnational corporations and other business enterprises;
- To compile a compendium of best practices of States and transnational corporations and other business enterprises.

## FREEDOM OF RELIGION OR BELIEF

### DEFINING RELIGION OR BELIEF

The word "religion," meaning to bind fast, comes from the Western Latin word religare. It is commonly, but not always, associated with traditional majority, minority or new religious beliefs in a transcendent deity or deities. In human rights discourse, however, the use of the term usually also includes support for the right to non-religious beliefs. In 1993 the Human Rights Committee, an independent body of 18 experts selected through a UN process, described religion or belief as "theistic, non-theistic and atheistic beliefs, as well as the right not to profess any religion or belief." Religions and other beliefs bring hope and consolation to billions of people, and hold great potential for peace and reconciliation. They have also, however, been the source of tension and conflict. This complexity, and the difficulty of defining "religion" and "belief," are showed by the still developing history of the protection of freedom of religion or belief in the context of international human rights.

#### A Complex and Contentious Issue

The struggle for religious liberty has been ongoing for centuries, and has led to innumerable, tragic conflicts. The twentieth century has seen the codification of common values related to freedom of religion and belief, though the struggle has not abated. The United Nations recognized the importance of freedom of religion or belief in the 1948 Universal Declaration of Human Rights, in which Article 18 states that "Everyone shall have the right to freedom of thought, conscience and religion. This right shall include freedom to have a religion or whatever belief of his choice."

Since the Universal Declaration, the attempt to develop an enforceable human rights instrument related to freedom of religion and belief has been unsuccessful. In 1966 the UN passed the International Covenant on Civil and Political Rights, expanding its prior statement to address the manifestation of religion or belief.

*Article 18 of this Covenant includes four paragraphs related to this issue*:

- Everyone shall have the right to freedom of thought, conscience and religion. This right shall include freedom to have or to adopt a religion or belief of his choice, and freedom either individually or in community with others and in public or private, to manifest his religion or belief in worship, observance, practice and teaching.

- No one shall be subject to coercion which would impair his freedom to have or to adopt a religion or belief of his choice.
- Freedom to manifest one's religion or belief may be subject only to such limitations as are prescribed by law and are necessary to protect public safety, order, health, morals or the fundamental rights and freedoms of others.
- The States Parties to the present Covenant undertake to have respect for the liberty of parents and, when applicable, legal guardians, to ensure the religious and moral education of their children in conformity with their own convictions.

Some of the articles of the Covenant on Civil and Political Rights regarding fundamental freedoms have become international conventions, which are legally binding treaties. In contrast, however, because of the complexity of the topic and the political issues involved, Article 18 of the Covenant on Civil and Political Rights has not been elaborated and codified in the same way that more detailed treaties have codified prohibitions against torture, discrimination against women, and race discrimination.

After twenty years of debate, intense struggle and hard work, the General Assembly in 1981 adopted without a vote the Declaration on the Elimination of All Forms of Intolerance and of Discrimination Based on Religion or Belief. While the 1981 Declaration lacks any enforcement procedures, it remains the most important contemporary codification of the principle of freedom of religion and belief.

## RIGHTS AT STAKE

The 1981 UN Declaration on the Elimination of All Forms of Intolerance and of Discrimination Based on Religion or Belief contains eight articles, three of which define specific rights. The remaining articles act in a supportive role by outlining measures to promote tolerance or prevent discrimination.

Taken together, the eight articles constitute a paradigm, an overall concept, to advocate for tolerance and to prevent discrimination based on religion or belief. While human rights are individual rights, the 1981 UN Declaration also identifies certain rights related to states, religious institutions, parents, legal guardians, children, and groups of persons.

Article 1: *Legal Definition.*

*This article repeats several rights from the Covenant on Civil and Political Rights's Article 18*:

- Right to thought, conscience, and religion or belief;
- Right to have a religion or whatever belief of your choice;
- Right either individually or in community with others, in private or

public, to manifest a religion or belief through worship, observance, practice and teaching;

- Right not to suffer coercion that impairs the freedom to choose a religion or belief;
- Right of the State to limit the manifestation of a religion or belief if based in law, and only as necessary to protect public safety, order, health, morals and the fundamental rights and freedoms of others.

Article 2: *Classification of Discrimination.*

This article identifies categories of potential discrimina-tors, affirming the right not to be subject to discrimination on the grounds of religion or belief by:

- States;
- Institutions;
- Groups of persons;
- Persons.

Article 3: *Link to Other Rights.*

This article links the 1981 UN Declaration to other international documents. Article 3 declares that discrimination based on religion or belief constitutes an affront to human dignity and a disavowal of the principles of the Charter of the United Nations, and shall be condemned as a violation of the human rights and fundamental freedoms proclaimed in the Universal Declaration of Human Rights, and enunciated in detail in:

- The International Covenant on Civil and Political Rights;
- The International Covenant on Economic, Social and Cultural Rights.

Article 4: *Possible Solutions.*

Article 4 declares that all States [including all sectors of civil society] shall take effective measures to prevent and eliminate discrimination based on religion or belief through:

- Actions in all fields of civil, economic, political, social, cultural life;
- Enacting or rescinding legislation where necessary to prohibit such discrimination;
- Taking all appropriate measures to combat intolerance based on religion or belief.

Article 5: *Parents, Guardians, Children.*

*At stake in the implementation of this article are the following rights*:

- Right of parents or legal guardians to bring the child up in their religion or belief;
- Right of the child to education in religion or belief, in accordance with the wishes of parents, and the right not to be compelled to receive education against their wishes;
- Right of the child to protection from discrimination and to education for tolerance;

- Right of the child's wishes when not under the care of parents or legal guardians;
- Right of the State to limit practices injurious to child's development or health.

Article 6: *Manifesting Religion or Belief.*

*At stake in the implementation of this article are the following rights*:

- Right to worship and assemble, and to establish and maintain places of worship;
- Right to establish and maintain appropriate charitable or humanitarian institutions;
- Right to make, acquire and use materials related to rites and customs;
- Right to write, issue and disseminate relevant publications in these areas;
- Right to teach a religion or belief in places suitable for these purposes;
- Right to solicit and receive voluntary financial and other contributions;
- Right to train, appoint, elect or designate appropriate leaders;
- Right to observe days of rest and celebrate holidays and ceremonies;
- Right to establish and maintain communication with individuals and communities at national and international levels.

Article 7: *National Legislation.*

This article declares that all of the rights at stake in the 1981 UN Declaration need to be accorded in national legislation in such a manner that everyone shall be able to avail themselves of such rights and freedoms in practice.

Article 8: *Existing Protections.*

This article specifies that the 1981 UN Declaration is non-binding on States so as to ensure that the Declaration does not negate existing legal protections on freedom of religion or belief.

Article 8 states that nothing in the Declaration shall be construed as restricting or negating any right defined in the Universal Declaration of Human Rights and International Covenants on Human Rights. The 1981 UN Declaration is a compromise between states after twenty years of complex discussion and debate, and after final passage by the General Assembly.

*Several sensitive issues are still in need of further clarification, including*:

- Religious or national law versus international law,
- Proselytism,
- Conscientious objection to military service,

- Status of women in religion or belief,
- Claims of superiority or inferiority of religions and beliefs,
- Choosing and changing a religious commitment,
- Religious registration and association laws,
- Public media and religion or belief, and the relationship of religion or belief to the state.

## INTERNATIONAL AND REGIONAL INSTRUMENTS OF PROTECTION

International legal instruments take the form of a treaty which may be binding on the contracting states. When negotiations are completed, the text of a treaty is established as authentic and definitive and is signed by the representatives of states.

There are various means by which a state expresses its consent to be bound by a treaty, with the most common being ratification or accession. A new treaty is ratified by those states that have negotiated the instrument, while a state that has not participated in the negotiations may, at a later stage, accede to the treaty.

The treaty enters into force when a pre-determined number of states have ratified or acceded to the treaty. When a state ratifies or accedes to a treaty, that state may make reservations to one or more articles of the treaty, unless the treaty prohibits this actions. Reservations are exceptions that a state makes to a treaty-provisions that it does not agree to follow-and may normally be withdrawn at any time. In some countries, international treaties take precedence over national law. In others, a specific law may be required to give an international treaty, although ratified or acceded to, the force of law.

Almost all states that have ratified or acceded to an international treaty may issue decrees, amend existing laws or introduce new legislation in order for the treaty to be fully effective on the national territory. While the 1981 Declaration was adopted as a non-binding human rights instrument, several states had reservations.

Romania, Poland, Bulgaria, Czechoslovakia and the then U.S.S.R. said that the 1981 UN Declaration did not take sufficient account of atheistic beliefs. Romania, Syria, Czechoslovakia, and the U.S.S.R. made a general reservation regarding provisions not in accordance with their national legislation.

Iraq entered a collective reservation on behalf of the Organization of the Islamic Conference as to the applicability of any provision or wording in the Declaration which might be contrary to Shari'a law or to legislation or acts based on Islamic law, and Syria and Iran endorsed this reservation.

### Monitoring Freedom of Religion or Belief

Many international treaties have a mechanism to monitor their implementation. As part of the Covenant on Civil and Political Rights, Article 18 is legally-binding and is monitored by the Human Rights Committee. As of 2002, there were 149 States Parties to this Covenant. Under an Optional Protocol, 102 States Parties recognize the authority of the Human Rights Committee to consider confidential communications from individuals claiming to be victims of violations of any rights proclaimed under the treaty. The 1981 UN Declaration on the Elimination of All Forms of Intolerance and of Discrimination Based on Religion or Belief is a non-binding declaration, and does not, therefore, have a treaty mechanism. Instead, in what is called an extra-conventional mechanism, the UN Commission on Human Rights appointed a Special Rapporteur for the 1981 UN Declaration. The Special Rapporteur is mandated to report annually to the Commission on the status of freedom of religion or belief worldwide.

# 10

# Passing Legislation for Human Rights

## INTRODUCTION

As the law-makers of a country, it is parliaments that ensure international human rights standards are met through domestic legislation. Bringing domestic laws in line with the standards required by treaty commitments usually requires parliament to pass legislation that specifically incorporates treaty provisions into domestic law.

This part also discusses a constitutional Bill of Rights with key human rights protections, and explains that all laws should accord with international law. The importance of prioritising key human rights issues such as poverty alleviation and justice sector reform, in budget allocations by providing substantial funds to support the work of national human rights institutions, and guaranteeing a transparent, participatory budget process is also discussed.

It concludes by highlighting ways the legislature can support the judiciary to protect human rights, as well as the responsibility of the judiciary to consistently maintain a human rights approach in its decision-making process.

## BILL OF RIGHTS: ENSHRINING HUMAN RIGHTS IN THE CONSTITUTION

Subject-specific domestic legislation is one way to protect and promote rights. One of the most effective national efforts is through a constitutional Bill of Rights. The national Constitution is the highest law of a country and overrides all other laws. Enshrining human rights in the Constitution, therefore, gives them enormous legal weight –all other laws must be in consonance with the standards set out in the Constitution. Most Commonwealth countries have a constitutional Bill of Rights. New Zealand and the UK are examples of countries that have relied upon common law traditions for safeguarding rights but in the modern context have legislated for specific protection of rights. Most Bills of Rights enshrine core values such as respect for human dignity; equality and non-discrimination; and the opportunity to realise one's potential through the exercise of fundamental freedoms. While many focus on civil and political rights, some notable examples, like the Bill of Rights in the South African Constitution, also include economic and social rights. Constitutions should ideally also enshrine the establishment of an independent human rights institution.

## PASSING COMPLEMENTARY LEGISLATION

Ratification of treaties requires that all domestic laws be brought up to the standards of the international commitment and be in harmony with it. In some countries, such as the United States, this is a simple matter because when a treaty is ratified, it is "self-executing" so the provisions in the treaty automatically become part of domestic law, such that the public can take the Federal government to court if it has failed to implement the treaty.

In Commonwealth countries though, even where a treaty has been ratified, this does not necessarily mean that the commitments in it can be automatically enforced in domestic courts. This is because while the executive might have the constitutional power to bind the State at international law, only the parliament has the power to change domestic law.

As such, parliament must pass legislation to specifically 'incorporate' the treaty provisions into domestic law. One recent example of this was the United Kingdom's enactment of the Human Rights Act 1998, which was specifically enacted to make the rights contained in the European Convention on Human Rights enforceable in UK courts. Likewise, Fiji's Human Rights Commission Act, 1999 for the purposes of the Fiji Human Rights Commission describes human rights as rights embodied in the United Nations Covenants and Conventions on Human Rights and includes the rights and freedoms set out in the Bill of Rights. Despite the obligation to pass laws that are consonant with treaty obligations many domestic considerations prevent or slow their passing. The conflict between personal laws, customary law and prevailing culture has been cited by some countries in explanation as to why they haven't passed laws that conform to treaty standards, although other countries have managed to do so.

## ENSURING ALL OTHER LEGISLATION MEETS HUMAN RIGHTS STANDARDS

In addition to legislation that specifically domesticates international treaties, all laws which parliament passes should be in accordance with international human rights standards. This requirement also applies to the constitutional Bill of Rights, if one exists. Specific human rights oversight committees set up to review legislation ensure it conforms to human rights standards. These committees are bolstered by legislation that specifically requires that all legislation meet minimum human rights standards. In the State of Queensland, in Australia, for example, the Legislative Standards Act 1992 enshrines fundamental legislative principles that "must be considered when legislation is drafted so that it does not infringe individual liberties". These principles include whether the legislation is consistent with the principles of natural justice and if it has sufficient regard for aboriginal traditions and customs, or provides for protection against selfincrimination. In the United Kingdom, the Human Rights Act 1998 specifically requires that all UK legislation should, if possible, fit with the European Convention on Human Rights. Because the UK does not permit judicial review of legislation, the courts cannot strike down inconsistent legislation, but if a court finds that a law is incompatible with the Convention, it can make a "declaration of incompatibility" and parliament must decide what action to take.

An example is when Section 23 of the Anti-Terrorism Crime and Security Act 2001, was ruled incompatible with the Human Rights Act 1998 and the European Convention on Human Rights, by the highest court in the country. This part allowed indefinite detention without trial, of foreign nationals suspected of involvement in international terrorism.

The Act makes it clear that parliamentarians have a key role to play in ensuring that all legislation is in line with universal standards. The Act also makes it unlawful for a public authority to violate Convention rights, unless it had no choice due to an Act of Parliament.

This explicit extension of the duty to respect human rights on to the bureaucracy is a major step forward in creating a domestic environment genuinely respectful of and committed to human rights.

## PROMOTING PRO-HUMAN RIGHTS BUDGETS

Allocations made in budgets show where a country's priorities lie. Optimum budget allocations towards poverty alleviation, human rights education, justice sector reforms, and socio-economic areas reflect the State's commitment to these areas and determine whether human rights can be truly upheld.

Budget allocations also indicate the relative importance given to institutions such as human rights commissions, minority commissions, women's commissions, police complaints commissions, human rights courts and ombudsmen – both to be established and to be maintained with sufficient resources to properly discharge their duties. Despite a strong mandate and excellent networks, human rights institutions are often unable to function to their true potential due to lack of funds. The difference between tokenism and true commitment of a government to human rights can often be seen through the funds available to these institutions. These priorities will be brought to the forefront through genuine consultation and participation of the people. By providing space for such participation and making sure that these views are incorporated into the budget, governments show their commitment to ensuring that both the process and final document are human-rights friendly. NGOs are increasingly engaging with the process through submissions, as well as analysing the final budget for adherence to human rights and social justice norms. One example is an initiative in Tanzania that has led to budget guidelines for government departments that now require that budget submissions be prepared with a gender focus. Since 1996, the Commonwealth Secretariat has also supported gender budget initiatives. In the pilot phase of their project, technical assistance was provided to Barbados, Fiji, St Kitts and Nevis, South Africa and Sri Lanka, for projects with the joint support of the Ministry for Finance and Ministry for Women's Affairs.

It must be recognized though that it is not just the community within the country that will influence the budget process, but also international bodies. Donors, for instance, whether through bi-lateral or multi-lateral agreements wield increasing leverage in setting the budgetary agenda in beneficiary countries.

The process of developing Poverty Reduction Strategy Papers (PRSPs), for instance, involves not just national stakeholders, but external development partners as well, particularly the IMF and World Bank. PRSPs aim to bring about a comprehensive national strategy for poverty reduction and describe the macroeconomic, structural and social policies and programmes that a country will pursue over several years, as well as external financing needs and the associated sources of financing.

These provide an opportunity for all stakeholders to ensure that poverty reduction is designed and implemented through a human rights framework and that explicit human rights activities are prioritized. A country's commitment to human rights is also gauged by willingness to contribute to international development agencies that promote human rights, democracy and good governance. Countries quite often make statements committing funds to international agencies but delay in releasing the money. Many crucial bodies such as the Office for the High Commissioner on Human Rights receive some general UN money but require voluntary contributions to function as designed. Financial contributions included in the budget reflect a State's commitment to international human rights.

# 11

# Corruption and Human Rights: Making the Connection

## WHY IT IS RELEVANT TO LINK HUMAN RIGHTS TO CORRUPTION

This stage explores the links between corruption and human rights on the assumption that, if corruption occurs where there is inclination and opportunity, a human rights approach may help to minimise opportunities for corrupt behaviour and make it more likely that those who are corrupt are caught and appropriately sanctioned. A human rights approach also focuses attention on people who are particularly at risk, provides a gender perspective, and offers elements of guidance for the design and implementation of anti-corruption policies. If corruption is shown to violate human rights, this will influence public attitudes. When people become more aware of the damage corruption does to public and individual interests, and the harm that even minor corruption can cause, they are more likely to support campaigns and programmes to prevent it. This is important because, despite strong rhetoric, the political impact of most anticorruption programmes has been low. Identifying the specific links between corruption and human rights may persuade key actors – public officials, parliamentarians, judges, prosecutors, lawyers, business people, bankers, accountants, the media and the public in general – to take a stronger stand against corruption. This may be so even in countries where reference to human rights is sensitive.

Human rights standards, as established in major international treaties and domestic legislation, impose obligations on states. Focusing on specific human rights will help to identify who is entitled to make claims when acts of corruption occur and who has a duty to take action against corruption and protect those harmed by it. A clear understanding of the practical connections between acts of corruption and human rights may empower those who have legitimate claims to demand their rights in relation to corruption, and may assist states and other public authorities to respect, protect and fulfil their human rights responsibilities at every level. Connecting acts of corruption to violations of human rights also creates new possibilities for action, especially if, as we will argue, acts of corruption can be challenged using the different national, regional and international mechanisms that exist to monitor compliance with human rights. In the last sixty years, following the adoption of the Universal Declaration of Human Rights (UDHR), many mechanisms have been created to hold states and individuals accountable for human rights violations. In addition to judicial accountability, parliamentary reporting plays an important role in many countries, while monitoring by civil society has become more extensive. Intergovernmental institutions have also developed, and the main UN mechanisms are now supported by regional mechanisms such as the European Court of Human Rights (ECtHR), the African Court on Human and Peoples' Rights (ACtHPR) and the Inter-American Court of Human Rights (I/A Court H.R.). The evolution of national human rights institutions is equally significant. When acts of corruption are linked to violations of human rights, all these institutions could act to force accountability and so create disincentives for corruption. While they do not replace traditional anti-corruption mechanisms – primarily the criminal law – they can give cases prominence, may force a state to take preventive action, or may deter corrupt officials from misusing their powers. They can therefore both raise awareness and have a deterrent effect. Taking a human rights approach is critically about empowering groups that are exposed to particular risks.

The human rights framework emphasises explicitly that vulnerable and disadvantaged groups must be protected from abuse. It does so by applying cross-cutting principles – in particular principles that focus on non-discrimination, participation and accountability – that have the effect of empowering people who are disadvantaged. Human rights law requires states to take these principles seriously. Populations should not be consulted in a superficial manner, for example; they should be allowed and encouraged to participate actively in efforts to fight corruption. A human rights perspective requires policy-makers to ask how the design or implementation of anticorruption programmes will affect people who are marginalised or impoverished, subject to social discrimination, or disadvantaged in other ways. Adhering to human rights principles implies identifying and overcoming obstacles (such as language differences, cultural beliefs, racism and gender discrimination) that make such people vulnerable to corruption. While there seems to be agreement that corruption has specific impacts on vulnerable and disadvantaged groups, the incorporation of vulnerability and gender in the design of anti-corruption programmes is still limited and exceptional. Making fuller use of human rights would help to strengthen these dimensions of policy.

The principle of nondiscrimination could be particularly useful as a guide to attain this objective. Under international treaties against corruption, anti-corruption measures must be compatible with human rights principles and should not adversely affect the rights of those involved. However, the treaties give little guidance on how officials are to reconcile their commitment to fight corruption with their obligation to promote and protect human rights. Analysing anti-corruption programmes from a human rights perspective may assist states to comply with human rights standards when they draft and implement laws and procedures to detect, investigate and adjudicate corruption cases. The International Council's second stage on corruption will address issues of implementation in more detail.

## VULNERABILITY AND DISADVANTAGE

While corruption violates the rights of all those affected by it, it has a disproportionate impact on people that belong to groups that are exposed to particular risks (such as minorities, indigenous peoples, migrant workers, disabled people, those with HIV/AIDS, refugees, prisoners and those who are poor). It also disproportionately affects women and children. Those who commit corrupt acts will attempt to protect themselves from detection and maintain their positions of power. In doing so, they are likely to further oppress people who are not in positions of power, including most members of the groups listed above. The latter tend both to be more exploited, and less able to defend themselves: in this sense, corruption reinforces their exclusion and the discrimination to which they are exposed. In some cases, it is their vulnerability that makes certain groups easy victims of corruption. For instance, corrupt officials may extract money from migrant workers who lack a residence permit by threatening them with deportation in the knowledge that they cannot complain. It seems that Roma people, when compared to other groups, are disproportionately asked to pay bribes when they seek access to health and education services. Corruption in such cases can magnify and exacerbate the pre-existing human rights problems of such groups.

### Women

Corruption impacts men and women differently and reinforces and perpetuates existing gender inequalities. Women's lack of access to political and economic power excludes them from networks that permit access to decision-making bodies. Where institutions are controlled by men, women do not have enough power to challenge corruption or clientelism. Corruption in the legislative and executive branches can allow discriminatory laws to stand, while corruption in the judicial branch can discriminate against women who do not have the means to pay bribes to gain access to the justice system. In some societies, women have traditionally been perceived as non-active participants in court processes (where they may be represented by their male relatives). Many non-formal or parallel decision-making processes, moreover, have no checks on corruption. Women's access to justice is compromised in other ways. Trafficking, for example, often involves the corruption of border officials, police and members of the judiciary. As illegal immigrants, often without proof of identification and subject to (sexual) violence, trafficked women are obviously hindered in seeking protection from courts. Many women also have fewer opportunities than men to achieve an education, or obtain land, credit and other productive assets. When they have access to work, they are often paid lower salaries. They tend to assume the domestic responsibilities of taking care of children and older adults, which means they are financially dependent, cannot work or are poorer. For all these reasons – but essentially because women are over-represented in the poorest social segments of society and under-represented in decision-making bodies – corruption and clientelism affect them in particular ways, often disproportionately. For example, corruption that diverts public resources from essential services or anti-poverty programmes will particularly harm the welfare of women and their dependents, who rely heavily on such services. In the same way, bribery that adds to the cost of public services will also disproportionately affect women, because they are on average less able to afford bribes, depend more on public services, and sometimes (for example during pregnancy) require services that men do not.

**Children**

Corruption may also have a disproportionate impact on children. While children possess in general the same civil, political, economic, social and cultural rights as adults, they also have certain rights specific to them. Most of these are identified in the 1989 United Nations Convention on the Rights of the Child (CRC), in Article 24 of the International Covenant on Civil and Political Rights (ICCPR), and in Article 10(3) of the International Covenant on Economic, Social and Cultural Rights (ICESCR). Corruption can violate many of the rights that children share with adults, including the right to life and the right to health. In addition, some rights, such as the right to education, are particularly important to children. As explained in more detail in the section on the right to education, corruption in the education sector very often violates the rights of children. Corrupt practices harm three other rights that are particularly relevant to children: a child's right to be protected during adoption procedures; the right to protection from trafficking and sexual exploitation; and the right to be protected from child labour.

**People Living in Poverty**

Corruption has a severely detrimental impact on the lives of people living in poverty when compared with higher income groups. Corruption not only affects economic growth and discourages foreign investment, thereby indirectly affecting the poor, but reduces the net income of those living in poverty, distorts policies, programmes and strategies that aim to meet their basic needs, and diverts public resources from investments in infrastructure that are crucial elements of strategies to lift them out of poverty. Where corruption is generalised, for example, poor people are as exposed as others to the small-scale bribery of public officials (notably in the healthcare, law enforcement and judicial sectors) but the effect on their purse will be heavier. Large-scale corruption, meanwhile, damages the quality of public services on which the poor depend particularly, to meet basic needs. Here again they are disproportionately affected.

### Indigenous People and Minorities

Indigenous people and minorities suffer particularly from corruption. They are often among the poorest and most disadvantaged groups in society. Indigenous women are additionally exposed to risk. Indigenous communities that are closely linked to land they live on collectively are especially vulnerable to corruption of infrastructure programmes that displace them, and smaller-scale corruption associated with land sales and registration. Many indigenous communities also lack access to education and are consequently less aware of their legal rights. Mechanisms for reporting and tackling corruption are often out of their reach as a result. Lack of access to justice compounds the risks of harm they face. Since indigenous voices are rarely heard in policy discussions, these populations often have little influence on the design and implementation of anti-corruption policies and programmes that could improve their status.

## HUMAN RIGHTS AS PREVENTIVE MEASURES

If weak human rights protection may create opportunities for corruption, policies that promote human rights may prevent corruption. This section briefly describes human rights principles that are relevant to the prevention of corruption.

### The Right to Freedom of Expression, Assembly and Association

These rights enable participation and are vital to efforts to combat corruption. Where governments permit information to flow freely, it should become easier to identify and denounce cases of corruption. However, since reporters and editors can also be bribed, protection of this right is not enough. Governments should also guarantee conditions for a diversity of independent media and protect the political independence of public service media. In the absence of a tradition of respect for freedom of expression, weak media are unable to expose corruption without exposing themselves to defamation lawsuits or risks to their personal security. Protection of the freedom to form and affiliate to formal and informal associations, such as human rights organisations, is also a vital element of anticorruption efforts.

### Political Rights

Where political rights are not effectively protected, opportunities for corruption increase. Low political participation creates conditions for impunity and corruption. The effective exercise of political rights counterbalances state power and its abuse, including corruption. In this regard, a gender-sensitive approach is important. As discussed, women are disproportionately affected by corruption and policies should guarantee their participation in decisionmaking.

**The Right to Information**

Until recently this right was interpreted as an obligation on states not to obstruct the flow of information. In 2002, however, the African Commission on Human and Peoples' Rights introduced explicitly the notion of a positive obligation to have access to information, and in 2006 the Inter-American Court of Human Rights (I/A Court H.R.) ruled unambiguously in favour of a right to access to public information. According to this ruling, states should make administrative documents public. Human rights organisations may play a role in helping to expand state interpretations of the right to access to information, and advocating where necessary for the inclusion of this right in constitutions and national laws. An access to information law should guarantee the right of all citizens to request and obtain public information, without being required to justify that request. In case of refusal, there should be effective mechanisms for filing administrative and judicial complaints. Access to information should be guaranteed for vulnerable groups, which often lack the economic resources or knowledge they need to obtain information from governments successfully. Some governments, in addition, tend to discriminate by putting up barriers or simply denying access. Human rights organisations can encourage and assist such groups to demand information to which they are entitled. More broadly, the same strategy can support broader efforts to prevent and expose corruption.

**The Right to Participate**

Human rights organisations may also help to promote active participation of people at every level of society and enable them to monitor how well government officials and other actors carry out their responsibilities. If lawyers, doctors, members of parliament, business executives, engineers, scientists, journalists, etc. cannot participate in public life or exercise their rights, they cannot conduct their work professionally. This can harm the realisation of rights at many levels and facilitate failures of performance and accountability, thus leading to corruption in these professions as well as in government. In addition, the human rights framework gives particular attention to the participation of groups that are disadvantaged or vulnerable. Public engagement in elections is only one aspect of participation: it is equally important to ensure that indigenous people participate in decisions relating to the use of their land and that slum dwellers participate in development decisions that affect their homes, and so forth. Interesting work has been done in a number of countries to improve the quality and probity of official decisions by using together the right to information and the right to participate. A second report by the ICHRP will examine in more detail how the right to participate might add force to anti-corruption strategies. The report confirms that the right to participation requires a strong legal framework and an open political system. In addition, when they act to combat corruption or promote human rights, individuals, communities and civil society organisations can make their governments more accountable.

## DEFINITIONS

The term "corruption" comes from the Latin word *corruptio* which means "moral decay, wicked behaviour, putridity or rottenness". The concept may have a physical reference, as in "[t]he destruction or spoiling of anything, especially by disintegration or by decomposition with its attendant unwholesomeness and loathsomeness; putrefaction"; or moral significance, as in "moral deterioration or decay... [the] [p]erversion or destruction of integrity in the discharge of public duties by bribery or favour...". These definitions are representative of two common shortcomings: they define corruption only in terms of bribery, or in terms that are very general. As a result, corruption definitions tend either to be too restrictive or excessively broad. In fact, this is not as contradictory as it may seem. Corruption has indeed broad causes and consequences. As Michael Johnston, a Professor at Colgate University, has stated: "In rapidly changing societies the limit between what is corrupt and what is not is not always clear and the term corruption may be applied broadly." Corruption demands a multidisciplinary approach, and many fields of study, from political science to economics, have addressed the issue.

Each has a different perception of the problem and therefore generates different policies: operational definitions tend therefore to start broad and become more specific as they try to render corruption measurable. A well-known classification distinguishes grand from petty corruption. *Grand corruption* refers to the corruption of heads of state, ministers, and top officials and usually involves large amounts of assets. *Petty corruption,* also called "low" and "street" corruption, indicates the kinds of corruption that people experience in their encounters with public officials and when they use public services (hospitals, schools, local licensing authorities, police, tax offices, etc.). It generally involves modest sums of money. Others have classified corruption by type. *Political corruption* involves lawmakers (monarchs, dictators, legislators) acting in their role as creators of the rules and standards by which a polity operates. Such officials seek bribes or funds for their political and personal benefit and provide favours to their supporters at the expense of broader public benefits. *Administrative corruption* includes the use of bribery and favouritism to lower taxes, escape regulations and win low-level procurement contracts. *Corporate corruption* occurs between private businesses and suppliers or private service providers. It also involves illegal behaviour by corporate officials for private monetary gain. *Institutionalised corruption* names the behaviour of those who exploit institutional positions to influence institutional processes and actions, such as law enforcement personnel and members of the judiciary; *operational corruption*, narrower, describes specific activities and goals. Another approach to definition has been specific to a given field of study.

In the economics field, for example, Robert Klitgaard has defined corruption in terms of an equation: Corruption = Monopoly Power + Discretion – Accountability. According to the United States Agency for International Development (USAID) *Handbook for Fighting Corruption*, corruption can assume various forms: "It encompasses unilateral abuses by government officials such as embezzlement and nepotism, as well as abuses linking public and private actors such as bribery, extortion, influence peddling and fraud. Corruption arises in both political and bureaucratic offices and can be petty or grand, organized or disorganized." Development banks and other national and international organisations have also variously defined corruption. Probably the most used definition is the one adopted by TI: "corruption is the abuse of entrusted power for private gain". However, to link corruption with human rights, a definition of corruption based on law is necessary. In the legal field, the term corruption is usually used to group certain criminal acts which correspond to the general notion of an abuse of entrusted power. International conventions against corruption reflect this, since they do not define and criminalise corruption but instead enumerate criminal acts that amount to corruption. Even here, they follow different approaches. For example, some conventions use the term "corruption" interchangeably with one of the most common criminal acts that encompass it: bribery.

This is true of the United Nations Convention against Transnational Organised Crime, the Council of Europe Civil Law Convention on Corruption, the Convention on the Fight against Corruption Involving Officials of the European Communities or Officials of Member States of the European Union (EU), and the Council of the European Union's Framework Decision on Combating Corruption in the Private Sector (EU Decision on Corruption in the Private Sector). The Organisation for Economic Co-operation and Development (OECD) Convention on Combating Bribery of Foreign Public Officials in International Business Transactions follows the same line, although the approach is reflected in the title. The UNCAC explicitly enumerates acts to be criminalised without stipulating that such acts amount to corruption. A similar approach is followed by the Council of Europe Criminal Law Convention on Corruption. A third group of conventions distinguishes corruption as a term to group criminal acts more explicitly from actual acts that involve corruption. Two such conventions are the Economic Community of West African States (ECOWAS) Protocol on the Fight against Corruption (ECOWAS Protocol against Corruption), and the Inter-American Convention against Corruption (IACAC). In Article 6, entitled "Acts of Corruption", both conventions provide a list of acts that constitute corruption. Two additional conventions distinguish even more clearly between corruption and the acts that constitute it.

The African Union (AU) Convention on Preventing and Combating Corruption (AU Convention against Corruption) states in Article 1 that "[c]orruption means the acts and practices including related offences proscribed in this Convention". Subsequently, it lists acts of corruption, such as the bribery of a national public official, abuse of function and embezzlement (Article 4). An even clearer differentiation is provided by the Southern African Development Community (SADC) Protocol against Corruption. This not only separates corruption and the acts that constitute it, but provides a general definition of corruption. Notwithstanding the different approaches taken by international conventions, it is clear that in law these do not consider corruption to be an individual and identifiable criminal act. When referred to in a legal context, corruption is the generic heading for a cluster of different and specific criminal acts. An appropriate *legal* definition of corruption would therefore be: "corruption is the list of acts criminalised by law under the heading 'Corruption'." It is therefore essential to identify the different acts that fall under the general heading of corruption.

## CORRUPT ACTS

By reviewing the agreements that states reached while adopting international conventions, it is possible to gain an idea of what they generally agree are "corrupt acts". The best such source is the UNCAC because it provides the most recent and comprehensive list of such acts. Moreover, it represents a wide range of views because it is the only anti-corruption treaty open to universal membership, all other conventions against corruption being regional. The following is the list of core corrupt acts. It is important to note, however, that this is not an exhaustive list. Progressive development could enlarge this list to include other acts in the future.

### Bribery

May be defined as the promise, offer or gift, to a public official, or the solicitation or acceptance by a public official, directly or indirectly, of an undue advantage, for the official himself or another person or entity, in order that the official act or refrain from acting in the exercise of his official duties. Several different forms of bribery are recognised. The act of offering a bribe is commonly referred to as active bribery and the act of accepting the bribe as passive bribery. In addition, the definition of bribery changes when the act involves a foreign public official, or when it takes place exclusively within the private sector. The bribery of foreign public officials and officials of public international organisations, also called transnational bribery, adds the condition that the undue advantage given to the official must be in the context of international business. Bribery in the private sector, or private-to-private bribery, may be defined as the promise, offering or giving of an undue advantage, directly or indirectly, to any person who directs or works, in any capacity, for a private sector entity; or the solicitation or acceptance of an undue advantage by any person who directs or works, in any capacity, for a private sector entity, for the person himself or herself or for another person, in order that he or she, in breach of his or her duties, acts or refrains from acting.

**Embezzlement**

May be defined as the misappropriation or other diversion by a public official, for purposes unrelated to those for which the assets were intended, for his benefit or for the benefit of another person or entity, of any property, public or private funds or securities or any other thing of value entrusted to the public official by virtue of his position. The embezzlement of property can also occur in the private sector in the course of economic, financial or commercial activities.

**Trading in Influence**

May be defined as the promise, offering or giving to a public official or any other person, or the solicitation or acceptance by a public official or any other person, directly or indirectly, of an undue advantage in order that the public official or the person abuse his real or supposed influence with a view to obtaining from an administration or public authority an undue advantage for the original instigator of the act or for any other person. For some it is irrelevant whether or not the influence is ultimately exerted and whether or not it leads to the intended result. Trading in influence is also commonly divided into its active form (giving an advantage in exchange for influence) and its passive form (requesting or accepting an advantage in exchange for influence).

**Abuse of Functions or Position**

May be defined as the performance of, or failure to perform, an act, in violation of the law, by a public official in the discharge of his or her functions, for the purpose of obtaining an undue advantage for himself or herself or for another person or entity.

**Illicit Enrichment**

May be defined as a significant increase in the assets of a public official that he or she cannot reasonably explain in relation to his or her lawful income. This is a particularly controversial matter. Some argue that criminalisation on such grounds infringes the principle of presumption of innocence and reverses the burden of proof, while certain judicial decisions take a contrary view.

## CORRUPTION AS A VIOLATION OF HUMAN RIGHTS

An analysis of corruption that draws on human rights will emphasise the harm to individuals that corruption causes. From this perspective, it is often taken for granted that corruption "violates" human rights. When people make this claim, they have a range of issues in mind. They mean that, when corruption is widespread, people do not have access to justice, are not secure and cannot protect their livelihoods. Court officials and the police pay more heed to bribes than to law. Hospitals do not heal people because the medical staff give better treatment to patients who pay backhanders or because clinics lack supplies due to corrupt public contracting procedures. Poor families cannot feed themselves because social security programmes are corrupt or distorted to support a patronage network. Schools cannot offer their students a sound education because the education budget has been looted and as a result teachers cannot be paid and books cannot be purchased. Farmers and market sellers cannot earn a living because police take a cut of their produce and sales. In numerous ways like these, corruption encourages discrimination, deprives vulnerable people of income, and prevents people from fulfilling their political, civil, social, cultural and economic rights. UN treaty bodies and UN special procedures have concluded that, where corruption is widespread, states cannot comply with their human rights obligations. Some international documents have even considered corruption to be a "crime against humanity", a category of crimes that includes genocide and torture. However, these statements are generally framed in broad terms. The extent to which acts of corruption directly violate human rights, or lead to violations, is rarely defined or explained. Most existing work examines the causes of corruption, mechanisms and policies to prevent it, and forms of technical cooperation to assist developing countries and countries in economic transition. Little work has been done to describe in precise terms what the links are between acts of corruption and violations of human rights. This stage therefore sets out an operational framework that tries to establish when a corrupt act violates human rights or leads to a violation of human rights. The aim is to provide a technique for analysing corruption in human rights terms. The presentation here is inevitably illustrative; a complete description of every possible link would be impossible. Readers are therefore invited to make use of the logic employed in this stage to assess other cases and other forms of corruption to see whether they violate human rights and, if they do, what rights they violate.

## DETERMINING WHEN HUMAN RIGHTS ARE VIOLATED

Because all forms of corrupt practice may in the long-run have an impact on human rights, it cannot be concluded mechanically that a given act of corruption violates a human right. This means that, to apply the human right framework usefully (that is to say, with potential effect in law), it is necessary to distinguish corrupt practices that directly violate a human right from corrupt practices that lead to violation of a human right (but do not themselves violate a right), and from corrupt practices where a causal link with a specific violation of rights cannot practically be established. A state is responsible for a human rights violation when it can be shown that its actions (or failure to act) do not conform with the requirements of international or domestic human rights norms. To determine whether a particular corrupt practice violates a human right, therefore, it is first necessary to establish the scope and content of the human right's obligation in question and whether it derives from domestic law, international treaty, custom, or general principles of law. In this stage we focus on obligations that states have voluntarily assumed because they have ratified international human rights treaties. Human rights obligations apply to all branches of government (executive, legislative and judicial) at all levels (national, regional and local). According to human rights jurisprudence, an act (or omission) is attributable to the state when committed, instigated, incited, encouraged or acquiesced in by any public authority or any other person acting in an official capacity. From an anti-corruption perspective, it is interesting to note that the UNCAC has a broad understanding of "public official" which includes "any person who performs a public function or provides a public service as defined in the domestic law of the State Party and as applied in the pertinent area of law of that State Party" (UNCAC, Article 2).

**Three Levels of State Obligation**

It is now commonly understood that states have three levels of obligation in relation to human rights: the obligations "to respect", "to protect" and "to fulfil". *The obligation to respect* requires the state to refrain from any measure that may deprive individuals of the enjoyment of their rights or their ability to satisfy those rights by their efforts. This type of obligation is often associated with civil and political rights (e.g. refraining from committing torture) but it applies to economic, social and cultural rights too. With regard to the right to adequate housing, for example, states have a duty to refrain from forced or arbitrary eviction. *The obligation to protect* requires the state to prevent violations of human rights by third parties. The obligation to protect is normally taken to be a central function of states, which have to prevent irreparable harm from being inflicted upon members of society. This requires states:

- To prevent violations of rights by individuals or other non-state actors;
- To avoid and eliminate incentives to violate rights by third parties; and
- To provide access to legal remedies when violations have occurred, in order to prevent further deprivations.

Non-compliance with this level of obligation may be a vital determinant of state responsibility in corruption cases. By failing to act, states may infringe rights. If they do not criminalise particular practices or fail to enforce certain criminal provisions, for example, they may not prevent, suppress or punish forms of corruption that cause or lead to violations of rights. The obligation to protect may also provide the link required to show that corrupt behaviour by a private actor triggers state responsibility. Although it might be difficult to establish, a state might be held responsible for violating a right, for example, if it failed to enact appropriate legislation to prevent or punish corruption committed by private corporations. Or a state might be judged negligent if employers breached labour laws (minimum wage requirements, health and safety regulations) and systematically bribed government labour inspectors to overlook this behaviour. In the case of transnational corporations, the home and host states might both have responsibilities, although the former are often better equipped to ensure that companies comply with human rights. This level of obligation is relevant to privatisation processes. The privatisation of public services (such as health, transport or telecommunications) may multiply opportunities for corruption and may harm the enjoyment of particular rights (access to clean water, for example). In some instances of privatisation, the state clearly retains direct responsibility for the service in question (for example, when state companies retain certain public functions after privatisation).

In others, the state devolves authority to private companies; but in these cases too it is still responsible for violations of rights that they commit, and will be liable if it fails to prevent corruption (or exposure to it) as privatisation occurs, or does not protect the rights of vulnerable groups who depend on the services in question. *The obligation to fulfil* requires the state to take measures to ensure that people under its jurisdiction can satisfy basic needs (as recognised in human rights instruments) that they cannot secure by their own efforts. Although this is the key state obligation in relation to economic, social and cultural rights, the duty to fulfil also arises in respect to civil and political rights. It is clear, for instance, that enforcing the prohibition of torture (which requires states to investigate and prosecute perpetrators, pass laws to punish them and take preventive measures such as police training), or providing the rights to a fair trial (which requires investment in courts and judges), to free and fair elections, and to legal assistance, all require considerable costs and investments. A violation of a human right therefore occurs when a state's acts, or failure to act, do not conform with that state's obligation to respect, protect or fulfil recognised human rights of persons under its jurisdiction. To assess a given state's behaviour in practice, however, it is necessary to determine in addition what specific conduct is required of the state in relation to each right. This will depend on the terms of the state's human rights obligations, as well as their interpretation and application; and this in turn should take into account the object and purpose of each obligation and the facts of each case. The term "violation" should only be used formally when a legal obligation exists. The use of this tripartite typology is a practical analytical tool to better understand the complexities of real situations. They are guidelines that assist us to approach the complex interconnections and interdependencies of the duties that must be complied with in order to achieve protection of human rights. In this regard, it is crucial to keep in mind that other obligations must be considered as well, at all three levels, such as the duty to establish norms, procedures and institutional machinery essential to the realisation of rights; and the duty to comply with human rights principles such as non-discrimination, transparency, participation and accountability.

## The Causal Link

### *Direct violations*

Corruption may be linked directly to a violation when a corrupt act is deliberately used as a means to violate a right. For example, a bribe offered to a judge directly affects the independence and impartiality of that judge and hence violates the right to a fair trial. When an official has not deliberately caused the harm in question, due diligence becomes the test. If a violation of human right was foreseeable, did officials exercise reasonable diligence (all the means at their disposal) to prevent it? In such cases, the responsibility of the state depends both on the specific circumstances and the right violated. Corruption may also directly violate a human right when a state (or somebody acting in an official capacity) acts or fails to act in a way that prevents individuals from having access to that right. To illustrate, when an individual must bribe a doctor to obtain medical treatment at a public hospital, or bribe a teacher at a public school to obtain a place for her child at school, corruption infringes the rights to health and education.

### *Indirect Violations (Corruption as a Necessary Condition)*

In other situations, corruption will be an essential factor contributing to a chain of events that eventually leads to violation of a right. In this case the right is violated by an act that derives from a corrupt act and the act of corruption is a necessary condition for the violation. This situation will arise, for example, if public officials allow the illegal importation of toxic waste from other countries in return for a bribe, and that waste is placed in, or close to, a residential area. The rights to life and health of residents of that place would be violated, indirectly, as a result of the bribery. These rights are not directly violated by the bribe in this example, but the bribe was an essential factor without which the violation would not have occurred. Even without a direct connection, therefore, corruption may be an essential contributing factor in a chain of events that leads to a violation, and so may violate human rights indirectly. Corruption often causes violations of women and children's rights in this way. When women or children are trafficked (particularly for sexual exploitation and abuse, abduction, sale, prostitution and pornography), those responsible commonly corrupt officials. Usually in return for bribes, the latter supply documents for crossing borders, or turn a blind eye to the trafficking activity. In these cases too, corruption is an essential condition and in its absence the violation would not occur. Corruption may also be an indirect cause where corrupt authorities seek to prevent the exposure of corruption. When a whistleblower (someone investigating or reporting a corruption case) is silenced by harassment, threats or imprisonment, or killed, the rights to liberty, freedom of expression, life, and freedom from torture or cruel, inhuman or degrading treatment may all be violated. In such a case, in addition to the original act of corruption that the whistleblower was trying to denounce, it is highly probable that the acts that subsequently infringed his or her rights would also have corruption as a cause (for example, corruption at the level of law enforcement). Again, acts of corruption will then be essential factors in the violation.

***Remote Violations (Where Corruption is one Factor Among Others)***

Sometimes corruption will play a more remote role. When corruption during an electoral process raises concerns about the accuracy of the final result, social unrest and protests may occur and these may be repressed violently. In such a case, the right to political participation may be violated directly, and repression of the social protests may also cause serious violations of human rights (for example, the rights to life, prohibition of torture and ill-treatment and freedom of assembly). Nonetheless, the electoral corruption would not necessarily be the only or determining cause of such riots or their repression. Many other factors might contribute and, to that extent, the corruption has a more remote link to the violations in question.

## LINKING ACTS OF CORRUPTION WITH SPECIFIC HUMAN RIGHTS

This stage provides an analytical tool that should assist in determining when and how violations of human rights and acts of corruption can be connected. It begins with a description of the scope and content of different human rights that have been developed by international human rights bodies. It goes on to provide specific examples of how the content of specific rights can be violated by acts of corruption, as the latter have been defined by the UNCAC. This is one of the several stages necessary to determine the links between acts of corruption and violations of human rights that we identified in the previous stage. The stage takes a human rights perspective and speaks in human rights language. The aim is to assist human rights organisations to address impacts of corruption on human rights, and to introduce international human rights standards to anti-corruption advocates. For practical reasons, this stage refers to human rights that have been recognised in widely ratified international human rights treaties, such as the International Covenant on Civil and Political Rights (ICCPR), the International Covenant on Economic, Social and Cultural Rights (ICESCR), and the Convention on the Rights of the Child (CRC), each of which imposes binding obligations on state parties. It is important to keep in mind that several of these rights are also found in regional human rights instruments, such as the Inter-American Convention on Human

Rights, the African Charter on Human and People's Rights (ACHPR), and the European Convention on Human Rights (ECHR), as well as in many domestic constitutions and laws. The stage examines some rights that are regularly harmed by corruption. It should be noted, however, that the impact of corruption on human rights is not restricted to the rights examined in this section. Corruption is frequently implicated in the violation of other rights (such as the right to life, or the prohibition of torture), in particular when corruption is present in the police, military and other law enforcement agencies. While we address each right separately, the interdependency of human rights should be kept in mind. In practice, corruption is likely to affect the enjoyment of several rights simultaneously. Failure to protect rights associated with political participation, for example, may have an impact on several economic, social and cultural rights because it may affect the design and implementation of social policies and thus the enjoyment of those rights.

## WHEN CORRUPTION MAY VIOLATE THE PRINCIPLES OF EQUALITY AND NON-DISCRIMINATION

The principles of equality and non-discrimination are fundamental principles of human rights. The principle that every individual is equal before the law and has the right to be protected by law on an equal basis is affirmed in all the main human rights treaties. These principles do not imply, however, that every difference in treatment implies discrimination. It is not discriminatory to differentiate, for example, if the criteria used are reasonable and objective, and the purpose is legitimate. Affirmative action, and other forms of preferential initiative, for instance, do not necessarily violate the principle of non-discrimination and in some instances may be required in order to remove discrimination. The UN Human Rights Committee has defined discrimination as "any distinction, exclusion, restriction or preference which is based on any ground such as race, colour, sex, language, religion, political or other opinion, national or social origin, property, birth or other status, and which has the purpose or effect of nullifying or impairing the recognition, enjoyment or exercise by all persons, on an equal footing, of all rights and freedoms". Four features of this definition are relevant with respect to corruption. First, acts of discrimination are defined widely ("any distinction, exclusion, restriction or preference"), and corrupt acts intrinsically distinguish, exclude or prefer. Second, the definition lists a number of "grounds" for discrimination (race, religion, colour, sex, etc.) but those grounds are not exclusive; inclusion of the term "or other status" shows this. As a result, discrimination on *any* ground is prohibited. Third, the definition of discrimination prohibits acts that have a discriminatory "purpose or effect". By definition, corruption has both a discriminatory purpose and a discriminatory effect.

Fourth, discrimination must bring about the specific result of nullifying or impairing the equal recognition, enjoyment or exercise of a human right, such as the right to life, right to education or right to health. Many corruption cases have such effects; they create distinctions, or exclude, restrict or prefer, in ways that impede individuals from exercising one or more rights. At the same time, discrimination can take place even if no specific right (apart from the right to equality) is affected. Article 26 of the ICCPR prohibits discrimination in law or in fact in any field regulated and protected by public authorities, and its application is not limited to those rights which are provided for in the ICCPR. When a person obtains privileged treatment by means of a bribe (when applying for an official document such as a passport or visa, for example, or clearing goods from customs without paying duties and taxes), no other human right is necessarily directly affected except the right to equality, i.e. the right to be treated equally when obtaining the visa or when clearing goods from customs.

This right stands independently from other human rights. Having said this, it is likely that privileged treatment of the abovementioned kinds would in fact affect other rights indirectly. For example, if many people do not pay custom clearances, the fees could rise, affecting poor families receiving goods from relatives abroad; if some people are fast-tracked in visa procedures, others could face delay; etc. In short, every individual is entitled to be treated equally by public officials; and if a person bribes a public official, that person acquires a privileged status in relation to other similarly placed individuals who have not partaken in bribery. Similarly, when a person is asked for a bribe in order to obtain a service to which that person is entitled without payment, that person suffers discrimination in relation to other individuals in the same situation. There is a violation of the right in both examples because similar cases are treated in a different manner and the difference in treatment results from corruption which is not an objective or reasonable justification. Corrupt practices commonly produce unequal and discriminatory outcomes with regard to human rights.

If corruption restricts a person's access to adequate housing, for instance, it is discriminatory. Housing should be accessible to all, and disadvantaged groups in particular should be granted some degree of priority. After eviction, people are often promised alternative housing, but they may subsequently be denied effective access because the officials in charge require bribes. Well-intentioned low cost housing programmes, designed to benefit disadvantaged groups, may be exploited to the economic advantage of officials in the same way. Corruption in the health sector often violates the right to equality and nondiscrimination. As described below, when bribes are requested from patients, their access to health is severely restricted; in such cases, states have a duty to act at once to ensure that the right to health can be accessed without discrimination. An interesting link between bribes paid to health workers and the accessibility and quality requirements of health services may be noted here. Sometimes, when a payment or gift is made to a health worker, it is difficult to say whether the purpose of the payment was to obtain treatment, to save time, to ensure proper treatment by corrupt means, or to express gratitude. There is a fine line here that should be analysed carefully. First of all, if a bribe was extorted by the health worker, or given as a condition of receiving adequate healthcare, the right to health has been violated. By contrast, secondly, if the payment was made out of gratitude or to obtain a superior quality of treatment, what matters is whether the patient would have received care to a good standard whether or not she made the payment or gift. Third, the difficulty remains that, even in such a situation, the right to equality (the prohibition on discrimination) applies in all cases. As a result, even if the bribe or informal payment has no effect on the treatment received, or on access to treatment, corrupt acts may still technically violate the right to health.

## WHEN ACTS OF CORRUPTION MAY VIOLATE THE RIGHTS TO A FAIR TRIAL AND TO AN EFFECTIVE REMEDY

The right to a fair trial is established in several human rights treaties as well as domestic legislation (e.g. ICCPR, Article 14; ECHR, Articles 6 and 7; ACHR, Articles 8 and 9; and ACHPR, Article 7). It is composed of a broad range of standards that provide for the fair, effective and efficient administration of justice. These standards address the administration of justice including the rights of the parties involved, the efficiency of procedure and effectiveness. We address each below. Again, it should be noted that, when referring to the scope and content of the right to due process, we are applying standards that human rights supervisory bodies have developed on the basis of treaties that are binding on states that have ratified them. As mentioned below, some important "soft law" standards are also relevant – like the Bangalore Principles of Judicial Conduct established by the Judicial Integrity Group. "Soft law" standards do not have the same binding authority as treaties. In the context of the judicial system, corruption may be defined as "acts or omissions that constitute the use of public authority for the private benefit of court personnel, and result in the improper and unfair delivery of judicial decisions. Such acts and omissions include bribery, extortion, intimidation, influence peddling and the abuse of court procedures for personal gain". "Private benefit" includes both financial or material gain, and non-material gain such as the furtherance of professional ambition.

This definition of judicial corruption covers a wide range of acts carried out by actors at different points in the judicial system (the judiciary, the police and prosecutors). For example a judge may be paid a bribe to exclude evidence that would otherwise lead to the conviction of a criminal. A court official may be paid a bribe to allocate a case to a sympathetic judge, to lose a case file, or to speed up the hearing of a case. Police can be bribed to tamper with criminal evidence. Prosecutors can be paid to avoid bringing a case forward or to assess the evidence in an unfair manner. Any actor within the judicial system is acting corruptly if he or she applies inappropriate influence affecting the impartiality of the judicial process. As we will see, such acts imply a direct violation of the right to due process. It may be that public perceptions of judicial corruption are incorrect or exaggerated. However, the judiciary cannot afford to ignore such perceptions: the causes need to be identified and remedied, because judicial authority finally depends on public acceptance of the moral integrity of judicial officials.

**Standards Relating to the Administration of Justice**

These standards require compliance with several principles, including the independence, competence and impartiality of tribunals. Corruption may jeopardise judicial independence in several ways. Corruption in appointment processes, for example, will interfere with the principles in several respects. Political interference in the judicial system occurs when those in political power use their influence (including threat, intimidation or bribery) to force or induce a judge (or other court official) to act and rule according to their interests and not in accordance with the application of the law. Political interference also occurs when judicial appointments, salaries and conditions of service are manipulated, allowing those in political power to have leverage over judges, prosecutors and court staff, thereby creating a judicial system which is pliant and deferential. Judges can be forced to stand down or reassigned from sensitive positions; they may not be promoted or may be physically intimidated or harmed. Political interference also includes the application of immunity laws to judges.

While corrupt judges can sometimes shelter behind outdated immunity laws, in the absence of an immunity law independent judges may become the target of vexatious cases mounted by the political authorities. Contempt laws can be used in a similar way to hound independent judges out of office, or protect corrupt ones unjustly. Bribery can be used by political powers to control judges, as suggested above. In this typology, however, it refers primarily to bribes that are demanded from, or given by, civil society actors, including vulnerable and low-income citizens who can ill afford to pay them. Every official in the system – a judge, court administrator or police investigating officer – can potentially solicit bribes for services that should be provided as a matter of normal duty. The principle of impartiality is of great importance: there must be impartiality in objective terms and there should be no appearance of partiality. In this context, it should be noted that corruption in the process of appointment of judges and judicial officials may have the effect of lowering their quality. Appointments should be based on personal qualifications, moral authority and competence; if they are influenced by corrupt interests, the judiciary is likely to become less able as well as less independent, and the rights of those who apply to the justice system will not be fully protected. In addition, corruption affects the administration of justice and the right to a fair trial when corrupt acts take place before a case reaches court, often at the investigation level. The police may manipulate evidence in favour of one of the parties, for example, or a prosecutor may alter the facts of a case. This is not a minor issue. The value of prosecuting and punishing acts of corruption can evaporate if evidence is mishandled.

**Standards Related to the Rights of the Parties Involved**

Other standards protect the rights of parties to a trial. Individual rights and principles related to the right to a fair trial include: the right to a public hearing and pronouncement of judgement; equality of arms; presumption of innocence; freedom from compulsory self-incrimination; the right to know the accusation; adequate time and facilities to prepare a defence; the right to legal assistance; the right to examine witnesses; the right to an interpreter; the right to appeal in criminal matters; the rights of juvenile offenders; no punishment without law; *ne bis in idem* (not to be punished twice for the same act); *ex post facto* (law that makes illegal an act that was not illegal when committed); and the right to compensation for miscarriage of justice. These are basic rights to procedural guarantees to which all human beings are entitled. If acts of corruption impair any of these elements, there would be a violation of the right to a fair trial. Acts of corruption might take the form of a bribe for a favourable judgement, or a more subtle infringement of the principle of equality during the trial process (such as impeding some parties from being in a procedurally equal position during a trial).

**Standards Related to Efficiency of the Procedure**

Standards that refer to efficiency require that hearings take place "within reasonable time". According to human rights bodies, the determination of the meaning of "undue delay" or "expeditious procedure" depends on the circumstances and complexity of the case as well as the conduct of the parties involved. The right to be tried without undue delay will be infringed if, for example, a judge is bribed to delay the proceedings as much as possible. Although in this case the right to a fair trial would be infringed by the bribe itself, in cases where there is insufficient evidence to prove that a judge has been bribed, violation of the requirement that hearings should take place in a "reasonable time" may enable a corrupt process to be challenged.

**Fair Trial when Investigating Corruption**

The right to a fair trial should naturally also be respected in corruption cases. The International Council's second stage will discuss in more detail how corruption may be combated while respecting human rights. It will examine the potential tensions between effective investigation of corruption and adherence to human rights principles, and signal the most important elements that need to be borne in mind if anti-corruption investigations, prosecutions and punishments are to comply with human rights. In reality, reconciling anti-corruption practices with human rights does not present insuperable difficulties; on the contrary, if care is taken, there is no reason why good anti-corruption practice should not be consistent with human rights. Some preliminary remarks may nevertheless be made here. The principle of presumption of innocence is highly relevant to corruption cases, and particularly to cases of illegal enrichment. The right to be presumed innocent requires that judges and juries and all other public officials refrain from prejudging any case. This means that public authorities, particularly prosecutors and police, should not make statements about the guilt or innocence of an accused before the outcome of the trial. It implies too that the authorities have a duty to prevent the news media or other powerful social groups from influencing the outcome of a case by pronouncing on its merits. In accordance with the presumption of innocence, the rules of evidence must ensure that the prosecution bears the burden of proof throughout a trial. This principle is extremely important in corruption cases where the prosecution has all the machinery of the state at its disposition.

The principle is clearly violated if an accused is not granted access to information that is necessary to prepare a defence, is denied access to expert witnesses, or is excluded from an appeal hearing at which the prosecutor was present. The right to a fair trial is also infringed when independent judges, prosecutors or members of anti-corruption commissions that are investigating cases of corruption are illegitimately dismissed or are prevented from carrying out their lawful functions by threats, inducements or an arbitrary reduction of funds. In a corruption case, an effective witness-protection system can have an important dissuasive impact and can increase denunciations and judicial investigation. Offering adequate protection to victims and witnesses in corruption cases is a very effective incentive for obtaining information that can help to investigate this kind of crime and obtain appropriate punishment for those responsible. In this context, the absence of firm witness-protection rules in many countries is a glaring weakness. Where intimidation, extortion, and threats against witnesses and their families cause witnesses to withdraw evidence, victims' rights and the right to a fair trial are violated, but harm is also done to the authority of the judicial system and its capacity to prosecute corruption effectively.

### Vulnerable Groups and the Right to a Fair Trial

Several factors prevent vulnerable and disadvantaged people from gaining access to courts and tribunals: they include economic costs, lack of information, complex and bureaucratic procedures, barriers of language and geographical distance. From a human rights perspective, it is important to consider the effect of judicial corruption on vulnerable and disadvantaged groups, because judicial systems that require citizens to pay bribes effectively exclude those who are very poor from access to justice, denying them opportunities to settle disputes impartially with neighbours or the authorities. Because they are generally poorer than men, women tend to bear the brunt of such injustice. According to human rights standards, states should adopt appropriate and effective legislative and administrative procedures and other appropriate measures that provide fair, effective and prompt access to justice. In addition, to prevent corruption at judicial level, states must put in place appropriate procedures that make access possible for groups at particular risk, including provision of information about their legal entitlements, legal aid, facilities that enable them to communicate in a language they understand, and mechanisms for reporting abuses and corruption.

Judicial corruption that takes the form of political interference in the selection of judges or the assignment of cases also has an impact on the poor, because they are disadvantaged relative to people who are well-connected or well off. Judicial corruption not only harms those seeking justice economically; it also undermines confidence in justice itself. In post-conflict societies the judicial infrastructure is often damaged. This also creates an environment in which corruption is likely to occur. Institutions espousing transparency and accountability are likely to be weak and, where a state is unable to pay adequate salaries, judicial officials are vulnerable to bribery. Because conflicts often have an ethnic or religious dimension, members of some minority or religious groups may be particularly subject to exploitation or corruption. After conflicts and where state institutions are weak, security and paramilitary forces are also likely to seek to influence judicial processes – by physically preventing people from gaining access to courts unless a bribe is paid, or influencing the outcome of cases by threatening judicial officials. While anti-corruption organisations have analysed these problems at length, human rights organisations have not yet engaged deeply with judicial corruption as a human rights issue. For their part, anti-corruption organisations may find it useful to apply human rights principles and methods to the work they do on judicial corruption.

**The Right to an Effective Remedy**

The right to an effective remedy is guaranteed by most international human rights instruments (e.g. ICCPR, Article 2(3); CEDAW, Articles 2 and 3; CERD, Article 6; ICESCR, Articles 2 and 3; CRC, Articles 12, 13 and 37(d)). It asserts that, when a human rights violation occurs, a state has a duty to provide victims with an effective remedy. Failure to do so can create a climate of impunity, particularly when states intentionally or regularly deny remedies. States are under an obligation to provide accessible, effective and enforceable remedies to uphold civil and political rights. A person claiming a remedy is entitled to have his or her claim determined and enforced by a competent domestic authority, and states must ensure that this can occur. Ending an ongoing violation is also an essential element of the right to an effective remedy. A state that fails to investigate allegations of violations or bring perpetrators to justice is in breach of the ICCPR. Effective administration of justice is essential to enjoyment of this right.

To achieve this, states must ensure that equality before the courts is established by law and guaranteed in practice. Corruption in the administration of justice infringes both the right to a fair trial and the right to an effective remedy. Suppose, for instance, that a woman, unfairly dismissed, brings a lawsuit against her employer, and that the employer then bribes the judge to obtain a favourable ruling. The woman's right to a fair trial and her right to an effective remedy for unfair dismissal are both violated. States must guarantee that remedies are accessible, effective and enforceable. This implies equal access to courts, fair and public hearings, and competent, impartial and independent judicial officials. In sum, from a human rights perspective a good system of fair trial requires compliance with numerous international human rights standards and norms. States are required to organise their judicial system in a manner that respects the requirements of due process. If states do not take measures to organize their judicial systems effectively and to give judges, court staff, prosecutors, attorneys and police officers sufficient capacity to deal with cases, they may create the conditions for corruption. If there is corruption in the justice system, it is probable that some of these standards are not respected. This may provide opportunities to challenge the process or specific decisions even in cases where a supposed act of corruption cannot be proven.

## WHEN CORRUPTION MAY VIOLATE THE RIGHTS OF POLITICAL PARTICIPATION

From a human rights perspective, the right to participation affirms that all citizens should be entitled to engage in decision-making processes that affect them. The major political expressions of the rights to participation are the freedom to vote and stand for elections, the right to equal access to public services, and the freedoms of association and assembly. These rights are enshrined in several human rights treaties (such as ICCPR, Article 25; CEDAW, Article 7; ECHR, Article 3 of the First Protocol; ACHR, Article 23; and ACHPR, Article 13). *The freedom to vote and stand for elections* refers to the right of every citizen to be involved in the conduct of public affairs, directly or through chosen representation.

People directly participate in the conduct of public affairs by exercising their right to vote or their right to be a candidate, at free and fair elections carried out on the basis of universal and equal suffrage by secret ballot that guarantees the free expression of the will of the electors. With regard to the right to vote, the state has the duty to ensure that individuals eligible to vote can exercise this right freely. Persons entitled to vote must be free to vote for any candidate without undue influence or coercion of any kind that may distort or inhibit the free expression of their will. Voters should be able to form opinions independently, free of violence or threat of violence, compulsion, inducement or manipulative interference. States must protect voters from any form of coercion or compulsion and from any unlawful or arbitrary interference with the voting process. *The right to equal access to public services* means that everyone has the right to equal access to the public services in his or her country and that access should be based on objective and reasonable criteria. *The right to freedom of association* allows individuals to join together to pursue collective interests in groups, such as sports clubs, political parties, NGOs and corporations.

The freedom of association affirms the right to form and join associations freely; but, in order for the right to be enjoyed, associations themselves must be free from excessive interference by governments. It is fairly straightforward to determine that bribing voters to persuade them to vote or refrain from voting interferes with the integrity of an election and therefore violates the right to vote. Bribing election officials to interfere with the electoral process, by stuffing ballot boxes in favour of a particular candidate or party and falsifying the count, violates the right to vote in a similar way. States must take effective measures to ensure that all persons entitled to vote are able to exercise their right. The UN Human Rights Committee has stated that any abusive interference with registration or voting, including intimidation or coercion of voters, should be prohibited by penal laws that must be strictly enforced.

The right to stand for election may be restricted by various corrupt means. An Electoral Commission may be co-opted politically, or be complicit in influence trading, or bribed, and may for all these reasons disqualify a candidate or refuse him or her permission to register. Trading in influence occurs when electoral commissioners abuse their position to obtain an undue advantage (monetary or otherwise) from a person who will benefit as a result. Corruption of this kind violates the right to stand for election. Corrupt practices can also negatively affect another right of political participation: the right to equal access to public service. Access to positions in the public service should be based on an objective and reasonable appointment process. Various forms of direct and indirect discriminatory practices exclude women, and so impede their ability to participate in political organisations and activities. In other cases, people engage in acts, such as bribery, that are recognised to be corrupt, to obtain public service employment. When they give or accept such bribes, they clearly violate the right to equal access to public service. In general, distinctions are not permitted between citizens in the enjoyment of this right on any ground. Any distinction should be on the basis of objective and reasonable criteria, and without discrimination. If individuals are refused employment, or lose their jobs in the public service because they will not bribe, their right to equal access to public service and their right to equality and nondiscrimination are both violated as a result of corruption. All the examples presented in this section violate the right of citizens to take part in the conduct of public affairs, directly or through chosen representation. By definition, corruption is incompatible with a free and fair electoral process or a merit-based approach to appointment to public service. As important, bribery, abuse of function and trading in influence infringe the free expression of the will of the electorate and as such directly violate the rights of all citizens, whether they are voters or candidates. Corruption also poses a threat to the broader normative and institutional framework of democratic governance. In a repressive regime where political participation is curtailed and accountability is poor, for example, the rights to life, liberty, security of the person, and freedom of expression and association are all less likely to be respected. In addition, the suppression of rights essential to political participation, such as freedom of expression and association, may increase opportunities for corruption. Promoting political freedoms and effective participation are likely to improve transparency and access to information.

## WHEN CORRUPTION MAY VIOLATE ECONOMIC, SOCIAL AND CULTURAL RIGHTS

It is especially important to give attention to the impact of corruption on economic, social and cultural rights. Corruption is likely to violate enjoyment of these rights because, as we will see, states have accepted, under human rights law, a wide range of duties to provide or regulate public services in relation to health, housing, water and education. These services generate large public contracts which not only create opportunities for corruption but have a disproportionate impact on vulnerable and disadvantaged groups, in particular women. Widespread corruption in health or educational services deters the poor from seeking healthcare and education, and depresses living standards and opportunities for poorer people in particular. Where states privatise services in areas such as healthcare, education and the water sector, the distinction between the public and private sector may become blurred. Nonetheless, even when public services are privatised, a state is still responsible for some violations of rights that private companies commit, and will be liable if it fails to prevent corruption (or exposure to it) as privatisation occurs, or does not protect the rights of vulnerable groups which depend on the services in question. It should be noted that the rights examined below serve as examples. Corruption will have an impact on the enjoyment of all economic, social and cultural rights. When assessing whether or not an act of corruption violates economic, social and cultural rights, two essential obligations should be taken into account: the duty that a state has to take steps to realise these rights progressively; and its duty to prioritise human rights when allocating resources. In addition, it is helpful to apply two analytical tools: the three levels of state obligation; and the principles of availability and accessibility.

### Progressive Realization

This issue merits specific analysis because it applies explicitly to all economic, social and cultural rights. When states ratify the ICESCR, they accept a general legal obligation to take steps to the maximum of their available resources to progressively achieve the full realisation of economic, social and cultural rights (ICESCR, Article 2). In doing so, a state accepts three obligations: to take immediate steps to make sure that economic, social and cultural rights will progressively become available to all those under its jurisdiction; to prohibit retrogressive measures; and to devote a maximum of available resources to this purpose. States must take deliberate, specific and targeted steps towards the goal of full realisation of the relevant rights. The obligation is an immediate one and states are required to adopt a range of different measures (such as enacting relevant legislation, providing judicial remedies, and taking administrative, financial, educational or social measures). States must move as quickly and effectively as possible towards full realisation; any deliberate retrogressive measures need to be justified by reference to the use of maximum available resources. Corruption implies that the state is not taking steps in the right direction. When funds are stolen by corrupt officials, or when access to healthcare, education and housing is dependent on bribes, a state's resources are clearly not being used maximally to realise economic, social and cultural rights. The UN Special Rapporteur on the right of everyone to the enjoyment of the highest attainable standard of physical and mental health, referring specifically to this, has argued that, when a state does not progress towards realising the right to health because of corruption in the health sector, it has failed to comply with its obligations concerning the right to health. The UN Committee on the Rights of the Child has noted that corruption reduces the resources available to implement the Convention on this right. It has suggested that states in which corruption is widespread cannot comply with their obligation to implement the economic, social and cultural rights of children as provided under Article 4 of the Convention. High level embezzlement of public funds would also reduce the resources for law enforcement that are needed to protect children from human trafficking and from sexual and labour exploitation.

**The Prohibition on Taking Deliberately Retrogressive Measures**

The UN Committee on Economic, Social and Cultural Rights (CESCR) has noted that "any deliberately retrogressive measures [...] would require the most careful consideration and would need to be fully justified by reference to the totality of the rights provided for in the Covenant and in the context of the full use of the maximum available resources". In order to understand the Committee's statement, it is important to analyse what constitutes a "deliberately retrogressive measure". The Committee has not provided a definition. However, some guidance is to be found in General Comment No. 4, which states that "[A] general decline in living and housing conditions, directly attributable to policy and legislative decisions by States Parties, and in the absence of accompanying compensatory measures, would be inconsistent with the obligations under the Covenant". It is therefore possible to argue that a "deliberate retrogressive measure" means any measure that implies a step back in the level of protection accorded to the rights contained in the Covenant resulting from an intentional decision by the state concerned.

## ThE Duty to Accord A Degree of Priority to Human Rights in the Allocation of Resources

Because resources are always limited, states need to prioritise. While they are entitled to decide where and how they allocate their resources, when they ratify human rights treaties, in particular the ICESCR, states assume obligations that limit their discretion. This follows from the obligation to take steps to realise economic, social and cultural rights progressively. If a state ratifies the ICESCR, it will not comply with its obligation under Article 2(1) of the Covenant if it does not give some priority to its implementation. It is bound therefore to acknowledge that its discretion on expenditure is not absolute.

## The Three Levels of State Obligations

As mentioned, states have an obligation to respect, protect and fulfil human rights. Regarding economic, social and cultural rights (ESC rights), the *obligation to respect* requires states to refrain from interfering directly or indirectly with these rights. The *obligation to protect* requires states to prevent third parties from interfering in any way with the enjoyment of ESC rights. The *obligation to fulfil* requires states to take positive measures to assist individuals and communities to enjoy their rights. The obligation to fulfil requires special attention. Governments comply with the duty to fulfil economic, social and cultural rights in several ways. These can involve a wide variety of operations, ranging from the provision of public services to the creation of social programmes for reducing poverty. All these activities give rise to opportunities for corruption and, where corruption occurs, it will have a disproportionate impact on the poor.

Social programmes redistribute sizeable resources through direct subsidies, income transfers and provision of services, and they represent a vital source of food, housing, health, jobs and income for people who live in poverty, even if the support they offer is insufficient to meet need. Wherever such programmes lack transparency, are weakly monitored, or are inappropriately discretionary, they offer major opportunities for patronage and other forms of corruption. In many parts of the world, social welfare programmes have become one of the instruments that are most highly valued by political parties to maintain or develop their support networks. Using targeted social programmes, political parties can favour certain groups and discriminate against others – a practice that neutralises the steady fulfilment of ESC rights, even though these rights have been formally recognised at national and international levels and the state has committed financial resources to their fulfilment. Ensuring that social programmes are properly regulated and accountable is the most effective way to reduce corruption. If accountability is to be sustained, moreover, it will be important to ensure that the beneficiaries of such programmes, including disadvantaged and marginalised populations, are consulted and involved in decisions about their design, implementation and monitoring. Participation needs to be authentic; members of the public need to have good access to information, and have opportunities to express their opinions, and have their opinions heard.

### The Principles of Availability and Accessibility

The practice of human rights has led to the development of standards for measuring fulfilment of social rights. Four standards – availability, accessibility, acceptability and adaptability – are generally used to assess the delivery of public services such as health, education, housing, food and drinking water. These standards protect the core content of economic, social and cultural rights. They ensure that public services are made available in sufficient quantity and quality to meet the needs of the community in question (availability); that services are allocated and provided to the whole community without discrimination, and are within reach (accessibility); that physical access to goods and services is safe; and that services are organised in ways that avoid discrimination. In addition, cost should not be prohibitive: for essential services (like water) this means that the poorest users should not be excluded from access by price. Corruption in the provision of public services affects and distorts the delivery of services in a wide variety of ways. It can cause under-provision, depress quality, increase cost, waste materials, generate fictitious expenditure and projects, or simply destroy the service or make it unavailable.

## WHEN CORRUPTION MAY VIOLATE THE RIGHT TO FOOD

The right to food, also referred to as the right of everyone to be free from hunger, is a component of the more general right to an adequate standard of living (ICESCR, Article 11(2)). The right to adequate food asserts that all people should be in a position to feed themselves. It should be made clear that the right to food does not imply that states must provide food to everyone. The obligation on a state is to take steps that will gradually make it possible for all people to feed themselves, will provide access to food in an equal and non-discriminatory way, and will assist people to obtain food if they are not in a position to feed themselves.

### Core Content of the Right to Food

According to the CESCR's General Comment 12, the core content of the right to food implies that food should be made *available* in a quantity and quality that is sufficient to satisfy the dietary needs of individuals. Individuals should be able to feed themselves from productive land or other natural resources, and distribution, processing and market systems should be able to move food from the site of production to where it is needed in accordance with demand. Food must be *safe* (free from adverse substances). This means that the government must set and enforce health and safety standards for food quality. Food should also be *acceptable* within a given culture. This implies the need to take into account, as far as possible, perceived non-nutrient values attached to food and food consumption and informed consumer concerns. *Accessibility* includes both economic and physical accessibility. *Economic accessibility* implies that personal or household financial costs associated with the acquisition of food for an adequate diet should be such that households can meet other basic needs. Socially vulnerable groups may need specific attention through special programmes. *Physical accessibility* implies that adequate food must be accessible to everyone, including physically vulnerable individuals, such as infants and young children, elderly people, the physically disabled, the terminally ill and persons with persistent medical problems, including the mentally ill.

Refugees, victims of natural disaster and other specially disadvantaged groups may need special attention and priority consideration. Corruption can seriously undermine the realisation of the right to food. The UN Special Rapporteur on the right to food identified corruption as one of the seven major economic obstacles that hinder or prevent the realisation of the right. In 1996, the Declaration of the World Food Summit expressly mentioned corruption as one of the causes of food insecurity. As it does with other ESC rights, corruption diverts essential resources from social spending and thus, directly or indirectly, hinders realisation of the right to food. In addition, corrupt practices related to the possession and use of land and natural resources can restrict the availability of food and violate the right. For example, if bribes are required to purchase or obtain a license to farm land, this may prejudice access to food.

The right will also be violated if land is allocated in a discriminatory manner as a result of corrupt practises. Indigenous populations may be particularly vulnerable to violations of their right to food as a result of corrupt sale or expropriation of land on which they depend. Logging, oil and mining ventures, many of which are frequently non-transparent about land acquisition, have displaced numerous indigenous communities from their ancestral lands, and in doing so have sometimes violated their right to food and other ESC rights. Corruption may also affect other elements of the right to food. Food security may be compromised if food producers obtain licenses by bribing the authorities; and the right to health (and life) may be compromised, if such food producers subsequently put adulterated or unsafe products on the market. Corruption in food programmes and schemes designed to meet the needs of socially vulnerable people may also prevent them from obtaining food; when a person embezzles funds from a food programme, or diverts food into the black market for personal profit, the right to food of those who are embezzled is clearly compromised.

## WHEN CORRUPTION MAY VIOLATE THE RIGHT TO ADEQUATE HOUSING

The right to adequate housing derives from the right to an adequate standard of living. It focuses on the obligation to ensure that everyone has housing that is safe, healthy and adequate (ICESCR, Article 11(1)). In addition, the right forbids discrimination in the field of housing, as well as forced or arbitrary evictions or acts of unjust dispossession. The right to adequate housing does not entail that the government has to build housing for the entire population or that housing must be provided free of charge to whoever requests it. It is primarily a right of access. What constitutes adequate is dependent on social, economic, climatic, ecological and other factors. However, certain minimum elements are integral to the right and should always be taken into account. Corruption may violate this right by restricting one or more of its elements.

### Core Content of the Right to Housing

The core elements of the right to housing have been defined by CESCR, General Comment No. 7. All persons should possess a degree of legal *security of tenure*, guaranteeing protection from forced eviction, harassment and threats. Housing must also be *affordable*: the price of housing should not be so high that households cannot meet other basic needs. Housing must be *habitable*. Houses must contain facilities essential for health, security, comfort, and nutrition, such as heating, safe drinking water, lighting, sanitation and washing facilities. They must be adequately spacious and protect from cold, rain, threats to health and structural hazards. Housing must be *accessible*, and disadvantaged groups in particular should be ensured some degree of priority in housing. *Location* matters too: housing should permit access to employment, healthcare services, schools, childcare centres and other social facilities; it should not be located in polluted areas.

Finally, housing policies should be culturally appropriate, enabling the expression of cultural identity. Corruption undermines security of tenure. Companies may bribe officials to grant leases on land that is already occupied. Officials or businesses may bribe homeowners directly to sell up, often throwing poor tenants on the street. Village leaders may be bribed into signing blank contracts with the local land administration, which then sells the land on to developers. Embezzlement of funds in a programme destined to build housing units, or bribery in the selection of contractors, may result in construction of substandard quality, impairing habitability. Accessibility too can be affected by corruption. In many countries, the easiest way to obtain a house is by bribing the relevant officials. Subsidised programmes may be hijacked by their administrators in case they demand payments before they agree to allocate or if they allocate to friends. Where land is owned by a provincial or regional government, informal settlements often squat public land. This creates conditions in which corruption, exploitative renting or abusive eviction can easily arise.

## WHEN CORRUPTION MAY VIOLATE THE RIGHT TO HEALTH

The right to health is included in several human rights treaties. Most notably, Article 12 of the ICESCR established the "right to the highest attainable standard of physical and mental health", defined as the "right to the enjoyment of a variety of facilities, goods, services and conditions necessary for the realisation of the highest attainable standard of health". While this right is broad, it does not imply that people have a right to be healthy. The right to health includes healthcare, but also the underlying determinants of health, such as safe drinking water, adequate sanitation, adequate supply of safe food, nutrition, housing, occupational health, environmental health and access to health-related information. Another core component of the right has been identified, which the state must guarantee under all circumstances regardless of its available resources: access to maternal and child healthcare, including family planning, immunisation against the major infectious diseases, appropriate treatment of common diseases and injuries, essential drugs, adequate supply of safe water and basic sanitation, and freedom from serious environmental health threats.

### Core Content of the Right to Health

The core elements of the right to health are set out in CESCR, General Comment No. 14. Health facilities, goods and services as well as programmes must be made *available* in sufficient quantity. States therefore need to ensure that the availability of health goods and facilities is not negatively affected by acts of corruption which, in the health sector, can have mortal consequences. Health facilities, goods and services must also be *accessible* to all persons without discrimination. Accessibility has four overlapping dimensions. *Nondiscrimination*: health facilities, goods and services must be within appropriate physical reach of all people, including vulnerable or marginalised groups. Health sector corruption can also lead to direct discrimination when healthcare providers and professionals treat patients differently, based on their income or their personal relationships with medical staff. *Physical access*: health facilities, goods and services must be within safe physical reach of all sections of the population, including vulnerable and marginalised groups. Health sector corruption may lead to decisions that are less favourable to a community.

For example, hospitals may be built in cheaper areas of a city, or in unhealthy locations, or in locations inaccessible by public transport. *Economic access* (affordability): whether they are provided by public or private institutions, health facilities, goods and services must be affordably priced. The affordability of health services is affected by corruption when, for example, health officials request fees for drugs that have been provided free of charge by pharmaceutical companies or donor organisations, or demand "informal payments" for treatment. When a person seeking a health service is asked for a bribe, this not only violates his or her right to health but also the principle of non-discrimination, because the bribe places the patient in a position of inequality *vis-à-vis* others. Women suffer most from corruption in the health sector because they tend to seek healthcare for themselves or for their children more often than men, and are more regularly exposed to corruption in the sector. Pregnant women and women with reproductive health problems, who have no money to pay bribes, are particularly likely to be at risk as a result. *Access to information*: patients and the public as a whole should have the right to seek, receive and impart information and ideas. States must take measures to ensure that patients are in a position to make informed choices and select appropriate providers at appropriate prices and standards of quality.

This component is particularly important in regard to the right to health due to the many asymmetries of health information. Physicians typically have more information than patients, while pharmaceutical companies frequently have more information than governments. *Acceptability*: health facilities must respect medical ethics and should be culturally appropriate. Among other things, health facilities must be designed to respect confidentiality and improve the health status of those concerned. States should put in place guarantees that ensure that health professionals do not abuse their position of power and thereby disregard the "acceptability" of the services they provide. *Quality*: health facilities must be scientifically and medically of good quality. Corruption can affect the quality of medicines, for example, when regulators are bribed to carry out less rigorous checks or to approve medicines without adequate investigation, or when hospital administrators purchase cheaper, less effective (or even expired) drugs and embezzle the difference in cost. States should ensure that the quality of health services is guaranteed at all levels of the health sector and that the quality of health services is not negatively affected by corruption. Corruption affecting the quality of health services and particularly the quality of medicines is a serious infringement not only of the right to health but also of the right to life. Corrupt practices in the pharmaceutical industry are particularly relevant. Unethical drug promotion can generate conflicts of interest for physicians and ultimately can harm patients' health.

If drug marketing by pharmaceutical companies is not well regulated, studies have shown that physicians may prescribe treatments under the influence of marketing inducements that may bring no benefit (and may even be harmful) to patients and the health system. If states do not guard against this kind of abuse, they will violate their duty to protect the right to health. In general terms, corruption in the health sector occurs in three main forms: in management of financial resources (budget allocation, etc.); in the distribution of medical supplies (purchasing, marketing); and in the relationships of health workers with patients.

## WHEN CORRUPTION MAY VIOLATE THE RIGHT TO EDUCATION

The right to education is guaranteed in several international instruments, notably Articles 13 and 14 of the ICESCR and Article 28 of the CRC. In general terms, this right has two main dimensions. The *social* dimension affirms the right to receive an education that reflects the aims and objectives identified in Article 13(1) of the ICESCR. States are required to make various levels of education available (primary, secondary and higher) and these should be easily accessible to all. Education also has a *freedom* dimension: it requires academic freedom and institutional autonomy and implies the personal freedom of individuals or their parents or guardians to choose educational institutions that reflect their educational, religious and moral convictions. This in turn implies that individuals should be free to establish and direct educational institutions.

### Core Content of the Right to Education

The core elements of the right to education are availability, accessibility, acceptability and adaptability (CESCR, General Comment No. 13). *Availability* requires states to ensure free and compulsory primary education to all, while secondary and higher education must be made available and accessible to all through the progressive introduction of free education. In addition, the provision of educational institutions and programmes must be adequate, and educational institutions and programmes must be equipped with what they need to function (buildings, trained and paid teachers, teaching materials, sanitation, drinking water, etc.). Corrupt practices in the education sector harm the availability of education.

Most notably, embezzlement removes resources required to equip educational institutions. *Accessibility* implies that education should be accessible to everyone without discrimination. It refers not only to physical but also economic access. In this context, all education should be affordable, and primary education should be free. *Acceptability* requires that the form and content of education programmes should be acceptable to students and parents (in terms of relevance, cultural appropriateness and quality). *Adaptability* implies that education should adapt to the needs of societies as they change. Corruption is frequent in the education sector. In most countries, educational institutions occupy a large place in the public sector. This creates many opportunities and incentives for corruption. Frequent forms of abuse include: rigged tenders and bids; embezzlement of funds; illegal registration fees; absenteeism; and examination fraud. Most corrupt practices in the education sector infringe one or more elements of the right to education. Corruption may restrict access to education in many ways. Children may be requested to make informal payments for services, for example, or required to pay a bribe on admission, or parents may be asked to pay the teacher fees for additional private lessons (covering material from the core curriculum that should be taught during the school day) or for correcting their child's work. In such cases, access to education is not based on equality but on ability to pay a bribe, which amounts to discrimination and puts vulnerable groups at particular disadvantage because they are least able to pay. All corrupt practices that entail the disbursement of money for primary education violate the right to education, because primary education should be free. Corruption that harms the quality of education affects its acceptability.

Corruption in procurement affects the acquisition of educational material, meals, buildings, and equipment, and usually lowers their quality. Corruption of recruitment procedures may result in the appointment of less qualified teachers, lowering the standard of education that pupils receive. These effects infringe the right to education. Corruption in the education system may discriminate against girl children and limit their opportunities. For example, when families living in poverty have to pay a bribe to send their children to school, many will prioritise the education of their male children at their daughters' expense, for religious, socio-cultural or economic reasons. Corruption in education is particularly damaging because it has long-term effects. It undermines access and harms the quantity and quality of education services and facilities. This has a disproportionate effect on vulnerable groups who, without access to education (or with access only to education of poor quality), stand little or no chance of breaking the cycle of poverty. As a result, corruption in the education sector is a catalyst for other serious rights violations. Children who drop out of school because their parents cannot afford bribes will earn less, and are more likely to work in more dangerous jobs and to live shorter lives. Moreover, if children are exposed to corruption in school, it is difficult to create a culture of transparency and integrity. The effects of corruption in education, like the effects of education, have lifelong, even generational consequences; it is therefore an area in which corruption has especially deep and pernicious effects.

## WHEN CORRUPTION MAY VIOLATE THE RIGHT TO WATER

The right to water and the right to an adequate standard of living are linked. Access to clean water is essential for fulfilment of the right to an adequate standard of living (ICESCR, Article 11) and the right to health (ICESCR, Article12). Without it, these rights are not attainable.

### Core Content of the Right to Water

The core content of the right to water is analysed in CESCR, General Comment No. 15. *Availability*: each person has the right to a water supply that is sufficient and continuous for personal and domestic use (such as drinking, personal sanitation, washing of clothes, food preparation, personal and household hygiene). Water must be of adequate quality. Water for personal or domestic use must be safe and free from micro-organisms, chemical substances and radiological hazards that constitute a threat to health. Furthermore, water should be of an acceptable colour, odour and taste for personal or domestic use. *Accessibility*: water facilities and services must be physically and economically accessible to everyone without discrimination. *Information accessibility* is defined as including the right to seek, receive and impart information concerning water issues. It has been argued that the shortage of clean water and rising water pollution are not caused by a lack of natural supply or engineering problems but by corruption. Corruption will violate the right to water when, for example, companies bribe state water regulators to allow them to draw excessive amounts from rivers and groundwater reservoirs, ultimately denying water access to neighbouring communities.

Corruption also occurs when citizens have to pay bribes in order to be connected to the national water grid, or to avoid drinking unclean water from sources such as rivers or dams. Women tend to use more water because of their roles as caretakers of the home. In poor female-headed households, lack of money to bribe water officials exposes them to unhygienic water sources, increasing their exposure to water-borne diseases. Where women are responsible for providing the household with water, interruptions of the supply due to corruption will mean that women have to walk further to fetch water. Corruption can harm the quality of water as well. If a company bribes a public inspector to overlook the discharge of waste into water resources, water supplies will be polluted and the right of people who depend on that water will be infringed. Again, the right of indigenous and minority populations to water is frequently threatened because many indigenous settlements are located by lakes or rivers.

## WHEN EMBEZZLEMENT OF FUNDS ALLOCATED TO SOCIAL PROGRAMMES MAY VIOLATE HUMAN RIGHTS

The claim that corruption violates human rights is usually based on reasoning that money lost to corruption could have been used to buy medicine, equip schools or supply water. It is therefore useful to analyse embezzlement in more detail, particularly the embezzlement of funds allocated to social programmes. This corrupt practice may affect a wide range of human rights. As described earlier, the right to health (ICESCR, Article 12) is usually understood in terms of the availability, accessibility, acceptability, and quality of public health and health-care facilities, goods, services and programmes. Health facilities, as well as goods and services, have to be available in sufficient quantity, must be accessible to everyone without discrimination, and must be scientifically and medically appropriate and of good quality. Most corruption cases affect several of these elements.

This is particularly true in the case of embezzlement of public funds by public officials. Part of the health budget can "disappear" before it is paid out by the Ministry of Finance to the Ministry of Health. More money may then be siphoned off in the course of channelling funds from the national government to provincial administrations, and eventually by the directors or managers of local hospitals. As these resources are drawn off by embezzlement and procurement fraud, less money remains to pay salaries, fund operations, and maintain equipment and buildings. Effects on staff, infrastructure and the quality of care will follow. In this way, corrupt acts, especially embezzlement, can simultaneously interfere with the availability, accessibility, and quality of the right to health. Embezzlement may also affect the food safety and dietary needs recognised in the right to food (ICESCR, Article 11(2)). When a public official misappropriates part of a subsidy scheme or other funds allocated to a food programme, and instead purchases low-cost and substandard food, the programme may fail to meet dietary needs and may even provide food that is unsafe to eat. Both effects will violate the right to food of beneficiaries.

Food must also be accessible to everyone; it must be affordable and physically accessible. In particular, it should be within reach of socially vulnerable groups (such as people who are particularly impoverished or without land) whose needs qualify them for special attention. Corruption undermines accessibility when it affects such programmes – and in practice assistance programmes of this kind are particularly vulnerable to corruption, because they have large budgets and large numbers of (relatively anonymous) clients, creating many opportunities and incentives for abuse. When an official embezzles funds that have been set aside to buy and distribute food, steals the food or sells it, the effect is to deprive people of food they need, to which they are entitled. The right to adequate food is clearly violated by such behaviour.

The embezzlement of education funds removes resources that are needed to equip educational institutions and pay teachers. The right to education (ICESCR, Articles 13 and 14) provides that educational institutions and programmes must be available in sufficient quantity. Availability also means that educational institutions and programmes must be equipped with what they require to function, including teachers who are trained and paid, teaching materials, buildings, sanitation facilities, drinking water, etc. Several different corrupt practices in the education sector harm the availability and quality of education. When funds are stolen, pupils suffer because educational equipment will be of lower quality and teachers will lack resources. Failure to pay teachers' salaries leads in turn to other corrupt practices, such as regular absenteeism or bribetaking. In this way, embezzlement creates new corruption. In these conditions, the state clearly does not comply with its obligation to fulfil the right to education and thus the right to education is violated. Funds to finance prison services are also embezzled. This practice has the same effect as in education: it depresses the quality of facilities, and the quality of the services provided.

All persons who are deprived of their liberty and placed in prisons, hospitals, detention camps, correctional institutions or elsewhere, have the right to be treated with humanity and dignity (ICCPR, Article 10). In prisons, this implies that each prisoner should have a minimum of personal floor space and access to a minimum cubic content of air, adequate sanitary facilities, clothing that is neither degrading nor humiliating, a separate bed and food of adequate nutritional value (United Nations Standard Minimum Rules for the Treatment of Prisoners). Embezzlement of prison funds can occur at many levels, from ministerial level to the warder. Corruption of this type will certainly affect the treatment of prisoners, possibly to a degree that will render their treatment inhumane in violation of human rights treaties (e.g. ICCPR, Article 10). This may happen, for example, if lack of funds results in a shortage of prison food, or failure to provide blankets or beds. In such a case, corruption can be associated with violation of the right of a person deprived of liberty to be treated humanely and with dignity. Embezzlement or misappropriation of assets may also affect the right to a fair trial and to an effective remedy (ICCPR, Articles 14 and 2(3)). Embezzlement deprives the justice system of resources and this will affect its quality and effectiveness. The same lack of resources may mean that insufficient staff are employed, which in turn may create a backlog of cases and slow procedures, infringing the right to be tried without undue delay as provided under Article 14(3)(c) of the ICCPR and consequently violating the right to a fair trial and an effective remedy. When public money goes missing, the state is not complying with one of its principal human rights obligations: to use the *maximum of its available resources* to achieve the full realisation of economic, social and cultural rights (ICESCR, Article 2(1)). In addition, embezzlement usually expropriates assets that were destined to provide goods or services to members of the public. In most cases, therefore, it prevents the state from fulfilling human rights obligations and is likely to result in human rights violations. The cumulative effect of corruption becomes evident especially in large scale social programmes. Numerous officials administer such programmes and, if corruption is endemic and widespread, levels of embezzlement can be very high.

## PROTECTING THE RIGHTS OF THOSE INVESTIGATING CORRUPTION

Some governments have used anti-corruption campaigns to suppress critics or political opponents, or curb the rights of those who combat corruption. When this occurs, instead of contributing towards increased transparency and accountability, anti-corruption campaigns may weaken democracy and public trust. In such cases, the human rights of those who are politically targeted may be violated. This stage examines protection of the human rights of anti-corruption advocates. It reviews rights that are often violated, and identifies human rights mechanisms that can be used to claim redress and create accountability. It also discusses issues that arise when anti-corruption campaigns become politicised, for example when they are exploited for electoral advantage. The stage concludes that it is necessary to protect the rights of anti-corruption advocates as well as reduce opportunities to exploit anti-corruption campaigns politically: these objectives offer key entry points for collaboration between human rights and anti-corruption organisations.

## THREATS TO HUMAN RIGHTS THAT ANTI-CORRUPTION ADVOCATES FACE

Those who campaign against corruption and call for transparent government often themselves become victims of human rights violations. Risks and threats take many forms. Journalists and anti-corruption defenders are often harassed, threatened and sometimes killed to prevent them from making corruption cases public. Whistleblowers are silenced by imprisonment, threats or violence. Sometimes those who investigate or stage instances of corruption find themselves facing criminal charges that have been fabricated or applied inappropriately (laws against dishonouring the government or subversion, for example, or national security laws). Prominent journalists or human rights advocates may be accused (falsely) of accepting bribes or misrepresenting their finances. Opposition candidates may be prevented from standing for election until they have cleared themselves of (bogus) corruption allegations. Such practices infringe not only the right to life, liberty and security, but also the right to freedom of opinion and expression and the right to seek and receive information without interference. They also discourage other individuals from denouncing corruption in the future. Media campaigns and pressure of public opinion may also cause authorities to feel obliged to punish people alleged to be responsible for acts of corruption, even when evidence to convict them is lacking. Judges, as well as prosecutors and other authorities who are responsible for prosecuting corruption cases, are often accused of being "soft" on corruption, or even complicit with it, if they do not punish alleged abuses swiftly and conspicuously. This can incline them to violate the guarantees of due legal process. While governments are entitled in law to deprive individuals of their liberty, they cannot do so in an illegal or arbitrary manner and use of that power must comply with legal standards of due process that are designed to prevent its abuse and misuse. Criminal procedure must be fair, and should comply with established legal standards. If these standards are not met, the human rights of those accused are violated. To prevent such outcomes, independent judges play a vital role in overseeing anti-corruption investigations, to ensure full compliance with due process guarantees. Independent civil society monitoring of the rights of those accused also provides an important element of protection. People accused of corruption have rights and are entitled to judicial guarantees.

### The Politicisation of anti-Corruption Campaigns

Anti-corruption campaigns do not operate in a political vacuum. Many anticorruption campaigns that claimed to tackle corruption (often at the highest levels of government) also promoted political interests. In Thailand in 2007, Bangladesh in 2007 and Fiji in 2006, elected heads of government were deposed by military leaders on grounds of corruption. Military involvement in anti-corruption programmes poses particular threats to human rights. The constitution is often suspended. Restrictions on civil liberties, such as freedom of assembly, are frequently imposed. Opposition politicians and activists are often unlawfully detained. In many instances press freedom is severely restricted.

## HUMAN RIGHTS MECHANISMS THAT PROTECT ANTI-CORRUPTION ADVOCATES AND PREVENT ABUSES

Human rights and anti-corruption organisations therefore have good reason to collaborate to protect the rights of anti-corruption advocates and reduce the risk that anti-corruption campaigns can be exploited politically. Those who campaign against corruption or call for transparent government do not necessarily think of themselves as human rights advocates and may not use the term "human rights" when describing their work. When they expose corruption cases they are nevertheless seeking to make institutions accountable, end impunity and improve the quality of government, and these activities are also human rights objectives.

Journalists too, may be acting as human rights defenders when they investigate and report on corruption cases. All such people need and deserve protection because of the work they do. Two of the UN mechanisms of protection are particularly relevant for anticorruption advocates: the treaty bodies and the "special procedures". The most useful "special procedures" are the UN Special Rapporteur on the situation of human rights defenders; the UN Special Rapporteur on the promotion and protection of the right to freedom of opinion and expression; the Working Group on Arbitrary Detention; and the UN Special Rapporteur on extrajudicial, summary or arbitrary execution. When the rights of an anti-corruption advocate are violated or threatened, it is possible to send a "communication" (a letter, fax or cable) to these bodies, documenting the violation in question. They can make concerns public and, where an advocate is in serious danger, can write to the authorities for clarification or request action that will guarantee the rights of the person at risk.

Anti-corruption advocates and organisations should be encouraged to use these mechanisms systematically. Several of the treaty bodies will receive complaints in case of violations of human rights, though as a general rule the petitioner must have exhausted domestic remedies. They have sometimes acted to protect individuals who have been threatened or subjected to ill-treatment after witnessing or denouncing corruption. The presence in a country of active human rights organisations and effective national human rights mechanisms will also help to protect against abuse. Where laws promote transparency, prevent impunity and guarantee access to information and freedom of expression, individuals and organisations who denounce corruption will be better protected and governments or private actors will find it more difficult to exploit anti-corruption laws for political objectives. If they decide to use UN human rights procedures, anti-corruption organisations may find it helpful to consult human rights advocates, many of whom are familiar with the mechanisms and with human rights law, and know what categories of case different mechanisms can address. Collaboration may usefully extend further, of course: human rights and anti-corruption organisations might cooperate to promote the adoption of improved laws on access to information, legal guarantees of freedom of opinion and expression, the independence of judicial authorities, plural media, and laws that properly balance national security concerns with the right to information.

## OPPORTUNITIES FOR COLLABORATION

In this stage we have highlighted the connections between acts of corruption and different violations of human rights, mentioning the risks that those who campaign against corruption face. A separate stage will discuss how human rights might be integrated practically in anti-corruption programmes, and the difficulties that anti-corruption specialists are likely to face when they make use of human rights. This stage highlights some opportunities for collaboration between those who promote and defend human rights and those who work to end corruption, and makes some recommendations.

### ENTRY POINTS

Civil society organisations, including NGOs, trade unions, business associations, think tanks, scholars and the media, play a crucial role in efforts both to combat corruption and to promote and protect human rights. Nevertheless, even though much of the work they do is complementary, with some important exceptions human rights and anti-corruption organisations do not regularly collaborate or share their knowledge and experiences. To an extent this is because anti-corruption organisations are perceived to work with governments and to be more "official", while human rights organisations are perceived to be more adversarial. Yet where levels of corruption are high, human rights are less likely to be respected: both types of organisations have good reason to promote civil and political rights that hold power to account and enable civil society to organise and work effectively. Nor are the relationships that human rights organisations have with governments always adversarial. Many civil society and government organisations act cooperatively to implement human rights reforms and human rights training. In short, opportunities exist for both human rights and anti-corruption organisations to collaborate in a broad range of activities – from participatory budgeting and tracking of public expenditure to the formation of citizens' advisory boards and lobbying and advocacy campaigns. Collaboration may nevertheless not be easy to achieve. One obstacle is that anti-corruption specialists often find the language and concepts of human rights alien and abstract. They generally do not use human rights mechanisms and complain that a "human rights approach" does not provide practical solutions. On the other side, people working on human rights largely ignore the specificity of different acts of corruption and the legal instruments available to combat it. Useful collaboration will require efforts on both sides to overcome differences of language and practice. Human rights organisations will need to find new ways of communicating their legal skills; adoption of rigorous but less abstract and legal forms of expression, for example.

**Raising Awareness and Empowering People**

Bottom-up, demand-driven approaches offer good opportunities for cooperation. Tested across the world from Amnesty International letter-writing campaigns to civil rights mass action and civil disobedience movements, these place public opinion and civil society at the centre of change. Though reform proposals are often easier to introduce from the top, sustained change is clearly more likely when it is supported and demanded by the public, because this promotes accountability and transparency. National human rights institutions can help to strengthen the impact of anticorruption organisations. Several successful examples of joint collaboration can already be cited. In general, they combine the traditional human rights practice of "naming and shaming" with the technical expertise of anti-corruption organisations.

**Enforcement of Existing Law and the Creation of New Law and Codes of Conduct**

Human rights and anti-corruption organisations could explore common interests in several areas. They could work to enact laws and develop policies that will reduce the secrecy of government decision-making processes and promote access to information and transparency; campaign for freedom of expression and plural media; and campaign to ratify anti-corruption treaties such as the UNCAC. Codes of conduct can set a standard for public servants by ensuring that they do not use their public office for private gain or show bias in carrying out their public duties. Human rights and anti-corruption organisations can also work together to develop firmer professional standards and codes of conduct, ideally in cooperation with law enforcement officials and members of the judiciary. In this regard, wider dissemination of the

Bangalore Principles of Judicial Conduct would be a useful common objective. They could also target other actors, such as bankers, accountants, real estate agents and other professionals, without whose assistance corruption and its proceeds cannot be concealed; and work to raise awareness among journalists and media professionals.

### Using Human Rights Mechanisms for Protection, Redress and Accountability

Various institutions and procedures exist that can hold states accountable for their policies and actions. Domestic mechanisms include those provided by NHRIs and parliamentary reporting; international mechanisms include those provided by the UN and regional human rights courts such as the European Court of Human Rights, the Inter-American Court of Human Rights, and the African Court on Human and Peoples' Rights, each of which can help to protect anti-corruption advocates when their rights have been prejudiced. In addition, where clear links between acts of corruption and human rights obligations can be established, the same mechanisms might sometimes be used to make those who commit acts of corruption more accountable. International mechanisms will not replace but can complement the essential role of criminal prosecution. In addition, human rights mechanisms may assist advocates to circumvent legal obstacles that prevent domestic prosecution. Some corrupt practices are not necessarily illegal: when these cannot be made subject to standard law enforcement, they can sometimes be addressed using human rights fora. To illustrate, in many judicial systems nepotism and political favouritism are not considered to fall under the concept of corruption in strictly legal terms, and therefore are not prohibited by law. However, such practices may result in a violation of the right to political participation or the right to equal access to public service. In these cases challenges on human rights grounds, using human rights mechanisms, may provide paths to reform or redress which a strictly legal approach would not offer. In addition, recourse to human rights may increase help to achieve public accountability (even if enforcement remains imperfect).

### Promoting Social Accountability – Budget and Statistical Analysis

One effective way to restrict corruption and protect human rights (and economic, social and cultural rights in particular) is to give the public and civil society better tools and more authority to assess social programmes in which they have an interest. Communities and civil society organisations have developed many ways to hold governments accountable, in addition to litigation and voting at elections. They include lobbying and advocacy, citizen advisory boards and budget analysis. Sharing experiences on how to implement these mechanisms effectively is another entry point for collaboration between human rights and anti-corruption organisations. For these mechanisms to work, disadvantaged groups in society need to be enabled to participate in their design, implementation and monitoring. Participation must be real, involving access to information and a degree of influence in the decision-making process. Budget analysis (a methodology for inquiring into government priorities by breaking down and comparing official expenditures on different items) and analysis of official statistical information are powerful tools for increasing transparency and compliance with human rights obligations. While human rights organisations are increasingly considering these tools, anti-corruption organisations have more experience of using them and can assist the former to develop their skills. Despite the potential of budget analysis, in many countries budget information is shrouded in secrecy. Whereas budget plans and processes of approval may be relatively public, governments are less often required to provide information about expenditure. Since corruption generally occurs when money is spent, it is therefore important to ensure that such information is accessible and of good quality. Both human rights and anti-corruption organisations have a common interest here, and could combine their efforts to persuade governments that they should collect accurate statistics on expenditure and make the information available.

**Monitoring Public Contracting and International Aid**

Human rights advocates working to end corruption should pay particular attention to public contracting. This implies monitoring contract procedures at every level, from municipal authorities, to provincial and national or federal government. While contracts at federal or national level are likely to be larger, local government contracts also involve considerable public expenditure and have impacts that are more directly obvious for the public. Public contracting, more than any other area, is a natural point of entry for cooperative work between human rights and anti-corruption organisations. Over the last ten years, for example, the national chapters of TI have developed tools and technical skills for monitoring complex public contracting processes. Human rights organisations could apply the language and practice of human rights to complement this technical work. Human rights and anti-corruption organisations could also join together to improve the transparency and accountability of international aid. Since donor governments are accountable to taxpayers in their countries and recipient governments to intended beneficiaries of aid, both movements can press for better information and compliance with human rights standards throughout the process of aid delivery. The need to do so will grow following the introduction of policies that will increase the scale on which aid donors directly fund national budgets.

**Litigation**

This stage has argued that, by connecting acts of corruption to violations of human rights, new channels of action can be created, especially if corruption can be challenged through the many national, regional and international mechanisms that exist for monitoring compliance with human rights. The same mechanisms can be used to protect anti-corruption advocates whose rights have been violated. Litigation also provides an opportunity for collaboration between human rights and anti-corruption organisations. Litigation can raise awareness, and can oblige states to take action against corruption. A successful lawsuit, in addition, may bring compensation for the victims and establish new legal rules that will help others. However, the effectiveness of litigation has limits. It will not always provide a solution. To be successful, cases require evidence of high quality and good cooperation between victims, lawyers and human rights advocates. Success usually requires too the services of a professional legal team, which can be expensive.

On the other side of the equation, courts may be corrupt, laws may be poorly drafted, the judicial system may be weak. Success is not guaranteed in the best of circumstances and those who most require protection are usually least able to launch expensive and time-consuming court cases. Public interest litigation could address some of these challenges. Some human rights organisations have gained considerable experience of public (or strategic) litigation that could be shared and disseminated. When it is appropriate, anti-corruption organisations should consider using public interest litigation, for example to recover assets. A particular limitation of litigation is the problem of evidence. By definition corruption is covert and leaves no paper trail. Collecting evidence is therefore a major challenge. We have also mentioned the limits of judicial redress. If litigation is to have effect, for victims or perpetrators, advocates also need to identify victims, secure their consent to a prosecution and perhaps recruit them as witnesses, all of which can prove difficult. In addition, where repressive regimes are involved, lawsuits may bring serious risks of harm for those involved. For a mixture of reasons, therefore, while litigation has value, its difficulties should not be underestimated and it should be carefully considered alongside other options for redress.

This said, it is a distinctive tool that is worth exploring in cases where other approaches have not brought results, and can be most effective when it is one element of a broader strategy. Some anti-corruption organisations are already focusing on litigation. In several countries, Advocacy and Legal Advice Centres (ALACs), run by TI national chapters, offer *pro bono* legal advice on corruption-related cases. This type of work resembles the traditional public interest litigation on human rights cases that is undertaken by many human rights organisations and university human rights law clinics. This too is an area ripe for collaboration. Organisations working with legal clinics and advice centres should keep in mind one risk: the possibility that, if ALACs become increasingly the first point of contact on corruption issues, this might have the effect of weakening official anti-corruption mechanisms and institutions. Finally, litigation should be seen as one element in a broader strategy designed to encourage social accountability and public participation.

In the absence of civil and political rights guarantees such as freedom to organise, access to information and access to the judicial system, it will be hard to fight corruption. Where corruption is prevalent, it will be equally hard to promote human rights. It is in the common interest of anti-corruption and human rights organisations to build a broader and more inclusive strategy that alone is likely to be effective.

## RECOMMENDATIONS TO NHRIS AND HUMAN RIGHTS ORGANISATIONS

NHRIs and other organisations that promote and protect human rights must find their own ways to address the impact of corruption. There is no "one fits all" solution. Nonetheless, they should be prepared to meet several challenges, and should be guided by human rights principles and values. While this section primarily addresses civil society organisations and NHRIs, its analysis is relevant to other bodies and organisations that monitor or regulate human rights or corruption. These include, for example, parliamentarians who oversee compliance with human rights standards or monitor anti-corruption policies and institutions (such as the Global Organization of Parliamentarians Against Corruption (GOPAC)).

### Apply Aew Analytical Techniques: Budget Monitoring

Embezzlement of public funds is frequent in both national and local government, notably from social budgets (health, education, housing, social security). NHRIs and other human rights organisations that wish to address corruption are likely to find that it will be useful to learn how to analyse budgets forensically. A great deal of work has been done recently to assess how public resources are spent. Budgets can be analysed at many levels, from a sectoral perspective (education, health, transport, infrastructure), or from the perspective of specific groups (minorities, women, indigenous communities, prisoners, etc.). This expertise can be applied to the issue of corruption. Indeed, a data and measurement revolution is underway in many areas of programming, from human development and poverty to good governance and anti-corruption reforms. This has implications for human rights. For practical and philosophical reasons, human rights organisations have always been wary of quantifying the fulfilment of human rights. Today, nevertheless, there is a growing need for sound statistics and their analysis, and human rights organisations will need not necessarily to collect but to advocate the collection, classification and analysis of quantitative as well as qualitative data.

### Strengthen New Alliances

Anti-corruption strategies require the creation of national and international alliances involving actors from across civil society, government and the private sector. Although they have already begun to develop new alliances and forms of cooperation, human rights organisations and NHRIs will need to strengthen their relationships with politicians and journalists, development and business associations, and grassroots and popular movements. This work requires human rights experts to find new ways of communicating their legal skills to a wider public, and in this instance to organisations working against corruption. NHRIs and human rights organisations should also develop their existing relationships with the judiciary and police – to provide training and advice on the impact of corruption, to assist with policy formation, and to ensure that anticorruption programmes are not used to suppress critical voices. In addition to monitoring anti-corruption programmes and policies (investigation, prosecution, enforcement, legislation, surveillance) to ensure that they conform with human rights principles, human rights advocates can work with anti-corruption institutions to improve the impact and quality of such programmes. NHRIs and human rights organisations should also seek to work in smart and innovative ways. For example, members of corrupt elites often travel abroad for medical treatment or education or to bank their money. Use of smart sanctions, that threaten such officials with prosecution or deny travel visas, can highlight issues of criminality and bring effective pressure to bear on individuals. If such actions are taken, they should not result in any human rights violations.

**Set an Example**

Of course, human rights organisations and NHRIs should be financially transparent themselves. They should be ready to disclose financial information and can set an example by opening their financial stages to public scrutiny, subjecting their accounts to independent audit and establishing mechanisms for internal financial control. Whenever NGOs participate in bidding processes for private or public funds, these should be transparent and open. Information needs to be socially contextualised. While financial information – sources of income, budgets, evaluations – should be available on websites, this may not be sufficient, because many people may be unable to access information, or submit their views, complaints or suggestions electronically. Organisations therefore need to make information available in an appropriate form to those who have a legitimate interest in their work. NGOs and other institutions also need to take steps to avoid becoming corrupt themselves. Codes of conduct that clearly identify and sanction corrupt forms of behaviour, promote good practises (on recruitment of staff for example), and protect staff when attempts are made to corrupt them, may be useful.

**Zoom in: Give Attention to Local Government**

Local governments deliver crucial public services (healthcare, education, infrastructure projects, etc.) that are especially vital for vulnerable and disadvantaged groups. Corruption can increase the cost of such services, lower their quality and distort their distribution. Clientelism and patronage are one of the greatest challenges at local government level. Human rights organisations and NHRIs should encourage local governments to be publicly accountable by promoting participatory budget analysis, social auditing and other innovative mechanisms. Human rights organisations can play an essential role in monitoring corruption in local governments and assisting communities and the public to identify and denounce it. When doing so, they should give special attention to disadvantaged groups, minorities and less organised groups. Women's participation may be essential to ensure that their rights are defended and that gender-sensitive policies are adopted. There are opportunities to use inventive techniques – use of radio and theatre, and adoption of participatory investigation techniques and innovative methods for gathering information.

To work effectively with excluded and marginalised groups, human rights and anti-corruption organisations will need to build relationships that overcome the understandable scepticism such groups often have of outsiders. These groups are likely to need to develop relationships over a long period, to work closely with people and organisations who are trusted in the communities concerned, and adopt approaches that allow members of the community to speak and act for themselves. When local government corruption is persistent and where national government has made commitments to human rights, human rights organisations should also work closely with ministries to ensure that they support appropriate interventions at local level, both to sanction corruption and ensure that sectoral services such as health, education and water are provided equitably and to a correct standard.

### Engage the Media

The media naturally play an important role because it is through international or local media that people generally become aware of human rights violations and corruption. Sensitising the media to corruption, and linking it to human rights violations, has enormous educational and advocacy potential. To combat corruption in the long-term, it will be essential to change the attitudes towards corruption of younger people. If the next generation grows up perceiving corruption to be normal, the battle has already been lost. The media have a great capacity to influence the development of anti-corruption awareness among young people.

## CHALLENGES HUMAN RIGHTS ORGANISATIONS MAY CONFRONT

Human rights organisations, including NHRIs, may confront a number of challenges when they try to address corruption from the perspective of human rights. While these will take specific forms according to context, they should be prepared for the following:

## Structural Corruption and Low Salaries

A human rights approach may not be well-received or understood in societies where corruption is endemic and public servants receive low salaries. Underpaid officials who corruptly receive a regular supplement to their salary may consider corruption necessary to safeguard a minimum level of pay or meet the needs of their families. Such conditions undoubtedly encourage acts of corruption by public officials. Parents who must struggle to get access to health services or to enrol their children in school will tend to pay bribes rather than be excluded from a service. There is a growing recognition that reorganising bureaucracies and increasing the accountability of public officials will not reduce corruption in the absence of broader civil service reform, in which raising public sector wages may be part of the package. Corrupt acts take place as a result of rational behaviour that responds to incentives and opportunities. Unless officials and the public are convinced that their rights will be guaranteed and implemented, those who suffer most from corruption may in fact prefer to consent to corruption, if the alternative is to be excluded from access to essential services.

## Ensuring Credibility

As noted, some governments use anti-corruption campaigns to suppress political opponents and human rights critics, or curb the rights of those who combat corruption. In these cases, far from increasing transparency and the accountability and quality of government, anti-corruption campaigns may weaken democracy and public trust. These situations create a particularly difficult environment for human rights NGOs to work in, because if they involve themselves in anti-corruption work they run the risk of becoming politically compromised or being corrupted themselves. In other cases, governments appear to take measures to counter corruption (by establishing anti-corruption agencies or passing legislation) but the measures are not effective or are not prosecuted with seriousness. In such cases, human rights NGOs again need to exercise care before they support reform processes. Does a new anti-corruption body have the powers and authority to be effective? Is it autonomous? Does it have financial resources and skilled staff? Does it have authority to prosecute? Other elements also need to be in place for effective action to be feasible. Are the media free? Are judges independent? Are civil society institutions robust and competent? Human rights NGOs will need to carefully analyse the social, legal and political context when they develop strategies for working on anti-corruption programmes or with anticorruption institutions.

They also need, obviously, to take the measure of government institutions, which are not monolithic. The executive, legislative and judicial branches of government offer different points of entry for work on corruption. Particular ministries, or provincial or local governments can become allies or obstacles to effective advocacy, investigation or other kinds of human rights work in this area.

**Combating Cynicism**

In practice, applying human rights to strengthen anti-corruption policies will come down in the end to putting individuals at the centre of anti-corruption programmes. To the degree that this is the case, one obstacle will be that many of those who are most in need of protection are not aware of their rights, and in particular of their economic, social and cultural rights. Rights-awareness training and confidence-building ought therefore to be an element of human rights programmes. If a woman does not know what health services she is entitled to receive, or which services should be free of cost, she will not know whether her doctor or other health officials are treating her correctly, or cheating her. If human rights NGOs wish to work on corruption effectively with and on behalf of groups who are poor or exposed to discrimination, they will probably need to develop new methods of working and new alliances that will enable them to have more sustained contacts at local and community level.

**The Limits of Access to Information Laws**

This stage has argued that human rights NGOs and NHRIs should advocate for greater transparency as a means to prevent corruption. At the same time, the adoption of access to information laws will have limited effects. Corrupt officials will simply become more careful. Despite positive examples from countries that have adopted access to information laws, in countries where government secrecy has been the norm and corruption has flourished, access to information laws alone are unlikely to achieve reform. Indeed, if access to information is elevated into the main tool against corruption, this could divert attention from the primary responsibility of government authorities (including prosecution services and courts). It may be wise to describe access to information less as a tool to identify cases of corruption, and more as a preventive mechanism that reduces the space in which government corruption can occur. To fulfil this role, the amount of information automatically available to the public should increase. The UNCAC requires states to promote transparency and establish mechanisms that will ensure respect for the right to information. It also requires states to provide and disseminate information about the functioning of the administration and about its anti-corruption policies measures. These provisions are important because they set standards that are not met in practice or in law in the majority of signatory states. Research shows that there is no commonly agreed standard about what budget information must be released, or what declarations of interest and assets should be made by officials, or indeed whether such declarations should be required. The World Bank gathers data on asset declarations but does not impose a standard for their collection and publication. The same is true for information concerning public procurement and government contracts. While national jurisprudence establishes what information contained in contracts should be released, there is no common comparative standard. This is an area where much work could usefully be done to promote coherent government policies and set minimum standards.

### Weak Prosecutors and Anti-Corruption Offices

Anti-corruption reforms promoted by the good governance agenda have called for the creation of new independent control institutions (the offices of Prosecutor, Attorney General and General Inspector). Creating control institutions, however, does not always guarantee greater accountability. Although they are now numerous and have developed a variety of institutional arrangements (in terms of location, autonomy, financing, rules of selection and appointment), many of the new control institutions do not have authority to impose legally binding sanctions. As a result, the impact of their stages, rulings or resolutions depends on the response of judicial authorities. Many of the new autonomous control institutions have failed to achieve their objectives at least partly because of lack of action by the judiciary. By and large, the problem seems to be due to the fact that some judicial authorities refuse to accept (or understand) the evidence provided by the anti-corruption agency. Often, this is due in turn to judicial corruption. As a consequence, the stages and rulings of independent anti-corruption agencies have sometimes not been supported, or have been reinterpreted, by judges, undermining their impact. Failures of prosecution can have a similar effect. If prosecutors are not independent, and investigate and convict on a selective basis, the independence and authority of the judiciary is also compromised. These are both areas to which human rights advocates should give attention.

### Working Beyond Borders

Much corruption is international; it involves the jurisdiction of two or more states. It may be associated with transnational organised crime (money laundering, drug trafficking); foreign states may be implicated; transnational companies may use corruption to obtain contracts. NHRIs and human rights organisations should develop alliances and working methods that enable them to address acts of corruption outside the jurisdiction of one state.

# Index